Report of the Inquiry into Child Abuse in Cleveland 1987

Presented to Parliament by the Secretary of State for Social Services by Command of Her Majesty July 1988

LONDON: HMSO
REPRINTED 1991: CORRECTIONS INCORPORATED
£20.00 net

Cm 412

The Right Honourable John Moore, MP
Secretary of State for Social Services

Dear Secretary of State,

You asked me to inquire into the arrangements for dealing with child abuse in Cleveland since 1 January 1987, including in particular cases of child sexual abuse. I now submit my Report and recommendations.

Yours sincerely,

Elizabeth Butler-Sloss

6 June 1988.

REPORT OF THE INQUIRY INTO CHILD ABUSE IN CLEVELAND 1987

Presented to the Secretary of State for Social Services by the Right Honourable Lord Justice Butler-Sloss DBE

CONTENTS

REPORT OF THE JUDICIAL INQUIRY INTO THE ARRANGEMENTS FOR DEALING WITH SUSPECTED CASES OF CHILD ABUSE IN CLEVELAND SINCE 1 JANUARY 1987

BACKGROUND TO THE INQUIRY

1. On the 9th July 1987, the Secretary of State for Social Services ordered that a Statutory Inquiry should be established under section 84 of the National Health Service Act 1977 and Section 76 of the Child Care Act 1980 to look into the arrangements for dealing with suspected cases of Child Abuse in Cleveland from the 1st January 1987.

2. The Inquiry was announced by the Minister for Health in the House of Commons on the 9th July 1987 (Hansard Volume 119 number 15 Column 526) and arises from an unprecedented rise in the diagnosis of child sexual abuse during the months of May and June 1987 in the County of Cleveland, principally at Middlesbrough General Hospital. Enormous concern was voiced not only by parents of the children involved but also by nurses, police, Members of Parliament and, through the medium of the press, the public both in Cleveland and nationally.

3. The Secretary of State for Social Services asked the Northern Regional Health Authority and the Social Services Inspectorate to provide reports as a matter of urgency. The Cleveland Constabulary also submitted a report. On the basis of the findings of those reports it was decided to set up a Statutory Public Inquiry, to be chaired by a High Court Judge and assisted by three Assessors.

4. I was asked to chair the Inquiry, with the following Terms of Reference:

"To examine the arrangements for dealing with suspected cases of child abuse in Cleveland since 1st January 1987, including in particular cases of child sexual abuse, and to make recommendations."

5. I have been assisted in my task by three distinguished Assessors: Professor David Hull, Professor of Child Health at Nottingham University; Mr John Chant, Director of Social Services for Somerset, and Mr Leonard Soper, recently retired as Chief Constable of Gloucestershire.

6. After the announcement of the setting up of the Inquiry on the 9th July, and the appointment of the Assessors and myself, we set about as a matter of urgency to arrange the start of the Inquiry as soon as possible. A public announcement was made on 22nd July 1987 inviting any person who wished to give evidence to apply to the Secretary to the Inquiry. A preliminary hearing was held on Tuesday 4th August in the Council Chamber of Middlesbrough Town Hall which has been our venue throughout.

7. I resolved, with the unanimous agreement of my Assessors, to start the hearing of the Inquiry with the utmost expedition, despite general concern that the information needed would not be ready and the representation on that occasion from the County Council Social Services Department, to adjourn for several weeks. The extent of public disquiet, reflected in the high level of media coverage, was clear. The pressure upon social workers, doctors, and parents, arising from the crisis, was enormous. It was apparent from the reports submitted to the Minister that there was a fundamental breakdown in communication with and co-operation between various disciplines which was impeding the proper approach to the care and protection of children in the area. Consequently there was a pressing need to ventilate the issues dividing the disciplines as quickly as possible in order to ascertain the facts, address the problems with some degree of urgency, and to try to offer guidelines to restore confidence in the working of those agencies both for the agencies themselves and for the public, locally and nationally. For these reasons we decided we had to begin hearing evidence as quickly as possible. During the course of the Inquiry we were aware of the considerable burdens it placed upon lawyers and organisations to provide the necessary documentation in a hurry, but we are convinced of the rightness of our decision to press on immediately.

8. As the Inquiry progressed the Assessors and I became increasingly aware of the large number of issues causing continuing difficulties which were not unique to Cleveland. We decided to invite evidence on some of those issues from a wider area and are indebted to the representatives of the organisations listed in the appendices for their submissions and to many experts for their advice to us.

9. The length of time spent hearing evidence was dictated by the necessity of a thorough investigation into a large number of complex and varied matters, all of which in our joint opinion merited consideration and comment in the report.

10. At the preliminary hearing on the 4th August I granted representation to the organisations and individuals listed at the end of this report. I invited parents of children involved in the crisis to be

represented throughout the Inquiry at the expense of public funds. I invited the Official Solicitor to act on behalf of the children concerned. His office set up a telephone "hotline" so that children could ring in and be heard.

11. It was the view of the Assessors and myself that in an Inquiry which was creating such widespread interest and concern it was our duty to present to the public in open session all the evidence to be called before us as far as this would be possible. It was only after considerable discussion and upon hearing the powerful plea of Counsel for the children that we resolved to hear the evidence of the parents in private session. This was to enable them to give their evidence freely without any danger of identification of any family and consequently any child. At the heart of this Inquiry we were concerned with the best interests of the children and we acceded to that application on those grounds.

12. The Inquiry lasted 74 days, starting on August 11th 1987 and ending on the 29th January 1988. We heard evidence in private session for 8 days, all of it given by parents, and thereafter the Inquiry was in public session every day although from time to time part of the day was in private session when we heard evidence which would identify a particular family.

13. We received both written and oral evidence and are grateful for the contributions of the many people who wrote to us. The Assessors and I together made various visits which are set out in the body of the Report, and the Assessors independently made visits.

We received much of the information in statistical form but had great difficulty in obtaining accurate and consistent figures in certain areas. We include in the appendices some of the information provided, for illustrative purposes, but we would wish to stress the dangers inherent in interpreting the figures too freely. It has not been possible to provide sufficient data about sexual abuse, a matter to which we refer in our recommendations. Out of interest therefore we include in the appendices an extract from the CIBA Foundation 'Child Sexual Abuse within the Family' on presentation and indicators of child sexual abuse and also the findings of the Leeds team given in their presentation to the Inquiry.

14. The Assessors and I have also read certain judgments relating to children referred to in the Inquiry, in wardship proceedings which have been heard and concluded before this Report was written. We were permitted to do this with the leave of the Judges trying the wardship cases.

15. As a result of the speed with which we started the Inquiry I have relied upon the Assessors to an even greater extent than I might have expected. In addition to the hours of sitting they have occupied many hours in evaluating documents, reading files and visiting establishments in order to direct the attention of the Treasury Solicitor to relevant evidence to place before the Inquiry. All the written material studied by them and visits made by them have been with the knowledge of the Treasury Solicitor.

16. I have not myself taken into account any matters which have not been placed before the Inquiry either in oral or written form, other than the judgments in wardship.

Acknowledgements

17. I owe an enormous debt of gratitude to Counsel for the Inquiry, Mr Matthew Thorpe Q.C and Mr Timothy Hartley. Throughout the Inquiry their calm, considered, reasoned guidance has been invaluable. I am aware of the long hours they have put in to have the conduct of the Inquiry in proper order.

18. I should like to pay particular tribute to the staff of the Treasury Solicitor's Office, who undertook with cheerful efficiency the monumental task of interviewing witnesses, taking statements, and collecting and sorting documents before and during the Inquiry. I am conscious of the fact that the speed with which the Inquiry was set into motion must have greatly added to the difficulty of their task. However, the Treasury Solicitors were not daunted by this additional difficulty imposed upon them, and thanks to them the Inquiry was able to get off to a prompt and useful start.

19. I should like to offer my thanks to Counsel representing all parties to the Inquiry. The Assessors and I were aware of the considerable difficulties they also faced in the preparation of and presentation of their respective clients' viewpoints. These they put forward with sensitivity and restraint and we are grateful to them for their assistance in unravelling the diverse strands of the problems with which we were faced.

20. I should like to offer my particular thanks to Mr Andrew Kirkwood representing the children on behalf of the Official Solicitor. His assistance during the course of the Inquiry was considerable and his submission at the conclusion has been invaluable.

22. I should like to offer my gratitude to the County of Cleveland for the assistance given to the Inquiry in identifying and securing a suitable venue at a time when the pressures were enormous. To the elected members of Middlesbrough Borough Council I owe an especial debt of gratitude—for I am conscious of the fact that they were deprived not only of their Council Chamber, but that the Inquiry staff deprived them of their newly refurbished offices for several months. I should like to offer both my apologies for the inconvenience caused and my thanks for the patience with which the inconvenience was borne.

23. The Assessors and I wish to pay tribute to Alan Davey and Mrs Pat Jackson, Secretary and Deputy Secretary to the Inquiry, for their cheerful and unstinting efforts behind the scenes to set up, organise and keep the Inquiry running smoothly under conditions of some considerable difficulty. The Assessors and I were very grateful not only to them but also to the enormous help given to us by their staff during the course of the Inquiry.

24. The writing of the Report has been a somewhat daunting task and we have all been conscious of the importance of completing it as soon as possible. It could not have been completed in four months without the dedication and tireless efforts of the Secretary and Deputy Secretary. I personally cannot thank them enough.

25. I cannot emphasise too much the gratitude I owe to the Assessors for their conscientious application to the awesome task we were set, which has extended far beyond the call of duty. The constant stimulation I received from their vigorously expressed wisdom kept me constantly alert to the issues and saved me from straying too far from the right track. I cannot adequately express the extent of the help I have received from them in writing the Report , both in time and in the contributions they made. It has been immense and indispensible.

26. The Assessors and I are unanimous in the conclusions and in the recommendations of the Report, which owe much to their wise advice.

27. Despite all the advice and assistance I have received, the Report remains my sole responsibility.

Child Abuse

SEXUAL ABUSE

Introduction

1. Child abuse, the non-accidental injury of a child, received increasing attention in this country in the 1960s, and followed upon its recognition in the United States. Public awareness of its nature and frequency grew in the 1970s. The background, early attitudes towards and subsequent general recognition of non-accidental injury has been set out in detail in various earlier reports on child abuse. A parallel can be drawn between the reluctance to recognise physical abuse in the United Kingdom in the 1960s and the reluctance by many to accept the reality of certain aspects of child sexual abuse in the 1980s.

2. Child abuse has many forms; the concerns may centre upon physical abuse, sexual and emotional abuse, or upon neglect. Dr Cameron in discussing the 3 categories of active child abuse:— physical, emotional, and sexual abuse, pointed out that, while it was helpful to the diagnostician to have distinct forms of child abuse in mind, not infrequently, in practice, a child is subject to more than one form of abuse. It is obviously important to recognise that the categories of abuse are not closed. Experts gave us figures indicating that as much as 30% of children referred because of other forms of abuse may also show medical evidence of sexual abuse.

3. Our terms of reference include all forms of child abuse. Those other than sexual abuse are referred to at page 11. The Inquiry's major concern was child sexual abuse and on this a considerable amount of written material and oral evidence was presented as to its nature, its occurrence, the circumstances, the immediate effect upon the children abused and the long term effects upon their lives.

Definitions of Child Sexual Abuse

4. The definition of child sexual abuse by Schechter and Roberge is widely quoted:—

"Sexual abuse is defined as the involvement of dependent, developmentally immature children and adolescents in sexual activities that they do not fully comprehend and to which they are unable to give informed consent or that violate the social taboos of family roles".

In other words it is the use of children by adults for sexual gratification. Dr Cameron described it as inappropriate behaviour which involved:—"the child being exploited by the adult either for direct physical gratification of sexual needs or for vicarious gratification."

This may take many forms. Mrazek and Mrazek set out a list:—

Exposure—viewing of sexual acts, pornography, and exhibitionism;

Molestation—fondling of genitals—child's or adult's;

Sexual intercourse—oral, vaginal or anal, on a non-assaultative and chronic basis; [eg in contrast to rape/the use of force]

Rape—acute assaultative forced intercourse.

5. Child sexual abuse may take place within the family circle or outside, for example, by a neighbour or a complete stranger. According to Dr Paul (1986) abuse within the family is the most common form. The type of sexual abuse, its degree of seriousness, the age of the child and whether it is within the family all affect not only the presentation but also the response to it by the community and the action required of the professionals charged with the duty of protecting the abused child. It is essential in any consideration of child sexual abuse to be clear at all times as to the definition and description being used.

Prevalence/Incidence

6. It has been impossible from the evidence provided to the Inquiry to arrive at any consensus or to obtain any reliable figures of the general prevalence of sexual abuse of children in the country or in Cleveland. Most data refer to allegations of abuse, or events in the protecting processes, e.g. the number on the child abuse register. A critique of U.K national statistics appeared in Health Trends and some of the figures presented to the Inquiry are given in the appendices. The data show that increasing numbers each year are being investigated because of the possibility of child sexual abuse and increasing numbers of adults are complaining that they were abused in childhood.

Dr Bentovim was in no doubt that the reason for the substantial increase in referral was due to increased diagnosis, the recognition that children who described abusive experience were not fantasising, and an increasing awareness of the pattern of physical and behavioural disorders of children, who had been subject to the traumatic experience of being abused, in many different professional groups .

7. We are strongly of the opinion that great caution should be exercised at the present time in accepting percentages as to the prevalence and incidence of sexual abuse. We received from published articles and oral evidence figures of 5%, 10% and upwards. Such figures depend on what is meant by sexual abuse. Some people have used the figure of 10% for serious sexual abuse, but there was before the Inquiry no evidence to support it.

Sexual Offences Against Children

8. It was suggested by some to the Inquiry that child sexual abuse is a new phenomenon of the 1980s. There has been difficulty and for many there remains difficulty in accepting its reality. We have no doubt about this from the variety of attitudes expressed in the evidence to the Inquiry including that from many of those immediately concerned with events in Cleveland. However Tardieu in Paris in the 1860s wrote at length on rape, incest and anal interference of young children. Parliament passed the Incest Act in 1908 as a result of concern expressed about children during the 19th century and crimes of incest and sexual assaults upon children within the family have been a regular feature of the criminal lists at the Assizes and continue to be so at the Crown Courts throughout the Country. There is perhaps a new recognition that young children are also subject to abuse and their plight has only just come to light. Doctors generally have not been looking at young children with the possibility of sexual abuse in mind, although Dr Paul in 1977 referred to serious assaults including anal abuse of very young children between 1 and 10 years old and by adults of both sexes. Sexual offences against children are listed and described in the following Table:

Rape	is forceable sexual intercourse with a girl without her consent. Penetration to any degree is sufficient.
Unlawful Sexual Intercourse	with a girl under the age of 16. There are two offences and the more serious is in respect of a girl under the age of 13, who cannot under any circumstances give consent. The less serious offence is between the ages of 13 and 16, and both the offence and the child's inability to give consent are subject to certain exceptions.
Incest	is sexual intercourse between a man and his grand-daughter, daughter, sister (half sister) or mother, or between a woman, 16 or over, and her grandfather, father, brother, (half brother) or son. The child cannot give consent.
Buggery	is unlawful sexual intercourse by penetration of the anus. Any degree of penetration is sufficient. Such an offence by a father against his minor son is buggery and not incest. The child cannot give consent.
Assault to commit buggery	this is an alternative and lesser offence.
Gross indecency	refers to acts between males and includes acts against children. Examples of gross indecency are, mutual masturbation, oral-genital contact. Physical contact is not always necessary.
Indecent assault	this must be an assault however minor accompanied by circumstances of indecency.
Indecent conduct with or towards a child	this is an act of indecency with or towards a child under 14 or the adult inciting a child to commit such an act.
Causing or encouraging pro-stitution of or indecent assault on a girl under 16	this must be done by the person having responsibility for the child.
Indecent Photographs of children	it is an offence to take or allow indecent photographs of a child to be taken; distribute such photographs or have in one's possession indecent photographs with a view to distribution or publication.

9. In the child care legislation some protection is given to children who may be living in the same household as a person convicted of a sexual offence. The first schedule to the Children and Young Persons Act 1933 sets out a list of offences, some of which are among those set out above. In care proceedings in the Juvenile Court the presence in the same household as the child of a person who has been convicted of one of the offences listed in Schedule 1 is a ground for making an application for a care order.

Presentation

10. Sexual abuse comes to the attention of police, social workers or doctors, (as well as others) in one of the following ways:— by allegation from an adult, complaint or a disclosure by the child of the sexual offences given in the table, or physical disorder or behavioural disturbance. The Inquiry was given numerous lists of the medical conditions which might result from sexual abuse of children. In 'Child Sexual Abuse Within The Family' published by the CIBA Foundation, physical and behavioural indicators are listed and these are to be found in Appendix E.

11. Whilst sexual abuse may cause such problems it is by no means the only cause, and the extent to which it is a significant factor in any one is at present unknown.

The Children

12. The Inquiry was provided with evidence about Cleveland children primarily in respect of allegations of the most serious offences of incest, unlawful sexual intercourse and buggery of girls and buggery of boys and indecent assault almost all within the family, including digital penetration, fondling, mutual masturbation, anal and oral/genital contact. From the evidence presented to the Inquiry a majority of children sexually abused in the U.K. are girls but there are significant numbers of boys. Dr Bentovim and his team at the Hospital for Sick Children at Great Ormond Street described 274 families they had seen between 1981 and 1986; within those families there were 411 sexually abused children and 362 non-sexually abused children; 77% were girls and 23% boys. The boys tended to be younger, more severely abused and for longer periods than the girls. On a follow up of 120 families there was a prosecution in 60%. The children were evenly distributed between all age groups and the abuse had occurred in some for short periods, and in others for 5 years or more. Seventy eight percent of the children had been subject to the more serious forms of abuse. In a considerable number of families there was more than one 'victim', in some families 3−5 'victims'.

13. The abuse may be one incident, occasional, a gradual but escalating level of abuse; or it may be frequent and regular. For some children it may become a way of life and only in adolescence do they realise they have not enjoyed a 'normal' family life. At the time it may not necessarily be experienced as distasteful by the child and it is only later that the child realises it is what it is. On the other hand it may be coercive and frightening from the beginning.

14. Some children appear to be specially vulnerable, for example those with physical or mental handicaps, others treated as scapegoats, or those who are particularly immature. It may occur where the older child has a parenting role. Alcohol, drugs, absence of the other parent from home; a single parent with succession of male partners, violence, marital or sexual difficulties may be factors. Other factors suggested include chaotic or inadequate families, or the sub-normality of a parent.

15. The children caught up in the crisis in Cleveland ranged in age from under a year to adolescence. It would be impossible to say how many sexually abused children in Cleveland were boys. But there were some boys sexually abused during the period and significant proportions in respect of whom allegations were made.

16. There were some unusual complaints, for example: one little girl of 7 complained that her father and girl friend squirted tea in a syringe up 'her front'; one little boy of 4 spoke of an iron bar being pushed up his bottom; one boy said he had a toilet roll pushed up as a punishment. In several instances children who were later found to have been abused at home engaged in sexualised behaviour towards each other or with other children at school.

Pressure to Keep the Secret

17. Many children who have been subject to sexual abuse are put under pressure from the perpetrator not to tell; there may be threats of violence to the child or that the perpetrator will commit suicide, of being taken away from home and put into care, threats that someone they love will be angry with them, or that

no-one would believe them. Children may elect not to talk because of a genuine affection for the perpetrator and an awareness of the consequences to the perpetrator, to the partner, to the family unit, or for an older child an understanding of the economic considerations in the break-up of the family and the loss of the wage earner. The secretive element persists. Professor Sir Martin Roth in evidence said:—"There is a powerful disincentive to disclosing the fact that one has been subject to sexual abuse. The person who discloses this has fears that he may be regarded as having permitted himself, as having collaborated in it, as having been lastingly damaged in a sexual way. He is likely to fear ridicule, humiliation, obloquy and so on".

18. This pressure upon the child not to tell and the desire of all to keep the secret is also apparent in the pressure brought upon children to retract once they have made a complaint. The pressure comes from the family, mother, siblings and the extended family as well as the abuser. The withdrawal of the complaint is a common situation with child complainants and presents particular difficulties for the police.

19. In Cleveland we heard of examples of pressure on children. A girl of 12 told the Official Solicitor that her step-father said no-one would believe her. A girl of 8 expressed relief at the death of her father who committed suicide after she revealed the abuse. One little girl of 5 told the police that her father had sexually abused her. According to a letter from her mother she explained why she had not told before:—"It was because my daddy told me I would lose my voice if I told anyone". The mother wrote:—"These are the things she has told me:—she was told, somebody will come and take her away, people would hit her for telling lies, Mammy will cry if you tell her."

The Children may become 'Double Victims'

20. Those who fear a child has been sexually abused naturally wish to protect the child from further assaults; to stop the abuser having the opportunity to abuse again. The ideal would be to protect the child within his or her home and neighbourhood, preferably after identifying and excluding the abuser. However, if, as is often the case, the perpetrator is unknown, or is suspected but denies the abuse, how can the child be protected? In practice, it is the child who is taken away from home, friends and school and it is the child who is placed in hospital, in a childrens' home or in a foster home, in strange surroundings and among strangers.

21. The plight of the 'double victim' is well illustrated by what happened to one of the children in Cleveland. The girl told the police that she had been sexually abused by her father. She said that the threat from the perpetrator was that she would be taken away from home and placed in care if she told anyone what was going on. As it happened the effect of the complaint was a place of safety order and she was removed from home, and suffered twice over. That child retracted her story.

22. The child who tells of sexual abuse within the family may be in serious physical danger. Dr Wynne spoke of a child she saw who was placed with friends after complaint of sexual abuse and was murdered. She said:—"There is often violence at the time of disclosure."

Abusers

23. Much of the abuse is contained within the family, and such facts as are available, any of them anecdotal, show a preponderance of fathers, then stepfathers, uncles, elder brothers. There is a view held that sexual abuse of a stepdaughter is not as heinous as abuse of a daughter.

24. There were examples in Cleveland of abuse by father, step-father, boyfriend, uncle, cousin, elder brother, baby-sitter and neighbour. There may be a single perpetrator or several abusers in one family. At least one girl in Cleveland was likely to have been abused both by her uncle and her father.

25. Sexual abuse of children by women has been reported but this was only alleged in the case of one child considered by the Inquiry. There were examples of children coming within the other definitions of abuse at the hands of mothers during the period investigated.

26. The adult is in a position of authority particularily if he is in the place of a parent and the child is not able to give true consent to any sexual advances. The adult is able to require a response, expect to receive it and where the demand is a sexual one he is abusing his parental authority. The approach to the child by the perpetrator may vary from intrusive and sometimes bizarre assaults upon children who from the beginning are afraid of violence or threats, to the over-loving relationship between father and child which slips into a

sexual one at a later stage. Professor Sir Martin Roth described one type of offender as:—"a severely psychopathic and sexually abnormal individual, (such as) a paedophile .....with other abnormalities of personality, and such an individual will be found in a relationship either as a stepfather or as a common law husband." He explained the jealousy that such a man might feel for the child's father and spoke of the likely inadequacy of some mothers who would not face the risk of confrontation and would turn a blind eye on the situation. He dealt with the opposite extreme of the widowed father with the adolescent daughter who had begun to assume maternal responsibilities and household duties.:—"From a normal daughter/father relationship in an isolated family, a bereaved husband may sometimes, not with any very great pathology in certain cases, slide, without any clearly formed intent, into a sexual relationship." He felt that the latter situation was more open to intervention with the possibility of providing treatment to the father within the context of family therapy and an attempt to conserve and re-establish the family. In between there are:—"fathers who are not normal fathers sometimes in middle or upper class families, who are not overtly pathological, who have a very strong sexual drive, whose sexual propensity is a relatively circumscribed abnormality of personality." Such a father might abuse several children in the family on the basis of an affectionate relationship, courting and then seducing them. He may be:—"very active sexually with his wife, (he) would be extremely jealous of her."

27. According to Dr Higgs in her evidence there is an element of compulsive behaviour in abusers. Research, much of in the United States' has looked at some offenders said to be compulsive abusers. This group is sometimes described as paedophiles or 'fixated' and contrasted with other offenders described as 'regressed', the latter group being believed to be more responsive to treatment. [see generally Finkelhor and Associates, Sourcebook on Child Sexual Abuse, and Sgroi, Handbook of Clinical Intervention in Sexual Abuse.] There is according to several witnesses a correlation between abusers and the abuse they themselves suffered as children.

Relationships within the Family

28. The mother, we are told, is by no means certain to be the protector of the child. Some may have themselves been abused as children. Some may be afraid of the man, inadequate personalities ill-equipped to give the child protection, or even prefer him to pay attention to the child rather than to themselves. Some mothers can not or will not believe it to be possible. There is a very acute dilemma for a mother in the conflict between her man and her child, in which the relationship with the man, the economic and other support which she receives from him may disincline her to accept the truth of the allegation. Some mothers choose sexual offenders as partners more than once.

Again quoting Professor Sir Martin Roth:—"In many cases mothers play a role in the genesis of the sexual abuse of their daughters. They may be too physically ill or inadequate in personality to provide proper care and protection for their children. In other cases mothers elect the eldest or one of the oldest daughters to the role of 'child mother'. The girl in her early teens or even earlier is expected to take the responsibility for the caring of younger children whose mothering role is allowed to slide into a sexual relationship with the father. This is tolerated with little or no protest. I refer to lack of protest of the part of the mother for a variety of reasons and the mother may in such cases deny what is happening. She conceals the truth from herself as well as others; the relationship continues and when the situation is brought to light it may be insisted by the mother that it had been unknown to her."

29. In the evidence presented to the Inquiry several children who described abuse indicated that their mothers either were present or knew what was going on.

The Lasting Effects of Sexual Abuse in Childhood

30. We have been provided with a considerable amount of written material on various aspects of the long term effects on the abused child. Much of that information only becomes available many years after the offences were committed and often when the subject is grown-up. We were extremely grateful to Professor Sir Martin Roth for coming to give evidence to the Inquiry and for his later written contribution. As a result of his oral evidence he received a considerable amount of correspondence from people abused as children and he sent us samples.

31. We were also indebted to Mr Frank Cook M.P. for his written and oral contribution, in particular evidence gathered from adults abused as children and their perceptions of the problem. (see page 11)

32. The Official Solicitor interviewed many children who were caught up in the crisis and his final submission on all aspects of the children has been invaluable. In particular he set out the experiences of one girl recently grown-up with whom we deal below. The Chairman also received individual letters which were made part of the Inquiry documents.

33. Professor Sir Martin Roth told us in evidence of the serious harm sexual abuse had done to some of his patients. He warned that "Those who have been intimidated by threats into incestuous relationships in childhood proved to be at high risk of abusing their own children thus transmitting the effects of deprivation. The ill effects are not confined to feelings of guilt, self-reproach and humiliation aroused after incest has begun or when its character has come to be appreciated. Emotional development may be seriously deranged or arrested and ability to form normal personal and sexual relationships to be fulfilled and happy in marriage and to prove emotionally equal to the responsibility of rearing children suffer lasting impairment. Although it is the more intrusive and more aggressive forms of abuse that cause the most grave damage, forms of incestuous relationship that leave no sign may inflict a lasting wound."

He was referring to the effect upon those who might not develop psychiatric disorder, but might have difficulty in forming:—"firm satisfactory and lasting emotional bonds with other individuals." Among adolescents it may manifest itself in:—"lack of confidence, lack of drive, in emotional ability, in uncertain identity, and perhaps uncertain orientation in a sexual sense. It may lead, through depressive responses to adversity or stress to impulsive suicidal attempts which may, on account of their impulsiveness, either fail because they have not been planned or go well beyond what had been vaguely intended and cause serious damage. Sometimes it can prove fatal."

Samantha's Story

34. During his investigations into the children in Cleveland the Official Solicitor interviewed a girl of 19 from the Cleveland area and her story provides a most helpful insight into many problems and issues raised by child sexual abuse. She chose to call herself Samantha and the Inquiry is grateful to her for allowing her story to be made public.

Samantha's mother died when she was very young and her father brought up her younger brother and herself singlehanded. He began to abuse her when she was 4. When she was little he covered her head and top half with a blanket and interfered with her vagina. By the age of 10 it was regular sexual intercourse and thereafter it included buggery and oral intercourse. "He made me say that I enjoyed it, that I wanted it. He wouldn't like any disagreement." As she got older she began to realise that this did not happen to other girls. She said that:—"it got to the stage that if I wanted a favour, to go out with a friend, or buy a new pair of shoes, I had to let him do it first."

She had no-one to confide in, no-one to turn to.:—"I thought any adult would not believe me—they would think I was making up a story. ... I didn't know what might happen. For my brother's sake I didn't want my family split up. ... I loved my father so much. I respected him as a father. But I was confused, didn't understand. I wanted it to stop. I hated that part of it so much."

The abuse continued several times a week. The father told her when she was 14 that many years earlier he had been to prison for a sexual offence with a minor. He also told her that he had been having sexual intercourse with her best friend who was also under 16.:—"After that, I thought that if I told anyone he would hit me."

She did well in exams at school. She did not mix much with other girls. Her father did not like her going out. He was:—"extremely possessive, jealous of me." She had no boy friends when she left school at 16. Her father would not let her. She also dreaded the idea.

She left school and went to college and there met a boy she called Andrew and became very fond of him. She found it very difficult to respond to the boyfriend's sexual advances and:—"The first time I was petrified, just shaking. He had realised from early on there was something wrong, something deeply worrying me. I wouldn't tell him. I could open up part of me, like lifting a curtain, but I couldn't tell him." Samantha was asked by her father if she had been to bed with Andrew and he threatened to throw her out of the house and beat her. He continued to abuse her sexually until 1985.

9

Eventually Samantha told Andrew and with his help and the help of a member of his family she went to the police. Her father was arrested. She went into care. Her father was tried and convicted.

Two police officers came and took her to the police station.:—" I was put in a room and left there, at times alone. It was as if I had done something wrong. I was seen by a police woman and gave her a statement, I was very frightened." She was at the police station for 3 hours. A police surgeon, a man, examined her.:—"I was not offered a woman doctor—I did whatever they said. I felt a wreck inside—I objected to a male doctor. But I was utterly shaken—it was all very traumatic." She was very upset by the knowledge that her father was also at the police station. A place of safety order was taken and she went to Andrew's relative. The next day she had to go back to the police station and go over her statement again. The police said that she might have lied:—"That got me really upset again."

Social Services were unable to place her brother and herself together and she had to go into a Children's Home. She spoke in glowing terms of the enormous help given to her by the staff of the Home and by her social worker. But she commented that she was with girls who had been involved in prostitution, glue sniffing, drugs and violence. She was unused to the foul language, arguing and challenges to fights:—"They were always on at you to try drugs, glue and smoking."

She had to go to the Juvenile Court several times for the care proceedings and her father was there on each occasion. His presence upset and worried her very much.

While in care she received messages from her father via her brother saying:—"it was all lies."

She had to attend the criminal trial which took place about 9 months later. She was at court for 2 days and gave evidence for 2 and a half hours. The public were in the gallery.:—"I felt on trial, my life being spilt out, this thing I was ashamed of, in front of people I didn't know." She was very upset at being attacked in cross-examination, and for the suggestion that if it were true she would not have done so well in her school exams:—"I said it had been going on, it was part of my life since I was four."

Her father was convicted and sentenced to 2 years imprisonment. He was released on parole after 8 months:—"That really cracked me up, after what I had had to go through for 12 years."

Samantha Raised 6 Points

1. *Sentencing.*

She felt the sentence was too lenient.

2. *Female staff.*

Police, doctors and Social Services should have female staff ready to help children.

3. *Confidentiality.*

"I was worried in case what I told people might be told to other people. I needed to feel that what I said was very secure. I could not trust many people."

4. *Childrens' Homes.*

She was unhappy with the mix of children at a time when she was very vulnerable. She felt a foster home would have been better. She did not feel the emotional neutrality of a children's home was preferable at that stage to the demands of life in another family.

5. *A topic to be accepted.*

She does not want other children to feel as she did that:—"I am the only one." It should be a subject that people can talk about and there should be people to whom children can talk.

6. *Help Generally.*

Samantha felt that in every school there should be male and female staff to whom children could talk about sexual matters and particularly abuse. Not just one person, otherwise other children will know what the child is going to talk about, several people so the child can choose. Those people should have some knowledge of sexual abuse. There should also be therapeutic help in every area to which children and adults alike can turn.

It was very courageous of Samantha to provide her story to the Official Solicitor and we felt it would be instructive to reproduce part of it in the Report.

Childhood Sexual Abuse Revealed as Adult

35. Frank Cook MP provided the Inquiry with information relating to a family who revealed only after many years the sexual abuse each of 3 brothers had suffered during childhood at the hands of their father. This did not come within the terms of reference of the Inquiry but the response to such revelations clearly presents problems. The perpetrator may remain in the community. Those abused may need counselling. The agencies may be presented with insuperable difficulties many years later and be unable to respond to the information presented. This is an area which we feel should be recognised and consideration given to it.

Public Response

36. Recognition of sexual abuse of children is becoming more widespread. But the subject undoubtedly presents problems for everyone. There is an emotional element from which no-one is immune, the effect of which however may be manifested in various ways. Dr Cameron said:—"Whenever a 'new' illness or treatment is described a flurry of excitement develops amongst professionals. This has certainly been the case with child sex abuse. However, in addition to the normal excitement generated by any 'new' condition, there is an added voyeuristic component arising from the universality of interest in sexual matters. Those who try to assist in this difficult field would do well to bear in mind the complex forces which can affect judgment and action in dealing with emotionally powerful material."

37. Some people have difficulty in believing that sexual abuse described in this chapter can be caused to children, particularily young children. Others cannot believe the perpetrators might be people they might know. Most people have some understandable unease or distaste for the subject.

Some feel the need to manage the denial of others by demonstrating its prevalence and engaging in active campaigns to eradicate it. The difficulties of recognition of sexual abuse of children and the threshold of suspicion at which action was to be taken were among the problems which arose in Cleveland in 1987.

PHYSICAL ABUSE

Introduction

38. The main areas of concern for children, as we have already set out at page 4 centre upon physical abuse, (non-accidental injury), emotional abuse, neglect and failure to thrive and concern about children living in the same household as known sexual offenders. Since the management of all aspects of child abuse are within our terms of reference, we looked at child abuse generally in Cleveland. But it was clear to us that little complaint or concern had been expressed about the way in which children believed to be victims of abuse other than sexual abuse were dealt with in the community. We did not, therefore, consider it appropriate to dwell upon this area.

39. It is not necessary to consider definitions, nor the course of growing awareness of this field of abuse, since it is comprehensively dealt with in numerous earlier reports.

Guidelines

40. In Cleveland in 1984 as set out in Chapter 3, guidelines were drawn up for the assistance of the agencies involved in the management of child victims of abuse. Those guidelines according to police, to social workers and health service staff worked well and effectively. As is set out in the chapter 4 the relations and communication between social workers and the police were harmonious and they worked well together. The guidelines provided a structure which appears to have been well-understood by all the agencies involved. They included referral to hospital and examination by paediatricians in cases where there was cause to be concerned about a child's injuries or general development. Otherwise, children were sometimes seen and referred by their general practitioners.

Involvement of Police Surgeons

41. We did not hear of any children examined by police surgeons in cases of physical abuse and that situation was confirmed by the senior Cleveland police surgeon.

Numbers Involved

42. During the period 1st January to 31st December 1987 321 children were referred to the Social Services Department by reason of physical abuse, 338 because of neglect and 40 other children because of concern that they were failing to thrive. This high volume of physical abuse work is a measure of the social problems of the area and an indication of the high load that has to be carried by social workers and other agencies in this field.

Cases Considered by the Inquiry

43. We considered a random selection of cases from the Social Services files, two cases which gained publicity during the hearing and received the attention of a local Member of Parliament, and read the judgement of Mr Justice Hollis in a wardship case heard in October.

We were impressed by the hard work and dedication of social workers, the skill of the paediatric services and the concern and co-operation of the Police in dealing with these difficult cases.

Cases Involving of Mr Bell

44. Mr Stuart Bell MP expressed concern about two cases.

In one, the mother had 5 previous children all of whom had been placed in turn in care by decisions of the Courts. The new baby and she were living in a hostel under the order of a Registrar in wardship proceedings. After a scene one afternoon involving her and a social worker among others at the hostel, the mother was arrested by the police. Thereafter, the social worker with the approval of the Registrar, placed the baby with foster parents. The mother was charged with criminal damage, bailed and on her return to the hostel found the baby had been removed. The wardship case has been heard. The child has been permanently removed from the mother, remains a ward of court and in the care of the County Council with leave from the Judge to place with long term foster parents with a view to adoption. We can see no cause for complaint in the management by social workers in that case, nor in particular in the removal of the child under the direction of the Registrar.

A six week old baby had been placed in the care of the Social Services Department following its admission to hospital with a fractured arm, fractured leg and other injuries. The child was made the subject of a care order and placed with foster parents. Later it was placed with prospective adopters, though the natural parents were still contesting their access to the child. The mother became pregnant and concern for the unborn baby led to a case conference to plan future action.

Later when the mother went into hospital, and in the light of the obvious cause for concern, the parents agreed that the child, when born, should remain in hospital. Despite that agreement, a social worker obtained a place of safety order and served it upon the mother some two hours after the birth of the child in the hospital. The plan agreed with parents involved their placement with the baby at a special unit in Newcastle. It was not the intention to separate the baby from the mother pending the assessment. The social worker who gave evidence about this case accepted that the obtaining of the place of safety order, when a firm agreement had been made with the parent, was in the circumstances, somewhat heavy-handed. This was an example of the Social Services Department's reliance upon the use of place of safety orders which is referred to in Part 1, chapter 4. In the context of the planning that had taken place with the family, the authoritarian intervention was premature and inappropriate at that moment.

Brittle Bones

45. In the case heard by Mr Justice Hollis, a baby boy, born in November 1986, was referred in January 1987 by a general practitioner to North Tees General Hospital and seen by Dr Dias, Consultant Paediatrician and Dr Dillon, Consultant Radiologist. The child had multiple fractures to the head, chest and legs. Mr Justice Hollis said in his judgement: "he was found to have a large number of fractures, periosteal reactions, and bruising to the facial area, plus a torn frenulum and possible fractures to his skull".

The Social Services Department, believing these to be non-accidental injuries caused by one or both parents, initiated care proceedings. After a brief stay in hospital he was placed with foster parents. The parents denied the allegations and in support of their contention that the child had brittle bones caused by copper deficiency, they called Dr Paterson.

Mr Justice Hollis did not accept the evidence as to the copper deficiency and preferred that of Dr Dias and Dr Dillon, supported by Dr Taitz. He was satisfied that: "the strong probability is, I am afraid, that these parents or one of them caused these injuries to a child with entirely normal bones".

Both parents continued to deny the abuse and he took the view that the possibility of rehabilitation in the future was really non-existent.

The response to non-accidental injury of a child by the health visitor, general practitioner, consultants at the hospital and by the social workers in this case was entirely appropriate and the arrangements satisfactory for the protection and care of the little boy.

Good Inter-agency Working

46. Two other cases involving physical abuse to young children, selected at random from the Social Services case records for the early part of 1987, illustrated effective operation of the child abuse guidelines, good inter-agency and multi-disciplinary working and sensitive social work practice.

1. Rehabilitation

In the first case, a boy aged 2.5 years presented to hospital with black eyes and extensive bruising. The child was allowed to return home to parents with additional support. Later, he presented again to the Day Nursery with bruising. The boy and his younger sister were received into care under a place of safety order. Eventually mother was able to recognise the difficulties she was experiencing. The younger child was returned home and steps were in hand to begin a programme of rehabilitation of the older boy.

2. Rejection and Sexual Abuse

In a second case, a fourteen month old baby girl had been seen by the family general practitioner following an episode in which the child was alleged to have fallen from her potty and stopped breathing. She was admitted to hospital where she was found to have extensive bruising. Subsequent examinations raised suspicion of sexual abuse and the child was referred to the second opinion panel where injuries consistent with sexual abuse were confirmed. Both the physical abuse and the possible sexual abuse were seen to be associated with a strong rejection of the child and the focus of work was built around helping the mother to relinquish her care of the child and build a satisfactory substitute family placement.

Whilst the case emerged on the basis of our random selection of cases where the primary presentation was of physical abuse, it nevertheless demonstrated the link which can exist between sexual and physical abuse. It also demonstrated that even at the height of the crisis in some areas of the County constructive working relationships between Dr Higgs, Dr Wyatt, Social Services and the Police were maintained.

Conclusion

47. In general we were satisfied with the arrangements and the inter-disciplinary working of the main agencies in Cleveland in their response to child abuse other than child sexual abuse.

THE STORY OF THE CLEVELAND 'CRISIS'

Prior to 1987

1. In Cleveland during 1985 and 1986 a number of people had been expressing concern about the response of the agencies to child sexual abuse, notably Mrs Dunn a nursing officer responsible for dealing with child abuse in South Tees. A working party of the Area Review Committee under the chairmanship of the National Society for the Prevention of Cruelty to Children representative, Mr Michie, had experienced difficulties in gaining agreement to revised guidelines from all the agencies, particularly from the Police. The efforts of the working party had been protracted but an acceptable draft had been placed in October 1986 before the committee shortly before its demise.

2. In June 1986 Cleveland County Council Social Services Department, as part of their programme to give child protection a greater priority, had appointed Mrs Richardson to the new post of Child Abuse Consultant.

January 1987

3. On the 1st January 1987 Dr Higgs arrived in Cleveland on her appointment as a consultant paediatrician in South Tees Health District. She was based mainly at the Maternity Hospital and at Middlesbrough General Hospital. There she joined, among others, Dr Wyatt and Dr Morrell. She also had sessions at North Tees General Hospital. Dr Higgs was concerned about the services available in Cleveland for deprived and abused children. Before her arrival in Middlesbrough, she had consulted Mrs Richardson on the prevalence of child abuse and the arrangements in Cleveland. She had expressed the hope of working in a community in a deprived area.

4. Soon after her arrival Dr Higgs called on the Director of Social Services, Mr Bishop, and met Mr Walton, his Senior Assistant Director, and Mrs Richardson. She joined in various multi-disciplinary and community projects and became vice-chairman of the newly formed Joint Child Abuse Committee which took over from the Area Review Committee.

5. Mrs Richardson was on the same committee and she was invited to chair a working party to bring up to date guidelines formulated in 1984 by the earlier committee, the Area Review Committee, for the various agencies to work together in the field of child abuse. The purpose of the new working party was to redraft the guidelines and to make more suitable arrangements for dealing with the special requirements of child sexual abuse.

6. Dr Higgs had, in the summer of 1986 in her previous post in Newcastle, examined two Cleveland children in the care of the Cleveland County Council. She suspected sexual abuse and on examination saw for the first time the phenomenon of what has been termed 'reflex relaxation and anal dilatation'. She had recently learnt from Dr Wynne, a consultant paediatrician at Leeds, that this sign is found in children subject to anal abuse. On the basis of various physical findings, including this sign, she diagnosed anal abuse.

February

7. Soon after her arrival in South Tees, her advice was sought about a little girl of 6 with vaginal bleeding. She had been taken by her mother to a doctor who as it happened was also a woman police surgeon. This doctor was concerned and consulted Mrs Richardson who initially recommended a police surgeon, but on learning that the referring doctor was herself a police surgeon, suggested Dr Higgs. Dr Higgs found evidence of vaginal and anal interference and the signs included anal dilatation. The child indicated that her grandfather was responsible. The police were called and arrested the grandfather, who denied the abuse. He was charged and bailed on the condition that he reside in a bail hostel, and the little girl returned home.

March

8. In March Dr Higgs examined the little girl again and found the signs had reappeared; she diagnosed further abuse and informed Social Services. The grandfather on this occasion could not be the perpetrator, and the little girl said it was her father. Social Services informed the Police. The Police were embarrassed by this revelation and dropped charges against the grandfather. Inspector Whitfield consulted the senior police surgeon, Dr Irvine. The police wanted him to examine the child. He telephoned Dr Higgs. He said she refused to let him examine the child. He expressed the firm view that the sign was unreliable as a basis for diagnosis. On the following day both Dr Higgs and Dr Irvine were at the case conference on the child. Dr Irvine again said he could not accept the grounds for the diagnosis and that Dr Higgs was placing too much reliance upon the observations of Drs Hobbs and Wynne.

9. Dr Irvine went away and consulted Dr Raine Roberts, a well-known police surgeon from Manchester; she supported his stand.

10. The little girl was admitted to hospital and a week later the sign was observed again by Dr Higgs. Dr Higgs saw this child a fourth time in June, when the child was with foster parents, and again the sign was present. Dr Higgs concluded on each occasion that this indicated there had been further sexual abuse.

11. Later in March a little boy of 2 was referred to hospital by his family practitioner as an emergency with constipation. Dr Higgs examined him and noted scars around the anus and the sign of anal dilatation. She considered the possibility of sexual abuse and asked his parents to bring in the elder brother aged 10 and sister aged 9 for examination. They were seen at hospital that evening and Dr Higgs found signs of anal abuse in the boy and anal and vaginal abuse in the girl. This was the first time that Dr Higgs had diagnosed sexual abuse on the basis of the physical signs alone. She asked Dr Morrell to examine the three children and he agreed with her conclusions. None of the children had made any complaint of abuse. After a request for a second opinion, Dr Higgs directed the children be taken to Leeds to be examined by Dr Wynne. She confirmed the physical findings and endorsed the diagnoses of sexual abuse.

12. Photographs of the children had been taken by a police photographer, and the Police later objected to the use of a police photographer for this purpose. Subsequently photographs of children were taken by a medical photographer.

13. The Police decided to interview the two elder children and did so on Saturday and Sunday; no social worker was present when the children were seen. The elder boy was believed at one time to be the possible perpetrator. According to his father he was 'grilled' by the Police. The boy was upset. This was a matter of some concern to the social workers later involved in the case.

14. Social workers obtained place of safety orders and the children were placed with separate foster parents. The two older children were interviewed on a number of occasions over a period of months, by social workers and a clinical psychologist, Mrs Bacon, who believed the children had been sexually abused and that they were making disclosures of abuse by their father. The children were made wards of court and after the hearing were returned home to their parents. The Judge held that they had not been sexually abused.

15. Dr Wyatt who had little previous experience in child sexual abuse was shown the sign by Dr Higgs on one of these three children and found it striking.

16. Some days later a seven year old girl was referred to Dr Higgs by her family practitioner because the child alleged that her father and his girl friend told her to take her clothes off, they played 'doctors' with her and squirted tea up her front. She had had a vaginal discharge for about 5 years. On examination there were abnormal signs relating to the vaginal opening.

April

17. In early April, a 3 year old girl was brought to the Accident and Emergency Department because a school nurse had noticed excessive bruising. She was admitted under the care of Dr Wyatt. He found signs consistent with sexual abuse and asked to see the two elder children. The boy was fine, but the 6 year old girl had anal and vaginal signs, including anal dilatation. This was the first time that Dr Wyatt had observed the sign in one of his patients. All three children went to foster parents and later the elder girl made complaints to her teacher and the foster mother of interference by her step-father.

18. The two children seen by Dr Higgs the previous summer in Newcastle had been placed with experienced foster parents in Cleveland. At the end of April Dr Higgs did a routine check-up preparatory to giving evidence in a pending Juvenile Court hearing. She found anal dilatation and diagnosed anal abuse. The parents had no access to the children for several months and suspicion fell on the foster family. The foster parents were asked to bring their three daughters to be examined in hospital and all were diagnosed as sexually abused.

19. The Director of Social Services, Mr Bishop, was informed that children in the care of the Council had been abused in a foster home and he asked for a second opinion. The 2 foster children and the 3 children of the foster parents were taken to Leeds and examined by Dr Wynne who confirmed the physical signs of sexual abuse in each child.

15

20. A number of children had gone through the foster household, both as foster children and some for whom the foster parents had acted as child minders. Social workers brought 6 more children to be examined by Dr Higgs. Together with the 2 foster children, the 3 children of the foster parents and these 6, 11 children in all were examined of which 10 were found by Dr Higgs to have signs of anal abuse and admitted to the ward.

21. Some of these children were no longer in the foster home or in contact with the foster father. None of the children in this group had made a complaint and no adult had made any allegation of sexual abuse. The children of the foster family became wards and were later returned home by the Judge.

May

22. The weekend after this group of children had been admitted to the ward happened to be the first Bank Holiday weekend in May and there was not the full complement of social workers available. Mrs Richardson helped social workers in the interviews of some of the children.

23. Other children entirely separate from those associated with the foster family were seen during the first week of May in Dr Higgs' outpatient clinic. On the 5th May, 7 of the children were diagnosed as sexually abused. One child, who suffered from a medical condition and was referred for excessive bruising, was a long term patient of Dr Wyatt. Dr Higgs found signs of anal and vaginal abuse and the child's two brothers were seen. A little girl of 1 was referred with rectal bleeding and bowel problems. On examination Dr Higgs found anal dilatation, fissures and a fresh scar. This child was seen by Dr Stanton and Dr Wynne who both confirmed Dr Higgs' findings. Another little girl of 2 was seen on a routine check-up for failure to thrive. She and two other related children were considered by Dr Higgs to have signs of anal abuse. She was already in care. The 3 children remained briefly on the ward and then went to a foster home. They became wards of court and later returned home on conditions by order of the Judge. A girl of 11 was referred by her family practitioner with poor weight gain and eating problems. Dr Higgs found signs of anal and vaginal abuse. Her young half-sister was called and was thought to have signs consistent with sexual abuse. The elder girl later made complaints against her step-father. After a wardship hearing she went to live with her natural father and his new wife. Her half sister went home. In total during the first week of May, 23 children were seen by Dr Higgs and diagnosed as sexually abused and admitted to the Middlesbrough General Hospital.

24. During May there was a steady stream of referrals to Dr Higgs and Dr Wyatt. These included children referred by social workers, health visitors, and a guardian ad litem. The reasons for referral included a mother who was worried that her boy friend might have sexually abused her child, who was found to have a very sore, red perineum, anal dilatation and multiple anal fissures. There were also several children with perineal injuries. In mid-May social workers brought in a family of 5 children for examination because of concern about sexual abuse. A boy aged 7 in the family had made a complaint to his mother and then to a social worker. That family was not admitted to hospital but went with their mother to a group home.

25. A week later social workers referred another family of 3 as a result of the comments of the eldest child of 10 at school and the concern of her headmistress. Dr Higgs examined the first child with the consent of the mother, and found signs she felt were consistent with sexual abuse. Before she could examine the second child, the father arrived on the ward and removed the 3 children. He took them to a secret address. He was at that time required to report daily to the police who were unable to persuade him to divulge the whereabouts of the children. However, he agreed to the examination of the children by a police surgeon, and Dr Beeby was taken to the secret address. He examined the children in an upstairs room and found no abnormality. They were then returned home by their father; removed on a place of safety order obtained by Social Services and taken back to hospital. This time Dr Higgs examined all 3 children and diagnosed sexual abuse in respect of all 3. The following day Dr Irvine examined the 3 children and agreed with the conclusions of Dr Beeby. Two weeks later, Dr McCowen, paediatrician from Northallerton, considered the signs suspicious and later in June Dr Roberts and Dr Paul examined the children and considered there was no abnormality. These children were first dealt with, at a very prolonged hearing, on an interim care application before the Teesside Juvenile Court and thereafter in wardship. The children were returned home but remain wards. The Social Services Department were extremely concerned at the removal of the children from the hospital ward by the father and the difficulties of tracing their whereabouts.

26. Also during May there were referrals to Dr Higgs other than by Social Services; for example, a Senior House Officer while examining a child of 2 with a febrile fit noted an abnormal anus. Dr Higgs found signs of anal and vaginal abuse in this child and her 2 sisters. The father was charged with several

sexual offences and committed suicide while awaiting trial. A Senior Clinical Medical Officer, as a result of concern in the neighbourhood about the possibility of sexual abuse, referred a family of 7 children, 4 of the children showed signs of sexual abuse and all 7 were admitted to the hospital. A nurse noticed an abnormal anus in a 2 year old boy admitted with asthma and Dr Higgs concluded that there were signs consistent with sexual abuse. He was examined by Dr Steiner who did not agree with Dr Higgs and the child returned home.

27. Over the second Bank Holiday weekend in May there was a new wave of admissions to Middlesbrough General Hospital. The numbers were augmented by the admission of the 7 children from one family and 3 children from another family. Altogether in May, 52 children from 17 families were examined for sexual abuse and 41 of them were considered to have physical signs of sexual abuse.

28. Most of the children had no medical problem requiring nursing or medical attention and their presence on the ward caused difficulties for the nurses. Social Services managed to place the children out of hospital with foster parents or in residential care, but their field workers were very stretched. Mrs de Lacy Dunne, the adoption and fostering officer, took control of all foster placements. By June she and her resources became overwhelmed and ran out of space for the children.

29. In May the hospital had the resources to cope, but it was an unprecedented number of children with an unfamiliar problem and alarm bells began to ring. Dr Drury, the Hospital Unit Manager had been informed of the numbers admitted in the first week of May. He got in touch with the Social Services Department to express his concern both at the numbers and the problems in the hospital, particularily for the nurses. Dr Drury met Dr Higgs and they discussed among other matters the disagreement between herself and Dr Irvine.

30. At a meeting in mid-May of the South Tees Community Health Council, Mr Urch, its Secretary, told Mr Bishop about mounting public anxiety over the admissions to hospital and the diagnosis of child sexual abuse.

31. Mrs Richardson, who had earlier predicted an increase in detection of sexual abuse, was alarmed by the numbers and the lack of resources to deal with them. On the 12th May, she wrote a memorandum to Mr Bishop referring to 'crisis', the likelihood that the numbers would increase and the need for more resources.

32. At the invitation of Mr Bishop she attended a meeting of the Social Services Directorate in mid-May. They discussed the alarming increase in referrals for child sexual abuse, but the differences between Dr Higgs and Dr Irvine and the controversy over the anal dilatation test and the diagnosis of sexual abuse were not referred to. Mrs Richardson did not recognise the importance of the dispute and did not inform the Director.

The Police in April and May

33. By the end of April and the beginning of May the Police were having doubts about the diagnosis of sexual abuse based upon the anal dilatation test. These doubts were reinforced by the strong views of Dr Irvine. At a meeting chaired by a Chief Superintendent on the 8th May, Dr Irvine was asked his views and made plain to senior police officers that he regarded the anal dilatation test as unreliable.

34. Also at the end of April, as a result of Dr Higgs requesting police photographers to photograph the ano-genital region of the 3 children in March, and on the instructions of Detective Superintendent White, Inspector Walls, the head of the Scientific Aids Department went to see Dr Higgs and explain the concern his Department had at taking these photographs. His photographers were embarrassed and felt the children were upset. The meeting was more in the nature of a confrontation, with Inspector Walls telling Dr Higgs what he thought. It did not improve relations between the Police and Dr Higgs.

35. Detective Superintendent White went twice in May to Middlesbrough General Hospital to discuss both the problem over the photographs and the difficulties caused by the diagnosis of child sexual abuse.

36. In the absence of prompt medical statements and with these doubts the Police investigated but without much confidence in the outcome. There was also a feeling, expressed by Inspector Makepeace of the Community Relations Department, that the good relations which he believed existed between police officers and social workers on the ground had deteriorated since the appointment of Mrs Richardson in her new role. These feelings among the Police gathered momentum.

Joint Child Abuse Committee Working Party—Meeting in May and its Consequences

37. The working party of the Joint Child Abuse Committee, chaired by Mrs Richardson (see paragraph 5 above), included a representative of the Police, Chief Inspector Taylor; a nursing officer, Mrs Dunn; Mr Michie from the NSPCC; an educational social worker, Mr Town and a probation officer. Between February and May they met on several occasions and agreed most of the outstanding issues which had troubled their predecessors on the Area Review Committee. The two main issues which remained were:

1. the degree of co-operation between the police and social workers in the investigation of sexual abuse;

2. who should perform the medical examination and whether the police surgeon should be consulted.

It was agreed that Mrs Richardson and Chief Inspector Taylor should arrange a meeting with Dr Higgs and Dr Irvine to try and come to an agreement on the issue which could be placed before the next meeting of the working party on the 1st June. The meeting was arranged for the 28th May.

38. At that meeting in addition to Mrs Richardson and Dr Higgs there were Dr Irvine, Detective Superintendent White, Inspector Makepeace, and Chief Inspector Taylor. The previous day Dr Irvine had for the first time examined children found by Dr Higgs to have been sexually abused. His negative findings confirmed Dr Irvine in his view as to the unreliability of the anal dilatation test. Dr Higgs had by then diagnosed as anally abused a considerable number of children, some confirmed by other paediatricians, and was convinced of the reliability of the test. When the meeting began to discuss the medical aspects of sexual abuse, Mrs Richardson put forward some new proposals, the effect of which was to provide for examination in all cases by the paediatrician. When challenged on this it became clear that Mrs Richardson did not see any future for police surgeons in the examination of children said to be sexually abused. Dr Irvine then said that Dr Higgs was incompetent and misguided and that her 'mentors' in Leeds, Drs Wynne and Hobbs, were equally misguided. Dr Higgs was firm in her viewpoint. Inspector Makepeace supported Dr Irvine and Mrs Richardson supported Dr Higgs. The meeting became heated and all those present found it disagreeable.

39. Detective Superintendent White expressed the Police conclusion that the police would treat the diagnosis of Dr Higgs with a degree of caution. Each group left the meeting with their preconceived ideas reinforced, and this led to a major breakdown in the relationship between the police and the social workers.

40. After the meeting Mrs Richardson and Mr Hughes together drafted a memorandum for Mr Bishop. It was largely the work of Mrs Richardson. Mr Bishop was given this memorandum and signed it on the 29th May. Its main effects were to provide for routine applications for place of safety orders in cases of suspected sexual abuse, to suspend access to the parents and to exclude the police surgeon from making a second examination.

41. Detective Superintendent White on the 29th May sent out a Force circular in which he instructed the Police to view Dr Higgs' diagnosis on sexual abuse with caution, and to look for substantial corroboration of her findings before taking positive action.

Although Superintendent White had told Mrs Richardson of the police response, neither agency officially informed the other of the steps they were taking.

42. The meeting of the working party of the Joint Child Abuse Committee was scheduled to take place on the 1st June. The Assistant Chief Constable Mr Smith instructed Chief Inspector Taylor not to attend. The working party went on in his absence and with no disagreement the proposals put forward on the 28th May were accepted by the working party as their recommendations to the Joint Child Abuse Committee on

the medical issue. They included: that the hospital was the most appropriate setting for the examination of a child by a paediatrician, and where a consultant paediatrician is able to give a statement to the Police it is not necessary for a police surgeon to re-examine the child.

June

43. In June children continued to be referred in ever growing numbers, mainly by Social Services. They included: children who had constipation, failure to thrive, an itchy bottom, urinary tract infection, bruised perineum, soiling etc. A nurse saw a gaping anus in a child admitted to hospital with tonsilitis and brought it to Dr Higgs' attention. There was a family of 7 children who had behavioural problems and poor growth, and several members of this family were diagnosed as showing signs of sexual abuse.

44. Dr Wyatt was asked by Social Services to see 2 boys from a special school who had been found with others indulging in inappropriate sexual behaviour. Dr Wyatt found signs of anal interference in both boys and offered to examine all the children in the special school. In the event the situation was dealt with by the Education Department. 6 of the children from 2 of the families concerned were admitted to the ward. One boy of 11 had considerable behavioural problems and had been under the care of a child psychiatrist for several years. In 4 further families the index (first) child examined during June had behavioural problems and had previously been seen by a child psychiatrist. Also about this time Dr Higgs saw a 3 year old girl with a vaginal discharge caused by gonorrhoea. The infection was present in her rectum. Her 2 year old brother also had a sexually transmitted infection. The girl had vaginal signs, both had signs of anal abuse. The childrens' uncle and a friend were convicted of sexual offences. Another little girl had anal warts. She had been referred by her family practitioner on suspicion of sexual abuse. The Independent Panel which examined this child came to the conclusion that the child should return home. The anal warts were not shown to be sexually transmitted.

45. During June children in two more foster homes were considered to have been sexually abused. In one case it was a handicapped child living with adoptive parents who was diagnosed as abused. Before informing the agencies Dr Higgs arranged for Dr Wynne to give a second opinion on the child and she confirmed the diagnosis. This child and his sister became wards and were returned home by the Judge on the basis that no sexual abuse had occurred.

46. Also during June, members of the Emergency Duty Team of social workers were asked to obtain place of safety orders late at night mainly by Dr Wyatt. In one case there had been an agreement with the parents that the children would remain on the ward; in another the children had been allowed to go home and had gone to bed and then had to be brought back to hospital. On one evening Dr Wyatt asked for 11 place of safety orders, 7 relating to a family already well-known to the Social Services.

47. On the evening of the 12th June Dr Wyatt was making a late evening round, a usual occurrence with him. Dr Higgs was on call and she went round the ward with him. The ward contained 12 children of 8 families where sexual abuse had been diagnosed. During that day between them they had identified 4 index children as sexually abused. Late that evening nurses told them of abnormal anal findings in two further children. They examined the children and diagnosed sexual abuse. Those two children had between them 8 siblings. They examined in all 4 children that night because of the possibility of sexual abuse. They were dissuaded from examining a 5th child because the nurse said that mother and child were asleep. Some nurses became upset about these examinations and two nurses made a written complaint.

48. The following day it was necessary to transfer 6 children to North Tees General Hospital because the wards in Middlesbrough General Hospital could not cope with the siblings of the children identified the night before.

49. The events of the 12th June and the consequential intake of the siblings created the third large wave of admissions.

50. On the 18th June there was a considerable number of parents at the hospital and there was a confrontation between Dr Wyatt and an angry father. The police were called and helped to calm the situation. The deputy administrator at the hospital took the parents to another building and helped them to set out their complaints for transmission to the hospital authorities.

51. The following day Mr Stuart Bell MP was told of the situation at the hospital and paid it several visits during the following week. He heard the parents' complaints. Some parents had just begun to form themselves into a parents' support group with the assistance of the Rev. Michael Wright.

52. During June there were meetings between professionals and the different disciplines to try to resolve the problems which arose.

— On the **1st June** Mr Bishop together with Mrs Richardson met Mr Donaldson, Dr Drury, Dr Ramiah, the new community physician, and Dr Higgs. Mr Bishop questioned Dr Higgs very closely on her diagnostic techniques and was satisfied that she was confident of what she was doing. None of the other doctors present queried her method of diagnosis.

— On the **5th June** the Chief Constable and the Assistant Chief Constable Mr Smith met Mr Bishop and Mr Walton, his senior Assistant Director, and they discussed the situation. Neither of the Chief Officers was entirely in the picture and the only suggestion made was for the deputies to meet the Crown Prosecution Service. This they did with no result. The Chief Constable and the Director made no arrangement to meet again and did not do so.

— Shortly after that Dr Higgs and Dr Wyatt called on Mr Bishop and refused to see anybody else. They praised him for his stand over child sexual abuse, and said that the detection of abuse was a breakthrough in the care of children and could explain many problems of child health which had previously not responded to treatment. He took the opportunity to tell them about the strain on the resources of the Department and asked them if they could proceed more slowly to allow Social Services to obtain more resources. They told him it was not professionally acceptable to them and that other agencies needed to recognise that this was a major development in child health.

— On the **11th June** Mr Cooke, the Clerk to the Justices went to see Mr Bishop. Many place of safety orders were expiring and applications were being made for interim care orders on the children. Two days before in the Teesside Juvenile Court there had been the unprecedented number of 45 applications for interim care orders. Mr Cooke asked Mr Bishop if he could arrange for 28 day applications for place of safety orders to be made to the magistrate. The numbers were compounded by the unusual opposition to the granting of the interim order. These applications were being contested and disputed medical evidence was having to be considered by the magistrates at an early stage in the proceedings. Mr Cooke noticed that this might have been due to the refusal or restriction of access to the parents which was also most unusual. A few days later Mr Cooke returned to see Mr Bishop, on this occasion accompanied by the Chairman of the Juvenile Panel, expressing the concerns of the Juvenile Bench about the numbers of cases which were threatening to overwhelm the Courts; the great concern of the magistrates at the refusal of access to parents; and the most unusual situation of disputed medical evidence. Again Mr Cooke suggested application for longer place of safety orders to relieve pressure on the courts. Later in June some disputed care applications were restarted in the High Court as wardship applications.

— On the **15th June** Mr Bishop consulted the Social Services Inspectorate as to whether second opinions might be obtained and was advised to go to the District Health Authority. He immediately got in touch with Mr Donaldson and asked him to arrange second opinions on the diagnoses of the two doctors.

— On the **16th June** Mr Donaldson consulted Dr Donaldson, the Regional Medical Officer of the Northern Regional Health Authority concerning the complaints of the two nurses about the evening of the 12th June and asked for advice and help. This was the first that Northern Region had heard of the crisis and they then became involved. Northern Region decided to deal with all the complaints about the two doctors. The following day Dr Donaldson and Mr Donaldson met and Mr Donaldson asked for help to deal with the request from Mr Bishop for second medical opinions.

— Also on the **16th June** there was a meeting of the Joint Child Abuse Consultative Committee at which senior representatives of Social Services and the Police attended. They did not tell the elected members about the difficulties being experienced between the two agencies. At the same time there were meetings between the Chief Executive and leading members of the County Council where the seriousness of the situation was fully explored.

— On the **18th June** after the incident with the parent on the ward, Mr Donaldson discussed the situation with both paediatricians and asked them to hold back. They refused and said that if they saw child sexual abuse they had a duty to act.

— Mr Donaldson then asked three senior consultants to interview the two doctors and find out if they were acting within the bounds of medical practice. At the meeting on the **23rd June** the two paediatricians assured the three consultants that they were acting correctly.

53. The Chairman of Northern Region, Professor Sir Bernard Tomlinson, became involved and he and Dr Donaldson invited the two paediatricians to the headquarters of the Regional Health Authority in Newcastle to find out if they were acting correctly. They had a four hour meeting. Drs Higgs and Wyatt

were given the complaints and asked to comment on them, which they said they would do after they had consulted their legal advisers. After the meeting at which the two doctors were cross-examined at length by the two Regional Officers, both Professor Sir Bernard Tomlinson and Dr Donaldson could find no reason to recommend their suspension from duties to the Regional Committee. There were thereafter various meetings which included legal advisers to consider the complaints and the position of the doctors.

54. The Northern Regional Health Authority took over the arrangements for second opinions requested by Social Services and with the help of Professor Kolvin, Consultant Child Psychiatrist at Newcastle, set up a panel of paediatricians and child psychiatrists to see jointly the children who had been diagnosed as sexually abused. They started to see children at the end of June. Thereafter Northern Region set up a second panel called the Regional Reference Group, made up of paediatricians within the area of Northern Region, to see any children who were subsequently diagnosed as sexually abused, in South Tees District.

55. By the end of June parents had arranged their own second opinions and a number of doctors, principally Dr Roberts from Manchester, Dr Paul from London and Dr Clarke from Liverpool, saw many of the children concerned.

56. On Friday **26th June** Dr Irvine was interviewed on television in the early evening and said that Dr Higgs was wrong in her diagnosis of sexual abuse in respect of a particular family.

57. Later that evening on the television programme Nightline, Mr Bishop and Mr Bell MP were among those who were present. Dr Irvines' interview was shown. Mr Bishop said he had no alternative but to act on the diagnosis of the paediatrician.

58. On the **29th June** Mr Bell put down a Private Notice Question in the House Of Commons asking the Minister if he would make a statement on the recent increase in the number of cases of alleged child abuse in Cleveland.

59. At the request of the Minister of State for Health reports were provided very quickly by the Social Services Inspectorate, the Northern Regional Health Authority. The Police provided a report for the Home Office.

60. At the end of June, with the help of Middlesbrough General Hospital, Social Services set up the Child Resource Centre in the grounds of the hospital and children and their parents were able to spend the day there and be interviewed there.

July

61. On the **1st July** the Joint Child Abuse Committee met to consider the recommendations of the working party. Mr Walton with the help of Mr Smith took charge of the draft guidelines and in a few days secured agreement to a revised draft which was almost immediately put into effect both by the Social Services and the Police. The agreed guidelines included: that the hospital is often the most appropriate setting for medical examination; that the child should be referred as soon as possible to a consultant paediatrician; that the roles of the police surgeon and paediatrician are complementary; early consultation is essential; there should be joint examination where possible.

62. Also on the **1st July** the Police set up the Child Abuse Unit at Yarm, to co-ordinate the investigation of child sexual abuse in the County.

63. On the **7th July** Mr Bell gave the Minister a 'dossier' of cases he had investigated. On the **9th July** the Minister announced in a statement to the House of Commons the setting up of a Statutory Inquiry.

64. In total 125 children were diagnosed as sexually abused between February and July 1987, 121 of them by Dr Higgs and Dr Wyatt—78 by Dr Higgs, 43 by Dr Wyatt. 67 of the children became wards of court. In the wardship cases 27 were dewarded and went home with the proceedings dismissed; 24 went home on conditions which included supervision orders on the children and conditions as to medical examination of the children and 2 of them went home on interim care orders. 9 other children who are wards of court remain in the care of the County Council and away from their families. Of those children not made wards of court, a further 27 were the subject of place of safety orders. In all 21 children remain in care. We understand that out of the 121 children, 98 are now at home.

PART ONE

PEOPLE AND EVENTS IN CLEVELAND

CHAPTER 1

The Children in Cleveland

1.1 It was perhaps inevitable that during the crisis in Cleveland attention was largely focussed upon the adults, both parents and professionals, and their interpretation of the experiences of the children involved. The crisis came to public gaze as a result of complaints of adults suspected of committing acts of sexual abuse. The voices of the children were not heard.

1.2 It was a decision of the Inquiry not to invite nor to permit any child to give evidence, in order to shield the children from the enormous burden of attending the Inquiry and speaking in the presence of upwards of 50 people if it were in private session. It would have been unthinkable to have heard them in public session. In our view, supported by the Official Solicitor, it was an unacceptable additional stress for children, many of whom, whether or not they had been sexually abused, had been adversely affected by subsequent events.

1.3 In order to redress this imbalance, the Inquiry invited the Official Solicitor to represent the children; to seek the views of children who wished to speak; to listen and record them and to put the children's views to witnesses where appropriate. In one or two instances professionals in the witness box were somewhat taken aback in what they were told of the children's impressions and responses to their experiences.

1.4 Although none of the children attended the Inquiry many were well aware of the existence and continuance of the Inquiry and we understand the Official Solicitor at their request took some children to see the Council Chamber where it was taking place.

1.5 The final submission of the Official Solicitor contained an account of interviews with children aged 8 or over. Out of the 165 children examined by the paediatricians at Middlesbrough General Hospital between January and July 1987, some 51 were over 8 years of age and 32 of them saw the Official Solicitor. The remaining 19 were thought likely to be badly affected by further discussions, or their parents did not want them to be troubled further, or they proved in some way difficult to trace. During the interviews the children were not asked about the question of sexual abuse, nor about sensitive topics such as family relationships, although some children volunteered such information. The Official Solicitor reported to the Inquiry that the children's stories reflected variously: "misunderstanding, mistrust, discomfort, anger, fear, praise, gratitude and sheer relief".

1.6 In the rest of this Report we set out the events and the responses of the adults which from time to time may appear to be entirely centred upon adult perceptions and concerns, and the arguments which surrounded them seemed to have little to do with the problems of the children themselves. In this chapter we have set out the impressions and perceptions of some children during the crisis, in an attempt not to fall into the same trap.

Two examples are marked with an asterisk, these children were not examined by Dr Higgs or Dr Wyatt at any stage. Before each account we have tried to set the child's story very briefly in context. Some of these stories are heard in other parts of the report. In those cases where the objective facts might not quite match the child's perceptions, the value of those perceptions is not diminished for our present purpose.

1.7 The Children's Stories

1 New Mum and Dad

This 8 year old girl was referred to Dr Higgs because of vaginal discharge. Sexual abuse was diagnosed. Her account of bizarre sexual behaviour involving her father and his girlfriend was given to a Woman Police Officer and a social worker.

In her foster home the girl was said to have initially displayed overt sexual behaviour, which had improved but she still displayed sexual behaviour towards men, and the family with whom she was placed had to take care that their young son was not abused by her.

When asked why she was not at home she said:

"They told my Mum that I was going to be fostered, and my mum was in a mood and she told uncle x and uncle y and my nanna."

She said her uncle had told Dr Higgs off. The doctor had been "terrible" to her uncle and nanna. She did not appear to be distressed, upset, worried or anxious about Dr Higgs, nor about her present or former social worker. She said Dr Higgs was "really all right". She could remember her examination which was not painful or uncomfortable, she was not worried by it and did not think about it much. She had told people all about things that had happened. She was expecting to have "a new Mum and Dad" until she was 18.

This child was made a ward of court. The Judge held that sexual abuse had occurred. The girl remains a ward and has been committed to the care of the Local Authority with no access to her own family.

2 Another Chance

This 8 year old boy was seen by Dr Wyatt after sexual abuse had been diagnosed on his sister, and a place of safety order was taken on the grounds that he might be at risk. Two other half sisters were also taken into care.

The boy arrived home on his sister's birthday to find a police car outside his house—not an uncommon sight, he said. Police officers and two social workers saw him upstairs and then took him to a foster home. He was taken to Middlesbrough General and was seen by a male doctor, who examined his bruises. His foster mother said that he wanted to return home and thought that his step-father should be given another chance. His sister did not want to return home. She was confused and talked about her experiences of being sexually abused.

These children and their baby sister born after proceedings started became wards. The three elder children are no longer at home. The baby has gone home on conditions but remains in the care of the County Council.

3 Ruined Birthday

A boy and girl aged 11 and 10 who were siblings of a younger child were examined by Dr Higgs.

The boy and girl were collected by their father and taken to hospital where they thought they would see their baby brother. They waited, were examined by Dr Higgs, and were then seen individually by Dr Higgs. The examination was short and caused no discomfort.

It was the boy's Birthday. He was visited by the police that night who questioned him throughout the following two days, on one of which he was to have had his birthday party. The day after the cancelled party, both children were taken in their father's car, accompanied by a social worker, to see Dr Wynne in Leeds. The children thought they would be going back to hospital, but they were taken to a foster home where they arrived later in the day.

The children had talks with their social worker and with Mrs Bacon about sexual abuse, and monthly medical check-ups. Photographs had been taken. They were seen by Dr Roberts and Dr Paul at the beginning of the school holiday. The boy had been at an International Scout camp, where, as a leader, he had been organising his patrol for judging before an important visitor. He had been removed from camp, and his mother was not able to attend the scout parent meeting. His sister was taken out of bed at 9.30 pm and brought by her social worker for the examination, which hurt and was very unpleasant. These examinations by Dr Roberts and Dr Paul were worse than previous ones. According to her foster mother the girl had suffered from nightmares before being taken into care, and had not had one since until this medical examination.

These children became wards. The Judge held that they had not been sexually abused. By consent they were dewarded.

4 Not believed

This girl was examined by Dr Higgs after a referral for failure to thrive and sexual abuse was diagnosed. A second opinion by Dr Roberts called the diagnosis into question. The girl told her social worker that her step-father had got into bed with her every Thursday night for two years.

The girl thinks she was referred to hospital because she suffered growth problems similar to those suffered by her half sister. She was examined by Dr Higgs who explained what the examination would entail. The examination did not hurt and caused no embarrassment. She stayed in hospital for about ten days and photographs were taken. She had been examined by Dr Higgs on two further occasions once at 11.00pm. She had been woken up for this but had not minded. She had been seen by Dr Roberts for a second opinion.

She had taken a long time to tell her female social worker what had happened to her—her step-father had told her no-one would believe her. She thought "it" had happened to her because her step-father did not like her. She had not been able to talk to her natural parents about what had happened to her. She felt under pressure because she had been asked where she would like to live—she found the choices she was being asked to make were difficult, not wanting to hurt anyone.

She was fond of her social worker, and found that they had helpful discussions. She felt happier than she had for a long time.

This child and her little half-sister were made wards of court. The Judge ordered by consent that both children remain wards. The elder child went to live with her natural father with reasonable access to her mother but no access to her step-father. Her half-sister was placed in the care and control of her mother, both children to be under the supervision of the County Council and the younger child to have regular medical examinations.

5 Mad

A family of three children, two girls, one aged 14 and the other aged 10, and a boy aged 11, were seen by Dr Higgs after the guardian ad litem was worried about the possibility of sexual abuse. There had been a history of Social Services involvement with the family for failure to thrive. The boy had severe behaviour problems. The mother reported the 14 year old girl masturbating the dog and wondered if the dog could be responsible for the abuse diagnosed in the younger girl. The two younger children were deemed by Professor Kolvin to be too disturbed to be interviewed.

The 14 year old girl said that she was examined for sexual abuse in 1986 by a male police surgeon, while care proceedings were in hand regarding her brother. Her mother had been there and a Woman Police Officer. She had been embarrassed by being examined by a man—it was "disgusting".

She was subject to a care order and her guardian ad litem sought a second medical opinion on her and her sister. On advice she refused to be examined by Dr Higgs, who had diagnosed that her sister had been abused. She agreed to be examined by Dr Grant if she could go home should the examination prove to be satisfactory. She refused to allow a social worker to be present and "passed the test". She has been unable to see her sister or her brother recently. She found it awkward to explain what was happening to her to fellow pupils when she was taken away from school. She had been sent to a special assessment unit and understood the referral was to assess if she was mad.

Care orders were made on these children, who were previously known to social services.

6 Dirty Things

This family of five were referred to Dr Higgs after the second eldest daughter had told her mother of sexual abuse. The father was a Schedule 1 offender. The elder daughter was on the verge of going into care as a result of her disturbed behaviour. The twelve year old spoke of full intercourse having taken place, and her father threatening to stab her. Three more of the children in this family spoke of similar experiences.

The two younger children, an 8 year old boy and a 9 year old girl were taken from home to a children's home by a social worker who had told them their father had been doing "dirty things". This happened when their mother was at work. One day they were collected from school and taken to hospital by a social worker. They asked why and were told to wait and see. Dr Higgs examined them after taking off their clothes. The examination had not hurt. Photographs were taken. They had been interviewed by Mrs Bacon but did not know why, and video recordings had been taken of them. The guardian ad litem said the children were crying out to go home.

The 12 and 13 year old girls said that a social worker used to visit their home at weekly intervals. One day they were taken away from school to meet Mrs Bacon whom they had seen previously. They went home and afterwards their father left. The elder girl was told she would have to go away for a few days. Their mother told the 12 year old to stay away from home so that the social workers could not get her. The 12 year old girl was eventually taken into care.

They were taken to see Dr Higgs by social workers. The 12 year-old was told that she was seeing Dr Higgs for a normal check-up, but it was a "sexual examination". The 15 year-old sister had been seen first and was upset afterwards. The social workers would not let her tell them why.

Dr Higgs did not introduce herself nor her colleague. She told them to strip—she inserted a stick and cotton wool into their "privates" and it hurt a little. They were rolled over for their bottoms to be examined and this did not hurt. The doctor did not call them by name. They were told to dress and tell the next one to go in. They returned to the community home but were not spoken to or told what was going on. They did not see their mother for 28 days while the place of safety order was in force and had recently seen their younger brother and sister for the first time in five weeks. They had not seen their 15 year-old sister since she was moved from the home two weeks previously. They did not miss her. The interview with the younger girl had been video recorded, and she said she was questioned "like a machine, boom, boom".

The 15 year old child was in a community home. She said that she had suffered abuse by her father for some time and had eventually told her mother. She begged her mother not to tell social workers but had been assured that she would not be received into care. Nevertheless, one evening a social worker took them all into care while their mother was out at work, apart from their 12 year old sister who was not at home at the time.

She was taken to hospital by a social worker, having understood that she was to have a routine medical because she had just been taken into care. At her examination Dr Higgs was somewhat brusque, poking at her "privates" with her hands and then examining her bottom. It had not hurt but was very embarrassing. Another person, a "young lass" was also present, but was not introduced.

After the examination she was told to dress and send in the next child. She was crying and the other children saw this. The social worker said it was not that bad, but the girl commented:

"How could she know? She weren't there."

Nothing further was said when they returned to the children's home. She had seen Mrs Bacon before being taken into care, but had not seen her since. She felt very bitter towards the social workers who deceived her before the medical examination.

These children were made subject to interim care orders and their father was prosecuted for indecent assault.

7 Suicide

The children in this family were felt to have been through too much already to be interviewed; their mother spoke for them. They were examined after the two year old was admitted to casualty with febrile convulsions. A senior house officer noted an abnormal anus. Dr Wyatt examined and diagnosed sexual abuse. The other children were admitted and sexual abuse was found after an examination by Dr Higgs and a police surgeon. Criminal charges were laid against the father, who committed suicide.

The children's mother said that the 8 year old had expressed relief at the death of her father, believing she would not have to discuss her experiences again.

8 Babysitter

A girl of 10 was referred to the social services by her headmistress after she told of her father's sexual activities which had been taking place in the girl's bedroom. She and her younger brother and sister were medically examined. Subsequent interviews revealed that the 10 year old girl had been abused also by someone outside the family.

28

The 10 year old knew that they were in care because their father had done "dirty things to their babysitter". He had done "dirty things" on her bed. She was anxious to get home and got upset at night. She said that if she went home there would be no more "dirty things" with her dad or anyone else. She said she could not take much more, everything was going round in her head. She had been told by a social worker that the family were not going home and had not explained why, and had merely explained it was up to the court. The girl had been examined by five doctors, including Dr Higgs, who told her that someone had touched her. The girl said that this was just not true.

The children were not distressed by their examinations, although the boy pulled a face when Dr Higgs' name was first mentioned.

The ten year old had told the younger girl of their father's behaviour and said that her sister knew why they were at the home, but was scared to say it. Whatever had been wrong with their day-to-day lives in the past it was the only life they had known and they wanted to return to it.

These children became wards of court. By consent the Judge ordered them to remain wards with care and control to the parents and a supervision order to Cleveland County Council. A number of conditions were attached including regular medical examinations.

9 Dislike of Doctors
The two girls aged 8 and 9 were examined by Dr Higgs after referral by the Social Services Department.

The two girls aged 8 and 9 arrived home from school to be told by their mother they would have to see Dr Higgs. The appointment was for 7.00pm but they waited in a cubicle until 9.00pm. Their parents were not allowed to see them. They were examined separately, it took "ages" and it hurt. They said their bottoms had been pulled right out. They were sent out and a lady and gentleman went in. After the doctors had spoken to their parents the children were told by the lady and gentleman that they would have to stay in hospital. They were not allowed to see their parents and no explanation was given to them as the reason for them having to stay.

The next day they were interviewed by a social worker and Dr Higgs was there—the younger girl would not speak to them. There were video recordings made of interviews—they had lost count. The younger girl complained that she had been woken up by Dr Higgs for photographs to be taken.

They had been examined by Dr Irvine, whom they had seen on T.V. The younger girl said that Dr Irvine hurt more than Dr Higgs. Her sister said the hurt was the same. The younger one had never liked doctors and did not want to see one again.

They were aggrieved that they were not allowed to see their mother whereas another child known to them who was also involved in the Inquiry had been receiving daily visits from her mother while in hospital.

They said their social worker was "alright", the younger girl did not like her guardian ad litem.

The uncle of these children was charged with indecent assault, he committed suicide in prison. The stepfather was charged with indecent assault and unlawful sexual intercourse.

10 School
This family of three brothers, aged 11, 12 and 14 were referred after concern at the elder boy's sexual activities at school. There was a number of boys involved. When interviewed they were in a children's home.

The twelve year old boy said he was taken for examination by Dr Wyatt, he "sort of liked him". He knew examinations of children who had been touched were taking place there. Dr Wyatt told him he had been touched. His examination hurt a bit. He did not like being photographed, but was told it was:

"So it could go to the Judge and get the person, but we (he and his brother) already told who did it."

He explained that he had thought the touching (by someone outside the family) had been a game. He described the abuse which had frightened him a bit. He discussed what had happened to him. He thought this information would help:

"put a stop to it...the men touching other people in their private parts. They can find the men and put them in to prison...for the rest of their lives as far as I can care."

He had been frightened of telling what happened originally. He was not upset at being away from home, but his elder brother was.

His elder brother said that he had bad feelings about those who had abused him—one of whom was in prison. He had had "nasty" things done to him for about seven years. Another boy involved had had things done to him lots of times. He now hated him and was frightened of him. He had never thought about telling his parents. The abuse came to light when his 11 year old brother was found abusing another boy.

When examined by Dr Wyatt his bottom hurt but then it always hurt. He did not like being photographed. He had returned to the school he had formerly attended and another boy involved in the abuse was still a pupil there—he did not like that.

An uncle of these children was arrested and charged with indecent assault.

11 Parental Anger

A boy was referred to Dr Wyatt following reported concern by his headmaster as to his sexual activity at school. The boy was being seen by a local psychiatrist and was described by various people as being very disturbed.

The boy had seen his parents for the first time on the day prior to the meeting. His father had been angry with him and had asked "why did you say those things". The officer in charge of the children's home in which he was placed said that the father had been verbally aggressive, accused the boy of lying and had blamed him for the death of his grandmother, which had upset and disturbed him.

He remembered having a medical examination and commented that Dr Higgs was "all right" and Dr Wyatt was "better". He said it was nicer being examined by a man.

He had enjoyed his time in hospital—there were lots of children there. He had stayed in hospital for a few days and could not remember if he was given any explanation as to why he was there. When he was on the ward he said he had one hour's schooling a day. He thought his mother had visited him once. His sister aged 4 was placed in a separate foster home—he did not mind this. He thought he would go to a new school but was not sure where he would stay at the weekends. He wanted to go home.

The officer in charge of the home said that the boy had to be watched all the time to prevent his sexual advances to other children. She expressed concern that at the time there were no plans for his future and that her establishment was not equipped to deal with a child like him.

These children became wards of court. The Judge held that sexual abuse had occurred. These children remain wards with care and control to Cleveland County Council.

12 Boredom and Confusion

These children—a girl aged 10 and her brothers aged 12 and 14—were admitted after Dr Wyatt diagnosed sexual abuse in the girl after an examination for an urinary tract infection. The 14 year old boy said that the father had on more than one occasion "put his finger up" but that was more than a year ago.

The little girl was very confused by events and could remember being examined by a doctor in hospital and her mother telling her she would have to stay in for a couple of nights. Her brothers also stayed in the hospital. She could remember being woken up to be examined and photographed. She said in a whisper that she found the examination "a bit embarrassing". A social worker had told her that she might be going into care, and had twice asked if anyone had put anything up her bottom. She had felt sad and bored in hospital and also sad because she wanted to go home. She said she would be worried now if she had to see another doctor in case the doctor might put her back into care.

The eldest boy said that he and his brother were collected from school and taken to hospital by their aunt, who had been unable to tell them why. He waited one and a half hours for an examination by Dr Wyatt, and was not told what form it would take. Dr Wyatt examined his "bum" and he felt "daft" and the examination hurt. His mother was present, and Dr Wyatt said "that's alright" and did not ask questions. He saw Dr Wyatt the following day and on about three or four other occasions. The doctor was friendly and asked if he had been interfered with. He always denied this . One night after about 12 o'clock his mother woke him up and Dr Higgs then examined his bottom and he was photographed. A nurse was the one who told him he would be admitted to hospital. His mother was crying when he was admitted, and she later told him that the doctor thought someone had been interfering with his bottom. He denied it, and she asked if he was sure. He had seen a social worker about four times whilst in hospital and had been questioned about his home, and he was annoyed and upset as no-one believed him. He had also been examined by Drs Roberts and Paul who had chatted to him generally.

He had found hospital boring, and had mostly sat around, with daily visits from his parents. At the time of the interview he was back home and had told friends that he had been away on his father's ship to avoid the embarrassment of them knowing what had happened to him. He had missed out on schooling and taking exams and had had to catch up. He now wanted to forget his experiences and get on with his life.

The 12-year old boy gave a similar account of what had happened—he was not upset by his medical examination, which was carried out by Dr Wyatt, and he had to get on a chair. His father had then moved him on a bed and had explained what was happening. His mother was too upset to explain anything. He had been interviewed by the police and asked if anyone had stuck anything up his bottom, as the doctors thought someone had. He said no-one had. He had vague recollections of being woken up and photographed at night when he was very sleepy. He could not remember whether Dr Higgs had examined his bottom. Dr Wyatt had talked to him, but not about abuse. He had talked to two social workers, and one had described abuse to him as someone sticking something up your bottom.

He too had not liked being in hospital, it was boring. He had missed school, and the hospital was very full, with some children sleeping on camp beds. He knew he was being kept in to make sure he had not been abused. He was now worried about going to hospital again "in case it all starts once more". He had been worried in hospital when a social worker said he might have to go to foster parents and he and his brother and sister might be placed separately. He was worried he might not be able to go home and it was very upsetting.

These children were wards. The Judge held that sexual abuse had not occurred and dewarded the children.

13 Abused mother

The following child had been subjected to sexual abuse in 1984 by a neighbour. The mother's co-habitee was a Schedule 1 offender but nothing had been known of it until it came to light during a case conference. Social Services requested an examination, and Dr Grant had suggested that Dr Higgs would be the best person to carry out the examination.

The girl said that she had been in care before and she understood that when she was examined she was being checked to make sure her mother was "not doing naughty things". She went to hospital with her mother and a social worker, who was very nice and kind. When she was examined Dr Higgs said that someone had been playing with her "front bottom". The examination hurt, because Dr Higgs used "a white thing with a bend". Dr Higgs did not ask who had done it, but the social worker had asked her this since.

Her mother had not been to see the home where she was living, and the girl did not think "they" would let her. No letters or telephone calls were received by her. The previous day she had just seen her father for the first time since she came into care. Her mother has told her that she had been abused as a child.

She had befriended other children in her home who had been involved in the Inquiry, and who had had "the same things done to them at the hospital". She wanted to go home.

This child became a ward. By consent the Judge ordered that she remained a ward with care and control to the parents and an order for supervision to Cleveland County Council. There was also a condition of regular medical examinations.

14 Rough Treatment

This 10 year old girl was referred to Social Services after a neighbour contacted the school. She was examined by Dr Oo, who got a second opinion from Dr Higgs, and Dr Irvine also examined her.

This girl remembers Drs Irvine, Oo and Higgs, although she would not say which one she liked best, or whether there was any part of the medical examinations which she did not enjoy. She would not elaborate about the police, although she confirmed she could remember them. She had enjoyed her stay in hospital, where she was for over a month, and she had not wanted to leave to go to foster parents because she liked the doctors and nurses.

The mother said that when her daughter was examined by Dr Irvine he had asked her to lie on her back and open her legs. She cried out that she would not as she thought the doctor was going to do what her father had asked her to do. He persuaded her gently, and a further examination was given under anaesthetic. Dr Higgs had been rough and her daughter had cried out "You are hurting me."

The girl had asked her social worker to be taken back into care.

This child returned home. Dr Irvine examined her and found no medical signs of abuse. The police found insufficient evidence for proceedings.

15 Disgusting

The children in this family—a girl aged 9 and her brother aged 7, were seen after Dr Wyatt had examined the boy referred by his GP for persistent soiling. This was during the period when admissions were reaching a peak. Sexual abuse was diagnosed in the boy and the girl was examined. The boy said that he and his sister used to sleep in "uncle's" bed. Uncle cuddled him but did not hurt him. Dr Roberts and Dr Paul did not find any medical evidence of sexual abuse.

The boy said that when he first went in to Dr Wyatt the doctor was "O.K." and had not been horrible until his sister went in and came out crying. The boy said that he had told his sister what the doctor would do and that he had "a big needle".

According to the girl Dr Wyatt had turned her over and wanted "to go into her front". She said Dr Wyatt was "talking not very nice". He was shouting, she was afraid. Dr Higgs, she said, had a "nasty face" but did not say anything nasty—it was Dr Wyatt who was speaking nastily.

Dr Wyatt said he wanted to examine her again and said he would tell her what he would do when he got there. The father described how his daughter became upset. Dr Wyatt shouted at her and her father returned her to the ward. Dr Wyatt later apologised.

The children stayed in hospital for two weeks and the girl said that she liked the nurses. The boy said that he liked it—the nurses chased him.

They had liked Drs Roberts and Paul who never shouted or forced them. Those doctors did not shout or force them, and their examination did not hurt. Dr Wyatt had hurt them.

The children said Dr Wyatt used to see them at 10.00pm and ask them if they were alright. He was being kinder then. They thought he was just being kind so they would go to him.

No-one told them what was going to happen, and Dr Wyatt changed the subject if it was mentioned. The boy said that Dr Wyatt was horrible although he was alright until Dr Higgs came in.

The children saw their parents every day they were in hospital.

The children had been seen on T.V. as they left hospital and featured in a newspaper. The boy said photographers looked through windows at the hospital and "got me on telly". The girl had been called a "child abuse kid" at school.

Looking back, the girl thought it all disgusting.

These children were made wards of court. The Judge ordered them to be dewarded and they returned home.

16 Cuddled

This family, with a girl aged 10 and her brother aged 5, were referred at the request of the Social Services after other children told the "lollipop lady" that the child's step-father exposed himself.

The girl said that she could remember Dr Wyatt examining her, and he was nice and explained what he was going to do. She had not minded Dr Higgs either, she was also nice, and had given her a cuddle. Dr Higgs had told her that she was worried that something had been put "up my bum". She had been photographed and seemed to proud to think they were part of a medical record. She had seen Dr Steiner and Professor Kolvin and had not minded that. She enjoyed being in hospital where there were lots of toys.

She had seen a social worker who had said she was sorry they could not go home but their father was there. She cried about that. Also they could not go on holiday because their father was going too.

Although her foster parents were nice, she wanted to go home. She did, however, say she would be worried about living with her father.

The step-father was arrested and charged with indecent exposure and inciting girls to commit acts of gross indecency.

17 Toilet Paper

This 12 year old boy was referred to Dr Wyatt by Social Services after disclosing physical abuse by his step-father to an Educational Welfare Officer and sexual abuse was diagnosed.

When asked why he was in care he said it was because he had been "caught pinching stuff...so they had that on me" and "there was another problem as well...my dad put toilet paper up my bottom". Social workers took him to see Dr Wyatt who examined his bruised spine and wanted to look at his bottom. His reaction was that "he was not having that" but agreed to be examined by Dr Higgs the following day. He could not explain why he changed his mind. He was not told why the doctors wanted to examine his bottom.

He was examined by Dr Wyatt in the presence of a social worker and nurse, and was photographed. He was not distressed by this, but had no idea why the photographs were taken.

He had not taken exception to Dr Wyatt and thought that Dr Higgs was very nice. He had told the police what had happened. He had refused to let Dr Clarke, a police surgeon examine him but had since changed his mind.

He saw his mother after being in care for about a month, and was allowed to see his natural father but not his step-father.

He would like to live with his natural father but his natural father did not want him, so he thought he would prefer to go home—he thought his step-father would not repeat the abuse. He was going to make it work and behave himself. "I've not touched any money I've seen laying around and have thought to myself "leave it out".

The step-father of this child was charged with physical assault but the police found insufficient evidence for other proceedings.

*18 Fear in Court

This fourteen year old girl told her teacher that she had been sexually abused by her mother's co-habitee and was referred to Social Services.

The girl's life had been made a misery by her step-father who had made her do work before and after school and was very domineering. He had physically assaulted her brother. The girl went to live with her grandmother for a time but rejoined her mother and co-habitee when they moved. The sexual abuse then started. With the encouragement of her friends, she spoke to her teacher and then to social workers and asked if she could be removed from home if her mother went into hospital, and she was then made the subject of a place of safety order.

She was interviewed by two WPCs, one of whom she really liked, was kind and put her at her ease.

She was worried about her younger brother who had suffered ill-treatment from the co-habitee. Her mother had threatened to seek police intervention about this, but she had not done so. She recalled that he was "knocked about pretty badly once".

Her attendance at court for the care proceedings had been upsetting. Her mother and co-habitee were there and although she did not have to speak to them, the occasion frightened her. She was moved to foster parents but did not settle and so she had initiated contact with her natural father. She went to live with him but the placement did not work out. Her step mother told her the family had been happy until she arrived. She was now living with her aunt.

She had attended a review conference and thought that note had been taken of her views and that she had a nice and helpful contact at the NSPCC.

The police in this case investigated but found insufficient evidence for proceeding.

19 Nightmares

A family of three children, a boy aged 9 and two sisters aged 12 and 3 were seen by Dr Higgs after a GP referral for the younger girl for "itchiness down below". The 9 year old boy was interviewed.

The boy was reluctant to talk to those who interviewed him and stared straight ahead during the interview, and would not leave the living room of his home to talk.

When Dr Higgs examined him, the examination had hurt a little but not a lot. He returned home but was woken up at 1.00 am to return to hospital. When asked what hospital was like, he wrinkled his nose. One nurse had been horrible. He stayed on the ward most of the time and had wanted to come home. He had been seen by police officers and the Woman Police Officer was alright.

When he came home he said "nothing" to his friends but his mother told him to tell the truth. He was then the subject of comments such as "You've had sex with a man," and "Show us where you were abused." These comments had now stopped. He had seen a reporter, and following the interview the boy appeared to be on the verge of tears.

His mother said he had nightmares after this experience and refused to talk about it.

These children were made wards of court. By consent they were dewarded and returned home.

20 Afraid to tell

This eight year old girl was referred after sexual abuse was diagnosed in a younger sibling, and was initially examined by Dr Wyatt. She told of abuse by a man outside the family who was later charged.

The girl went to hospital with a social worker and with her mother and did not feel scared. She was put into a room to sleep or watch television, and her mother went home. She was with two of her younger sisters.

She had seen two doctors, a man and a lady who looked at her bottom and were both nice. She was not embarrassed but it hurt.

She had seen a police lady several times who had asked if someone had hurt her bottom. She did not tell at first because she feared she might be hurt again, but now she felt safe. She had been visited by her parents in hospital and no-one had told her how long she would be there. She returned to hospital weekly and has had outings. She thought the nurses were nice.

The police charged a suspect from outside the family with indecent assault. The girl was previously known to Social Services, and at the time of writing was at home on trial.

21 Glad to be in care

This 16 year old girl alleged that she had been abused by her step-father.

The girl said that she was in care because she had been "sex-abused by her step-dad". Her abuse came to light when she started "messing around" with her wrists. She told her friends at school, then the police, and then the Social Services. She was taken into care. She was treated "all right" at the children's home where she was placed, and liked her social worker but could not stand the police. She had been interviewed on one occasion but charges against her step-father were dropped. Her social worker believed the allegations, but her mother did not. Her sister had been abused which her mother knew but did nothing. She was glad to be in care, as she did not want to go home because her step-father was still there. She only saw her mother at the care hearings.

This child was previously known to the Social Services, and was still in care at the time of writing. She admitted intercourse with boyfriends. Her step-father was interviewed by the police but there was insufficient evidence for proceedings.

CHAPTER 2

Parents

2.1 The crisis in Cleveland came to public knowledge as a result of the complaints of parents about the allegations of sexual abuse of their children, together with the removal of their children unexpectedly under place of safety orders, the denial of access to them, the lack of consultation and the fact that they often did not know what was going on. These factors left them feeling shocked, angry, distressed and seemingly powerless to affect the course of events which was overtaking them.

2.2 Among the families affected were those well-known to the Social Services Department, with long-standing family problems and a history of social work intervention, but no previous allegations of sexual abuse. There were parents with previous convictions for sexual offences against children (Schedule 1 offenders). There were families with children who were failing to thrive. There were also families previously entirely unknown to the Social Services Department. In addition there were families well-known and well-respected by Social Services who fulfilled that necessary and invaluable role of foster parents. There were single parents, mothers with boyfriends, married couples all caught up in the crisis. Their voices were not not heard publicly until the latter part of June. Then the Rev Michael Wright, Dr Irvine, and Mr Stuart Bell MP, with the assistance of enormous media coverage, gave their point of view and some of their stories across the country. The parents' reaction to the crisis is in chapter 9 .

2.3 In this chapter we seek to record the perceptions of parents as they were caught up in the crisis, and as they were communicated to us in written and oral evidence, provided by 38 families. These parents had criticisms to make about the way in which they were treated by professionals. The criticism was mainly directed at the two doctors and social workers. Parents from 11 families gave oral evidence to the Inquiry in private session. Some parents expressed relief and gratitude at the discovery of hitherto unknown sexual abuse of their children from either within or outside the family. Their views were expressed through letters sent to the Inquiry and from conversations with the Official Solicitor.

2.4. The views of the parents are presented as they were given to the Inquiry. The accuracy of their accounts were not tested in evidence in any depth and the comments recorded represent the views of 11 families only. The same people are quoted several times on different topics. These parents paint a picture of the strong feelings which existed in Cleveland during the crisis.

Their comments are set out under the heading of themes rather than under individual families.

Relationships with Doctors

Brief Examinations

2.5 A number of parents expressed their concern that the medical examination of their children was very brief and that the paediatricians appeared not prepared to take acount of any medical history. One mother said:

"Dr Higgs examined them all over very quickly and she examined their bottoms very quickly"

and later:

"We did try (to tell Dr Higgs about their medical histories) but Dr Higgs was not interested. She did not know any of their medical histories at all".

A mother of a two year old girl said:

"She (Dr Higgs) checked her over, two seconds and said she had been sexually abused as well. She just put her thumbs on her bottom, pulled her bottom apart".

The parents of one girl claimed no reference was made to their daughter's medical records or family background and that the examination took about 5 minutes. The parents of another girl wrote that the child's medical records were missing and that the examination by Dr Higgs "took 30 seconds".

Index Children

2.6 The above cases arose most frequently in the families where other children in the family had already been diagnosed as sexually abused. We did hear of some examples where in examining an index child the paediatricians took full medical histories and recorded them in their notes. One mother who had referred to Dr Higgs taking a brief history, when shown the medical record, said:

"When I referred to the (brief) examination, I was referring to the examination of his bottom".

Dismissal of Medical Symptoms

2.7 Parents made reference to what they saw as a dismissal of medical symptoms on the basis that these would disappear with the cessation of sexual abuse. The parents of one family complained that Dr Higgs, in dealing with their youngest child, refused to discuss the child's bowel problems saying they were directly related to the abuse and would clear up when the abuse ceased. A mother said in evidence that she told Dr Wyatt of her child's constipation but that Dr Wyatt said this was not relevant to his diagnosis of sexual abuse. Another said that Dr Wyatt told her that her daughter's bowel problems would cease if the child was placed in a place of safety away from her and her husband. Another said that, in response to her request for treatment of her child's bowel problems, Dr Higgs said it was "child abuse, there was no other explanation" and it would clear up in 14 days. Parents complained that following a diagnosis of sexual abuse bowel disorders were not treated.Others told us that when the children eventually returned home their original bowel problems still existed.

Medication

2.8 Some parents complained that other forms of medication or treatment which their children were undergoing were not available or were ignored whilst the children were in hospital or foster care and they largely attributed this to the paediatricians' concentration on and preoccupation with sexual abuse. One mother complained that the needs of her sons who was on a gluten-free, dairy-free diet, had not been met in hospital and that her husband had to purchase more suitable food from outside. She also said that when her two children were moved to another hospital anti-biotics and medicine which they were taking did not accompany them. Another describing the examination of her son by Dr Higgs said "She also told me he had worms, incidentally which she did not offer to treat....." The mother of a child undergoing physiotherapy and exercises for her arms complained that the child received no treatment in hospital and that no arrangements were made for the physiotherapy to continue whilst the child was in foster care. Another mother said she told Dr Higgs of the medication her son was taking for asthma but that when she approached the nurses the child was not receiving the liquid sedative previously prescribed and she went on to say that when the child returned home she had to take him back to her GP for continued medication.

Times of examinations

2.9 A number of parents in their evidence commented unfavourably upon the times that medical examinations took place, either in terms of the inconvenience or inappropriateness of the time or in terms of the length of time children and parents had to wait for the doctors. The mother of a 2 year old girl under the long term care of Dr Wyatt, in an affidavit, described the cancellation of 2 appointments in April and May 1987 followed by the making of an appointment for 17th June and said: "When I attended on 17th June I was told that Dr Wyatt was not available". She then made a further appointment for 22nd June when her daughter was seen by the doctor. Several parents gave evidence about waiting at hospital with their children for periods of between one-and-a-half and three hours before being seen by the paediatricians. A mother told the Inquiry of her daughter and two foster children being collected from her home after 10pm and being taken to the hospital for examination that same night by Dr Wyatt. Another told of making arrangements, after a diagnosis of sexual abuse upon her youngest child, for the collection of her two elder children after school. She said, that when the children were brought to hospital:

"... we hung around for at least a couple of hours.... and there was no sign of Dr Higgs at all".

Her husband then took the children home to give them a meal and the mother told us:

"Dr Higgs arrived at 7pm and said she had come to examine the children. I said they had gone home. So she said I would have to ring up and ask my husband to bring them back to hospital".

The children were returned to the hospital, examined by Dr Higgs and diagnosed as having been sexually abused. The children remained at the hospital but the parents said it was 11.30 pm that night before beds were provided for them.

Second Medical Opinions

2.10 A general view among the parents giving or providing evidence to the Inquiry was that they met resistance and difficulty in obtaining an independent medical opinion. A number complained that they received no advice from doctors or social workers on their right to another medical opinion or the procedure to be followed if they wished to obtain one. One father said:

"I was later to find, as I see it, a crucial part of the place of safety order is that to some extent one still retains certain parental rights, particularly as regards access to other medical opinion. That was never explained to me".

The wishes of some parents were achieved once they were legally represented. The parents of one child in written evidence, said a second opinion was suggested by their solicitor and:

"after some reluctance from Social Services it was agreed".

One father wrote that he was not advised on the matter of a second opinion and did not obtain one until his solicitor "asked for one at Court". Some parents with legal advice arranged for their children to be made wards of court in order to obtain a second medical opinion.

2.11 Most of the parents seeking a second medical opinion were looking for one which would challenge or refute the diagnosis of sexual abuse made by Dr Higgs or Dr Wyatt. Thus they objected to and were not prepared to accept the doctors' views that another paediatrician of a like opinion as to the significance of anal dilatation, whether from the same hospital or elsewhere, constituted an independent second opinion. A mother said:

"My husband asked for a medical opinion on our behalf the first day. He objected to going to Leeds (for examination by Dr Wynne) and asked for an independent opinion of our own from Newcastle. He did not know where we were going to go, but he did not want to go to Leeds. We were refused absolutely".

Her husband later said in his evidence that it was Dr Wyatt who refused his request.

Another mother said

".....we told Dr Wyatt we wanted a second opinion. He told us we already had two opinions, his own and Dr Higgs, and that they worked independently and that another opinion was not in the interests of our daughter".

One father was dissatisfied with the presence of Dr Higgs at an independent medical examination of his daughter and although it was put to him in cross-examination that Dr Higgs was present at the request of the examining doctor, he said:

"If that is what you call an independent examination, that is a farce".

Consent to examinations

2.12 A number of parents complained that their consent was not sought or not obtained for medical examinations; or for the taking of photographs; or for disclosure work to be carried out with their children. These complaints were also directed at social workers.

2.13 A parent complained that Dr Higgs, carrying out her first full examination of a child under long term care of Dr Wyatt, did not seek consent to examine the child's anus. A father complained that Dr Higgs examined his son without consent but in this case hospital records showed that the examination took place 2 days after the child had been admitted to hospital and after a registrar had expressed concern to the consultant about the child.

2.14 One mother said:

"Dr Higgs asked if she could take some photographs and we said 'Yes' if it helps find out what is the matter".

There were also several instances where, although the subject of complaint and an absence of evidence of consent being formally obtained, parents were present and in a position to question or object.

2.15 The parents of one family complained that consent was not obtained for their children to be photographed but the mother gave evidence of being present when the photographs were taken. A mother in a written submission complained that she did not give consent for her 5 year old son to be photographed but wrote that she was present together with a nurse and Dr Higgs and Dr Wyatt. However the only evidence to the Inquiry of any formality being considered in obtaining the consent of parents came from one family when the mother agreed in cross-examination that she and her husband had consented to their children's interviews by a psychologist being video-recorded and said "I believe we were told we would have to sign a form to that effect and I do not think we have ever done so".

2.16 There was evidence from a number of parents that requests for children to be examined were put in such a way that it would be difficult to accept that consent was freely obtained or given because the parents saw little alternative but to accept or agree to what was proposed. The parents of one family described two social workers arriving at their home and seeking their agreement to the medical examination of their 3 children. The parents agreed to the medical examination but requested a doctor other than Dr Higgs. That request was refused and according to the mother:

"Mrs Dunn said that there was only one doctor in Teeside qualified for that sort of examination and that was Dr Higgs and we had no choice, otherwise they would take a place of safety order on our children".

A mother whose 4 year old son had been examined by Dr Wyatt was told by him that he wished Dr Wynne to examine the boy. She was asked:

"Were you told what would happen if you did not agree to (him) being seen by Dr Wynne?"

and replied:

"Yes, I was. I was told that they had not gone to Social Services but if I refused to go down to Leeds he would ring Social Services".

2.17 Grandparents, who were bringing up their 10 year old grandson, told the Inquiry:

"We were simply told by a social worker, Mr Garland, that (our grandson) had to be examined and our permission was not sought".

2.18 The parents of two boys said:

".... Mr Pearce, social worker, came to our home and said that arrangements had been made for both (our sons) to attend a medical examination at Middlesbrough General Hospital".

The mother of two children told the Inquiry of social workers asking her to take her children to Middlesbrough General Hospital for examination by Dr Higgs. She said y she told the social workers "No you can take them to see anybody you like, any other doctor in the country. I do not want Dr Higgs examining my kids" and she went on "They said 'If that's your attitude, I'll go back to the office and take place a safety order and we'll take them that way".

Previous good relationships with the Doctors

2.19 Many of the families legally represented in the Inquiry had children who had been under long term care of the paediatricians and had been attending regularly the Middlesbrough General Hospital, the majority over a period of a year or more. All except 2 families were under the care of Dr Wyatt or Dr Higgs. Most, because of his longer period of appointment, were patients of Dr Wyatt.

2.20 The mothers of 3 families, in describing their relationship with Dr Wyatt over a long period prior to the diagnosis of sexual abuse on their children paid tribute to him. One found him a "friendly, helpful and approachable man". Another said:

"...he had a good manner with my daughter. He did not just talk to me, he talked to her as well".

The third said she always found Dr Wyatt "understanding and helpful" and agreed there was "a very good mother/doctor relationship".

The grandmother of one child described Dr Wyatt as "smashing", and said he was wonderful with children and gained their confidence.

Gratitude

2.21 Some parents were grateful to the doctors for bringing to light sexual abuse of which they had previously been unaware. One mother, whose husband was charged and who committed suicide in prison, was full of praise for Dr Higgs, as she had no idea her children were being abused until the diagnosis was made. She said that Dr Higgs explained what was happening at all times and had acted with kindness throughout. Another rang the Official Solicitor to say that she had no complaints about the way in which she had been treated. Another mother whose two daughters were diagnosed as being sexually abused was full of praise for Dr Wyatt and was concerned that there was a vendetta against him and Dr Higgs. She found Dr Higgs helpful, kind, and gentle. She was unhappy about an examination undertaken by Dr Clarke, a police surgeon, at her husband's request. She said that in contrast to Dr Wyatt, Dr Clarke was rough and hurt the children. One child had screamed and had to be held in a head lock whilst she was examined. Dr Clarke found no abuse.

Another mother told of Dr Higgs' kind, gentle approach, and that she spent a lot of time reassuring her daughter.

Relationships with Social Workers

2.22 Social Services, inevitably perhaps because they were dealing directly with dissatisfied and unhappy parents, shared with the doctors the main thrust of the parents complaints.

Place of Safety Orders

2.23 A number of parents who gave evidence to the Inquiry referred to place of safety orders being used as a threat to achieve the wishes of the doctors or social workers. Some said that orders were unnecessary. Others complained of the timing or the method or circumstances in which orders were served.

Doormat

2.24 A father described a meeting with Dr Higgs and Dr Wyatt following the diagnosis of his daughter as having been sexually abused and his resistance to bringing his son to the hospital for examination. He said he was told he had no choice and went on:

"I was told that he may be placed in the care of the Local Authority if we did not have him examined".

His wife told of returning to the hospital next morning and of Dr Wyatt saying:

"If you dare to take your child out of the hospital she will be placed straight into care".

A place of safety order was obtained this day and the mother said:

"(that evening) I arrived home and opened the door to find a place of safety order on my doormat".

Pregnancy

2.25 In the case of a 3 year old girl, diagnosed by Dr Wyatt as being sexually abused, the mother was 17 weeks pregnant. The parents felt under pressure to accept the diagnosis in a conversation with social workers which touched on the wife's pregnancy. The father said that nothing was said directly but described asides between the social workers as taking the form of:

"We want to get this sorted out before the next baby comes along"

and he saw this and a similar statement made at the first hearing before the Magistrates' Court as implying that the expected child might be taken into care at birth. To another set of parents the matter was put specifically. Their two children had been taken into care and were subject of an interim care order when they received a letter from a social worker which referred to children she might have in the future and which included: "....there would be no guarantees from us that you would be entrusted to look after any child you may have". The mother said she was pregnant at this time but as a consequence of receiving this letter the pregnancy was terminated.

Back within the hour

2.26 The parents of 2 children said that social workers were insensitive and unthinking when they walked into a hospital cubicle at 10.30pm and, in the presence of their children aged 9 and 10 years, said they intended to obtain place of safety orders and "would be back within the hour".

Brown Envelope

2.27 The father of a 2 year old boy who had been diagnosed by Dr Higgs as sexually abused but who, with his parents' agreement, remained in hospital, told of being visited at ten minutes to midnight by two police officers and a social worker who served a place of safety order in respect of the child in hospital. In documentary evidence the parents of a year old daughter described returning to hospital to find a social worker waiting and being taken to the sister's office and given a brown envelope. They said the envelope contained a place of safety order and that the social worker simply and without explanation handed them the letter and left.

Lying in wait

2.28 The parents of 3 children diagnosed as sexually abused, also told us:

"We were told place of safety orders would not be applied for as we were leaving the children on the ward but when we got up next morning at 8 am a social worker was waiting with orders outside our house."

Welcome Order

2.29 One mother expressed relief and gratitude to social services for the taking of a place of safety order. She said that she approved of the taking of a place of safety order because her husband, the suspected perpetrator, had threatened to remove the child.

Access

2.30 Some parents had unrestricted access; others were very upset at the restrictions on access, or on what they saw as an inconsistency of approach. Some suffered the anguish of denial of all access to their children.

Unrestricted Access

2.31 Several parents provided evidence of unrestricted access. One mother described going to the foster home with the social worker and when asked about access, said:

"He left it up to ourselves and the foster mother......"

and added that the unrestricted access included her husband "everytime".

Inconsistency of Access

2.32 Others told of having unrestricted access in hospital but of arrangements being changed when the children were moved to foster care. A mother said that whilst her children were in Middlesbrough General Hospital she and her husband had unrestriced access and there had been no objection to her or her husband sleeping in the hospital room with the children but she said that when the children were removed from hospital the social worker did not tell the parents where the children were going and thereafter access was "a constant source of conflict". She said that subsequently access was to be supervised for one hour per week but arrangements were often cancelled or changed for no apparent reason.

Restricted Access

2.33 The mother of a 3 year old girl found restricted access particularly distressing. She described staying with her child for the five days the girl was detained in hospital but said that when the child was removed to foster care her access was limited to one hour per week under supervision at the Social Services family centre. She said "I asked for more access but it was not allowed" and "I thought it was awful.....(I was) particularly concerned about the effect on her".

Denial of Access

2.34 The parents of three children aged 9, 7 and just under 2 years, described the total denial of access to their children both whilst in hospital and in foster care until the children were made wards of court, three weeks after the place of safety order was taken out. The father told of attending the hospital with clothes for the children and being stopped by a nurse who said:

"I'm sorry Dr Higgs won't let you in".

The parents said they were not told when or where the children were taken from hospital to foster homes and when the mother was asked whether she or her husband had sought access, she replied "Yes we did. We repeatedly made attempts".

Dispute over access granted

2.35 There were differences, which the Inquiry was unable to reconcile, between the recollection of some parents as set out in written complaints and the records contained in the schedule provided by Drs Higgs and Wyatt. The parents of 3 children who were admitted to Middlesbrough General Hospital said:

"(We were)told that (we) could only see them for a few minutes. We were told to leave".

The doctors schedule refers to access being "voluntarily restricted". The parents of two children wrote of their son and daughter being "taken onto the wards, out of our care" and of having no access, whereas the doctors schedule refers to 'open visiting'.

Case Conferences

2.36 Many parents felt strongly that they should be heard at case conferences. A number told the Inquiry that they were informed that case conferences were to be held. Some said they were told they could not attend. Others said they were informed they could attend but would not be admitted or would not be heard whilst the meeting was in progress. Some said they were told the results of case conferences. Others complained they were told neither of case conferences nor of decisions reached there.

Not Told

2.37 A mother in evidence said she and her husband were not told that a case conference was to be held but that on a Monday she had a telephone call from a social worker telling her that a conference had been held the previous Friday. She said that when she asked why she and her husband hadn't been told of the case conference, the social worker said:

"they did not have to tell us if they did not want to".

Little said

2.38 In written evidence the father of three young girls, diagnosed as showing signs consistent with sexual abuse, in describing the parents' attendance at a case conference, wrote "Came in at the end. Was informed about what the situation was—very little said. I complained at not being allowed in from beginning to put my point of view across".

Letter

2.39 The mother of a 1 year old girl told of being informed that she and her husband could attend the case conference but would only be permitted into the conference at its end when "half the people would not be there." She said that as a result she wrote a letter which the social worker told her was read out at the meeting.

Not permitted

2.40 Another mother said she asked if she and her husband could attend the first case conference concerning their child. She was told this was not permitted but they could visit the Social Services office afterwards and would be told the result. She therefore wrote out the child's medical history and asked that it be put before the conference. She told the Inquiry she also asked for their general practitioner to be present but learned later that the doctor was only informed on the morning of the conference and was thus unable to attend.

Praise of Social Workers

2.41 Some parents in evidence paid compliments to social workers. One mother told of being a foster parent and of having a good working relationship with social workers, health visitors and others. Another referred to Mrs Alison McPherson making arrangements for access visits and said ".....generally we got on well with the social workers.....". She later went on to say that Mrs McPherson spent a great deal of time in discussion with her and her husband and said "She was very hardworking". When later the child of this family returned to its home the parents expressed appreciation by sending flowers on behalf of the child to Mrs McPherson. One father asked for a general view of the manner in which his child's case had been handled, said "Once Mr Roberts started on his investigations, Mr Roberts was very good. I have no qualms about Mr Roberts at all. He tried to explain as much as possible to us".

Another speaking of the Area Officer, Mr Burnard, said

"Mr Burnard was one, possibly the only person ......who did appear to be quite happy to talk. .....he certainly did seem to have the time and was available and I felt one could ring him, so that seemed quite helpful at that time".

Problems with legal advice

2.42. Confronted with the diagnosis of the doctors and with place of safety orders it was clear that parents felt a need to be told of their legal standing and rights. Some consulted their solicitor at a very early stage, in some instances before a place of safety order was obtained. A small number of parents complained of not being told to seek legal advice but the overwhelming majority provided evidence to the Inquiry of being advised, largely by social workers but on occasion by the police, to obtain legal advice from a solicitor.

Problems with Money

2.43 Some parents told of additional financial burdens brought about by the situation in which they found themselves. Legal costs were clearly the major consideration but not exclusively so. In written evidence an unemployed father said he had been granted legal aid but additional travelling costs to visit and to attend Court could not be easily found. Another referred to additional costs of transport and to loss of earnings.

2.44 A mother who gave evidence referred to legal costs being in "thousands rather than hundreds". Another gave evidence of the difficulties she and her husband were meeting in obtaining legal aid and was asked:

"Do you feel your endeavours to obtain legal advice and services has been inhibited by lack of financial resources?". She replied:

"I think it is getting to be that way now".

The family were later to be compelled to take out a second mortgage on their house in order to pay for legal costs.

Disclosure Work

2.45 A number of parents were unhappy about "disclosure work" being carried out with their children. Many felt uninformed as to the number, nature and extent of the disclosure interviews and saw them as part of a pattern designed to exert pressure upon them, the parents, and possibly force admissions. The involvement of some parents at a later stage in some of the interview sessions did nothing to alleviate their concern. One mother told the Inquiry that her request for more access to her daughter was rejected by social workers and "They said it was because of the disclosure work". Another asked, in cross-examination:

"Do you know how many disclosure interviews they (her children) had taken part in?"

replied:

"No. I do not.... I would not have had any means of knowing when the children had been seen".

Empty Chair

2.46 Her husband, referring to a family interview session, said: "It was clear from the outset.....that what we were there to do was to do one of two things, either elicit a confession from myself in some way in front of my children, or get my wife to agree with the children that she too considered that I had sexually abused them. This was done, as I say, in front of the children. There was a slight, almost sick note about it, in terms of there was an empty seat placed there which we were told was for (another absent child)".

2.47 These parents were particularly upset when they were asked to watch a small part of a video-recording which was being interpreted as a disclosure by a child that the father was the abuser. The child was distressed and the mother, in particular, saw this as a "pre-planned tactic" to obtain an admission of guilt.

Paediatricians and disclosure work

2.48 The Inquiry heard and received evidence from several parents who were critical and suspicious of the paediatricians' interviews of children alone at or about the time of the medical examinations. One mother related circumstances in which she and her two children were to stay in Middlesbrough General Hospital overnight, after examination and diagnosis of sexual abuse, and where between 10pm and 11pm Dr Higgs interviewed separately the two children alone, saying:

"Dr Higgs came and took (my daughter) off on her own"

and later:

"Dr Higgs then took (my son) off on his own".

These interviews were recorded by Dr Higgs in her medical notes.

2.49 Another mother told of being present when Dr Higgs took the medical history of her 12 year old daughter but not being present for the medical examination. She said:

"Dr Higgs asked me to leave. (She asked) if she could have a talk with (my daughter) on her own because she was at the age where they liked to talk to them on their own".

The doctor afterwards told the mother that the child "had been repeatedly sexually abused".

2.50 The parents of an 8 year old boy complained that after a medical examination the mother was told to leave the room and the boy was interviewed by Drs Wyatt and Higgs, and that they were not told what was said to the boy.

2.51 Another father said that:

"my wife and I were then left alone approximately 1 hour while Dr Higgs and Wyatt went to talk to (our 7 year old daughter)".

General Comments about Professionals

Isolation/Lack of Consideration

2.52 Most deeply felt by the parents was a sense of isolation and what they saw as a lack of consideration for them by doctors and social workers and some described the effect of the diagnosis and the removal of the children from the home and their parents' care upon relationships with family and friends. The parents' complaints were threefold:-

1. They were denied or unable to obtain information about their children or what was happening or what was planned for the future;

2. That social workers were not interested in and not enquiring into the family environment and history; and

3. That paediatricians and social workers had concluded that the parent (usually father) or parents were abusers and, until that was accepted by one or both, were indifferent, unresponsive and lacked compassion.

Lack of Information

2.53 The father of one family referred to making numerous calls to social services but to being met with:

"what can only be described as utter stonewalling".

The parents of another family in a letter of complaint to Social Services wrote:

"Once the children were removed from hospital we were left totally alone, not knowing what was happening and not having been told of any future contact with Social Services or when we would see our children".

Attempts by lawyers to obtain information

2.54 Parents also referred in their evidence to attempts by their legal representatives to obtain information. The parents of two families gave evidence of unsuccessful legal steps taken to obtain the production of documents. The parents of 3 children tendered documentary evidence including correspondence entered into by their solicitor. In one letter to the Director of Social Services the solicitor wrote:

"We feel compelled to place on record and on behalf of the parents the appalling lack of precise and detailed information which has been conveyed to us and them regarding the welfare of the children and the decision making process since these children were taken into care".

Lack of wider assessment

2.55 The mother of 3 children in evidence told the Inquiry that the psychologist interviewing her 2 elder children said to her:

"she did not consider it necessary to do a history of the family".

This mother went on to say that no contact had been made with the childrens' school and that she and her husband were particularly aggrieved by County Council press publicity that they were providing support to families because "These people just were not talking to us".

2.56 The father of another family was asked:

"What did you feel about the contact between yourselves and social workers?"

He replied:

"They just did not want to know anything, they were not interested in finding out about the family, the family background, the children, about the home environment, about us".

The parents of a young girl in documentary evidence wrote of asking a social worker team leader to "come and interview us, teacher, friends, etc" and of being told "such procedure was not necessary".

2.57 The father of a family wrote that he was told by a social worker that his children had been abused and that he was the prime suspect and in documentary evidence the fathers of three other families were said to have been "accused" by doctor and/or social worker. In documentary evidence also another family referred to particular antagonism between the social worker and the father. They said that this resulted in a local Councillor writing to the Director of Social Services suggesting the replacement of the social worker but that this letter was unanswered except through the same social worker who told them she would not be replaced. The mother of a 3 year old girl in evidence described her feelings at a discussion with a Social Services Area Manager which centred around the long term future of her daughter and she said "We felt that what we were saying was not being taken into account...... We felt desperate at that point". The father of 3 children told the Inquiry of a meeting with social workers at which he expressed disquiet at the lack of contact. He said he was told "We do not come to you, you come to us" and that "they were willing to work with us but until we accept responsibility for what has happened they would not do so". His wife said of another meeting with a social worker "(I inferred there was) no future for me at all with my children if I continued to support my husband"; and later "....they were saying to me that they would have to consider long-term arrangements. I was being told that my children were going to be taken away for ever and ever"

Comments on South Tees Health Authority

2.58 A number of parents referred to the courtesy with which their complaints were received and the assistance they were given in formulating and submitting their complaints by District Managers. Some parents referred to assistance and comfort given to them by nurses. One mother told the Inquiry of assistance given to her by two ward sisters, one making arrangements for a social worker to come and talk to her, and another advising her on the matter of a second opinion by another doctor. Another mother acknowledged receiving "courtesy and kindness from junior doctors and nursing staff at Middlesbrough General Hospital".

Comments on the Police

2.59 With the exception of one family where the parents considered the police interviews of their children to be insensitive, parents made little or no complaint against the police even though in some cases one or both parents were arrested, detained and interrogated concerning possible sexual abuse of their children. This was less than surprising because it was clear from the parents' evidence that, by the time the crisis had been reached, police officers were displaying or expressing the doubts and reservations they held concerning the medical diagnosis. One father told the Inquiry that he went to the police on the advice of another parent and said "I think to some parents they were even providing almost a pastoral system".

Mr Stuart Bell M.P.

2.60 One mother, expressed gratitiude to Dr Higgs for diagnosing sexual abuse and was happy with the action taken by Social Services in removing her child as protection from her husband who was a suspected abuser and unknown to her was a Schedule 1 offender. She said that Mr Stuart Bell M.P. had spoken to her husband and believed her husband when he said that he had not committed sexual abuse. Mr Bell telephoned her and would not accept her point of view. She told the Official Solicitor that Mr Bell said:

"the bairn's been told to say she was abused".

He told her he had seen her Social Services file, which she found very upsetting. He was not prepared to listen to her. She said that she had a similar problem with the Rev Michael Wright, but that he subsequently came to believe her rather than her husband.

Suicides

2.61 A father and an uncle who were charged with abusing their children committed suicide while in prison. One of the mothers spoke of her child's relief after the death of her father. One man said that he tried to kill himself three times while he was under suspicion of having abused his children.

Conclusions

2.62. As we said at the beginning of this chapter there was only limited testing of the evidence given by parents. No attempt is made in this report to judge, weigh or evaluate the complaints of individual parents. These have been dealt with outside the Inquiry by the Northern Regional Health Authority. The Inquiry in some instances had additional information which was not available to the parents which provided an explanation and put a different complexion on a particular set of circumstances. We were aware in regard to the parents evidence as in other evidence presented to us that it was impossible for us to hear all sides of a particular situation, and that from time to time we might hear a partial or even distorted version of events.

2.63. In other parts of the report we consider the general issues raised by parents' complaints. The major criticisms of the two doctors relating to examination of children are looked at at page 114, consent to examination of children at page 194 and 195, second medical opinions at page 196, 197. The main criticisms of the social workers and Social Services Department on place of safety orders are looked at at page 68, absence of information at page 67, access at page 69 and case conferences at page 58.

2.64. We recognise that the experience of parents involved in the crisis in Cleveland evoked the strongest of human emotions, that of the feeling of a parent, especially a mother, for a very young child and the immediate shock, dismay and disbelief at the time of diagnosis may well be equalled, if not surpassed by enforced, continuous and sometimes lengthy separation from the children, coupled with uncertainty and doubt about the future. At this period for reasons which are set out elsewhere these parents were left alone and without professional support.

2.65. Whether the parents were abusers, possible abusers or ordinary people caught up in the result of a misdiagnosis, this situation of isolation and lack of support, was a most worrying feature in the Cleveland crisis.

CHAPTER 3

Inter-Agency Bodies—Cleveland Area Review Committee and Joint Child Abuse Committee

3.1 Cleveland Area Review Committee

The Cleveland Area Review Committee [ARC] was the main consultative forum for co-ordinating multi-agency response to child abuse—mainly child physical abuse. It was set up in December 1974 in response to DHSS circular LASSL (74) 13, as a multi-disciplinary group with wide membership to evolve procedures for dealing with suspected cases of child abuse, the organisation of the child abuse register and the general system of liaison between the different agencies involved

3.2 The ARC was chaired by Mr Walton, Senior Assistant Director of the Social Services Department.

3.3 In 1984, the Area Review Committee issued a Manual of Procedures to guide the work of all local agencies involved in child abuse. In common with most manuals adopted by Area Review Committees across the Country the guidelines did not specifically deal with problems related to child sexual abuse.

3.4 The purpose of the manual was to co-ordinate the work of the various agencies involved. Each service, Health, Education, Police, Social Services and the NSPCC was required to define its own practice guidelines and these were then drawn together by the Area Review Committee to ensure an effective pattern of local operation.

3.5 The Area Review Committee agreed that personnel should be identified in the Health Service and Social Services as Designated Officers for the purposes of co-ordinating work relating to child abuse. These key people in Health and Social Services had ready access and contact with the Police Inspectors responsible for the work of the Community Relations Departments within the Police Divisions.

3.6 In the 1984 Procedures Manual, the section relating to medical examinations of children believed to have been abused or at risk of abuse, stated under the heading "Procedure Carried Out by Social Work; Staff Initial Action".

"If there is concern about the physical care or neglect or ill-treatment of the child then a detailed medical examination should be arranged. Contact should be made with the child's general practitioner or if unavailable, by admission to hospital".

3.7 Under "Cleveland Health Services, Guidelines for Doctors", instructions were given for the management of suspected cases of physical abuse which provided for the child's admission to a paediatric ward if there was any reasonable doubt that the injuries were other than purely accidental.

ARC Working Party

3.8. The ARC became increasingly aware that their existing guidelines offered no assistance to those working in the newly emergent field of child sexual abuse. Having recognised the problem the Committee set about formulating guidelines to cover this area.

3.9 In February 1985 a working party was established. Mr Michie of the NSPCC was Chairman and its membership was drawn from all the agencies involved in the investigation and treatment of child sexual abuse with other professionals attending as and when specific issues were discussed.

Key Issues

3.10 There were 3 issues which the working party saw as being of key significance:

(i) who should examine children thought to be the victims of sexual abuse? Should it be consultant paediatricians or police surgeons?

(ii) where should children be examined: hospital, general practitioners surgery or police station?

(iii) the propriety and practicality of police and social workers working jointly or co-operatively in investigating allegations of sexual abuse.

3.11 These issues and the difficulty of achieving agreement about them were the underlying causes of the problems experienced by social workers and police in their efforts to work together. The difficulties met in resolving the different views genuinely held by the respective agencies, should not detract from the fact that in Cleveland early efforts were being made to deal with the problem of child sexual abuse.

3.12 According to Mrs Summerbell the intention of the health and social work professionals involved in the working party was:

"to ensure that child sexual abuse was brought into the child health arena."

3.13 That sentiment reflected the views of agencies concerned to establish practice guidelines that gave first consideration to the interests of the child. Initially the police representatives, drawn from the Community Relations Department were willing to consider the proposals.

3.14 However, after Police Community Relations representatives reported back, a senior officer from the C.I.D. attended the working party, and it became clear that he and others held rather different views. Thereafter progress became slower for reasons set out in the Police chapter.

Difficulties Over Place of Examination

3.15 According to the minutes of the working party on the 19th April 1985 it was felt that all allegations of child sexual abuse should be reported to the Social Services Department through the Police Community Relations Departments.

3.16. Early consultation between police and social workers was thought to be essential together with joint decisions being taken about how further intervention should proceed. In the minutes it was recognised that this would require a significant change in attitude as well as policy.

3.17 In May 1985 the working party recommended that all medical examinations take place in hospital and that the examination be carried out by a paediatrician or police surgeon if experienced in this kind of work.

3.18 In June 1985 Dectective Superintendent Pears of the C.I.D. attended the working party and stated that the Police were implementing the Home Office circular in relation to examination of victims of sexual offences at a police station and only two police stations were considered suitable. Unlike his colleague Inspector Dale who had represented the Police on the working party and had good grasp of the issues, he did not see any reason to change the practice of police surgeons examining victims in their surgeries. He pointed to the availability of three female police surgeons. He further said that the Police could not agree to joint investigation. This being so, he would not agree to joint consultation, because he saw this as a curtailment of the right of the police to independent action. He agreed to joint discussion before any action was taken, wherever possible.

3.19 There was a fundamental difference of approach and perspective between the views of some senior police officers and the other agencies. The good progress in resolving difficulties made by representatives of the working party was set back by decisions taken by senior police officers without wider consultation and which were presented to other agencies as Force policy. Those involved in such decision making never appear to have been aware of the reasons for the working party's proposals nor understood what it was striving to achieve. The Police had little experience of the problem of sexual abuse of very young children and they were not aware of the extent to which the representatives of Social Services, Health and voluntary agencies on the working party had moved in their recognition of the problems of child sexual abuse. There never appears to have been a meeting of minds throughout the long drawn out process of agreeing new guidelines.

Attendance of Police Surgeons and Paediatrician

3.20 The senior police surgeon, Dr Irvine and Dr Morrell a paediatrican from Middlesbrough General Hospital were invited to attend one of the working party meetings. Dr Irvine consulted with the Assistant Chief Constable Mr Smith who decided that he should not attend. This was probably a misunderstanding by senior police officers as to the role he was expected to play.

3.21 However later in February Dr Irvine and Dr Oo, a paediatrician from North Tees did attend a meeting. While Dr Irvine felt that the recommendations as to hospital were inflexible and pointed out what he saw as disadvantages to the child in an automatic referral to hospital, the working party eventually agreed that police stations should not be used for the examination of children. It was agreed that a hospital would be the most appropriate setting for the medical examination, initial treatment and care of a child who may have been subjected to sexual abuse. However, in cases where the early involvement of the police surgeon was indicated, the surgery might be the appropriate place for the examination to be performed.

Compromises

3.22 The long hours of discussion over 15 months resulted in recommendations which were based on attempts to reach a compromise. On the 9th June 1986, a meeting of designated officers approved the recommendations of the working party with some amendments in relation to the involvement of the police and the police surgeon. Those included the requirement that a police surgeon should be consulted on every occasion.

3.23 On the two issues which had taken up so much time the recommendations were as follows:

Under 1 "INITIAL ACTION ON DISCLOSURE AND INVESTIGATION"

(iv) "All allegations of child sexual abuse should be discussed jointly by the police and social worker, before the process of investigation begins, unless the circumstances of the referral, or other factors, clearly indicate the need for a different approach. This consultation could result in a joint police/social work approach to the case."

In correspondence between Mr Walton and Chief Inspector Dale in December 1986 about the proposed revision of the draft procedures manual by the new Joint Child Abuse Committee, the latter wrote in a letter under the heading Joint Interviews

"It is not police policy to allow joint police and social worker interviews of child victims. This matter was very thoroughly discussed at meetings of the working party chaired by Mr Michie, mentioned earlier, and that decision was made at a very senior level in the Cleveland Constabulary. However, it must not be inferred from that decision that close co-operation should not take place, but reaffirms the police responsibility for the investigation and prosecution of offenders."

Under 2. "MEDICAL EXAMINATION"

(i) "Hospital is the most appropriate setting for the medical examination, initial treatment and care of a child who may have been subjected to sexual abuse. However, in cases where the early involvement of the police surgeon is indicated, the surgery may be the appropriate place for the examination to be performed. The police surgeon must be consulted in every case."

Establishment of Joint Child Abuse Committee (JCAC)

3.24 As a result of the DHSS paper "Working Together" in April 1986 the ARC set up a working party to consider the implications and recommended the replacement of the ARC by the proposed JCAC to take effect from 1987.

3.25 Mrs Richardson who had played a prominent role in the Social Services review of its child care strategy was largely instrumental in setting up the new JCAC.

3.26 The proposals of the working party on child sexual abuse were presented to the ARC in October 1986 but in the event neither considered nor implemented because the ARC was replaced by the JCAC.

Joint Child Abuse Committee

3.27 The DHSS consultative document "Working Together" recommended that Area Review Committees be redesignated Joint Child Abuse Committees (JCACs) and that they should be accountable to the Joint Consultative Committee (JCC) for that area. This was said to be to enable issues identified by the JCAC as requiring joint review of health or local authority services to be considered within the joint planning mechanism of the health and local authorities.

3.28 The draft circular recommended that an early task of JCACs should be to review existing policies and procedures.

3.29 Cleveland ARC took the recommendations of the draft circular very seriously and decided to redesignate themselves a JCAC before the circular was published in final form.

3.30 In February 1987 the Cleveland JCAC held its first meeting. Mr Walton was its first chairman. Dr Higgs was appointed a full member and was elected Vice-chairman.

Composition of Working Party

3.31 One of its first tasks was to set up a working party to tackle the up-dating of the Child Abuse Procedures Manual in all its aspects as a matter of urgency. On this occasion the working party was chaired by the Child Abuse Consultant, Mrs Richardson. The members of the working party, in addition to Mrs Richardson, were Mr Michie of the NSPCC, Mrs Dunn a Nursing Officer, Chief Inspector Taylor of the Police Community Relations Department, Mr Town the Chief Education Social Worker and a representative of the probation service.

3.32 The meetings and the motivation of this working party have been the subject of considerable criticism and suspicion both from the Police and the senior police surgeon in relation to its recommendations as to medical examination.

3.33 The working party met on six occasions between the 18th February and the 1st June. No formal minutes were kept but from the evidence of Mrs Richardson and contemporaneous letters and other documents we have a picture of its progress.

3.34 In March the draft produced for discussion was almost identical with the ARC working party and included the words in the Child Sexual Abuse Medical Section,

"The police surgeon must be consulted in every case."

3.35 By April the differences in medical opinion were becoming obvious and were already causing difficulties. During April at another meeting Mrs Richardson discussed with Mr Michie of the NSPCC the problems raised over the preceding month as a result of conflicting views held by Dr Higgs and Dr Irvine. At the suggestion of Mr Walton, Mr Michie was requested to reconvene the ARC working party on sexual abuse. He declined and, according to Mrs Richardson, felt it was inappropriate due to the failure of that working party to reach agreement, particularly with Dr Irvine. His advice was to deal with it through the JCAC.

3.36 By the meeting of the 29th April the working party had completed a major part of the revision and were ready to consider the guidelines in cases of sexual abuse. They put forward a new recommendation for strategy meetings, but were not able to consider medical examinations without some professional assistance. Chief Inspector Taylor and Mrs Richardson were asked to arrange a meeting with Dr Irvine and Dr Higgs. It was specially arranged to try to reach some sort of consensus and to advise the working party on the guidelines to be introduced. The intention was for Mrs Richardson and Mr Taylor to report back to the working party on the 1st June and to present the draft manual to a specially convened meeting of the JCAC on the 1st July.

3.37 Mrs Richardson was spurred on to hold the meeting of the 28th May by the reports which she had been receiving of the difficulties experienced by social workers in the field. She did not discuss the purpose of this important meeting with the Director or senior staff in the Department beforehand.

3.38 We were surprised that she had, without wider consultation within the Social Services Department, organised a set-piece confrontation which in the event she was unable to manage effectively. It was doomed to failure and it was naive of her as the convenor not to have appreciated it. The outcome polarised differences of professional opinion and provoked a major breakdown in inter-agency working relationships.

Meeting of 28th May

3.39 The meeting took place on the 28th May. Chief Inspector Taylor attended with Detective Superintendent White and Inspector Makepeace. Mrs Richardson was the sole representative of Social Services. Dr Higgs and Dr Irvine were also present. Mrs Richardson was the only one present to keep a note which was very brief. The consequences of this meeting are set out in other chapters [Police, Social Services]

3.40 There remained two areas of disagreement and both were for discussion. According to Mrs Richardson's note and evidence she attempted once again to explore with the police representatives the possibility of working in a planned and joint way as far as the child victims of sexual abuse were concerned.

Joint Investigation

3.41 They first discussed joint investigation of the child by social worker and police. The Police position of interviewing possible perpetrators entirely on their own was fully accepted. The Police were willing to consider joint interviews of children.

3.42 According to Mrs Richardson's note the Police response was outlined by Chief Inspector Makepeace. He was of the view that working in a planned and joint way was not practicable; he thought investigation needed to proceed with urgency; the role of the Police was primarily to investigate a crime and therefore the Police must be in overall charge of the investigation from beginning to end. He was not prepared to consider it. Mrs Richardson's evidence and note recorded that the absence of agreement on the point of strategy meetings was noted for referral back to the working party.

3.43 This attitude of the Police on the point of joint police/social worker approach to an allegation reaffirmed the lack of movement by the Police despite the ARC agreement nearly a year earlier.

3.44 From this inauspicious start the meeting moved to the consideration of medical examinations on which no agreement was reached. The meeting degenerated into a heated dispute between Dr Higgs and Dr Irvine. From the various versions the Inquiry has received it is clear that Dr Irvine became frustrated and angry and consequently very loud. Dr Higgs remained very quiet and calm and confronted his anger and exasperation with cool, distant objectivity. He became infuriated and according to Mrs Richardson, called Dr Higgs incompetent and misguided, and "her mentors—Wynne and Hobbs—equally misguided."

3.45 Dr Irvine agreed in evidence that he had said something to that effect. He alleged bias by the Social Services Department and that they were equally responsible for removing children from innocent parents by acting on Dr Higgs' diagnosis. When challenged by Dr Irvine to say whom she supported, Mrs Richardson became partisan in support of Dr Higgs. According to her she said:—"The Social Services Department worked closely with the consultant paediatricians and were bound to act on receipt of information from them—she had no reason to doubt Dr Higgs' diagnosis She alarmed the Police who formed the impression, correctly, that she was 100% behind Dr Higgs and that the police surgeon would be wholly excluded.

3.46 Mr White acted to calm things down and to control the meeting. In summary he said it was clear that medical opinion was diametrically opposed and this left Cleveland Constabulary no alternative but to issue a Force directive to treat Dr Higgs' work with a degree of caution. Mrs Richardson believed that some directive to that effect had already been issued by the Police. She found the meeting upsetting but clearly she exerted no moderating influence during the dispute; rather she added fuel to the flames by her wholehearted and unquestioning support of Dr Higgs. Her role at the meeting considerably exacerbated the already serious breakdown in police-social worker relations. It is however clear that she has never reflected upon that aspect.

3.47 The decisions taken by the Police and Social Services after the meeting created greater misunderstanding and led to allegations of conspiracy and collusion between the Social Services Department, particularly Mrs Richardson and Dr Higgs, which have no foundation in the facts presented to the Inquiry.

3.48 There were other unfortunate consequences, one of which was the ill-advised instruction by Mr Smith to Mr Taylor not to attend the meeting of the working party on the 1st June which met in his absence. The members present were placed in a dilemma. There was some urgency to prepare a draft for consideration by the specially convened meeting of the JCAC on the 1st July. It is difficult to gauge how much of the flavour of the meeting of the 28th May, and the depth of feelings unleashed, were communicated by Mrs Richardson to the meeting on the 1st June. But even if she gave the other members of the working party little assistance in that regard, (as is possible), they were aware that the non-attendance of Mr Taylor was a deliberate decision of his superiors and therefore to proceed in his absence meant that they would not have an united recommendation to present to the JCAC and that it was most probable it would be opposed by one of the most important participants in the future procedure.

3.49 The proposed draft required the Police to agree to the exclusion of the police surgeon from most cases of suspected child sexual abuse. After considerable discussion the working party decided to proceed and to agree the draft in his absence. This decision was equally ill advised.

The recommended draft read as follows:

"i. Hospital is the most appropriate setting for the medical examination, initial treatment and care of a child who may have been subjected to sexual abuse. The child should be referred directly to a Consultant Paediatrician. Where a Consultant Paediatrician is able to give a statement to the Police, it will not be necessary for the police surgeon to re-examine the child."

3.50 This was the draft which was referred to by Mr Stuart Bell MP and also by the Police in their press statement and by the senior police surgeon in his interviews with the media.

3.51 In a letter to Chief Inspector Taylor, dated 11th June, Mrs Richardson enclosed the draft for the consideration of the Police. She said the working party were sorry that he was unable to attend the final meeting on the 1st June :—"due to local circumstances." She went on :—"The medical investigation was revised according to what is perceived as good practice, without regard to any current local issues. The role of the police surgeon is therefore as a member of a team of specially trained and nominated doctors available for this purpose."

3.52 There were no more meetings of the working party and the draft manual was presented to the special meeting of the JCAC.

3.53 On the 1st July, Mr Walton, who had been in the thick of the crisis created by numerous referrals of children diagnosed as sexually abused most of whom were in the care of the Local Authority under place of safety orders, took charge of the draft manual. He and Mr Smith in an intensive effort over the next two days or so, in discussion with the other members of the JCAC, rapidly evolved a draft on the disputed areas which was accepted by all.

3.54 It was agreed that the procedure relating to sexual abuse should be immediately implemented even before the projected meeting of the JCAC on the 7th August. There was some dissent from Hartlepool which had remained outside the problems affecting the other areas.

3.55 Finally on the 7th August 1987 the Procedures Manual was agreed by all members of the JCAC. The relevant passages are as follows:

The Procedures Manual for the Management of Child Abuse

"Definition of Child Abuse ......(page5)

Harm by parents or carers (i.e. persons who, while not parents, have actual custody of a child) either by direct acts, or by a failure to provide proper care, or both." Included in the definition were a) physical injury, b) neglect, c) failure to thrive and emotional abuse, d) children in the same household, e) sexual abuse, f) potential abuse.

At page 41 "Guidelines for All Agencies in the Management of Sexual Abuse"

A. Initial Action On Suspicion and Disclosure

(ii) The Police should inform Social Services of all allegations of child sexual abuse, through the Community Relations officer. Similarly, the Police should be informed of allegations received by other agencies.

(iii) All referrals should be passed through agency line management: .....

(iv) Any suspicion or allegation should routinely be discussed...... Consultation.....

(v) If the process of consultation substantiates the allegation or suspicion, then a strategy meeting should be called .....

B. Strategy Meeting.

C. Investigation

(ii) The investigation with regard to the child should be undertaken jointly by Police and Social Workers. The investigation of the alleged perpetrator is a police matter.

D. Medical Examination

(i) Hospital is often the most appropriate setting for the medical examination but any appropriately equipped setting may be used. The child should be referred as soon as possible to a consultant paediatrician.

(ii) The roles of the police surgeon and paediatrician are complementary in the diagnosis of child sexual abuse. That of the police surgeon is the collection of evidence for any future prosecution. The role of the paediatrician is to plan the care of the child and advise child protection agencies regarding the welfare of the child. Early consultation is essential.

(iii) When the Police have requested an opinion of the police surgeon, the consultant paediatrician and the police surgeon should jointly agree how the evidence the latter requires will be obtained. Where examination by more than one medical practitioner is required, there should be joint examination where possible, in order to keep the number of intimate examinations to the minimum.

(iv) When a child is diagnosed as having been sexually abused during an examination for some other condition, the doctor should then proceed on the basis of the recommendation A above: "Initial action on Disclosure"

(v) [recognises need for training and recommends rota of suitably trained doctors.]"

Present Position of the JCAC

3.56 We had some helpful evidence from Mr Beckwith from the North Tees Health Authority. As a result of his view that the composition of the JCAC did not adequately reflect either the managerial interest in problems nor reflect the psychiatric viewpoint, Mr Beckwith has set up and chaired a child abuse working party independent of the subgroup of the JCAC. He felt with some justification that the present composition of the JCAC did not have sufficient executive power to be able adequately to influence the outcome of recommendations which were worthy of serious consideration. He pointed out that they had requested more senior representation on the JCAC but even with that increased representation they were answerable in Cleveland to 3 separate JCCs, a situation not expressly contemplated by the DHSS paper 'Working Together'. This envisaged one JCC covering one Local Authority and all the District Health Authorities within that Local Authority boundary.

3.57 In fact at present there is one JCAC, one Local Authority, one Police Force but three Health Authorities and three JCCs.

3.58 We were given no information about the formation or interests of the JCCs but it is obvious that there would be difficulties in co-ordinating arrangements approved by the JCAC and its subgroups with all three JCCs for an unified policy on any particular subject.

General Comments on ARC and JCAC

3.59 The working party of the ARC highlighted genuine differences of approach and attitudes before 1987 and the difficulties for the various disciplines to understand each others' differing roles and responsibilities.

3.60 Despite the agreement of the working party of the ARC as to general principles in June 1986, the length of those discussions, and the difficulties in reaching broad agreement, precluded any detailed consideration of how they would actually work in practice.

3.61 We are satisfied that there remained genuine unresolved issues of attitude and procedure despite the apparent agreement. From the evidence before the Inquiry the ARC recommendations were seen differently by the different disciplines and involved such a degree of compromise that they were likely if implemented to present difficulties in practice. For example the glimpse given by Chief Inspector Makepeace's re-statement of the position adopted by the Police ever since the original working party started to look at this issue of planned collaborative work in 1985 simply serves to show the extent to which senior police officers were entrenched on this point.

3.62 The Area Review Committee and the Joint Child Abuse Committee proved for the most part an ineffective mechanism to co-ordinate the work of the key agencies in the field of child sexual abuse.

3.63 A number of factors contributed to this failure. Like many Area Review Committees across the country, having successfully established guidelines for the co-ordination of physical abuse, the committee had difficulty in defining its future role and function in isolation from its constituent agencies.

3.64 There was some evidence before the Inquiry to suggest that representatives attending may have more concern to protect what they saw as departmental interests than to commit themselves to the prime purpose of establishing an effective co-ordinating mechanism.

3.65 The role of the Joint Child Abuse Committee throughout the crisis in Cleveland demonstrates the ambivalence that its constituent members had towards it. The function of the committee was not recognised by the senior management and none sought to use it to resolve the underlying conflicts until early in July. Earlier attempts in May and June were unsuccessful. In July, the Chairman Mr Walton, and Mr Smith were both given clear authority by their agencies to seek a solution to the procedural conflicts which surrounded the medical examination of children and that they did by hard work and firm commitment within four days.

The Future

3.66 The major agencies involved in the committee had no responsiblity for it and the representatives did not have the ability to bind their respective agencies to implement the policy approved by the committee. This may be a reason why the JCAC was not to any extent involved in the resolution of the crisis.

3.67 To be effective, the committee needed its purpose to be defined and agreed between the Chief Officers and Senior Managers of all participating agencies. Representatives had to have sufficient delegated authority to commit their agency. Each agency needs to have formulated the basic principles and framework of its own practice and be committed to the importance of co-ordinating work with others.

3.68 The role and function of any sub-group or working party needs to be properly defined and authorised, so as to ensure that the prime role and purpose of the Co-ordinating Committee is not dissipated.

3.69 The chairmanship should be held by a person of calibre, sufficiently experienced in both practice and policy issues to ensure that problems are properly considered and resolved. One way of ensuring a greater commitment would be for the chairmanship to rotate on a biennial basis between senior staff of the agencies involved reporting direct to each authority.

CHAPTER 4

Social Services Department

4.1 The Social Services Department of the County of Cleveland is managed through a Divisional structure, North and South (See Appendix M). North Division is roughly equal to the North Tees and Hartlepool Health Districts. In addition the Divisions are split into a number of Social Service areas which broadly correspond to the four Boroughs of Stockton, Hartlepool, Middlesbrough and Langbaurgh.

4.2 Mr Bishop is Director of Social Services with Mr Walton as his Senior Assistant Director, and together they are responsible for some 4,677 staff. Mr Green is the Divisional director for North Cleveland and Mr Roberts is the Divisional director for South Cleveland.

4.3 The total budget for Social Services in Cleveland for 1987/88 was set at £33.1m. The area served by Cleveland Social Services is an area with a high level of unemployment, approximately 26% in Middlesbrough, with a higher than average proportion of the population under the age of 16.

General Practice in Cleveland Prior to January 1987

4.4 Prior to 1987 the Social Services Department of Cleveland County considered themselves to be a positive and forward looking authority in the field of child care, and were careful to respond to DHSS circulars and to developments elsewhere which might affect them.

4.5 In addition they had been prompt to take constructive action on criticisms of specific shortcomings in child care set out in an Audit Commission investigation in 1985, which highlighted the number and proportion of children in care who were placed in residential homes.

Priority Given to Child Care

4.6 In November 1985 a decision was taken to give child care priority over other services in the Department. During 1986 the Department made a number of important changes in child care practice. The purpose of the changes and improvements in services was to improve the levels of support to families experiencing difficulty in providing adequate standards of parenting; to ensure that as many of the children in care as possible were cared for in substitute families rather than in residential homes; and to improve the co-ordination of services in the field of child abuse. Additional social workers were allocated to each area, and in each area a senior experienced social worker was appointed designated officer for the purpose of co-ordinating the work of the area in child abuse.

4.7 Record keeping was standardised and regularily monitored. Additional clerical staff were provided to ensure that case conferences were properly administered and recorded. The evidence of these changes was before us in the Inquiry in the high standard of record-keeping seen both in individual case files and records of case conference discussion. In view of the criticisms that have been made about record-keeping in other Inquiries, Cleveland's achievements in ensuring a high standard of record-keeping was especially welcome and of great assistance to us in conducting the Inquiry. However, they failed to keep up to date records of place of safety orders granted.

4.8 In addition to these improvements in levels and standards of social work practice and administration in the area social services office, two new posts designed to co-ordinate policy on a county-wide basis were established.

New Posts

4.9 The first new post was that of co-ordinator for Adoption and Fostering Services to which Mrs de Lacey Dunne was appointed. The second post of Child Abuse Consultant was filled on the 1st June 1986 by Mrs Richardson.

4.10 Together with the Child Care Adviser, Mr Hughes, who was appointed in July 1986 and took up post in October, Mrs de Lacey Dunne and Mrs Richardson provided a core group of experienced social workers able to give advice on child care matters to both the area based social workers and the central managers of the Social Services Department.

In addition they each had responsibility for service development in their area of special responsibility.

Co-ordination on Child Abuse

4.11 Staff of the Social Services Department together with colleagues in the Health Service, such as nursing officers who were designated with a special responsibility for the co-ordination of child abuse, were alert to problems associated with the growing recognition of sexual abuse of young children. This was seen in the work of the Area Review Committee (See previous chapter).

4.12 Throughout 1986, the Social Services Department continued to provide training for social workers, team leaders and area officers in relation to the growing problems of child sexual abuse. The work of Dr Hobbs and Dr Wynne in Leeds in describing the relevance of anal examinations in the diagnosis of sexual abuse was discussed and made the subject of seminars in the region.

A Child in Trust—the report into the death of Jasmine Beckford

4.13 The publication of the Jasmine Beckford Report and the publicity which surrounded it, prompted the Social Services Department further to review its child care strategy. The Director of Social Services regarded the report "as an absolutely vital document to study and resolved that, if at all possible, Cleveland Social Services would learn from the unfortunate instances made elsewhere and ensure that we did not made similar mistakes which could result in children being avoidably abused".

4.14 This review was led by the Child Abuse Consultant, Mrs Richardson, now established in her new post. The completion of the review resulted in proposals being put before the Social Services Committee in January 1987 to establish child protection teams in each of the Social Service Areas. The intention was to use both staff drawn from within the Social Services Department and agency arrangements with voluntary organisations to ensure the development of this service.

4.15 The publication of the Beckford Report added impetus to training programmes and involved staff of all grades. Team leaders and social workers who worked with the most difficult child care cases had received some preliminary training in child sexual abuse by 1987. The training was broadly based and not specifically directed or informative about anal abuse as a form of child sexual abuse. Mrs Richardson played a significant part in initiating the training programme for workers in the field of child sexual abuse.

Dr Higgs' Arrival

4.16 In January 1987, Dr Higgs was appointed to Middlesbrough General Hospital. She was known to have an interest in child sexual abuse. Her special interest in a community-based approach to her paediatric work was welcomed by some social workers who were encouraged by her appointment and some 5 or 6 cases of long-standing concern were identified for referral to her.

4.17 In October 1986, she had attended as an observer a meeting of the Area Review Committee (ARC). In January shortly after her arrival she visited the Social Services Department and met Mr Bishop, Mr Walton and Mrs Richardson. She offered assistance to professionals dealing with child abuse by providing consultancy, advice and diagnosis for any child about whom the Department was concerned.

Working Relationships

4.18 While guidelines for dealing with children suspected of being the victims of sexual abuse were being considered at a fairly high level in the ARC (later the JCAC) from the evidence of senior social workers we learned that those in the field had cordial working relationships with other practitioners such as Police, Health, Education and the NSPCC in dealing with cases of physical abuse and some forms of sexual abuse.

4.19 Case conferences were generally well attended with full discussion and recording of decisions, well thought out liaison in planning work in individual cases. They told us that the police were prepared to take account of views expressed by case conferences in coming to decisions about prosecutions and that the quality of working relationships at local level was generally high. The established pattern of referrals was working well.

4.20 Cases of physical abuse, through whichever agency they presented,—Police, Social Services, NSPCC, GP, Accident and Emergency, were seen by consultant paediatricians who attended case conferences and if necessary appeared in court proceedings.

Cases of Sexual Abuse

4.21 There were few cases of sexual abuse, but those which occurred fell into a distinct pattern. Cases involving incestuous or improper behaviour with older teenage girls within the family and molestation by strangers usually went to the Police direct. The abuse or suspected abuse of young children was rare but when it occurred was more usually picked up by health visitors or teachers or social workers and eventually referred to paediatricians. Depending on the nature of the referral, the police surgeon might or might not be involved. Cases of anal abuse were rare, and those initiated by a medical finding without prior complaint from the child or a third party were unheard of.

Guidelines

4.22 Whilst there was variation between the Social Services areas and their related Health Districts and Police Divisions as to the amount and level of work undertaken together, the existing guidelines drawn in 1984 were seen by social workers as an effective tool in the co-ordination of work in the field of physical child abuse and neglect.

4.23 There appeared to be a broad measure of understanding about the nature of the problems associated with the physical abuse and child neglect. The various agencies involved shared feelings of concern and had respect for one another's role and responsibility and there was a good level of inter-agency trust; coupled with participation in decision-making.

4.24 On the 2nd February 1987 Mrs Richardson convened a meeting involving key personnel from the Police Community Relations Department, Divisional staff and the relevant managers of the corresponding Social Services districts together with representatives of the NSPCC. The meeting undertook a general review of co-ordination and general practice across the county. In most areas, both Police and Social Services representatives reported good liaison, and moves towards early consultation and joint working. Some problems over delays in response were identified and agreements in principle on the desirability of joint training and the sharing of referrals were reached. Superintendent Saunders in clarifying that current Force policy was of liaison only, indicated that Police Standing Orders were to be amended to include the recommendations of the former ARC working party on sexual abuse which had not yet been circulated within the Police Force.

4.25 The field-workers and their managers were encouraged by the progress they had so far made. Social workers became angered and felt under-mined and disillusioned by the breakdown in inter-agency working relationships when it occurred.

Changes in the Use of Place of Safety Orders

4.26 Changes were occurring in relation to the use of place of safety orders. A move away from applying for orders for 28 days had begun. Practice varied across Social Services areas. In at least one area, it was common for 7 day orders to be sought. In other Social Services areas, 14 and 21 day orders were applied for.

4.27 Our attention was drawn to a Social Services manual that indicated that whilst circumstances should be the determining factor in the length of order, it nevertheless highlighted that there was a strong body of opinion that 7 day orders should be the normal application. Social workers and Area Officers in evidence emphasised that change was afoot and in some area offices their practice was not to seek a place of safety order on an automatic basis. They assured us that they considered the circumstances of each individual case and, if at all possible, proceeded by way of co-operation with parents. Nevertheless, it appeared to us that in the Social Services Department, child care practice traditionally relied heavily upon the use of statutory-based interventions and on place of safety orders. There was some progress being made to reduce the length of time of place of safety orders. Such progress as there was in this direction broke down in May and June as a consequence of the memorandum issued by the Director of Social Services on 29 May (See Page 65).

Case Conferences

4.28 Case Conferences in Cleveland were well organised and generally well attended by those who had a direct concern or involvement with the child. A noticeable shortcoming in the arrangements was the lack of involvement of a legal representative even in complex cases. On occasions the Social Services Court Liaison

Officers attempted to fulfill the role of adviser in the preparation of cases for presentation in Court.(See chapter 10).

4.29 Discussion and decisions in relation to registration and recommendations in respect of future action were carefully documented and recorded.

4.30 Within the Social Services Department and other agencies, opinions about the appropriateness of directly involving parents in attendance at case conferences reflected the divided views which exists nationally. There were those who believed that the presence of parents for part or all of the conferences would inhibit the free exchange of confidential information and professional opinion which was essential to the task of the case conferences. Others believed that the conference could be conducted in a manner which achieved their objective but gave the parents the opportunity to attend.

4.31 The general practice varied considerably between areas. In the Eston area, it was not uncommon for parents to be involved throughout the case conference. This was usually in cases of physical abuse where the abuser had been identified but some attempts had been made at adopting similar practice in cases of sexual abuse.

4.32 In other areas, a more common practice was for the Chairman of the case conference to see the parents at the end of the conference to advise them of the conclusions reached and recommendations made. In some areas, it was left to individual social workers to ensure that parents' views were represented and they were informed of the outcome of the case conference. During the crisis parents felt a strong sense of grievance that conferences were making recommendations and decisions about them and their children without, as they saw, it their views being heard.

4.33 There were 175 case conferences held on child abuse in Cleveland in the period April-August. Parents were not involved in attendance at any of these case conferences related to child sexual abuse. In a number of cases parents were seen by the case conference Chairman to explain the decisions that had been reached.

4.34 In those cases where social work involvement had been limited to the securing of a place of safety order, parents felt that their views and circumstances were not being effectively presented to the case conference and they felt powerless to influence events.

4.35 The guidelines agreed by the ARC in 1984 were silent on the issue of parental attendance at case conferences. However, the draft guidelines drawn up as a result of the review initiated by Mrs Richardson in early 1987 clearly advised that parents should be informed of case conferences and included in the meeting after initial professional discussion unless there is good reason not to do so. These recommendations were formally adopted by all the agencies represented at the JCAC in August 1987.

Problems Emerging in 1987

4.36 The tensions and fundamental differences of view which characterised the position of senior middle managers of Police and Social Services were masked by the long established working relationships of staff in the field. Two cases in March however threw differences between the police and social workers into sharp relief, polarising their positions. They affected the ability of the two agencies to respond appropriately to the large numbers of cases that were subsequently identified.

4.37 The first case which arose on the 17th February involved a 6 year old girl. This child had been seen by a clinical medical officer who was also a police surgeon at a health clinic. She sought advice from Mrs Richardson and together they decided to refer the child to the consultant paediatrician, Dr Higgs at North Tees. Mrs Richardson was careful to liaise with the police over this arrangement. Whilst expressing some reservation, the police nevertheless concurred—(for fuller details see Chapter 6). Dr Higgs diagnosed sexual abuse, both vaginal and anal, and the child was admitted to hospital and her grandfather arrested and charged. The subsequent diagnosis by Dr Higgs of a further episode of abuse on the 10th March when the grandfather could not have had access to the child caused the senior police surgeon to question the basis of Dr Higgs' diagnosis. Their disagreement on the interpretation of the sign of anal dilatation, and whether it could be regarded as diagnostic of sexual abuse, was recorded at the case conference on the child and clearly posed difficulties both for the Police and for social workers. Later the credibility of the diagnosis was further stretched by third and fourth episodes of abuse diagnosed, one in hospital shortly thereafter and the fourth in June in the foster home.

4.38 The second case occurred on the Thursday 19th March when a two year old boy was referred to Dr Higgs by the family general practitioner for advice on treatment of acute constipation. A diagnosis of anal sexual abuse was made and similar findings confirmed in the older children who had been brought to the hospital on the following day at the doctor's request.

4.39 The children were referred to the Stockton area office of Social Services. Mrs Summerbell, the senior area officer, took the responsibility of informing the police of the referral. She asked the Community Relations Department to contact Dr Higgs at the hospital. The Police made arrangements with Dr Higgs to take a statement from her that evening after her examination of the older children. This was obtained by a CID officer late at night. The Police telephoned the duty social worker on the Emergency Duty Team. The detail of the conversation was unknown to us. The Police and the Emergency Duty Team communicated with one another on the basis of indicating action to be taken but do not appear to have set out to agree with one another a joint approach to the investigation of the problem. Later the Police interviewed the older children in the presence of their father. Initially the eldest child was thought to be the perpetrator. When he told of his experience later social workers formed the view that he had been unfairly treated in the police interview. As this boy's story was further examined, it became clear that he was unlikely to be the perpetrator of offences against his sister, however incidentally. He could not have been the perpetrator of his own alleged abuse (see also chapter 6).

4.40 At a subsequent case conference, social workers, particularly Mrs Richardson, were critical of the way in which the referral had been managed. Dr Higgs had spoken to her about a lack of response she had received initially from both the Social Services Department and the Police when the referral was made. Mrs Richardson was critical both of the way in which the child had been interviewed by the Police and the fact that the interview had taken place in the presence of his father—a possible perpetrator of the offence. Her criticisms of the Police provoked angry responses and led to her receiving a telephone call from Detective Inspector Scott which she experienced as:—"most intimidating".

4.41 The management of this case was badly handled by both Police and Social Services from the start. It did not get better.

4.42 The three children involved were placed in separate foster homes, in part influenced by the fact that initially there was concern that the elder boy may have been responsible for the offences.

4.43 The children were engaged in formalised 'disclosure work'. Social workers from the Area Office together with a clinical psychologist based at the hospital undertook this work using techniques based on the principles of family therapy. Initially the children were seen individually, but usually the two elder children were seen together. Later they were seen with their mother and then together with both parents.

4.44 As a result of the examination of the children by three consultant paediatricians each of whom had formed the view that the physical signs found on the children were consistent with sexual abuse, the psychologist and the social workers involved with the children worked from the presumption that the children had been abused. [see page 154].

4.45 During April there were several cases of sexual abuse referred but they did not present any particular problems.

The Development of the Crisis

4.46 The end April/beginning May marked the watershed in the development of the crisis.

4.47 On the 30th April two children who were in the care of the Social Services Department, one of whom had been diagnosed in July 1986 by Dr Higgs as having been anally abused, were seen by her for the purpose of completing a report for the court. She diagnosed further medical signs consistent with a more recent incident of sexual abuse. Her diagnosis was confirmed by Dr Morrell. The children of the foster parents were examined by Dr Higgs and were found to have physical signs which she diagnosed as sexual abuse.

4.48 The diagnosis of sexual abuse to these children just prior to the Bank Holiday caused difficulty in ensuring that adequate numbers of social workers were available to do the follow-up work on the children. Mrs Richardson sought to help by reverting to the role of social work practitioner, and interviewed children together with a woman police officer and Dr Higgs. A decision was taken to initiate wardship proceedings on the 5 children of the two families. The Police view was that they were unable to proceed further in criminal proceedings on the basis of what they had heard the children say and the evidence available. Whilst the two agencies had worked well together on the investigation of the presenting diagnosis, the fact that they, quite properly, adopted different outcomes led to further tension.

4.49 The diagnoses gave rise to serious concern within the Social Services Department. The Director was informed and through him the Chairman of the Committee. There was a pending appeal by the parents of the foster children against termination of access which gave an added measure of pressure to the concern to establish the facts surrounding this diagnosis.

4.50 The new diagnosis involving foster parents sent alarm bells ringing. The consequences of such allegations for the children involved and for the Authority was seen to be very serious. The Director instructed that an independent second opinion be obtained. Arrangements had already been put in hand by Dr Higgs and Mrs Richardson to send the children to be seen by Dr Wynne at Leeds who confirmed the diagnosis. That confirmation was communicated to the Director. There was consultation about the position of other foster children who had been at the home. The next day, with Mr Bishop's approval, Mrs Richardson consulted with an Inspector at the regional office of the DHSS Social Services Inspectorate.

4.51 On the 3rd May a special planning meeting was held to discuss the steps necessary for the further protection of the children involved and any further action. Two solicitors were present, the childrens' solicitor and a solicitor from private practice instructed directly by the Social Services Department. Dr Higgs, Mrs Richardson, the Area Officer, the social worker directly involved together with the guardian ad litem of the foster children and a consultant social worker, Mrs Madge Bray, completed the planning group. Reports of the meeting do not suggest any testing of the evidence by the solicitors present. Most of the discussion centred around the timing of the application for wardship in relation to the children of the foster parents. The likelihood of the medical evidence being the subject of challenge was recognised and a decision was made to call in, for examination by Dr Higgs, the children who had contact with the household. The planning group also concluded that the court should be asked to appoint as guardian ad litem for the children of the foster parents, the person present at the planning meeting who was already undertaking that role in respect of the foster children.

4.52 There was a lack of objectivity in the evaluations of the problems which faced them. There is no evidence that the solicitors advised caution and the eagerness with which the other professionals sought to proceed was inappropriate. The arrangement they sought to make in respect of the appointment of a guardian ad litem and a solicitor for the children of the foster family might have seriously compromised the proper independence of the guardian ad litem.

4.53 Notwithstanding the fact that Social Services were already facing difficulties as a result of the number of children admitted to hospital with a diagnosis consistent with sexual abuse, the decision of the planning group to bring to the hospital for examination all children in care but sent home on trial who had been with the foster home during the past year was implemented. These children were examined by Dr Higgs, who on finding signs consistent with anal abuse, formed the view that such abuse was of more recent origin than their stay in the foster home concerned. As a result yet more children, those who were members of the household in which the children were currently resident, were brought to the hospital for examination. In all 9 children were examined in this way and 8 of them were found to be showing signs consistent with anal abuse.

4.54 The alternative argument of accepting that after a long period of time it was unlikely that physical signs of abuse would exist and that unless the social workers currently involved were aware of disturbed behaviour or other signs there was little purpose in doing more than advising parents quietly, appears not to have been considered. Parents could have been advised to take their children first to their general practitioner, referring on to the paediatrician only where there was cause for concern. This in fact, happened in relation to children who had been cared for in the foster-home on a daily basis with the foster parents acting as child minders. None of them was found to have signs consistent with abuse.

4.55 In the event, the course adopted by the Department appeared at that time to have been justified by the high proportion of new cases identified by the process. However, in the evidence put forward, it was unlikely that the signs these children were currently showing, if indicative of sexual abuse, could in any event have resulted from abuse alleged to have ocurred in the foster-home.

Bank Holiday Weekend in May

4.56 The crisis was mounting. Between the 1st and 8th May 23 children were admitted to Middlesbrough General Hospital. Since most of the admissions had taken place over the Bank Holiday weekend, when only staff from the emergency duty team were available, social workers were unable to give much help to parents. Most of the children retained in hospital had been made the subject of place of safety orders.

Many of the children were associated with the foster home investigation. The size of this group put everyone under considerable pressure over the Bank Holiday period. The emergency team was unable to do more than fetch and carry children for examination.

4.57 Other children were diagnosed by Dr Higgs as showing signs of sexual abuse after being examined during their attendance at paediatric out-patient clinics.

11 children from 6 different families were diagnosed in this way and admitted to the hospital. Taken together, the children connected with the foster home and those from the out-patient clinics formed a substantial group of children in whom signs of sexual abuse had been diagnosed without there being a complaint either from the child or from a third party.

4.58 The admission of a large number of children to the hospital was brought to the attention of the Director and senior managers of the Social Services Department immediately on the 5th May. No analysis of where the children came from or how they got to hospital appears to have been prepared or asked for. At this time, senior staff were preoccupied with the implications of alleged abuse occurring in a well-established foster-home and children allegedly reabused whilst in care.

Health Service Concern

4.59 The Unit Manager at the hospital, Dr Drury, contacted the Social Services Department to express his concern about the numbers of children being admitted to hospital, many being held there on place of safety orders. There was also concern being expressed by the Community Health Council at the presence of active, healthy—if possibly abused—children on the ward, which caused significant management problems.

Relationships Between Police and Social Workers

4.60 The breakdown of relationships between the Police and the social workers varied in different areas. The relationship with the Community Relations Department was reasonably good, but the police approach to and reluctance to accept the diagnosis of Dr Higgs and Dr Wyatt raised tensions markedly. Social Services took the view that referrals directed to their service by Dr Higgs were diagnoses responsibly made by a consultant whose skill and experience was respected. Social workers were reluctant to accept the necessity for an internal digital examination of the kind carried out by the senior police surgeon and from their evidence accepted they did little to facilitate them. In fact it is clear that between Dr Higgs and Mrs Richardson and a number of other social workers they did not wish second opinion examinations to be carried out by Dr Irvine.

4.61 The process of breakdown was now becoming clear. There was a rising conflict between agencies attempting to grapple with a serious and delicate problem without an agreed systematic approach. Its absence was to become increasingly apparent in the playing out of personalised conflicts which bedevilled the management of individual cases. In this climate, Mrs Richardson became a focus for the anger and frustration being felt by the Police and the senior police surgeon. Without a system agreed between the agencies, the overall position could not be effectively managed or controlled. Failure and frustration was attributed to the non-cooperation of agencies or individuals.

Role of Senior Management

4.62 In their concern to deal with the wider implications of the allegations against the foster parents, senior staff left the detailed discussions and management of individual cases to Area Directors and to Mrs Richardson. The degree to which they were aware of executive decisions being taken in the planning meeting on 3rd May was unclear. Mrs Richardson sought approval from Mr Walton for the necessary financial authority to cover the legal expenses of warding the children. Whilst in theory her role was advisory there can be little doubt that she exerted a major influence over the direction of events in this and other cases.

4.63 Throughout the next two months there was a steady pattern of referrals in the clinics of Dr Higgs and Dr Wyatt from social work staff of the various area offices. There were many examples of children telling teachers and day nursery staff and on one occasion the "lollipop lady" who operated the school crossing patrol—about things which were happening to them at home which properly needed futher inquiry.

4.64 Foster parents reported that a number of children were displaying highly sexualised behaviour inappropriate to their age. As Dr Higgs' interest became known, several of these children were referred to her.

4.65 With no agreed response between the agencies, services were hopelessly overloaded. The sense of urgency with which matters were pursued whilst understandable was inappropriate; matters would have been better handled in a calm, planned and organised manner. That could not be achieved without somebody within the organisation taking effective control to regulate the position. Without effective managment the practitioners in both social work and medicine were being overwhelmed by their own activities.

Mrs Richardson Contacts Mr Bishop

4.66 Mrs Richardson was now alarmed. She sent a memorandum to Mr Bishop in which she said:—"The increase in detection of child sexual abuse has now become critical. As you will be aware 18 sexually abused children were admitted to Middlesbrough General Hospital during a seven-day period beginning on 1.5.87, highlighting major discrepancies in the Department's ability to respond in concert with the police and health services. Already there are new cases pending and this increase in referrals is likely to continue. Urgent plans are needed to examine both short and long-term issues." The memorandum went on to suggest an urgent meeting with the District General Manager to examine the "shared implications" for the Health and Social Services. It recommended the setting up of a "task force" of nominated social workers to deal with the children referred. She urged the provision of a play facility for children at the hospital and comfortable rooms for interviewing the children with video facilities.

Fostering Arrangements

4.67 Middle managers in the Social Services Department were charged with the responsibility of drawing together resources to move the children on from the hospital. Area-based fostering officers were faced with real difficulty in coping with the sudden increase in demand. In order to secure appropriate placements and movement the co-ordination of fostering placements and resources was centralised.

4.68 Mrs de Lacey Dunne assumed central control of all fostering placements throughout May, June and July. Together with Mrs Richardson she visited the hospital on the 8th May to see what could be done. Dr Higgs did not think it was appropriate to discharge many of the children immediately because of continuing medical investigations. But during the course of the following week, all the children requiring to be placed, were placed with foster parents.

4.69 The phenomenon of children being admitted in waves occurred twice more. On each occasion the pattern was the same, a large group of children from the community, from a large family, foster home, or school, combined with a number of children diagnosed as a result of attendance at a paediatric out-patient clinic on a Friday. The second time it happened, the weekend 22-24 May, was a weekend when the capacity of Social Services to respond was at a low ebb. When it happened for a third time on the weekend 12-14 June, the fostering resources were thrown into crisis. Mrs de Lacey Dunne told us:-"As far as fostering was concerned, we were in a state of crisis. The situation was untenable; we had reached the level of looking for beds for children, rather than placing children appropriately." She gave us examples:

— The use of newly approved foster parents for complicated cases without adequate preparation;

— The taking advantage of the kind-heartedness of foster parents or placing more children than they could cope with—then having to move children again when the foster parents could not manage;

— The separation of brothers and sisters who should have been placed together;

— The impossibility of giving any real thought to matching the needs of the child with what the foster family had to offer;"

4.70 The pressure experienced by fostering officers, their great anxiety at the compromises they were forced to make by pressure of the volume of work they were having to adapt to, ran as a common thread through the experience of the practitioners who were trying to cope with the volume of work being generated.

Mr Bishop Speaks to the Community Health Council and the Social Services Committee

4.71 On the 12th May Mr Bishop had agreed to speak to a meeting of the South Tees Community Health Council. Following a general talk on provision of social services in the community he was faced with questions expressing public concern about what was happening at the hospital in relation to the diagnosis of sexual abuse. The secretary of the Community Health Council, Mr Urch, became a strong critic of Dr Higgs' practice and on this evening both he and his members expressed their worries directly to Mr Bishop.

4.72 Since he was unaware of the differences of viewpoint expressed by Dr Higgs and Dr Irvine at the case conference in March, Mr Bishop at that time had no reason to question the basis on which the diagnoses were being made. Indeed in the case where he had given instructions for a second medical opinion, the diagnosis of Dr Higgs had been confirmed by Dr Wynne in Leeds. He had no grounds upon which to advise the Social Services Committee of any doubt about the basis of the diagnosis and he did not do so at the meeting on 13th May.

There he made a verbal report on the increase in the number of cases of child sexual abuse and that 21 children had been admitted to hospital in the previous week. The Director emphasised that the matter was causing a great deal of concern, that the Social Services Department was trying to work closely with schools, the police, health visitors and doctors. He alerted the Committee to the possibility that if the current level of referral did not decrease, he might have to seek additional funding. He promised a full report to the next meeting of the Committee on the 24th June.

4.73 At operational level social workers and Police were working hard to follow up cases that had been diagnosed and to deal with new cases. In some areas, according to evidence from social workers, relationships built on personal trust and mutual respect withstood the pressures that were placed on both groups by increased numbers of referrals of sexual abuse, arising from medical signs alone with no complaint by the child or a third party.

Urgency of Diagnosis

4.74 It was the consultant paediatrician's usual practice to tell parents of the diagnosis and its implications at the time it was made. Social workers responded by securing the child's admission to hospital with a place of safety order. Often police officers were faced with parents who were angry and outraged. In the absence of a confirmation by the child or other supporting evidence the Police were unable to take action. Mrs Richardson was aware of the increasing tension in the relationships between social workers and the Police. But her impression was that much of the conflict was subterranean until the end of May. She attended a meeting of the senior management team on the 19th May to discuss the issue of sexual abuse. Mr Bishop told us:—"At this time the particular form of sexual abuse that was being referred to us was, frankly, something we found very difficult to accept could be happening to very young children and we were trying to find out exactly what was happening to the children and how it was being detected."

4.75 Mrs Richardson knew that Dr Higgs was using techniques based on the work of Dr Wynne and Dr Hobbs in Leeds. She did not warn her seniors of the fact that there was a divergence of views among medical practitioners, particularily between Dr Higgs and Dr Irvine, nor of the dangers ahead. Mr Bishop's recollection of the message that came across was:—"Incredible as it may seem, this is something that is happening in our midst and medical opinion establishes it."

Conflicting Evidence

4.76 Increasingly, the Police responded by insisting that children be re-examined by a police surgeon. Social workers and paediatricians did not accept the need for further examinations by a police surgeon. Dr Higgs and Dr Wyatt made a general practice of confirming one another's diagnosis. On occasions second opinions were given by Dr Morrell and Dr Oo. In some cases children had been sent to Leeds for formal second opinion making a third examination, which on each occasion confirmed the diagnosis. It was in this context that the Social Services came initially to regard the diagnosis as reliable.

4.77 The divergence of medical opinion was presented at case conferences where it posed considerable problems. The conference could be faced with one diagnosis confirmed by two and sometimes three consultant paediatricians, and on the other with the view of a police surgeon that abuse had not taken place. This had first happened at the case conference in March. In each case faced with the disagreement social workers felt they would be failing in their duty to protect the child if they did not act on the diagnosis of the consultant paediatrician.

4.78 As working relationships between the Social Services Department and Police deteriorated rigid stances were adopted. Problems arose in cases that were relatively straightforward. In the third week in May a little girl was taken to a doctor at a child health clinic with signs suggestive of vaginal abuse and referred to Dr Higgs, who made a diagnosis of sexual abuse. The child had already been seen by two doctors, but the police wanted a further examination by a police surgeon. There appeared to the social workers to be delays in investigating the perpetrator, whom the social workers understood was eventually arrested after going to the police station of his own accord. There were arguments between social workers and police about how and by whom the 4 year old was to be interviewed. They were unable to agree with one another whether to work either co-operatively or jointly.

4.79 The second wave of 14 children over the weekend 22nd to 24th May further added to the anxiety in the Social Services Department.

4.80 The difficulties experienced in the practical management of cases during this period became frustrating for individual social workers. Some situations received a lot of attention. In one case, a girl of 10 told her headmistress of sexual activities in her home which eventually led social workers to refer her to Dr Higgs for examination. Her mother who brought her two other children to the ward consented to the examination. During the course of the examination the children's father removed them from the ward and secreted them away. Social services sought and obtained place of safety orders. With the assistance and co-operation of the Police the children were eventually examined by a police surgeon, Dr Beeby who found no signs of sexual abuse. They were returned to the hospital where they were examined by Dr Higgs who confirmed her original diagnosis on the girl of 10 and found signs of sexual abuse in respect of the other two children. The next day, the 27th May, the senior police surgeon, Dr Irvine, examined all three children and found no signs of sexual abuse. The children were later examined by three more doctors. The experience in this case, in which the father removed children believed to be at risk from the hospital, reinforced the views of social workers as to the importance of seeking a place of safety order.

Meeting of 28 May and Breakdown of Relations

4.81 The incident of the missing children had a wider significance. It was not a good beginning for the meeting planned the following day by Mrs Richardson in her role as co-ordinator of the working party on the JCAC charged with the task of bringing up to date guidelines in child abuse. [see chapter 3] She had arranged the meeting with the hope that an opportunity to air differences might resolve them.

4.82 This meeting was crucial. We have dealt with the meeting in detail elsewhere, but the outcome polarised differences of professional opinion, particularily between the Police and Social Services, and provoked a major breakdown between Police and Social Services. Considering the importance of the meeting and the circumstances in which it was taking place we were surprised that Mrs Richardson did not discuss its purpose with the Director or other senior staff beforehand.

4.83 After the meeting Mrs Richardson and Dr Higgs went to see Mr Walton who took the view that this was a matter for the Director and sent Mrs Richardson on to see Mr Bishop.

On the same day the Child Care Adviser, Mr Hughes, met Mr Walton to discuss how best to assist social workers who were expressing feelings of frustration and anger over the number of examinations that children were being subjected to.

Mr Bishop gives Direction

4.84 On the 29th May, Mrs Richardson and Mr Hughes drafted a memorandum which they placed before Mr Bishop. It was difficult to establish how much discussion there had been between senior managers and Mr Bishop about the terms of the memorandum and its effect. Our impression was that there was little. Mr Bishop emphasised to us his anxiety to take steps to protect the children involved from the growing climate of conflict. He was concerned to learn of the differences which had occurred at the meeting the previous day. He was told that the Police were going to view the diagnosis of Dr Higgs based on anal signs with caution. It was not clear to us whether he had been told of telephone conversations between Mrs Richardson and Dr Higgs. They were worried that the differences of professional opinion might leave the children at risk. Mrs Richardson reassured Dr Higgs telling her that an instruction was going to be issued. The next day Mr Bishop issued the memorandum. It had a critical effect, but he told us in evidence that he did not see it as a very important document. Senior staff of Social Services were unsure what would be the effect of the decision taken by the police on Dr Higgs' diagnosis. They were worried that if the Police did not act in situations where suspicion fell on parents as perpetrators of the abuse, children would be left at risk. They took the view that the decision taken by the Police might well have the result of parents immediately discharging children from hospital and for that reason social workers needed to seek place of safety orders to protect the children.

4.85 The memorandum directed the exclusion of police surgeons from examining children referred to social services for reasons of sexual abuse. The key role in medical examination and diagnosis was accorded to the consultant paediatrician. It stressed the importance of obtaining a disclosure from the child, and the need to restrict access to parents. Emphasis was placed on the importance of informing the Police of all cases and continuing efforts to involve them in conducting a joint police/social worker interview with the child.

4.86 The full directions of the memorandum were:—"

"*Management of Child Sexual Abuse*

In order to safeguard the welfare of children, pending guidelines from the Joint Child Abuse Committee, the following steps should be taken in cases of alleged or suspected sexual abuse:

1 Medical examinations should be carried out in hospital by a consultant paediatrician.

2 Initial protective action should be via admission to hospital. Where the consultant paediatrician is of the opinion that there is medical evidence of sexual abuse, an immediate place of safety order should be taken to protect the child's interests during investigation.

3 The Police should be informed in all cases. Every effort should be made to conduct a joint police/social worker investigation with the child.

4 The obtaining of a disclosure from the child should be the key focus.

The child should be interviewed as promptly as possible, preferably not in the presence of a parent, which may inhibit disclosure. Parental access may therefore, need to be suspended or restricted during initial investigations.

5 Any siblings should also be seen and medically examined.

6 Repeat examinations should be avoided. Where a statement is available from a clinician, it is not necessary for the police surgeon to re-examine the child. Forensic tests should be arranged in consultation with the consultant paediatrician, who will be able to assist the police surgeon as necessary.

Mr M Bishop

County Director of Social Services

29 May 1987"

The Chief Constable Gives Direction

4.87 The same day the Police issued a directive advising officers to treat any diagnosis of Dr Higgs based upon 'anal reflex dilatation' with caution and to look for substantial corroboration of her findings before taking positive steps. [see chapter 6]

Divergent Instructions

4.88 The issue of divergent instructions increased the difficulties of operational staff in both organisations. The failure to resolve problems and co-ordinate action at middle and senior management levels in both organisations increased the difficulties of social workers and Police on the ground.

4.89 The contents of the Social Services memorandum, and the reasons for issuing it in order to protect the child were never communicated to the Police.

4.90 The effect was significant. In the view of Mr Horne the Area Officer for Eston the conflict of instruction was the reason for the breakdown in relationships with the Police in the field. He told us: "when we were faced with difficulties of medical opinion in cases, I believe the two agencies involved—the Social Services and the Police took two different courses of action, which ultimately became divergent; on the one hand, the Social Services Department certainly in my area took the decision to continue to take seriously and to act upon a diagnosis of one of the paediatricians, and having taking that decision we needed then rigorourly to assess and investigate, to confirm or disconfirm that original allegation. I believe on the other hand, that perhaps the Police, given that medical conflict, took a decision to view with more caution the original allegation by the paediatrician, which was obviously a decision which was their right to take in terms of criminal investigations and perhaps a very proper decision. I cannot comment on that. What it did give us though, was a situation which differed from the previous degree of co-operation and team approach in full investigation of any form of allegation of abuse in Langbaurgh, towards one where investigations was being left to the Social Services Department rather than being joint investigation".

Use of Place of Safety Orders

4.91 The memorandum issued by the Director had a profound effect on practice in certain areas, particularly Middlesbrough, but less so in those areas which were less affected by the crisis, such as North Tees, and no effect on Hartlepool.

4.92 With the Police reluctant to investigate possible perpetrators without the child being examined by a police surgeon, or a written statement from Dr Higgs, often not forthcoming for a considerable period, a clear statement of abuse by the child assumed disproportionate importance for social workers. The place of safety order appeared to be used to control parental access and in order to facilitate disclosure interviews with children. There was a high level of concern that if parents had open access to children, pressure would be brought to bear on the child not to tell what had been happening. The memorandum issued by the Director continued to emphasise the importance of joint work with the Police. Social workers' general practice of not interviewing parents until they had been seen by the Police continued.

4.93 Most of the place of safety orders were taken out by social workers during working hours. But 49 of them were taken by the Emergency Duty Team.

The Emergency Duty Team

4.94 The social work service provided by Cleveland County Council outside of normal office hours is delivered through a small group of staff who form the Emergency Duty Team based at the Department's Headquarters in Middlesbrough.

4.95 The team of four full-time and two part-time workers are deployed so that there are two social workers on duty part of the time and one on duty overnight. At the weekends, two social workers are on duty during the day on Saturday whilst during the remainder of the weekend, only one worker is available. Mr Howie, the Adviser in Mental Health, acts as the Team's link to the Department. During the period when they are on duty team members are responsible for providing service to a population of 600,000. In emergencies back-up social workers can be called in on a bleeper system.

4.96 The staff of the night duty team were experienced social workers though not all of them held a professional qualification in social work. The arrangements for their professional support to deal with complex cases appeared somewhat haphazard though team members were quite clear that if they needed help or support they would seek it by telephoning senior staff, including if necessary, the Director.

4.97 The social workers of the Emergency Duty Team were involved in dealing with requests from Dr Wyatt and Dr Higgs to seek place of safety orders in respect of children who had been examined at the hospital and, on occasions, were requested to take action in respect of bringing siblings to the hospital for examination. Prior to May/June 1987, they were rarely called upon to consider seeking place of safety orders in respect of children who were in-patients at the hospital. They indicated that if such situations did arise, they would be primarily guided by the willingness or otherwise of parents to leave their children in hospital overnight, so that matter could be dealt with properly the next day. Where it was thought necessary to seek a place of safety order, Magistrates granted orders for relatively short periods, often as little as seven days.

4.98 The position changed significantly in early June. Members of the Emergency Duty Team were faced with pressing requests, mostly from Dr Wyatt but on one occasion by Dr Higgs, to seek place of safety orders in respect of children they had examined at the hospital and concluded were being sexually abused.

4.99 At 10.10 pm on Friday 5th June, Dr Wyatt contacted a social worker on the Emergency Duty Team requesting a place of safety order on three children who had been examined earlier in the day and diagnosed as sexually abused. The referral coincided with the 10.30 pm change-over of staff. The incoming social worker phoned the hospital, but was unable to speak to Dr Wyatt who was busy. She spoke to Dr Higgs who outlined the circumstances in which the examination of one child in the family for an urinary complaint had led to the mother being invited to bring the other children to the hospital when all three were diagnosed as being sexually abused. Dr Higgs told the social worker that Dr Wyatt wanted an immediate place of safety order. The social worker did not raise any questions in relation to the diagnosis. She was aware of the departmental instruction to take a place of safety order on children who had been diagnosed as sexually abused, and acted upon it.

4.100 The social worker did not speak with the child's mother prior to making the application. Had she done so, she would have learnt that one of her colleagues from the Medical Social Work Team had been involved in making a preliminary assessment of the case earlier in the day and had concluded that a place of safety order was not necessary. The child's mother had co-operated in bringing the siblings for examination, and was prepared to allow the children to stay in hospital whilst further enquiries were made. The child's father was aboard a ship anchored off Tees Bay. The social worker left messages with the ward staff about the agreement reached with the children's mother. Staff were advised to contact the Emergency Duty Team if difficulties arose, such as the parents threatening to remove the children from the ward. Later that evening the child's father was contacted by telephone and he came ashore. Whilst it was clear that the parents were convinced that their children had not been abused, it was not suggested that a change of plan had been made necessary because parents had withdrawn their co-operation.

4.101 A further case referred that night involved a small girl who had been referred to the hospital following a report to the school nurse about a vaginal injury caused by falling on a toy. The child and mother had been in hospital since mid-morning. Dr Wyatt's examination had shown anal dilatation and he expressed the opinion that she had been sexually abused. A younger brother was examined, he showed no sign of abuse. The child's mother was upset and angry at the diagnosis. She left the hospital with the younger baby. The social worker from the Emergency Duty Team sought and obtained a place of safety order, by her account at 1.00 am in the morning. They delivered the place of safety order the next morning only to find that the mother was not at home. She was so upset that she had gone to stay with a relative. The social worker posted the place of safety order through the letter box. There was no accompanying note. The order was found by the mother on her return later that morning. The mother did not understand the order and was alarmed by it. She rushed back to the hospital where the ward sister contacted the Emergency Duty Team. A social worker visited the mother at the hospital to explain the implications of the order and advise her on her rights. On this occasion the mother found the social worker helpful.

4.102 A week later, on 13th June, further referrals from Dr Wyatt were received by the staff of the Emergency Duty Team. In a phone call received at 6.00 pm Dr Wyatt requested place of safety orders on eleven children. Seven children belonged to one family already well-known to the Social Services Department. Two of the children belonging to the family group had been seen at the hospital and diagnosed as sexually abused. The doctor wished the other children in the family to be examined. The social worker did not question the appropriateness of a late evening emergency intervention in a family that was well-known and had a long history of contact with social services. On the strength of the place of safety order the other five children were brought to the hospital for examination where three of the children were believed to be showing signs of sexual abuse.

4.103 On the same evening a further three children, two being siblings of a baby who had been examined for a chronic bowel problem at the paediatric out-patient clinic held that day, were also made the subject of a place of safety order. The social worker told us that the parents appeared to be numb and did not know what was happening. She explained her decision to make the application by referring to the direction given to the staff of the Social Services Department in the memorandum of 29th May.

4.104 Finally, on that same evening, one other child was to be made subject to a place of safety order. He had been taken to the casualty ward having bumped his head. On examination he was found to have other bruising consistent with non-accidental injury—and signs thought to be consistent with sexual abuse. In this case the social worker emphasised that in her view, the physical signs alone were sufficient to require the protection of the child whilst matters were further investigated.

4.105 A further incident arose late at night on 17th June. As a result of a call received from Dr Wyatt at 10.30 pm, the duty social worker visited Ward 9 at Middlesbrough Hospital. The social worker was told by the staff nurse that Dr Wyatt wished two children to be made the subject of place of safety orders. Three children had been examined earlier in the day. One had been admitted but due to a misunderstanding the other two who had been found to have signs indicating sexual abuse had been allowed to go home. The mother had remained in hospital with the younger child who had been brought to the hospital for investigation of a chest complaint. She claimed her other children were with her niece but said she was uncertain as to the precise address. Dr Wyatt was firmly of the opinion that the children should be returned to the ward that night. The social worker thought to proceed at such a late hour was unreasonable particularly as, to admit the children, other children would need to be moved from one ward to another. She expressed her concern about what she was being asked to do to Dr Wyatt. He re-iterated his diagnosis and told the social worker that she would have to take full responsibility if she chose not to act. The social worker did not feel able to stand out against the firmness of Dr Wyatt's view. She did not seek any support advice from senior staff in her own Department. Eventually, after having sought and obtained a place of safety order, she went with the children's mother to collect them from their own home where they were in the care of their father. The children were roused from their sleep and taken to the hospital and admitted in the early hours of the morning.

4.106 The team members were unhappy about the new demands being made on them and raised their anxieties at a formal meeting of the Emergency Duty Team held in the afternoon of the 18th June. We received an account of that meeting from Mr Howie, which indicated that the social workers had sought "guidance on child sexual abuse because of the rumours that were circulating that the Doctors had changed the policy guidelines and members required clarification". The staff emphasised that they wanted child care courses and training.

A memorandum of guidance was issued by Mr Howie on 25th June after consulting with Mr Hughes and Mr Moms', the Court Liaison Officer. This dealt specifically with situations in which place of safety orders were to be applied for to secure the examination of the siblings of a child diagnosed as abused by a Consultant. The Emergency Duty Team were told:

"If parents refuse to allow examinations, ask the consultant whether they are prepared to put in writing that the children's situation, from a medical point of view, necessitates an immediate medical examination and if so take a place of safety order and take the children to hospital. Do not sign authorisation for medical examination but leave to the doctor. If the consultant will not give such written consent, then if in your judgement, history and situation suggests children need immediate protection then take a place of safety order, but no medical examination".

4.107 For the most part, the social workers did as the consultants requested. On those occasions when they did demur, such as being requested to bring children from their beds to the hospital in the early hours of the morning, they did not feel able to stand by their views in the face of a firmly restated opinion from the consultant concerned. We were concerned to find that even as late as 25th June, when the number of children had overwhelmed the department's resources, the middle managers of the Social Services Department were still directing field staff to take immediate place of safety orders.

4.108 It was difficult for the social workers to resist not only the requests of the consultants but also their own departmental instructions. The problems they faced called for a direct involvement of more senior management to advise them and to make plain both to the consultants and social workers the level of intervention that was appropriate when a diagnosis of sexual abuse was made. The fact that such a response was not forthcoming, and that staff were left to cope with each case as it came along, put them in an impossible position.

4.109 Their request for training appears to have gone unheeded.

4.110 The fact that they did not contact senior staff for consultation and advice when faced with such an unusual request as to seek eleven place of safety orders suggested the need for improvements to be made to the training, management and support for the Emergency Duty Team.

Parents Complaints on Place of Safety Orders

4.111 We have no reason to doubt that as a general practice social workers sought co-operation from parents before applying for place of safety orders. In circumstances where they believed that parents might not co-operate, an explanation that a place of safety order would be applied for in the absence of agreement, although it might be seen by the parents concerned as a threat, would be a correct step to take.

4.112 But during 1987 in a number of cases the criticisms made by parents about the way in which they were presented with place of safety orders was borne out by the accounts given to the Inquiry by the social workers involved. There is a strong correlation between the complaints made by parents and the account of events given by social workers on the Emergency Duty Team. We question the extent to which it was necessary for staff to act on a basis of crisis late at night in the cases referred to earlier, in circumstances where there could be only inadequate communication between parents and social workers.

4.113 We heard from social workers that at the time of serving the place of safety orders they explained what the orders meant and advised parents to seek legal advice. However, it was likely at such a moment of shock and distress parents would have great difficulty in understanding the implications of the explanations given. A form of notice in clear and simple language is needed setting out the meaning and implications of the order and the way it affects parental rights.

Parents' Complaints About Access

4.114 Complaints about access were a distressing feature of the evidence to the Inquiry. It was a matter which particularily worried the magistrates hearing the applications for care orders. It had been the practice of the Social Services Department in the past, on the obtaining of a place of safety order, in general to allow access to parents. During 1987 some parents had open access but in other cases parents were denied access during the investigation phase when children were being interviewed, as a result of the perceived need to separate child from parent for the purpose of disclosure work. This very much upset the parents involved. Access on the hospital ward generally presented fewer problems than parental visits to foster homes. In the hospital supervision was generally available. In the foster home, the foster parents' capacity to cope with a newly placed child and regular if not daily visiting from a distressed parent was a factor which had to be taken into account. Parents found this change in the pattern of visits both hard to understand and to accept.

4.115 In many cases only supervised access was allowed. Visits took place in child and family centres away from the foster home. Such arrangements made heavy demands on social workers time and as the number of children in care rose the problem of supervising access visits became an acute one. In an attempt to help with this problem, six social work visitors were appointed on a temporary basis. From the viewpoint of the parents the situation was most unsatisfactory.

Mr Bishop Meets the Paediatricians

4.116 On the 1st June Mr Bishop and Mr Walton met Mr Donaldson, General Manager of the District Health Authority and Dr Higgs to discuss the problems which were being experienced by the Health and Social Services. The newly appointed Community Physician and Dr Drury the Unit General Manager at Middlesbrough General Hospital were both present. Mr Bishop told us that at this meeting critical questions were asked of Dr Higgs. He pressed her for an explanation of her diagnostic techniques and sought clear explanations from her to the effect that the signs she was seeing could not be attributed to causes other than sexual abuse. He said:—"It was not a heated discussion. It was a cool, professional assessment of questions that we wanted to ask of her and we received cool, balanced, very carefully thought-out replies. .... We were giving her a fairly intensive grilling, those of us who were not au fait with her thinking." Dr Higgs told us:- "I felt confident about the diagnosis that I made". Neither of the other doctors present at the meeting expressed any reservations about Dr Higgs' replies to Mr Bishop's questions or about the diagnosis.

4.117 A few days later Dr Higgs and Dr Wyatt called on him in his office, refusing to speak to other staff and insisting on seeing him. He gave us this account of that meeting:—"Their concern was to praise the Department for reacting so firmly to the diagnosis of sex abuse and to express the hope that our strong response would continue. They believed, particularily Dr Wyatt, that the detection of child sex abuse was a major breakthrough in the care of children and could explain many problems of child health which had previously not responded to treatment. I took this opportunity to raise the question concerning examination of children for sex abuse who had been referred for other symptoms such as asthma, as I had heard that such examinations had taken place. Both doctors assured me that they would not examine for sexual abuse as a matter of routine but if a child had been referred with forms of chronic or long-standing complaints, and if other causes for the symptoms could not be established, then sexual abuse would be considered as a possible cause of the symptom and investigate further by medical examination."

He sought change and co-operation from them:—"I proceeded to suggest to both doctors that I was not qualified to question their diagnoses but that the effect of uncovering so much sex abuse of children was placing serious strain on other services. The existing resources could not cope with their numbers of referrals and I wondered whether there was any way in which they could reduce diagnoses to allow us to obtain the resources which would enable us to provide a proper service for children and families.

4.118 The doctors said that this was not professionally acceptable to them and that other services needed to realise that this was a major development in child health which required an appropriate new initiative in terms of resources and effort to ensure that the opportunity was not missed to create a whole new integrated service to identify and combat the effects of child sex abuse."

4.119 He was not able to secure their agreement to change and they concluded the meeting recognising that problems lay ahead that would need to be faced by all.

The Director's Scepticism Reassured

4.120 These contacts with Dr Higgs and to a lesser extent with Dr Wyatt appear to have reassured Mr Bishop who had a growing sense of concern about the basis of the diagnosis. His view of the controversial nature of the diagnosis was a limited one. He still saw the difficulties as essentially a personal difference of view and conflict between Dr Higgs and Dr Irvine. He saw Dr Higgs as a committed, responsible, thoroughly professional practitioner and gave weight to her opinion. He saw no reason at that time not to do so. He knew other paediatricians, notably Dr Wynne, had confirmed her diagnoses in certain children. He was not aware of the wider medical controversy over the interpretation of the sign of anal dilation until the end of June.

4.121 Mr Bishop ensured that the Chairman and Vice-Chairman of the Social Services Committee were kept informed of developments. As he did not see the medical diagnosis as controversial, the focus of his attention and reports to others was how the Social Services Department and the staff could cope with the volume of work and ensure that children were protected from the extreme form of sexual abuse indicated by the diagnosis. Together with the Chief Executive, he visited staff in area officers to hear at first hand the problems they were experiencing.

Meeting with the Police

4.122 On the 5th June Mr Bishop, accompanied by Mr Walton, visited the Chief Constable in his office. Mr Smith was also present. The meeting had been initiated by Mr Bishop when they met socially on the 22nd May. Mrs Richardson had made some written suggestions for the meeting. There was however, no agenda, little other preparation and no notes taken. They did not agree in evidence as to what was actually said. In the light of the difficulties at operational level of both agencies and the importance of the meeting the apparent lack of preparation by both parties was surprising. [see also chapter 6]

4.123 The discussion appears to have centred upon the professional problems that were being caused to both organisations by the differing diagnoses of police surgeons and paediatricians. Neither side stood back to ask which of them might or might not be right nor to consider together how they might try to resolve the differences between the two agencies. They attempted to some extent to consider the consequences but never looked at the cause of their profound disagreement. Neither side appears to have reported to the other what was actually happening. Neither side told the other of their respective directions issued to their staff on the 29th May. The possibility of taking steps to ensure co-operation between Police and social workers appears not to have been discussed. The differences were wide. Without preparatory work and no-one to direct their attention to the underlying issues no progress was made. Eventually, it was suggested that both parties should discuss the problems arising from disagreement over the diagnosis with the Crown Prosecution Service.

4.124 The Police informed Social Services of their intention to set up a specialist team to work on child sexual abuse. Neither side suggested any discussion as to involvement of or liaison between the new team and Social Services. Mr Bishop, however welcomed the development. There was no arrangement for Mr Bishop and Mr Payne to meet again.

Crown Prosecution Services Consulted

4.125 Mr Walton, on behalf of Mr Bishop, attended the meeting with the police representatives and the Crown Prosecution Service. That meeting did nothing to advance a solution other than to make suggestions about using other consultants. Mr Walton's note of this meeting read:—"Mr Smith thought that Dr Higgs—and I emphasise this—was employed by the Social Services Department. The Police asked Social Services if they would use other consultants to give a more balanced picture. Social services pointed out that the Northern Regional Health Authority offered the consultant service and we could not pick and choose between them."

4.126 They failed to appreciate that much of the problem arose out of the consultants' practice rather than from referrals. It is right however to point out the approach of Mrs Richardson, undoubtedly communicated by her to social workers, of preferring to call upon Dr Higgs' experience in cases of child sexual abuse.

4.127 These meetings did little to identify problems or solutions or bring the organisations together or to provide any instructions or decisions to be followed.

Children Abused in Foster Homes

4.128 During June further diagnoses of sexual abuse were made relating to children in foster homes.

4.129 Early in June a mentally handicapped child who had been adopted by his former foster-parents was diagnosed as sexually abused by Dr Wyatt. His opinion was confirmed by Dr Wynne. The child's mother told us of her sense of outrage and disbelief of the diagnosis. She had been fostering three children who had previously been diagnosed as abused. Her daughter and her adopted child were admitted to hospital on place of safety orders notwithstanding the Social Services detailed knowledge of the family and formal approval of them as adoptive parents. The foster-children were moved to alternative placements. In the previous two years the family had provided short-term care for twenty-five children. On this occasion no attempt was made to bring forward for examination children who had been previously placed in the home nor were the most recently-placed children who were alleged to have been abused re-examined.

4.130 Towards the end of June the six year old girl who had been first diagnosed as sexually abused in February (see page 14), was examined by Dr Higgs on a follow-up visit to the hospital. On completion of her examination Dr Higgs advised the social worker accompanying the child that in her opinion, the child had been subject to further sexual abuse. The foster parents were devastated by the diagnosis and the fact that the child was to be immediately removed from their care. The foster-mother reacted by feeling physically sick. We saw little evidence of support being given to the foster parents involved to cope with the after-math of this experience (See page 75).

4.131 In the middle of June, Dr Higgs examined three children who had been in care since the previous October. The reasons for the children being in care related to poor standards of care and failure to thrive. The question of sexual abuse of the eldest child was raised in the context of a medical report requested by the guardian ad litem. It was not central to the grounds upon which care proceedings were being pursued. Dr Higgs examined the children and diagnosed signs of anal abuse in all three children and vaginal signs in the two elder girls. The examinations were initiated by the Social Services Department. Subsequently the children were re-examined by another doctor at the request of the parents' solicitors. He found no sign of abuse. Social Services re-referred the children to Dr Higgs in July, who confirmed her original diagnosis. The children were then referred for a further examination by two doctors from the Regional Reference Panel (see chapter 8). That examination confirmed that the older child had been sexually abused at an earlier stage. Their findings—in respect of the other two children—were that the minor abnormalities seen in both children fell well within the normal range of appearances for children of their age.

4.132 In his report the consultant concerned said of the young boy who had been removed from a very caring foster home "there is strong evidence that he has been considerably disturbed by the examinations that have been carried out since the beginning of June".

4.133 There was an over-reaction to a suggestion of past sexual abuse irrelevant to the current needs of those children. Everyone involved seems to have lost sight of the interests of the children altogether. Since these children were already in care, the value placed upon medical examinations and diagnosis might perhaps have been weighed with more care in relation to the best interests of the children involved. For the youngest child of the family and his foster parents, a great deal of stress and trauma was caused, as he was not returned, to what was clearly a successful placement for him, for several months.

4.134 Since the children were required to be examined in accordance with Boarding Out Regulations it was unfortunate they were not examined at the time of their placement in the foster home, the reason being that they had previously been examined in hospital. The result was that there was uncertainty as to their medical condition at the moment of placement with the foster parents, and whether or not there was any change afterwards.

4.135 The possibility of sexual abuse arising in a foster-home must properly give rise to a high level of concern in the Social Services Department. As a Public Authority charged with a statutory responsibility to protect children at risk of abuse, for abuse to occur whilst children were in care was a very serious matter. On the first occasion such a suggestion arose, the Social Services reacted by requiring an examination of all the children previously placed in the foster-home. Three further suggestions of children being abused in foster homes within a six-week period should in itself, in our view, have raised questions about the validity of the diagnosis. The fact that foster parents have been through a selection process which would have involved making careful enquiries into their background and the taking of references does not seem to have weighed with social workers in deciding how they should respond to the medical opinions expressed by the consultant paediatricians involved. As a result, children whose lives had already suffered disruption were moved again without any preparation.

Further Effects of Place of Safety Orders

4.136 As a result of restriction of or denial of access, applications for interim care orders began to be contested with conflicting medical evidence from paediatricians and police surgeons. Mr Cooke, the Clerk to the Teesside Justices, and the Chairman of the Juvenile Panel sought an urgent meeting with Mr Bishop (see chapter 10).

Problems arose with the Guardians ad Litem Panel (See chapter 10).

The Third Wave

4.137 During the eight-day period, 12th-20th June, a third wave of admissions occurred. A total of 33 children from 17 families were admitted to Middlesbrough General Hospital on a diagnosis of sexual abuse. Some referrals involved children already known to the Social Services Department.

4.138 The latest wave created a major crisis for the Social Services Department. Fostering resources in particular could no longer be matched to need, however haphazardly.

4.139 In the areas problems were becoming intractable. On the 19th June, Mr Burnand, an experienced Area Officer, wrote a memorandum to Mr Walton, setting out his growing sense of frustration. He wrote:—"I am extremely concerned about the current dispute between the Police and their surgeons and the consultant paediatricians and this intruded into two case conferences which I chaired yesterday." He described them, in one of which he said the diagnosis of another paediatrician was not accepted and the Police were not prepared to act on the information unless a police surgeon was permitted to re-examine the children. He went on:—

"This situation is becoming increasingly bitter and my colleagues and I are being subjected to further pressures which are not of our making and which, I feel, should be clarified at a much higher level."

4.140 His views were endorsed by Mr Horne giving his account of the dilemma. He said: "we were therefore faced with the alternative of accepting one diagnosis and rejecting another, or of maintaining the protection of children referred to us whilst working with the child and family to seek confirmation or otherwise of the original diagnosis. Both as a Social Services Department and within the child abuse case conference system, we choose the latter course rather than attempt, as lay people, to make a judgement on conflicting medical views".

4.141 There is no doubt that he was reflecting the feelings of field staff.

Difficulties Faced by Social Workers

4.142 The volume of work, the incidence of re-abuse, the breakdown of working relationships with the Police and the media converage left even experienced social workers feeling angry and disillusioned. The views were summmed up in evidence by an experienced social worker who said:

"I feel angry about the crisis. I feel that we had to change our attitudes because sexual abuse is a very difficult field to cope with ... we have also questioned a lot of things that have gone on. We have questioned what on earth are we doing to children. I do not think any social worker, whatever the press say, brings children into care without a lot of thought. Certainly, I do not like bringing children into care and I do not like keeping them in".

4.143 The difficulties which faced social workers on both a professional and personal level were emphasised to the Inquiry by Mr Horne. He told us of the problems in dealing with a high rate of referrals, and how as a consequence, it became necessary to deploy staff with less experience. He catalogued the pressures of working with parents who were upset and angry and with children who were frightened and upset. He underlined the impact on morale when staff were faced with undertaking complex work in a climate of hostile media and public response. He explained his anxiety at the need to deploy staff unprepared by any training or experience to face a flood of referrals and drew particular attention to the demanding nature of social work practice in the field of child sexual abuse. He described the problems which social workers must face in coming to an understanding of child sexual abuse.

"Whilst working for a considerable time with children and parents where severe physical abuse has taken place, it has been possible to accept the nature of this abuse as something which happens in families when certain strains, stresses and predisposing factors are present. It is possible in this sense, for a worker to "understand" the abusive behaviour. However, in working with sexual abuse, I believe I am not untypical of colleagues in finding great difficulty in understanding in this same way, sexually abusive behaviour. [it is]....a difficult and demanding task not only because of the problems of multi-agency working or of medical conflict but because of the nature of the activities involved. For example, the idea as in the case cited of someone inserting tea in the vagina of a child aged 7, is not only a factor to be acknowledged and take into account in a cold process of investigation or assessment—it represents a shock to the sensibilities of all who hear it".

4.144 The effect of such allegations and occurrences undermined the social workers' confidence in their own practice. In Mr Horne's words, "we felt that our previous faith in our practices and expertise in family assessment had been suddenly shaken in terms of our ability to assess indicators of possible sexual abuse. Again this contrasts to our relative confidence in assessing the dangerousness as regards physical abuse. The allegations of re-abuse of children in foster homes had a major impact. "Within a three-day period", our view of foster parents had changed from potential permanent caretakers for children in our care to suspected abusers of those children. The repercussions of such a rapid enforced re-evaluation were immense in terms of disbelief, shock and a questioning of how we had appeared to have mis-assessed the situation so badly. We felt that our whole faith in our assessment techniques was shaken and questioned, how could we tell what was or was not a potentially or actual sexually abusive situation or who was or was not an abuser.

We attempted to resolve this difficulty rapidly and professionally by maintaining an open mind regarding possible abusers and avoiding statements of the "Oh but he couldn't possibly be" nature."

4.145 The attitude of key managers and the Child Abuse Consultant suggested that the way to resolve the conflict was to 'suspend disbelief'. Often in suspending disbelief, social workers fell into the trap of suspending all critical appraisal and without their general skills in assessment being properly utilised, saw their task narrowly as securing the protection of the child. It was not a helpful approach. Ultimately children can only be protected on the basis of evidence that can be tested in Court. The need was for a broadly based assessment against which the conclusions based on the physical signs could be tested.

4.146 The practice of social workers delaying seeing parents until they had first been seen by Police created special problems in the crisis.

Disclosure Work

4.147 The breakdown in working relationships between the agencies resulted in delays in communicating the outcomes of enquiries being made about perpetrators and the problems over establishing common patterns of joint working with the Police underlined the social workers' concentration on work with the child.

4.148 Considerable emphasis was given to 'disclosure work' with children, many of whom were quite young. Sometimes this work was done jointly with police officers, at other times by social workers acting alone. Interviews often involved the use of anatomically complete dolls, the use of video equipment and on some occasions, the use of family therapy techniques. [see chapter 12]. Staff felt under pressure to seek confirmation from children of the diagnoses or if the diagnosis was accepted by the professionals to help children disclose the experiences they had encountered for therapeutic reasons. The boundaries between diagnostic/assessment work and longer term therapeutic objectives were often confused. The basis upon which any information obtained in this way could be used as evidence in court proceedings was not generally understood. Many social workers were conscious of the fact that they did not have the special experience and skill in communicating with young children needed for work of this nature.

4.149 Mr Duncan, a team leader, said:—"We had very few people who did have that sort of training or experience, and so it was the practice for social workers to try and get on and do the job themselves and fulfil the need where it was seen and sort of tutor themselves in order to do it. .... It was a rapidly opening area of sexual abuse, of which there was nobody with any experience and people to their credit felt they had to do the best they could in the situation and they got on with doing the best they could."

4.150 Without the resources, experience, skill and overwhelmed by the numbers of referrals the best efforts of many staff fell short of the skills that were required.

4.151 On one occasion, minutes of a case conference showed that Mrs Richardson had recommended 'disclosure work' with a child and suggested a social worker known to the child to assist in carrying it out. The social worker concerned was willing to take part :—"but wished it recorded that she was very unhappy at undertaking this form of work without having had any training." We heard that the social worker acquired some of the 'literature' on the subject from which to instruct herself on 'disclosure work' which in the event she was not required to carry out.

4.152 Mrs Richardson herself helped with the first foster family and over the period, paediatricians, police, social workers, a clinical psychologist and later play therapists engaged in this type of interview with the children. [see chapter 12]

Outside Help

4.153 Throughout the evolving crisis, the Social Services Department faced serious difficulties in finding sufficient staff with the necessary experience and skill in the field of child sexual abuse.

4.154 With Mrs Richardson's assistance, Mr Bishop attempted to remedy the position by securing the services of independent social work practitioners recognised as having skill and experience in the field of sexual abuse. This was done initially through the involvement of Mrs Madge Bray who undertook "disclosure work" with some of the children from the foster-home, and later through the involvement of Miss Glassbrook as the manager of the Children's Resource Centre.

4.155 Both of these social work practitioners were experienced in the field of child sexual abuse. Both were skilled and talented in direct work with children, taking great care to see problems from the child's perspective. Their techniques and skills were essentially those of play-therapists and relied heavily on the use of the imaginative relationships they offered, toys, anatomically complete dolls, drawings and fantasy play to facilitate communication with young children. We were impressed with their sensitivity, commitment and skills. We were uneasy at the extent to which conclusions were based on an interpretation of fantasy play or drawings. We recognise that such methods may have much to commend them in a therapeutic sense. We received expert evidence which indicated that it is unwise to rely upon such approaches as a basis for forming a view that a child has been sexually abused. This is considered in chapter 12.

Opening of Childrens Resource Centre

4.156 On the 22nd June Mrs Richardson introduced Miss Deborah Glassbrook to Mr Bishop and he offered her a temporary appointment to head an unit within Middlesbrough General Hospital to work with children and parents. This was established and its doors were opened to families within a week from the arrival of Miss Glassbrook. The establishment of the Childrens' Resource Centre did much to relieve the pressure on the hospital ward. Situated as it was within the hospital grounds it provided an environment in which the needs of active children who were not physically ill could be properly met and an environment in which families and social workers could meet as part of the assessment process in a more relaxed way. According to Mr Bishop and many of his staff the opening of the Children's Resource Centre on the 29th

June was one of the most important steps taken to defuse the situation and help to end the crisis. Under Miss Glassbrook's guidance and leadership it undoubtedly made an important contribution to the resolution of the crisis. The Assessors and I visited the Centre.

Social Work Practice and the Needs of the Family

4.157 From the written and oral evidence before the Inquiry, including social work records and case conference notes, it is clear that considerable time and care was spent by social workers in seeking to meet what they saw to be the needs of the child; but little time seems to have been allocated to assessing parents. In addition to this practice however, many areas of Cleveland had adopted a practice, common to other parts of the Country, where social workers deferred the contact with parents who might be regarded as potential abusers until the initial inquiries to be made by the Police had been concluded. There can be little doubt that this practice contributed to the parents' feelings of isolation and lack of information. With one or two notable exceptions to this general statement, there was a strong focus on the needs of the child in isolation from the family and this was a common pattern. Social workers concentrated their efforts on the immediate need to protect the child rather than an assessment of the family.

4.158 We would suggest that a child's needs and best interests cannot be fully considered in isolation from knowledge about, and full understanding of, all the circumstances relating to its parents. Their strength and weaknesses as individuals, their functioning as a couple, their capacity as parents, and the known risks which any facet of their behaviour or attitude may have for the child concerned or any other children in the family must be taken into account. Balanced judgments cannot be made without careful appraisal. It is a sad fact that in very few of the social work files of the families seen by us, was there evidence of social workers taking a full social history of the family so as to inform both their own views and decisions and more widely, those of the case conferences they attended. As the crisis grew, the difficulties of thoroughly completing such a task in the limited timescales and in the context of the considerable pressure that staff were working under, was understandable. However, such considerations did not apply to cases that were referred earlier in March, April and the beginning of May.

4.159 This lack of basic understanding of the unique features of each family as a family meant that parents felt alienated by what they saw as an apparent lack of willingness to understand their point of view. This emerged as a main criticism by parents. It also appears to have led to a situation where important judgments about the future were based on the child's and parents' reaction to the present rather than any analysis or understanding of their functioning as individuals and as a family unit. We would suggest that the gathering of knowledge upon which to base carefully considered judgments together with cautious use of professional authority and statutory powers are more likely to be in the best interests of vulnerable children than patterns of professional practice which alienate parents and isolate children at the centre of confict.

Steps to Resolution

4.160 In an attempt to manage the growing problems, Mr Bishop decided to do two things.

4.161 First, on the 15th June, he took urgent steps to establish arrangements for second opinions on the diagnoses of sexual abuse. He discussed the plan for second opinions with the Social Services Inspectorate who sought advice from the DHSS, and he was advised that any arrangement would primarily be the responsibility of the District Health Authority most directly involved. He immediately got in touch with Mr Donaldson, at South Tees requesting him to make arrangements as a matter of urgency. This was referred to the Northern Region Health Authority. [see chapter 8] There were great difficulties in setting up the Second Opinion Panel which were eventually overcome and the members of it began to see children and review their cases on the 26th June.

4.162 Secondly, he established a special child abuse group within the management team to monitor and co-ordinate the operational response to the increased pattern of referral of sexual abuse under the chairmanship of Mr Walton. Between 15th June and 11th August, the child abuse group met on 16 occasions under Mr Walton's chairmanship. Meetings were often held on a daily basis. Membership of the group involved the Headquarters-based Divisional Directors and the Child Care and Child Abuse Advisers, together with a Court Liaison Officer. Only one Area Officer was involved.

4.163 For the most part, the group attempted to co-ordinate the work of social workers in the field who were coping with the problems which emerged. Attempts were made to clarify the role the Second Opinion Panel and later, the Reference Group, were to play, and to give guidance to social workers on the protocol to be observed in working with these groups. Advice was given on the issue of medical examination of children by the doctors appointed by the parents' solicitors.

4.164 At the meeting of the child abuse group held on 30th June, it was agreed to establish a Central Information Bank.

There was an absence of reliable information with which to attempt some accurate analysis of what was occurring and this resulted in senior managers re-acting to events as they unfolded rather than taking effective control of the problem with which they were faced.

4.165 By the time the Social Services Department attempted to set up a reliable information base defining the nature and the scale of the referral pattern involving child sexual abuse, other factors were operating to bring the crisis under control. Decisions about individual cases were properly delegated to area officers. Whilst senior managers did their best to deploy resources and support staff with advice and guidance, firmer direction and control of both the way in which referrals were received and dealt with was needed. At the height of the crisis, managerial lines of control and communication needed to be shortened. As it was, area staff faced problems they were unable to resolve whilst staff at Headquarters sought to assist by addressing logistical issues rather than taking control.

The Media

4.166 During this time, in late June, the public and media interest was at its peak. Such intense interest from the media absorbed huge amounts of time. As the spotlight of media attention fixed on the Social Services Department, senior managers and social work staff alike found themselves under intense pressure. The degree of media attention added considerably to the difficulties which faced them in finding a solution to the problems which were besetting their services. (See chapter 9)

Problems on the Wards

4.167 There were evident difficulties in coping with the numbers of children on the wards. Mr Bishop joined with Mr Donaldson in meeting Dr Higgs and Dr Wyatt to discuss the alternatives which could be made available. They were not able to identify any immediate solutions. Tentative plans to re-open a ward in another hospital were discarded.

Parents' Concerns

4.168 Parents whose children had been diagnosed as sexually abused were increasingly expressing their distress and anger direct to media commentators in the press and on television. A group of parents began to meet to provide support for one another . On the 18th June feelings ran very high on ward 9 and the police were called to calm the atmosphere. A clergyman, the Rev Michael Wright became involved in giving support to parents; he went to see Mr Bishop three times on their behalf. Mr Bishop told him about the arrangements to provide second opinions. The Rev Michael Wright prepared a letter to the press which he showed first to Mr Bishop since he was employed by the Cleveland Social Service Department.

4.169 At his first meeting the Rev Michael Wright had not told Mr Bishop of his proposal to invite Mr Bell M.P. and Mr Devlin M.P. to a meeting when they had met on the previous Friday. When they met again on the Monday, he did not tell Mr Bishop that the meeting had taken place. Both were agreed that their meeting had largely consisted of Mr Bishop listening carefully to the points and information which the Rev Michael Wright wished to share with him. In the circumstances, it seemed an odd omission not to have mentioned the meeting with the M.P.s. It was a point the Rev Michael Wright was unable to explain.

Mr Stuart Bell MP Intervenes

4.170 Mr Stuart Bell, MP was alerted to the growing anxiety and visited Middlesbrough General Hospital on the evening of the 19th June and the following day and spoke to parents. He got in touch with Mr Bishop. Mr Bell suggested that the County Council should co-operate with his idea of taking out an injunction banning the County Council from taking place of safety orders. Mr Bishop's view was that this was an impractical step. After discussion Mr Bell agreed not to pursue it. Mr Bishop told Mr Bell of the steps he was taking to try to establish a panel of experts to provide a second opinion on the medical diagnoses. He suggested that Mr Bell should meet Dr Higgs. He felt that Mr Bell would find her very convincing. He advised Mr Bell not to take the side of the parents.

Joint Child Abuse Consultative Committee

4.171 On the 16th June a special meeting of the Joint Child Abuse Consultative Committee (JCACC) was called in response to the crisis. County Councillors, and Officers representing Social Services, Police, Education and Finance Departments attended. Mr Walton gave a report on the increase in cases of child sexual abuse and said that there had been 60 confirmed cases of child sexual abuse since the beginning of May. Mrs Richardson was also present at the meeting.

4.172 The minutes of the meeting record that:—"It was considered that the situation could largely be attributed to improved detection and diagnosis ..."

The opinion was expressed that the present higher levels of referrals were likely to continue. The pressures on all Departments and Social Services in particular, were emphasised. The fact the referrals of children were based on a diagnostic sign that was controversial or the subject of dispute was not referred to by Mr Walton, nor by Mrs Richardson nor by Superintendent Saunders. Members were told that there was good co-ordination between the Departments of the County Council and outside agencies. Superintendent Saunders, speaking for the Chief Constable emphasised that the Police did respond to serious allegations of serious criminal offences in respect of child abuse.

4.173 Insofar as the elected Members were not told of the medical controversy nor of the difficulties being experienced by the Police and social workers at operational level nor of the directives issued both by Police and Social Services Department, the picture presented to them was incomplete and somewhat misleading. Since the meeting appeared to have been called for the specific purpose of ensuring that members of the committee were informed of developments the presentation of so partial a picture was inadequate. It is difficult to assess whether the reports presented showed an inability or an unwillingness on the part of the officers present to express the reality of the difficulties facing their services in responding to the crisis. In view of the reluctance of officers to air their differences before Members, there would seem little point in having a consultative committee which not only lacked executive authority but also was provided with such a limited view of events. Some elected Members of this newly formed committee were unfamiliar with the information presented to them and expressed the wish for more information to give them a better understanding of the problems of child abuse.

State of Crisis

4.174 On the same morning as the members of the JCACC met, Mr Bishop was reporting to the Chief Executive that a state of crisis existed in the Social Services Department, that all the foster homes were entirely full and that appropriate childrens' homes were almost full.

4.175 The Chief Executive responded promptly. The next day he called a meeting of senior officers from Social Services, Police and Education. The Chairman of the Social Services Committee and the Leader of the Council were present. The differences between the police surgeon and the paediatricians were discussed at this meeting and the reservations of the Police about the basis of the disputed diagnosis were made plain by the Assistant Chief Constable, Mr Smith.

4.176 According to Mr Bishop the question of police surgeons being denied access to examine children diagnosed by Dr Higgs were not raised at this meeting. The meeting concluded with general support for Mr Bishop's assertion that when children were diagnosed as sexually abused, the Social Services Department had no alternative other than to consider a place of safety order until further proper investigation could take place. He was authorised to spend what money was necessary in order to prepare a contingency plan to cope with the continuing crisis.

Increasing Pressures

4.177 The pressures on Social Services at this time were immense. There was the involvement of Mr Bell, MP; the Rev Michael Wright was co-ordinating the parents' group; there was constant pressure for information from the media. Some parents sought interviews with Mr Bishop and were seen by him. Solicitors for other parents were making representations. Meetings were held and agreements reached over procedures to initiate wardship proceedings. Contact was made with other agencies and departments to try to find experienced staff to work at the Resource Centre. Mr Bishop met Miss Marjorie Mowlem, MP for Redcar. It was difficult to retain a clear sense of purpose or initiative in such circumstances. The arrangements for a second opinion were extended by the Regional Health Authority to provide a second opinion on any child diagnosed as sexually abused in the South Tees area. There was little time for considered analysis of problems while the crisis continued to escalate.

Report to Social Services Committee

4.178 The meeting of the Social Services Committee held on the 24th June reflected the growing pattern of confusion. The report promised to the Committee by the Director at the meeting of the 13th May was submitted. It had been prepared some 10 to 15 days previously for circulation with the agenda papers. The report was based on facts collated up to the 24th May. It further illustrated the position by highlighting the fact that in the first 8 days of June there had been 26 inquiries of the Child Abuse Register. The report drew attention to the following issues:

— that the level of referrals was such that it was no longer possible to ensure that only staff who were qualified and experienced dealt with child abuse cases;

— acute problems were being experienced in finding suitable homes for sexually abused children, as a result, some children were staying in hospital longer than they otherwise would;

— suitable premises and equipment were needed to allow recorded interviews with children to be made;

— there were not enough staff in field, residential or day care settings were trained in child abuse;

— children and their families would need long term help.

The report recommended that proposals for strengthening the child care resources of the Department previously planned to be implemented on a phased basis over two years should be brought forward and implemented with immediate effect. This recommendation, and a recommendation that further discussions with a view to establishing a child abuse unit in each area be pursued, were approved.

4.179 The cost in a full year of these proposals led to Mr Bell, MP. to allege that the Director of Social Services and Senior Managers were intent on using the crisis as an exercise in "empire building".

4.180 The report stated that the increase in referrals of child sexual abuse were:

"largely attributable to improved detection and diagnosis" and expressed the view that the level of referrals was likely to remain high.

4.181 Prior to the meeting on the 24th June Mr Bishop met the Chief Executive and the Chairman of the Social Services Committee. The purpose of their meeting was to bring themselves up to date and to discuss the matters to be put before the meeting that afternoon. They agreed that Mr Bishop would speak to media representatives in view of the unusually intense media interest. Mr Bishop left for a lunch time meeting with the Regional Health Authority in Newcastle and returned in time for the afternoon meeting. He had perhaps understandably little recollection of the details of the meeting save that there was an intense discussion. He could not remember whether the division of medical opinion was pointed out to the committee and agreed that if it had not been discussed, with the advantage of hindsight, that was unfortunate. His mind was undoubtedly on the establishment of the independent panel, his intention to allow children on interim care orders to be examined by doctors chosen by their parents, and the work to be done at the Resource Centre. If, as seems probable, the divergence of medical opinion was not brought to the attention of the Committee that was probably a reflection of the view that there still was uncertainty about the real nature of the dispute and that it was in any event a problem outside the competence of the Social Services Department and would be dealt with by the Second Opinion Panel.

4.182 On the same day Dr Paul and Dr Roberts examined a number of children on behalf of parents and were firmly of the view that the children they examined had not been sexually abused.

4.183 Reviewing the position with legal representatives the following day, Mr Bishop agreed that the children concerned should be made wards of court and that the conflicts of medical evidence be dealt with in the High Court.

More Dealings With Mr Bell

4.184 On the Friday evening the Director appeared on a programme on Tyne Tees Television. Mr Bell, MP was also on the programme (See chapter 9). At the end of the programme Mr Bishop and Mr Walton invited Mr Bell to visit the offices of Social Services and talk about the issues. According to Mr Walton

Mr Bell refused. They then asked Mr Bell whether he would be prepared, as a public figure, to assure parents that the Second Opinion Panel was completely neutral. Mr Walton said:—"In fact Mr Bell in a little outburst, said, 'As long as that woman (Dr Wynne) is on the panel there is no way that I would ask anyone to look at children, to be seen by the panel'........Personally I felt very, very saddened because of 25 years in service we have always been able to work with our MPs, to talk to them, to invite them into the office. We have our differences of opinion—obviously you do—but we have always been able to talk them out, and we have always worked very closely. It was the first time in my career I have ever known an MP to take that line and refuse to come in." Mr Bell never did visit the Social Services Department. His dossier of cases was never shown to them prior to its production to the Inquiry as part of the written evidence. The following week Mr Bell raised the matter in the House of Commons.

Mr Walton was asked:—"I think it is right as a matter of record, that the next you heard from or of Mr Bell was when he made those remarks in the House of Commons when he accused the Department of conspiring and colluding with the doctors? ... "Yes."

"What effect did this type of media interest or coverage have upon your ability as a Department to control or deal with the crisis.?"

"It certainly had a demoralising effect on staff, from social workers right up to ourselves. ...... I think it alienated the parents from the Department which I think was absolutely diabolical."

Social Services Inspectorate

4.185 Following Mr Bell's questions in the House the Secretary of State for Health and Social Security commissioned a fact-finding team from the Social Services Inspectorate to provide a report as a matter of urgency. That report, which was produced in 4 days, provided a helpful framework of evidence to assist in our Inquiry.

Mr Bishop

4.186 Mr Bishop has been Director of Social Services in Cleveland since 1982. He is an experienced Chief Officer of his Department.

Our comments on the way he conducted his responsibilities during the crisis need to be set in the context of a proper understanding of the full range and scale of his responsibilities.

The Social Services Department provides a wide range of personal care services to people who are elderly, or are physically handicapped, or mentally handicapped or recovering from mental illness as well as a full range of services to assist families and protect children.

Since 1983, there has been no formal post of Deputy Director, though in practice, this role was increasingly filled by Mr Walton, the Senior Assistant Director.

Decisions about individual cases involving child care matters, as is usual, were delegated to Area Officers. These Area Officers had a line of managerial accountability to Mr Bishop through two Divisional Officers and the Senior Assistant Director, Mr Walton. Both Senior Officers and Area Staff looked to the Child Care Adviser, Mr Hughes, and the Child Abuse Consultant, Mrs Richardson for specialist advice in the child care field.

Mr Bishop relied on that chain of command to deal with the day to day needs of cases being referred to the Department. Likewise, he expected to have drawn to his attention any cases of special difficulty in meeting children's needs, any cases of special difficulty likely to have implications for the good name of the authority, any significant change in the pattern of referrals requiring or indicating a need to review the way resources were deployed.

It would normally only be in exceptional circumstances that Mr Bishop would become involved in decisions about individual cases.

Mr Bishop kept himself up to date with developments in the child care field. When the report into the circumstances of the death of Jasmine Beckford was published, he read it and resolved to ensure that his Department would learn from mistakes made elsewhere which resulted in children being avoidably abused.

Mr Bishop's first involvement in the problems directly connected to the crisis occurred on 9th April when he interviewed a social worker about children whose parents were appealing against a decision to terminate access. These were the foster children referred to on page 60.

Three weeks later, this case and the allegation involving the foster-parents brought matters to his attention. His immediate response was to seek a second opinion, and this confirmed Dr Higgs' diagnosis.

After being advised by Mrs Richardson that the situation was becoming critical, there was no evidence that he made any arrangements in May to ensure a detailed day to day monitoring of the position.

By the third week of May he was aware of the increasing numbers and the growing tensions and difficulties with the Police. He approached the Chief Constable for a meeting but a further two weeks passed before they actually met. In the meantime, he was not consulted about the meeting of 28th May.

The following day on 29th May, he signed and issued the memorandum which constrained the professional practice of his social workers. The importance of issuing some guidance to staff had been urged on him by Mrs Richardson. Mr Bishop agreed that he was not au fait with the detailed knowledge of some of the issues that had led to the document being prepared. He did not discuss the content of the memorandum with anyone other than Mrs Richardson. She was not a line manager and he would have been wise to test the advice she was giving him by discussing it with his senior staff holding operational responsibilities. He viewed the memorandum as child-centred and child protective. He signed it and in evidence before us took full responsibility for it.

It was said, in his final submission to the Inquiry, the failure to notify the police of this memorandum may now appear unwise but viewed against the sense of distrust in which the police held the Social Services, it was entirely understandable. That is not a view which we can share. Both Mr Bishop and the Chief Constable, Mr Payne, must bear a responsibility for failing to recognise and seek to resolve the differences which were impeding the effectiveness of staff in their respective organisations. Mr Bishop's initiative in seeking a meeting with the Chief Constable fulfilled part of the requirement. But admirable though it was in intention, the outcome was inconclusive and ineffective. Both Chief Officers must have known that a meeting with the Crown Prosecution Service could not solve the difficulties their respective services were experiencing in working together. In agreeing to that, they were in effect agreeing to go their separate ways. Mr Bishop made no further arrangement to meet Mr Payne, and another 10 days passed before he took steps to control the situation.

It was the impetus of later publicity and a great deal of detailed work by the Assistant Chief Constable Mr Smith and Mr Walton, which allowed progress to be made in resolving the differences between the Police and Social Services. Mr Bishop could have provided a greater sense of urgency to get to the bottom of the problem, to understand whether the police were being obstructive or did in fact, have a point of view which justified some compromise or accommodation.

It was clear from the tone of evidence before the Inquiry that Mr Bishop and the Chief Constable face an uphill task in rebuilding sensible inter-agency working relationships. Whilst staff at an operational level in both services had made real efforts to work together, there was evidence of over cautious attitudes amongst some middle and senior ranking police officers and a lack of understanding of the realities which have to be faced by the police on the part of some middle and senior managers in the Social Services Department. In such a circumstance, it must fall to the responsibility of the respective Chief Officers to build bridges and trust between the two services.

At no time in the crisis was any attempt made to bring all three agencies—Health, Social Services and Police, together. Mr Bishop was well placed to initiate such a meeting; it was sad that he did not think to do so.

Later he sought co-operation from Drs Higgs and Wyatt in slowing down the rate at which children were being diagnosed. He could not secure their co-operation and the position deteriorated further.

Throughout the developing crisis in Cleveland, Mr Bishop did what he could to support his social workers. He relied heavily on Mrs Richardson throughout for professional advice. But as the problem escalated, he would have been wiser to have tested the advice she was giving him by consulting more widely, if necessary outside his own Department. The absence of any mechanism to monitor and control the position left him always in a position of having a partial picture and reacting to events rather than controlling them.

Having accepted the validity of Dr Higgs' diagnosis all his actions were directed to supporting his staff in what he saw as their primary duty to protect children. He was motivated by a concern that neither individual social workers nor the Department should be criticised for failing to act on such a serious allegation. He accepted the premise that the diagnosis required an immediate response from Social Service to control the position with a place of safety order whilst further investigation took place. He advised the Chief Executive that this was his view and believed there was no alternative way to proceed. His memorandum led to a peremptory use of authority which alienated parents and made the proper task of social workers impractical, that is to say the carrying out of a full assessment of the family.

After a third wave of admissions in June he lost faith in the medical practitioners and took urgent steps to secure both a second opinion and a validation of any further diagnoses.

Eventually the sheer weight of numbers and the loss of public confidence created a situation where he had to take control.

After the third wave, he acted purposefully to bring the matter under control by seeking the establishment of a second opinion panel. Once the crisis of June was upon the Department he had a duty to the children in care and to the staff trying to cope under extreme pressure to obtain the appropriate resources. We saw no evidence whatever of empire building or departmental aggrandisement.

The establishment of the Child Resource Centre at the Hospital was achieved within a matter of weeks and was an example of his capacity to get things done. The arrangements made with the Childrens' Society to deal with the delays in the appointment of guardians ad litems brought a prompt resolution to what had been an intractable problem.

Mrs Susan Richardson

4.187 Mrs Susan Richardson was appointed a Child Abuse Consultant in Cleveland Social Services in the Summer of 1986. Her duties were to act as custodian of the Child Abuse Register, which involved her in monitoring the procedures for registration; to provide specialist advice to managers of other Departments on matters related to the development of services to children at risk; and to act as a Case Work Consultant to Area Officers and Social Workers in providing advice on the management of complex individual cases.

Mrs Richardson had fifteen years' experience as a practising social worker. Her previous post had been that of a Team Leader in an area office. Her commitment was to social work practice. She had not previously had senior managerial responsibility. She came to her new post without any previous experience of carrying responsibility for a specific area of service on a county-wide basis.

Mrs Richardson had undertaken post-qualification training in family therapy, a specialised technique of social work practice. She had a wide background of experience in child abuse. She played an active part in the local branch of the British Association for the Study and Prevention of Child Abuse and Neglect. She was widely respected by her colleagues as a social work practitioner.

Through her experience in the field of child abuse, she had become knowledgeable about the problems of child sexual abuse. She saw sexual abuse as a unique constellation of trauma. In her view there was nothing quite like it in terms of the damage it does. She attended lectures in March, April and May of 1987 at which the work of Drs Wynne and Hobbs into the phenomenon of anal dilatation was presented.

She had firm views about child sexual abuse. She saw sexual abuse as "essentially the misuse of power by an adult against a child. So in any investigation the adult concerned is likely to continue to misuse and exploit the power and it is difficult to carry out an effective investigation unless you are proceeding from an authoritative base."

Having formed that view she was sceptical about the prospects of working with families "I feel the policy of investigating sexual abuse by family co-operation is a bit of a myth."

Where sexual abuse had been diagnosed she thought the only way to achieve effective management of a family was to take control by means of a place of safety order. Whilst she sought to distance herself by saying that such decisions were the responsibility of the Area Manager, there can be little doubt as to the advice she gave in the management of individual cases. The memorandum she prepared for the Director's signature on 29th May, following her ill-fated meeting between Dr Higgs and Dr Irvine, reflected her views on the need to take control through the provision of the place of safety order.

Mrs Richardson worked alongside Dr Higgs. From her own direct experience she believed that the things the children had said substantiated the diagnosis. She was quite firm in her belief in the validity of the diagnosis. From her discussions with people in other authorities she believed the number of cases coming to light in Cleveland was not unusual. She took the view that with Dr Higgs' skill they were bringing to light a hidden problem.

She advised social workers, the Director and Dr Higgs of the importance of taking control of the situation through the use of a place of safety order. She was concerned to ensure children were protected. She told us that the possibility of misdiagnosis had not occurred to her: when pressed to consider the possible effects she told us "I cannot deny that the damage separating from their families does to children is awful. I would not like to choose which is the worst damage. If I had to choose I would say that the damage done by sexual abuse is far greater."

She did not doubt the diagnosis and she did not regard the rate of discovery as unusual. The advice she gave to the senior management team was based on these beliefs. She said "I advised Mr Bishop and Mr Walton that I believed it was a hitherto largely undetected problem and there was bound to be a lot of disbelief surrounding it from a whole range of people."

Her approach to the problem, shown in her memorandum to the Director on 12 May, can be contrasted with the caution with which she approached her new responsibilities in July of the previous year. That caution appears to have disappeared in the face of her commitment to a new approach. In July 1986 she had made a file note of her concerns:

— that there was no coherent system of assessment and treatment and in some areas, inexperienced workers were having to carry high risk cases.

— that there was a shortage of skilled and experienced staff.

— that there was already a basic problem of overload.

— that there was a shortage of extended resources particularly medical consultants and external assessment facilities.

The appointment of Dr Higgs had gone some way to compensate the last point but the others remained.

In March 1987, she compiled a further report highlighting several difficulties in the management of child sexual abuse within the Department. She listed the problems as:

(i) Joint investigation;

(ii) Avoidance of repeat interviewing and/or examination

(iii) Obtaining sufficient evidence for legal proceedings in respect of child or perpetrator;

(iv) Lack of treatment resources for children and adults.

With her detailed knowledge of the problems the Department was facing in 1986 in dealing with even the current level of child abuse referrals, it might have been reasonable to expect her to adopt a rather more cautious approach to the prospect of a high rate of referrals of child sexual abuse. There was no evidence that in 1987 she sought to exercise a restraining influence on the processes of work.

Mrs Richardson worked hard to achieve improvements. She tried to use the mechanism of the Joint Child Abuse Committee to take other agencies, particularly the Police, with her. She was frustrated by their lack of enthusiasm and seemed unable to appreciate how wary they would inevitably be of her strongly motivated commitment. She was aware of the "theory of denial" which is said to be a barrier to the recognition of the reality of child sexual abuse. The efforts she made with Dr Higgs to win over the scepticism of the Police and the police surgeons had the opposite effect.

What people needed was to build up practical experience in a measured way, establishing trust, developing skills and joint working relationships. Mrs Richardson's commitment to the protection of children and recognition of the problems of child sexual abuse led her forward at a faster rate than the Police were prepared or able to go. In that context, she must bear a significant share of responsibility for the breakdown in relationship between the two Departments.

When pressed as to how she would regard a situation in which a child had no behavioural problems, where the parents appeared to be good parents, where there were no surrounding circumstances to suggest abuse had taken place but a diagnosis of sexual abuse was made on purely physical signs, Mrs Richardson agreed in evidence that in such a case, the Social Services Department should investigate; if having investigated, the situation was found to be as described then she would regard the outcome as inconclusive. The possibility of sexual abuse could not be ruled out but in the circumstances, it would be extremely unlikely that the Department would be in the position to take matters further. But there was little reflection of this view in the advice she gave.

Mrs Richardson was at pains to point out to us that she was primarily concerned to approach her responsibilities in a child-centred way. She was less concerned with things which she regarded as being "adult agendas". There was much in her attitude and approach which would have been commendable if she was acting as advocate for child's rights organisation. But the reality was that she occupied a position of some considerable importance and influence in a public authority. Her position was such as to require her to weigh any advice she gave not only with the interest of children but also the rights and responsibilities of parents, the proper consideration of the use of statutory authority, the good name of Cleveland Social Services Department and the wider public interest.

In the closing submission made on Mrs Richardson's behalf it was said "that some might seek to argue that what happened in Cleveland was caused in part by the conjunction forced on them by their jobs of a number of persons from different, though relating, disciplines, all holding strong views about child abuse. Even if the evidence supports this thesis, no single one of those persons can be blamed for the common thread in their backgrounds and the coincidence and necessity which brings her into contact with the others."

In the part she played in subsequent events, she did not have the managerial skills, or the foresight to control or contain the escalation of problems that eventually overwhelmed the department.

Mrs Richardson and Dr Higgs

4.188   The suggestion of conspiracy and collusion between Dr Higgs and Mrs Richardson denoting bad faith and some sort of impropriety has been raised from time to time during the evidence to the Inquiry as it was before it began. It has been alleged by Mr Bell M.P., taken up by the media and the Police, and never withdrawn.

From all the evidence before the Inquiry, oral and written statements, minutes of meetings, correspondence, there has not been a shred of evidence to support any collusion, conspiracy, bad faith or impropriety.

Before 1987 they had met once or twice. They were both members of BASPCAN in the North East. They exchanged occasional letters. Before the crisis beginning in May there was no evidence of their meeting other than professionally. They went together to the Leeds Seminar on the 12th May. Mrs Richardson described their working relationship as fruitful, but it was not close. They undoubtedly saw each other a similar approach to child care and an awareness of the problems of sexual abuse and and were sympathetic to each other's perceived goals. Mrs Richardson put Dr Higgs forward to the Department in memoranda as the paediatrician to consult but that was in response to her view of Dr Higgs.

She said:—"Our contact has been positive from the first."

When asked why she suggested Dr Higgs in a memorandum of the 27th May she said:—"Dr Higgs is one of the few people along with myself who were available to make the kind of contribution which I felt was needed to any meeting looking at the future of planning management of these cases in particular. I thought it an advantage to have Dr Higgs involved from the same perspective as myself as one who was closely involved with children."

"She shared your beliefs, she shared your goals, and together you might achieve more than you on your own?"

"Yes, that is true. I think it is very important to have input from people with a real knowledge and understanding and perspective on this problem."

"And perhaps a commitment, too?"

"Yes, and a commitment."

She also said:—"Certainly throughout the Department I think Dr Higgs was being selected by us to see children on our behalf".

Mrs Richardson shared with Dr Higgs and indeed with Mrs Marjorie Dunn a common resolve and the same convictions and all three have forceful personalities.

That however is the sum of the evidence of Mrs Richardson's contact and relationship with Dr Higgs.

Conclusions: Comments on Social Work Practice

4.189   The criticism of parents about their contacts with social workers during 1987, understandable and much of it justified. It must however be seen in the context and climate in which social work practice took place at that time.

As we have already set out earlier in this report, from about 1984 many professionals were concerned about the need to recognise the existence of child sexual abuse. The report of the ARC working party published in 1986 gave considerable emphasis to the importance of a multi-disciplinary approach in the assessment and management of referrals involving child sexual abuse. It also underlined the necessity of undertaking a full psycho-social assessment of the family before arriving at firm decisions about the future of the child.

In these earlier recommendations the question of the child's removal from home was a matter to be carefully considered in the context of each individual case and circumstance. Decisions would rest on factors such as whether the alleged offender was residing away from home, the view formed of the mother's part in the alleged offence and assessments of her ability to protect the child. Social workers were increasingly involved in the professional assessments of the needs of individual children, and as we saw from the files before the Inquiry there were numerous examples of good work being done to support many families facing multiple problems in their care of their children. Procedures for dealing with physical child abuse were also well established.

The practice of 1987 was very different from the prudent advice of the working party in 1986. The public climate had changed. The media focus on child sexual abuse in association with the NSPCC Centennial Appeal, the television launch of Childline and its assertion of the numbers of children sexually abused together with the work of the BASPCAN all contributed to this climate of increased awareness.

During the same period, proceedings associated with the deaths of Jasmine Beckford, Tyra Henry and Kimberley Carlisle led to public criticism of social workers for failing to act promptly and positively to secure the protection of children. These events had the effect in Cleveland of creating a renewed sense of determination to ensure that if serious risks to children were seen, effective steps would be taken to intervene. Social workers were becoming more aware of child sexual abuse and they had been led to believe that the scepticism of the past had resulted in significant numbers of children been left in situations of continuing abuse. They had been reminded by the Beckford report of the importance which social workers should attach to their child protection responsibilities. Social workers and their managers were anxious not to have been seen to fail the children involved by leaving them in situations of risk.

Some general and non-specific training was given which did not provide any detail of the practice to be followed when intervening in such cases.

The new techniques adopted by Dr Higgs and later Dr Wyatt resulted in authoritative statements that children had been sexually abused. The medical findings were of the most serious forms of sexual abuse, both vaginal and anal. The diagnosis was made when the children were at the hospital. Social workers were faced initially not with removing the children from their homes, but with the responsibility of deciding whether to allow them to return home in the face of such a serious allegation implying abuse within the family.

Social workers did not regard themselves as competent to question the basis of the medical diagnosis from a consultant paediatrician whom they treated with the respect due to that status. Few felt able to query the basis of the diagnostic findings on the basis of a co-equal professional relationship. When presented at case conferences with opposing medical views, they felt obliged to follow the diagnosis of the consultant paediatrician and take steps to protect the child. In many cases the social workers were not only presented with a diagnosis but also a firm request for a place of safety order from the consultants, and after the 29th May they had the instructions received from the Director of Social Services. Thereafter social workers had no real opportunity to exercise their own individual professional judgment and responsibility.

Under the guidance of senior staff, and in the absence of any specific complaint by a child or allegation by an adult and without the wider assessment, social workers treated the diagnosis of sexual abuse as a matter which in all cases and all circumstances required an immediate emergency intervention to protect the child's health and safety. The procedures and practice adopted failed to recognise that child sexual abuse has different characteristics from physical abuse. It requires cautious measured intervention which will allow the risks of a false positive finding to be balanced against those of a false negative and which will produce the evidence required by the court to secure the future welfare of the child concerned.

They adopted a procedure where there was no assessment of the individual circumstances of each case or any alternative to an application to a magistrate. The attitude of key managers and the Child Abuse Consultant suggested that the way to resolve the conflict was to 'suspend disbelief'. Often in suspending all critical appraisal and without their general skills in assessment being properly utilised, they saw their task narrowly as securing the protection of the child. It was not a helpful approach. The primary responsibility for the standard of practice in this respect of practice must lie with the Advisers, Senior Managers and the Director of Social Services whose instructions to seek an immediate place of safety order on receipt of a diagnosis of sexual abuse guided social work practice in Cleveland.

There has been no evidence before the Inquiry to lead the Assessors and myself to the view that any social worker has acted other than in good faith.

In their final submisssion to the Inquiry the Social Services Department point out:

"It is ironic that the County Council's Social Services Department should have been pilloried in the media, not for under-acting as in the Jasmine Beckford and Kimberley Carlisle cases, but for over-reacting to the diagnosis presented to them with such confidence and firmness by the Paediatricians. As Mr Justice Hollis, said at page 6 of the judgement of 30th July 1987:

"The Social Services, of course, always have a thankless task. If they are over-cautious and take children away from their families, they are pilloried for doing so. If they do not take such caution and do not take a child away from its family and something terrible happens to the child, then likewise they are pilloried; so it is a very difficult position they find themselves in."

We have taken those observations very much to heart in our observations of the Social Services Department. We accept the general findings of the report of the Social Services Inspectorate and in particular "In general, Cleveland has been trying to maintain a high standard of services to families and children in desperately difficult circumstances".

On the ground during the crisis, the social workers did their best under great pressure and in stressful conditions. Their resources of manpower, skill and experience were inadequate to deal with the height of the crisis.

The social workers of Cleveland Social Services Department will be among the first to recognise that it is the skill and experience of social workers rather than a high level of commitment to child protection procedures which are in the best interests of the children we seek to protect. The position was well summarised by Mr Roycroft, President of the Association of Directors of Social Services who told us:

"The Cleveland case, of course, begs the question of how any Department would cope logistically under a high bombardment rate. Cleveland, like many other Social Services Departments, has established well understood procedures and has a group of staff with the appropriate skills to begin to respond to the problems of child sexual abuse. But like most Departments, when faced with a flood of requests for investigation, they would of necessity have to deploy staff who were less knowledgeable and skilled and be faced with a situation where the implementation of procedures might adversely impinge on good, and in the case of most Social Workers, preferred professional practice.

As an informed outsider looking in on the crisis in Cleveland, I recognise that my colleagues, will on reflection, see things which could have been done better, perhaps not done at all, or avoided."

Educational Social Workers

4.190 The Inquiry heard from Mr Town, Chief Educational Social Worker, as to the role of the educational social work service in relation to child sexual abuse. The service is part of the County Education Department. Mr Town told us that the role of schools fell into three main areas:

— Watching out for signs of abuse and reporting those signs appropriately and without delay.

— Monitoring the progress of those children who have been registered as being abused

— Raising the awareness of children of their right to personal safety.

4.191 Prior to 1987 if a school had reason to suspect a child was at risk and the child was not known to Social Services, the Social Services Department was informed and a investigation would be carried out by the educational social worker for the school, supervised by their senior officer in the Education Department. This involved seeing the child at school, interviewing the parents, and arranging with the parents for a child to have a medical examination. If during any of these stages the child was thought to have been abused then the Social Services Department and the Police Community Relations Department were contacted. A representative from the school and the educational social worker would attend the case conference and subsequent reviews.

4.192 After January 1987 we were told that new procedures were introduced, which had the effect that the educational social worker would not investigate suspected child sexual abuse cases, but would pass on the referral to the Social Services Department. They might investigate some cases of physical abuse but only after consultation with the Social Services Department.

4.193 These changes were made as a response to the draft DHSS guidelines "Working Together". Mr Town told us that in responding to those guidelines the County Education Department had stressed that the document undervalued the work of the educational social work service and suggested that they had a larger role to play.

4.194 He emphasised the important role that the educational social worker might have in weeding out 'false positives' of child abuse. He said:

"Children often present themselves at school with bruises or a variety of marks and injuries. It would be wrong to invoke the full child protection procedures in the majority of these cases when a preliminary investigation by the school and/or the educational social worker may well establish that the injuries have been caused accidentally."

4.195 Mr Town stressed that there were good working relationships with the Social Services Department, especially at local level.

CHAPTER 5

National Society for the Prevention of Cruelty to Children

5.1 We heard evidence from Mr Michie, who is the team leader of the Cleveland and Durham Child Protection Team of the NSPCC. Mr Michie joined the NSPCC in 1980 after 30 years in social work. He has been the team leader since 1984.

5.2 Mr Michie is responsible to the Regional Social Work Manager of the Northern Region for the management of the NSPCC resources in Cleveland and Durham and the provision of the Child Protection Services.

5.3 He told us that he is responsible for five teams. His case work staff are qualified social workers.

General Involvement of NSPCC in Cleveland

5.4 Mr Michie said that the NSPCC in Cleveland were working with other agencies in the following respects:

— Investigation

— Case work and assessment

— Assisting inter-agency co-operation

— Consultation

— Education and Training

Mr Michie has been involved in every working party set up by the ARC and JCAC and was chairman of the ARC working party (see chapter on ARC/JCAC). We heard that the NSPCC were or had been involved in at least five cases which were before the Inquiry.

5.5 The NSPCC played a minor part in the events leading to the crisis and we received no comments about it. The Society at one stage sought representation at the Inquiry in order to give us the benefit of their considerable expertise in dealing with child sexual abuse. Their lack of involvement in the events likely to be considered in the Inquiry, coupled with considerations of the high costs which would be incurred, led us to ask the Society to consider if such representation would be necessary. In the event they provided a written submission on the Society's work with child sexual abuse which we were grateful to receive and have carefully considered.

5.6 In addition we received copies of reports and draft working papers from regional groups of the NSPCC which gave evidence to their expertise in the field of child sexual abuse and proved helpful to us in considering our recommendations.

CHAPTER 6

Police

Background

6.1 Police cover and services for the County of Cleveland are provided by the Cleveland Constabulary. The Force Headquarters is situated at Middlesbrough and the Chief Constable is Mr Payne. The authorised establishment of the Force includes 1474 police officers. The senior management team consists of the Chief Constable, Deputy Chief Constable, and two Assistant Chief Constables.

6.2 The Deputy Chief Constable is Mr Ord. His responsibilities include Community Relations and there is at Force Headquarters a Community Relations Branch under the command of Superintendent Saunders. The Superintendent's deputy from March 1985 until January 1987 was Chief Inspector Dale. He was replaced by Chief Inspector Taylor.

6.3 The duties of the Headquarters Community Relations Branch comprise the co-ordination of work and the provision of guidance to the Force on a number of community related matters including physical abuse of children.

6.4 One of the two Assistant Chief Constables, Mr Smith, holds the post of Assistant Chief Constable (Operations) and is thus responsible for all Police operational matters including the investigation of serious crime. A Criminal Investigation Department provides special resources, on a Force wide basis, for use in the investigation of crime. At Force Headquarters the Criminal Investigation Department is commanded by a Detective Chief Superintendent who, at the beginning of 1987 was assisted by two Detective Superintendents, one of whom, Detective Superintendent White, was responsible for advising the Chief Officers of the Force on matters related to sexual offences against children.

6.5 One of the specialist departments within the Criminal Investigation Department is the Scientific Aids Department. Police photographers work under the control of this Department headed by Detective Inspector Walls.

6.6 At the beginning of 1987 the Force consisted of four territorial Divisions—Hartlepool, Stockton, Middlesbrough and Langbaurgh, each headed by a Chief Superintendent. The boundaries of the four Divisions were the same as the boundaries of the four District Councils in the County. Each territorial Division has a Divisional Criminal Investigation Department and a Divisional Community Relations Department.

6.7 The responsibilities of the Divisional Community Relations Department embrace a wide range of duties including crime prevention, road safety, schools liaison and the monitoring and investigation of child abuse. Until the 1st July 1987, in the investigation of serious physical abuse of children, officers of the Community Relations Department were assisted by Detective officers of the Divisional C.I.D. The officer in charge of Middlesbrough Community Relations Department is Inspector Makepeace.

6.8 On the 1st of July 1987 the Force structure was changed, and the number of territorial Divisions reduced to three by the merger of Hartlepool and Stockton.

6.9 On the same day a Central Child Abuse Unit, to investigate cases of alleged child sexual abuse throughout the county, was set up at Yarm. The Unit consists of two Detective Sergeants and six Detective Constables, in equal numbers of male and female officers, under the command of Detective Inspector Wilson. According to Mr Smith its terms of reference are "to investigate all allegations of child sexual abuse and serious violent assaults on children coming to the notice of the police". The Unit investigates all reports of sexual offences throughout the Force area. Cases of physical abuse are referred in the initial stages to the Divisional Community Relations Department but serious assaults or those which also incorporate sexual abuse are referred to the Central Unit.

6.10 The Assessors and I visited the Hartlepool Police Community Relations Department and the Central Child Abuse Unit at Yarm. The Police Assessor also visited a second Divisional Community Relations Department.

The Position Before 1987

6.11 One of the principal points made in the Police evidence is that prior to the arrival of the Social Services Child Abuse Consultant in June 1986, arrangements for dealing with child sexual abuse were effective and relationships with Social Services good. Previous arrangements, which had existed for a number of years, appeared to be so for those cases of sexual abuse in which the Police had a clear and traditional role to play—sexual offences involving teenage children most frequently perpetrated by adults from outside the family. However, with increased awareness of the problem of the sexual abuse of younger children within the family the need for a more complex and sensitive type of interagency intervention and co-operation required alteration of existing arrangements. Cleveland Constabulary were slow to respond to this need and, as in time other agencies moved to meet this new challenge, there was difficulty in carrying the Police along with the new arrangements.

6.12 The Police were represented on the Area Review Committee and agreed a Procedures Manual for child physical abuse which was published in April 1984, but saw themselves as the sole agency charged with the investigation of sexual offences against children and they invariably took the lead in such investigations. After the publication of the 1984 Procedures Manual they followed the guidelines on child (physical) abuse but, in dealing with sexual offences against children, followed their own Force Orders and Home Office Circulars concerning victims of rape and serious sexual offences. Child physical abuse was handled by officers of the Community Relations Departments and some minor sexual offences were handled also by officers of these departments. However, in serious cases of physical and in sexual abuse the C.I.D was involved.

6.13 We were told, in sexual offences against children, the Social Services Department were consulted where the Police thought it appropriate. With rare exceptions if there was a case conference representatives of the Community Relations Departments, usually the Inspectors, attended. In serious cases the investigating C.I.D. Officer would also usually attend the initial case conference. By the Force procedure decisions as to proceedings in criminal cases were generally reached by the Divisional Detective Chief Inspector with any cases of difficulty being referred to the Divisional Chief Superintendent. On occasion recommendations of case conferences as to the desirability of proceeding to prosecution, where the case conference felt it was not in the interests of the child, were accepted by the Police.

6.14 During meetings of the Area Review Committee in 1986 and after consideration of the DHSS Circular "Child Abuse—Working Together" the Force representatives on the ARC reconsidered their role in investigations and came to accept the principle of a joint approach with social workers. Although new guidelines had not been published, at an operational level by mid to late 1986, the Police believed that a joint approach was being implemented and believed both agencies to be working well albeit against a background of a comparatively small number of cases. This view was endorsed by some social workers (see Chapter 4). At ground level the Police tell us that relationships with social workers were generally good and we can confirm for example that when we visited Hartlepool we were particularly impressed by the obviously cordial arrangements between the Hartlepool Community Police and the local social workers. From the evidence presented to the Inquiry we have no reason to doubt that similar good relations existed elsewhere throughout the County.

6.15 The working relationships with social workers was described in evidence by Mr Makepeace, who said that he found the Area Officers with whom he worked to be:

"extremely competent expert people, extremely professional people who were only too anxious to ensure that the problem of child abuse was properly investigated, and that the best interests of the children involved were taken care of."

He described their relationships as amicable:

"It even went so far that we exchanged home telephone numbers and sometimes ex directory, so if there was a problem from either discipline, we could resolve that very, very quickly before it in any way, shape or form affected adversely the interests of the children."

6.16 Inter-agency co-operation had existed on the ground for a number of years. We heard evidence that some professionals involved had known each other for twenty years or so. Trusted and easy working relationships had been established. New faces with new ideas would inevitably have difficulty initiating change.

6.17 Police at operational level appeared to be unaware of the growing concern to have specific guidelines of a multi-disciplinary nature to deal with child sexual abuse. In his evidence, although aware that discussions were going on, Mr Makepeace saw no need whatever to change the existing arrangements or to up-date the 1984 guidelines. Given the close personal relationship he enjoyed with some members of Social Services, this is understandable.

6.18 However, Mr Saunders, who regularly attended meetings of the Area Review Committee and its Working Party, did recognise the need for change. He was receptive to it, and in 1985 presented a paper at a Training Day held by Cleveland Social Services, which showed a sensitive regard to the issues and particular problems which child sexual abuse within the family presented to the police. One of his conclusions was:

"the management of sexual abuse cases needs a high level of professionalism".

6.19 In November 1986 Mr Saunders addressed the Joint Consultative Committee outlining police procedures in child abuse cases, which among other things stressed the need for joint working and recognised the need for the involvement of other agencies, with the Police acting as partners in a multi-agency response. We heard no evidence that the views of Mr Saunders were ever acknowledged by senior officers.

6.20 The evidence we have heard suggests that the officer representing the Force C.I.D on the Area Review Committee working party, Detective Superintendent Pears, and other senior officers were much more cautious in their approach to multi-disciplinary working in sexual abuse cases.

6.21 Senior police officers had two specific concerns. First they felt that investigation of sexual offences against children was a matter in which the Police had great experience whereas the Social Services did not.

6.22 The other main difference between the two agencies had to do with medical examination—whilst the Police were willing to accept the evidence of any suitably qualified medical practitioner, they wished to retain the provision for the engagement of police surgeons in cases which they considered to be appropriate. They were approaching the problem of child sexual abuse through procedures designed to deal with rape or other cases of serious sexual assault, often with older girls, where they had previously relied upon the police surgeon to collect and give forensic evidence. Social Services, who were developing strategies to approach the problem of sexual abuse of young children in the family from a different viewpoint, did not consider that such provision in these cases was necessary. Because the Police failed to explain the reasons which lay behind their requirement for the use of the police surgeon there was no meeting of minds between the two agencies.

6.23 When, in June 1986, new draft guidelines were eventually agreed by the Area Review Committee working party, they placed a clear emphasis on joint action between the agencies and they provided for the police surgeon to be consulted in every case. It was put to Mr Saunders that the document represented an uneasy compromise but in response he said:

"It was not an uneasy compromise. I still think that was a good document. It was produced by the working party and it was accepted by every member of the working party. My recollection was that we were proud to have been associated with it. I should add perhaps that document was placed before my Chief Officers for their agreement, because this suggested or meant a change in force policy as it affected the investigation of child sexual abuse. It was accepted by my chief officers."

We heard no evidence of consultation with police officers at operational level. Before these guidelines could be accepted, the Area Review Committee was replaced by the Joint Child Abuse Committee and a new working party formed.

6.24 The Police accept in their closing submission that they were slow to change their approach to these problems and reluctant to agree the new emphasis on inter-agency participation in the investigation of child sexual abuse. With the exception of Mr Saunders, we heard little evidence that the Force had recognised or considered in depth the complexities of child sexual abuse, especially the sexual abuse of a child of such tender years as to be unable to give evidence in a criminal court. We were given little confidence that the Force had been willing or committed to dealing with the problem of child sexual abuse, even before the arrival of the Social Services Child Abuse Consultant in 1986.

6.25. Although there was no evidence before 1987 of any specific case being affected thereby, senior police officers appeared to be unaware of the Home Office Circular No 179/1976 requiring decisions, when there was dispute or difficulty in reconciling agency views on investigation or prosecution, to be referred to Chief Officer level. There appeared to be no Force Order setting out a procedure to meet the recommendations of this Circular. It was not until after the crisis that there was any formalised inter-disciplinary consultation and no procedure was agreed for such consultation.

6.26 The failure to consider and understand the complexities of child sexual abuse led to an entrenched stand to resist changes in procedures and thus caused delays in the development of new guidelines. The Police resisted recommendations for change in the manner and place of medical examination of child victims of sexual abuse and for joint investigations by police and social workers.

6.27 There were undoubted strains in the system and difficulties in reaching agreement on procedures prior to 1987. These were not sufficiently recognised by the Police at the Inquiry.

Police Distrust of Mrs Richardson

6.28 The Police view was that the "good relations" between the Force and the Social Services Department started to deteriorate with the appointment of the Child Abuse Consultant to the Social Services Department in June 1986. Mr Makepeace maintained that working relationships remained sound but that there was a change in atmosphere following Mrs Richardson's appointment. This change he believed to be reflected in a sense of unhappiness among some Area Officers and those social workers he had contact with:

"It is difficult to describe, but can I say that there came a time when there seemed to be a cooling of relationships, not in any visible way, but a sense experienced by the investigating officers and myself in communication with social workers and Area Officers of something of a distancing between the Police and the Social Services. My attempts to identify that problem in actual fact were always related back to the appointment of Sue Richardson, and I was told by a number of people that, not so much of what was going on, but a reassurance that 'never mind, we believe you, we trust you, we'll work together through this'."

6.29 Mr Makepeace told us of one occasion in 1986 when Mrs Richardson voiced criticism of the failure of a police officer to attend a case conference. Although the Police felt the criticism to be unjustified, it was the manner of it which upset them rather than the criticism itself. He said:

"I accept criticism where it is justly and constructively put forward, but what was concerning me was the attitude of the people, the Area Officers, the social workers, who were expressing their concern about that attitude in relation to the police".

Because of his feelings and those of the Officers of his Department, he, early in 1987, brought the matter verbally to the attention of his superior officers.

Mr Ord said in evidence:

"Saunders particularly, and one or two other people on the odd occasion, expressed some concern to me about Mrs Richardson. They saw Mrs Richardson as a very strong-willed and determined woman, a woman who did not necessarily agree with what they were saying, and the fact that she was disagreeing and the fact that she had a strong personality, could be seen as something of a difficulty".

Police Distrust of the Diagnois

6.30 The Cleveland police were first involved in a diagnosis of anal and vaginal abuse by Dr Higgs in February. On 17th February the 6 year old girl referred to earlier was seen by Dr Longwill, a Police Surgeon, at a clinic in a health centre. The child had physical signs which caused her mother to think that someone might have interfered with her. Dr Longwill was uneasy and contacted Mrs Richardson who according to Dr Longwill suggested that she contact Dr Higgs. Inspector Whitfield of the Community Relations Department who had been informed of the arrangements, told Mrs Richardson that the Police required the presence of a police surgeon. When it was pointed out that Dr Longwill was a police surgeon, Inspector Whitfield arranged for Dr Irvine to 'oversee' the examination in view of Dr Longwill's 'relative inexperience' in cases of sexual abuse. In the event a joint examination was carried out with Dr Higgs on 17th February 1987, Dr Irvine making a brief appearance to show Dr Longwill how to carry out the appropriate tests. There was nothing at the time to suggest any animosity, although in a later statement to the Police Dr Irvine spoke of 'a diagnosis by committee' taking place, a rather pejorative description of a joint examination which for some reason was highlighted in the police summary of the case. Dr Longwill and Dr Higgs diagnosed sexual abuse.

6.31 The child subsequently indicated to a police officer and to a social worker that the perpetrator was her grandfather. On this basis he was arrested and although he denied any offence he was charged and subsequently bailed by the Magistrates Court on condition that he live in a bail hostel. A case conference was held on 19th February, at which Mr Whitfield expressed unhappiness at the lack of admission of an offence by the grandfather, and suggested that the further details of the child's disclosure had been prompted by leading questions by the social worker when the police officer was not present. The child returned home but then on 10th March during a check-up at the hospital Dr Higgs diagnosed further anal abuse during a period when the grandfather had no access to the child. Mr Whitfield and Dr Irvine spoke to Dr Higgs on the telephone that night, and at a case conference on 11th March which Dr Irvine attended, upon being shown some slides of the child's injuries he stated that the anal signs shown could have explanations other than abuse. He asked if he could examine the child but Dr Higgs was not prepared to agree to further physical examination of the child. The child then remained in hospital where, on 16th March, Dr Higgs diagnosed yet further recent abuse and, following this examination, the child indicated that the perpetrator was and previously had been her father.

6.32 These revelations were described by the Police as embarrassing and one Police Officer described it to a social worker as leaving "egg on their face". The Police who had arrested the grandfather, on the basis primarily of Dr Longwill's findings and the statement to a police officer and social worker of his involvement despite his denial, subsequently withdrew proceedings against him. Whether the embarrassment of the Police can be attributed to the second diagnosis is open to question. It was the result of the second examination of the little girl on the 10th March that caused the Police to start to doubt Dr Higgs' diagnosis and they turned to their senior police surgeon Dr Irvine.

6.33 During the course of the case conference on 11th March it became clear to the police representatives that Dr Higgs and Dr Irvine held very different views as to the significance and interpretation of medical signs, especially anal dilatation. The Police had confidence in Dr Irvine with whom they had worked for a number of years, and they accepted his views. When some time later, on 23rd June, Dr Higgs once again found in this same child gross anal dilation, and diagnosed further recent sexual abuse, on this occasion while the child had been in foster care, the Police were convinced that their stance had been justified. The reabuse of this child was the first time that a medical diagnosis of physical injury of sexual abuse in the absence of disclosure was the basis of action taken by Social Services Department.

6.34 On 20th March 1987 the two year old child referred to earlier was seen by Dr Higgs who diagnosed anal abuse both in him and his elder siblings. At the suggestion that his elder brother might be the perpetrator the older boy was interviewed for six hours in the presence of his father by the Police. Social Services thought the interviews inappropriate and insensitive, especially the interview of the eldest child in the presence of his father. The child also expressed some unhappiness at the manner of his interview. The Police view was that at that time there was nothing to indicate that the father might be the perpetrator and because Social Services staff were not inmmediately available they felt they had no alternative but to pursue their inquiries. This was the first occasion that the Police were being presented with evidence of anal abuse from medical findings alone. It was clear to us from all the evidence that there was a breakdown in communication between Police and Social Services on this occasion.

6.35 The criticism from social workers and parents that the interviews were inappropriate and insensitive, was not entirely justified in the light of the information available to the police at the time. With hindsight the Police would have preferred to have conducted them differently. With the exception of this case, we have heard nothing to lead us to a view other than that the Police generally interview children who are said to be victims of abuse in an entirely suitable and sensitive way. Those officers most likely to be engaged in such a delicate task might however benefit from further guidance.

6.36 At a later stage, after interviews which were being interpreted as disclosure sessions and which were recorded on video, social workers assumed that the Police would act upon the information obtained from them. In May, Mr White watched a video session involving the two elder children and was disturbed by it. The Police felt that social workers appeared not to understand the constraints upon the Police in conducting investigations and instigating criminal proceedings.

6.37 The Assessors and I watched some of the video sessions with the two elder children and we ourselves were concerned. We looked carefully at the areas which were seen by those involved as producing relevant disclosures but we were convinced that these were not likely to be acceptable in court as indicating the truth of the matter.

Increasing Distrust with the Diagnosis

6.38 During April the differences between the Police and social workers and the growing concern of the Police over the validity of the diagnoses of Dr Higgs came to the attention of senior police officers. The circumstances and the form of diagnosis by Dr Higgs were confronting the Police with a new phenomenon. They were accustomed to receiving referrals for involvement in the investigation of sexual offences by complaint from the victim either directly or through a third party or agency such as parent, social worker, health visitor, school etc. This was called, by Mr White, the traditional route. The reports now coming to them were from non-traditional routes:

(i) They originated from the examination of the child at hospital by a paediatrician;

(ii) In some cases the referral to the paediatrician appeared to be unconnected with sexual abuse;

(iii) In some cases the child was of such tender years that any complaint or disclosure by the child was unlikely to be obtained in the conventional manner. Thus the introduction of such evidence into a criminal trial presented the Police with formidable difficulties. These difficulties did not appear to the Police to be comprehended by the social workers or the doctors.

Crisis

6.39 According to the Police, the crisis arose from the diagnosis of sexual abuse by Dr Higgs and Dr Wyatt by means of reliance placed upon the test of anal dilatation. As a result of that test, significantly large numbers of children were being diagnosed as sexually abused and admitted to Middlesbrough General Hospital. The Police were therefore being required to investigate a considerable number of very serious allegations, including buggery of very young children, with grave consequences for the perpetrators if apprehended. In some cases the Police found no further evidence in support of the initial diagnosis upon which they could take action. In time, in the minds of investigating officers the lack of further evidence cast doubt on the diagnosis itself. The Police appeared to be unaware that the suspicion was raised in many cases by other agencies and referred to Drs Higgs and Wyatt for physical examination.

6.40 Although, in the eyes of social workers, a suspected perpetrator was sometimes identified there were great difficulties for the Police in pursuing investigations in the absence of further pointers. According to Mr Makepeace:

"Initially, because of the good relationships that we have had in the past, and in all honesty, we usually acted on the word of the two paediatricians from where we got the majority of these referrals. In the early stages we did, and the staff were coming back saying "This is just not right; we're not getting the vibrations. My gut reaction is all against what is going on here.""

6.41 The procedure of the paediatricians in immediately telling the parents of the diagnosis and of some social workers in immediately removing the children from the parents under a place of safety order destroyed, as the Police saw it, the impact of their initial interviews and added to the problems.

Problems in May and June

6.42 It is hardly surprising that during the pressures in May and June there occurred a number of incidents, minor in themselves and amounting mainly to failures in communication between the two agencies, which exacerbated the fraying relationships between police and social workers. Social workers were concerned that investigations should start promptly and found it difficult to understand why the Police required written statements from paediatricians before pursuing inquiries and saw this and the reluctance of Police to arrest suspects on medical evidence alone as inconsistent with previous police practice and co-operation with their service. In the regrettable absence of any consultative process and of discussions between police and social services, the different approaches and respective perceptions of both agencies were unappreciated by each other. The issues remained unresolved and substantially contributed to the breakdown of relations.

6.43 The Police took no positive and constructive steps to improve understanding by social workers and paediatricians of the difficulties facing the Police and the limitations of possible police action in the circumstances of many cases being presented to them.

6.44 The Police accepted in their submission that during the crisis there was some strain on their manpower that on occasion delayed their response and investigation and that there were failures in communication.

The Police and Dr Higgs' Statements

6.45 When Dr Higgs worked in Newcastle she was used to the Police coming and taking down her statements for her to sign. In the early stages this practice was followed in Cleveland, but as the pressure on Dr Higgs' time increased she was on occasions unable to keep appointments with police officers. The Police asked her to complete her written statement and forward it to them. However, as her availability was reduced, there were delays, sometimes considerable, before statements were received by Police. Dr Higgs appeared to expect them to act upon her verbal report. Both she and Dr Wyatt were unable or unwilling to give priority to the supply of written statements of their opinions, and failed to understand the difficulties this created for the Police.

Photographs

6.46 During March and April police photographers were asked by Dr Higgs to take photographs of child victims who had been diagnosed as sexually abused, the like of which, according to one police witness, had never been taken before.

6.47 These included photographs of the anus at the moment of dilatation. The police photographers were upset and they complained, saying that they thought the photographs were causing the children embarrassment, and that the process of photography was causing distress. They were particularly referring to intimate photographs which they thought did not illustrate any injury. Following the meeting on 28th April Mr White sent Mr Walls, Head of the Force Scientific Aids Department, to see Dr Higgs to express the view of his team.

6.48 Having seen Mr Walls in the witness box, his visit to Dr Higgs was clearly more in the nature of a confrontation than an effort to achieve greater mutual understanding. He said he would not hand over photographs to Dr Higgs:

"Because in my opinion they should never have been taken and they showed nothing of evidential value which could not be described verbally".

We have no doubt that the police photographers were upset, but they were being supported by their senior officers in circumstances which had no sound basis or support in Force instructions or policy. This approach was a part of the picture being built up in the minds of police officers as to the behaviour and reliability of Dr Higgs.

6.49 Mr White was sufficiently concerned about the photographs and the difficulties of diagnosis to visit Middlesbrough General Hospital on 5th May and call on Mr Crown, Senior Administrator to talk about these matters and then to pay a return visit on 13th May to talk to Dr Drury, the Hospital Unit Manager, about diagnosis. During the evidence before the Inquiry the Police came to accept that photographers might not be best qualified to judge the evidential value of such photographs.

6.50 On the 8th May there was a meeting at Stockton held by Mr Scott, the Divisional Commander and attended by Mr Saunders of the Force Headquarters Community Relations Department, Mr White, Mr Whitfield and Dr Irvine to discuss, as they saw them, the problems arising from Dr Higgs' diagnosis of child sexual abuse. Dr Irvine expressed, according to Mr White, violent opposition to the diagnosis of Dr Higgs and the police officers were much influenced by the strongly held view of their senior police surgeon. On the 29th May, immediately after the meeting of the 28th May, referred to below, Dr Irvine saw Mr Smith, the Assistant Chief Constable and reiterated his view that this method of diagnosis was controversial and unreliable.

Meeting on 28th May

6.51 On the afternoon of the 28th May the meeting arranged by Mrs Richardson included 3 police officers, Mr White, Mr Taylor and Mr Makepeace. The Police were already in sympathy with Dr Irvine's view of the diagnosis before the three officers attended this meeting, the outcome of which was simply to reinforce the preconceptions of those in disagreement (see chapter 3).

6.52 Following the meeting Mr Makepeace submitted a report which included comments upon the disputed medical diagnosis. He wrote:—

"It soon became very clear that Dr Higgs is one of only three or so doctors in the country whose clinical practice and interpretation is at variance with the vast majority of medical opinion. Dr Irvine was of the view that she was frequently in error which often resulted in care proceedings against innocent families which effectively tore them apart.

What was worrying was the obvious lack of objectivity on the part of Mrs Richardson. She openly supported Dr Higgs 100% and even attempted to correct Dr Irvine, rather foolishly,on matters which really involved expert medical opinion. Dr Higgs gave me the distinct impression of being besotted with her own convictions, citing similar problems of recognition by an American doctor, who tried to gain credence of his evidence of child physical abuse. There was a definite sense of the evangelical present in Dr Higgs' attitude and without doubt Mrs Richardson is a convert and ardent follower."

6.53 Mr White was very disturbed by the meeting. His attempts to calm it had been unsuccessful. He realised that there was no possibility of co-operation between Dr Higgs and Dr Irvine. On the 29th May he sent his account of the meeting to the Assistant Chief Constable, Mr Smith. He wrote:—

"We turned to item 3 (medical examination). Our discussion of this was preceded by Mrs Richardson stating 'There are a number of amendments required here.' It then became clear that the amendments in fact would amount to the non-involvement of police surgeons in child sexual abuse cases, Dr Higgs to be used exclusively. It is fair to say that the meeting then degenerated into a slanging match between Drs Higgs and Irvine with each doubting the other's competence and qualifications. Mrs Richardson frequently interrupted to condemn Dr Irvine's views".

6.54 He set out the views of Mrs Richardson at length and his recollection was that they included the following:

"Dr Higgs' diagnosis cannot be disputed, she is an expert in the field. She is 100% behind Dr Higgs and will endeavour to refer all cases to her". He then added "I asked Mrs Richardson, in view of what she had said, what the role of the police surgeon would be in sexual abuse cases. She stated that she did not believe he had a part to play, Dr Higgs would carry out every examination and her diagnosis would be accepted."

6.55 Mr White also sent out a confidential memorandum to Divisional Commanders on the 29th May. In it he stated:—

"As you are aware the medical findings of Dr Higgs in respect of child sexual abuse are causing problems to the Police. The main area of concern appears to be her interpretation of the 'anal reflex dilatory action'. Dr Higgs is of the opinion that this is a clear and undisputed sign of sexual abuse. She is fully supported in this belief by members of the Social Services. It appears that there is a considerable body of eminent medical opinion which disagrees with Dr Higgs' diagnosis. Officers dealing with such reported cases should proceed with caution and look for substantial corroboration of her findings before taking positive action.

Dr Higgs is a well qualified paediatrician who deals with many cases where her findings are not in dispute. Our actions in such cases are well established and will continue."

6.56 The effect of the police directive of 29th May appears to have been that the Police would join in an initial joint interview with the child but in the absence of further evidence they took account of the directive of 29th May and took a cautious approach in pursuing the matter. Although it is clear that Mr White had told Dr Higgs in the presence of Mrs Richardson of his intention to treat her diagnosis 'with caution', it was regrettable that there was no formal notification to the Social Services Department of the police views nor of the issue of the important memorandum to Divisional Commanders.

6.57 From the same date without communication to the Police, Social Services adopted a policy of refusal of access to the police surgeon. The Police were faced with reports of offences which they felt they were effectively precluded from further investigating. These events caused a serious strain in relationships between Police and Social Services.

Meetings in June

6.57 The next meeting of the JCAC working party had been arranged for the 1st June. As a direct result of the meeting of the 28th May and the report received from Mr White, Mr Smith decided that the police representative on the working party, Mr Taylor should not attend that meeting. The decision was influenced by the fact that a meeting had been arranged for the 5th June between the Chief Constable and the Director of Social Services. The Police accept that with hindsight the decision not to attend the meeting on the 1st June was ill-advised and did not help the situation. The new draft guidelines sent by Mrs Richardson to Mr Taylor were construed by them as an attempt to exclude the police surgeon and the Police to a large extent from some areas of the investigation into child sexual abuse. By not attending the meeting in 1st June they had precluded themselves from objecting at the appropriate time to the revised draft presented without opposition at that meeting but thereafter complained about it in a press statement.

6.59 On the 5th June the meeting between the Chief Constable and the Director of Social Services took place in a cordial atmosphere. Mr Walton and Mr Smith attended. Surprisingly, in the light of events leading to its calling, the meeting was unstructured in that there was no agenda, no notes were taken and there were no formal proposals at its conclusion. They discussed the increase in the incidence of reported cases of child sexual abuse and the practical difficulties which had arisen. According to Mr Payne, both Mr Bishop and Mr Walton expressed confidence in Dr Higgs and said they were obliged to refer cases to her because of her position as community paediatrician at Middlesbrough General Hospital and to act upon her diagnosis. They suggested that her evidence should be sufficient for police use in criminal proceedings. Mr Smith said that Mr Bishop stressed that medical examinations were a matter for Dr Higgs and he felt that both Mr Bishop and Mr Walton saw no locus for the police surgeon in the examination of the children. The participants were in dispute over their recollections of what was said. It seems as though there may have been two meetings going on at one stage, with each Chief Officer talking to the other's senior assistant. The apparent lack of preparation by both parties for this important meeting was disquieting. The heads of the agencies were at no time fully in the picture and the meeting did not address the underlying problems.

6.60 On the 11th June Mr Smith chaired a meeting attended by Mr White, Mr Walton and Mr Morris together with representatives of the Crown Prosecution Service. The meeting examined the needs of the Police in the terms of the material and corroborative evidence necessary to launch a criminal prosecution but did little to resolve the differences between the two agencies. The Police continued to press for the involvement of the police surgeon and resisted any suggestion that a second opinion should be obtained from either Dr Wynne or Dr Hobbs at Leeds. The Social Services representatives continued to express their belief that Dr Higgs' evidence should be sufficient for police purposes.

6.61 On 16th June, Mr Saunders was among those who attended a special meeting of the Joint Child Abuse Committee. When the elected members were told by Mr Walton of good inter-agency working between Social Services and other agencies, he did not alert the meeting to the difficulties between the Police and Social Services on the disagreement over the diagnosis. However he did say he was surprised that in the course of discussion Mrs Richardson suggested that the Police were not coping and he felt that Mrs Richardson was hostile to him.

6.62 On the 17th June Mr Smith, with Mr White, attended a meeting at the Middlesbrough Town Hall. The main purpose of the meeting was to examine the logistical problems being encountered by the Social Services. Present were Mr Hanson, Leader of Cleveland County Council, Mr Stevenson, the Chief Executive, Mr Bishop, Mr Walton and other senior officers of the County Council. The Police took the opportunity to highlight the difficulties and the differences of opinion on medical examination and diagnosis. Also on the 17th June Superintendent Saunders and Chief Inspector Taylor attended a meeting of the JCAC . On the agenda was a proposed discussion on the draft Procedures Manual and it was the intention of the police to raise under this item the unacceptability to them of the new proposals for the medical examination of children. However the agenda was set aside to enable the conference to discuss the current crisis.

Public Disturbance

6.63 On the 18th June the Police were called to Middlesbrough General Hospital to deal with a disturbance by parents who were voicing their discontent and displeasure in the Paediatric Ward. The Police attended but were not required to intervene although they remained present to help to provide a calmer atmsophere (see chapter 8 on Nurses).

Publicity

6.64 There was by this time enormous press media interest and publicity. Pressure upon the Police to respond was resisted by them until the 29th June. On that day Mr Stuart Bell MP tabled a question in the House of Commons. Mr Bell referred to the Police and beforehand he spoke to Mr Ord by telephone. Mr

Ord said that he was very surprised at the information possessed by Mr Bell and was concerned about what he was going to say. He said that while he tried to dissuade Mr Bell from making some of the allegations there were also things which he felt the Police would not deny if they were said. As a result the Police decided to issue a formal press statement. This was drafted by Mr Ord and read as follows:

"Whilst we are not aware how Mr Stuart Bell came by his information, we can confirm the facts on which he based the questions he tabled in the House of Commons on the afternoon of 29th June 1987 are correct.

Firstly, we can confirm that after the statutory agencies had approved the guidelines for use in Cleveland, to their mutual satisfaction, a second edition was produced by Mrs Richardson and Dr Higgs which was substantially different to the first and unnacceptable to the police.

Secondly, we can confirm there have been occasions when the police surgeon has been denied access to children, allegedly sexually abused and access has been denied by Dr Higgs.

We have carefully avoided entering the debate so far because we see the problem as one essentially of differing medical opinion. The consequences of that difference of opinion are a matter for the Health Authority and Social Services.

Recently there have been differences of opinion between on the one hand a member of the Social Services and a doctor and on the other the Police. The differences centre on second examinations by the Police Surgeon and the proper role of the Police as investigators. We were discussing those differences before the present debate achieved national interest and we will strive to continue our discussions."

6.65 The Police were under intense pressure from the media. Their press release however did nothing to dampen the disagreement between the agencies. There were two major inaccuracies in the press release drafted by Mr Ord which were unfortunate.

(i) Guidelines

There were no approved guidelines. The working party's draft guidelines had not been agreed or approved by the JCAC.

(ii) Dr Higgs' Involvement

Although Dr Higgs was Vice-Chairman of the JCAC she was not a member of the JCAC working party nor had she attended any of its meetings and nor is there evidence to suggest that she had taken part in the drafting of the disputed medical procedures.

6.66 On the 30th June Mr Ord and Mr Smith attended a meeting with the Leader and senior officers of the County Council prior to the County Council holding their own press conference. By this time the Police had gone public and the differences were communicated to the Press. The refusal of the Police to share a platform with Social Services at short notice to meet the Press was understandable and their attendance would have been likely to have emphasised the differences. The Police were firmly of the view that the draft guidelines, agreed to in their absence from the working party meeting on the 1st June had been implemented by Social Services. They were unaware at that time of Mr Bishop's memorandum of the 29th May. [see chapter 4]

6.67 The JCAC met on the 1st July and was attended by the Assistant Chief Constable Mr Smith, Mr White and Mr Saunders. The meeting was chaired by Mr Walton. The meeting agreed that a further small working party including Mr Smith should revise the draft guidelines. Mr Smith played a major role in the agreement reached after consultations on a new set of guidelines. The new proposals accepted at the JCAC at the beginning of August were immediately implemented by the Police.

6.68 At the meeting of the 1st July there was certainly some sense of urgency to resolve the differences. The Procedures agreed at that time do not appear yet to have been tested under strain.

Yarm

6.69 The setting up of the Child Abuse Unit at Yarm had been contemplated by the Police for some time. Its establishment on 1 July was timely. The Inquiry was supplied with statistics of the work carried out by the Yarm unit from the date of its inception to 31st December 1987, by which time it had investigated a total of 148 cases, involving 183 children, including 7 transferred to the Unit on the 1st July. 57 cases were recorded as "In Family Abuse" of which 22 according to police records justified further investigation.

6.70 We were concerned that the unit may have been set up without sufficient consideration as to the scope of its duties and its contacts both with the various Community Relations Departments and with Social Services. We heard no evidence of discussions with Social Services or other outside agencies. There was an obvious lack of consistency between various police officers in their evidence as to the work undertaken by the unit. Despite this, those running the unit have evolved what appears to be a workable arrangement. We were generally impressed by the aptitude and dedication of individual officers in the Unit and in the Community Relations Departments, but we found, understandably perhaps, some feeling of a sense of loss in the Community Relations Department because the officers concerned saw that some of their responsibilities had been taken away. At the time of our visit to Yarm the officers there told us that the new guidelines were strictly followed where, in accordance with the definition within those guidelines, the offence was one committed within the family or caring agency. Where offences fell outside that definition the officers used their own judgement as to the procedure to be followed and the nature of the involvement of other agencies.

6.71 There were areas in which we saw the possibility of either difficulty or reduced efficiency. The close personal relationships between social workers and police officers at working level, which is very local and which in many instances were maintained throughout the crisis of 1987, are less easily maintained when the police officers work from a distant central office. There had at that stage been little contact with the Social Services Child Resource Centre at Middlesbrough General Hospital, an omission which appeared surprising to us. Lines of communication are extended and there is separation of the operational investigating officers from sources of necessary and useful information in the shape of both the officers of the Community Relations Departments and the records they maintain. It is fair to say that Detective Inspector Wilson and his team at Yarm were conscious of the dangers and were working to establish the right relations and lines of communication with Social Services, but we think it would be appropriate for the Chief Constable, after a suitable period of time, to review the new arrangements to ensure that what is being sought is being achieved. The Chief Constable in his evidence said that he was prepared, in the light of additional experience, to modify further his Force policies and practices and this is encouraging.

6.72 In evidence, Mr Ord reflected the view of Mr White that the new unit at Yarm constituted a new Police approach to dealing with child sexual abuse. He amplified this by describing the new approach as providing a selected team of officers who would bring the most professional approach to the problem. Somewhat to our surprise he did not see it necessary to develop the working of the unit at Yarm to reflect new thinking in terms of police relationships with other agencies and he was rather cautious in considering the value of developments elsewhere. In fact the evidence we heard from the senior officers of the Cleveland Constabulary indicated but little knowledge of the work being done in other Forces. We were however told that Detective Inspector Wilson of the Yarm Unit visited Bexley on 21st October 1987 and, in his final submission, Counsel for Cleveland County Council referred to a joint visit to Bexley by the Chief Constable and the Director of Social Services on 22nd December 1987. There clearly would be benefit if the Chief Constable, when considering how further to modify his Force policies and practices took a still broader view and added to Cleveland Constabulary's own experience the knowledge gained by other Forces.

Conclusions

6.73. A major source of dispute between the Police and other agencies throughout was the diagnosis of anal abuse on the basis of the anal dilatation test, and the subsequent evidential value of this test. The Police were receiving strong encouragement for their own reservations from Dr Irvine. They were much influenced by his strong condemnation of Dr Higgs' methods. This led them to require the involvement of the police surgeon in many cases from March 1987. They later became inflexible in their insistence on the use of a police surgeon and Dr Irvine in particular. The reason most frequently put forward was that this was for a forensic medical examination, but it is widely agreed that forensic evidence is not likely to be present after about 72 hours. The senior police surgeon, Dr Irvine said :

"In general terms, 72 hours or three days is seen as a limit ......as a rough guide, three days"

Further we were told it is present in at most 10% of such cases. The Police witnesses agreed that it was unlikely to be found in most of the cases diagnosed by Dr Higgs, and certainly not by the time they invited the police surgeon to examine the children. They were in fact asking for the senior police surgeon to examine for the purpose of providing a second opinion on the diagnosis of the paediatrician, to confirm or, as must have been increasingly obvious in the light of Dr Irvine's declared views, to discount the diagnosis. This was the response by the Police to the position in which they found themselves, the implications of which they did not appear to have thought out. We do however recognise that they were in the difficulty of receiving extremely serious allegations, most of them against parents, in circumstances in which they could take no effective action.

6.74 Their attitude is stated most clearly in their final submission:

"The effective acceptance by Dr Higgs that her diagnostic technique was controversial ruled out the degree of reliability that the police were bound to seek. They were anxious to have a clearer and more reliable picture in each case as to whether or not there was evidence of anal interference. It was impossible to know whether or not in individual cases from which he was excluded the police surgeon could have found some sign of interference. But it was impossible to proceed to arrest in many cases where Drs Higgs and Wyatt indicated a diagnosis of sexual abuse with no supporting evidence. If the Police had found relevant signs the matter would have been pursued and may have resulted in admissions."

6.75 As soon as doubt was cast upon the reliability of the diagnosis of Dr Higgs it was reasonable for the Police to require a second opinion. The Police were accustomed to relying upon their senior police surgeon, Dr Irvine, to provide the expert medical opinion upon which they could rely with confidence in criminal proceedings. It was natural that they should initially turn to him in this instance. However, after the meeting of the 8th May with Chief Superintendent Scott and with the knowledge of the depth of feeling exhibited by Dr Irvine in his dispute with Dr Higgs, senior officers should have reflected upon the wisdom of relying thereafter exclusively upon his advice. There was a clear division of medical opinion, as a consequence of which the Police and Social Services were moving in different directions bound to bring them into conflict.

6.76 The Police should have taken some action to avoid this conflict. There was a clear need to advise Social Services and paediatricians as to the limitations on possible police action where there was a lack of evidence to satisfy the burden of proof in criminal proceedings. In particular there was a need to explain the additional legal requirement for evidence of corrobative for proceedings of sexual offences. Consultation in depth and at a high level was required primarily with Social Services and the Police should have taken a lead or at least indicated a willingness to become involved in such a process.

6.77 Since the diagnosis of the paediatrician was open to question it would have been reasonable for them to suggest a second opinion and either on their own or in conjunction with Social Services to seek an outside authoritative medical opinion. It was the responsibility of senior staff and the respective chief officers to try to resolve the dispute and to make sure other agencies understand the problems involved. Instead the Police concentrated their energies on managing the reaction and not in identifying and resolving the problem. Equally with Social Services there was a significant failure to identify the underlying cause. With the issue of Mr Bishop's memorandum to social services staff the two agencies had each adopted without notifying the other, a formal stance which was likely to affect the mode of operation of the other. The Police retired into their entrenched position, requiring the attendance of the senior police surgeon in the certain knowledge, if they had reflected upon the consequences, that they would be refused. In the circumstances the requirement of examination of children by Dr Irvine was an inappropriate mechanism. With the notable exception of Mr White, who by his visit to Dr Drury made an attempt to seek a solution, the Police made no effort to resolve the problem. Apart from the inconclusive meeting of the 5th June, arranged at the request of Mr Bishop, Mr Payne appears to have taken no further part in the crisis.

6.78 The Police have been rightly concerned with the evidential questions raised by the conflict in medical opinion and the effect of it upon criminal proceedings. It is an important element but not the only or paramount one for consideration. The Police failed to give sufficient weight to the responsibilities of the Social Services Department after a diagnosis of sexual abuse had been made and their statutory duty towards the child. In complying with their statutory duty and where they believed a child's welfare required it, the Social Services Department had to obtain a court order in order to have the authority to deal with the child appropriately. The civil evidential requirements both in Juvenile Court proceedings and in wardship are different from the criminal courts and the standard of proof is not as high. The social workers therefore were not only entitled to proceed in cases where the police felt unable to act but had a duty to the child to do so. This duty may not always have been fully appreciated by the Police.

6.79 The Police gave evidence (through Mr Saunders) that their concern for the welfare of the child extended beyond their anxiety to mount a successful prosecution, and this broader approach to the role of police in society was seen and reflected in our visits to Community Relations Departments. However as the crisis developed in Cleveland the Police, faced with some clear difficulties, concentrated their thoughts on the problems of prosecution and, with the support of their senior police surgeon, on the conflict over the diagnosis. In so doing they were losing sight of their wider responsibilities for the interests and welfare of the children involved.

6.80 In their final submission the Police paid a disproportionate amount of attention to the position and influence of Mrs Richardson, and placed great stress upon the 'difficulties' caused to them by a forceful personality who disagreed with the way in which the Force had been working for a number of years. It is inevitable that in working together two agencies will at times have separate points of view and see things from different positions. This was clearly happening here. It is a necessary part of working together to explain these positions and to make allowances for other views, perceptions, or ways of working as circumstances change and even the problem itself changes. This joint working was never achieved between the Police and Social Services in Cleveland, and a part of the reason may be the over-emphasis placed on Mrs Richardson's contribution which distracted the Police from wider considerations. Professional priorities and values were forgotten as the inter-agency squabble became increasingly personal. The interests of the children became completely submerged.

6.81 The Police tell us that they now accept unequivocally the principle of joint investigation of child sexual abuse together with Cleveland Social Services, and the need for inter-agency co-operation in order to meet a child's on-going needs. We are by no means convinced that the implications are either understood or accepted at all levels throughout the Force, including at the unit at Yarm; in particular that the question of prosecution may be only one of a number of matters to be faced and that the protection and welfare of the child are important elements in the overall considerations. It appears to us that it was the crisis in 1987 which forced the Police somewhat reluctantly into a multi-disciplinary stance. There is a need for the Police Force in Cleveland to try to understand the full implications of true joint working, which will make the many genuine attempts they have made to try and address the problem of child sexual abuse more effective in the future, and allow each agency to build on their strengths.

CHAPTER 7

Police Surgeons

Introduction

7.1 In the County of Cleveland there are 16 police surgeons: four divisional police surgeons in Middlesbrough, Stockton, Langbaurgh and Hartlepool, 4 deputies and 8 female police surgeons who were appointed in 1986 and 1987 in response to the need for female doctors in cases of victims of sexual offences. Since the female surgeons are all relatively inexperienced a divisional police surgeon or deputy is normally called out to advise as necessary. From the evidence it appears that police surgeons are rarely involved in cases of child physical abuse. They have traditionally played a greater role in cases of sexual offences against children. The major part of this work in Cleveland has been done by two divisional police surgeons, Dr Irvine and Dr Beeby.

Dr Irvine

Background

7.2 Dr Irvine qualified as a registered medical practitioner in 1966 and has since been in general practice. He has been a police surgeon for 13 years, attached to Stockton, and was appointed senior police surgeon in Cleveland in 1982, an honorary appointment to enable the Chief Constable to deal with one police surgeon who would represent the collective views of police surgeons in the County.

7.3 When he was appointed police surgeon he had received no formal training in the work of police surgeons. At his own expense he attended a number of courses and obtained the Diploma in Medical Jurisprudence. He has been on the Council of the Association of Police Surgeons and has lectured on the role of the police surgeon both in Cleveland and elsewhere. He considers himself to be experienced and knowledgeable on all aspects of work within the ambit of a police surgeon including sexual offences against children.

7.4 His experience in the field of child sexual abuse has been in the realm of a police surgeon examining a child on the instructions of the police for the purpose of police investigations and the taking of forensic samples. He has not had and would not expect to have any future care of a child who is not his patient.

Role of Police Surgeon

7.5 According to his evidence the duties of a police surgeon in the context of child sexual abuse are:—

"1. To attend any suitable place to examine the child

2. To take any necessary forensic samples

3. To prepare and submit a written report to the police (as quickly as possible, within a day or two)

4. To attend and give evidence at the request of the police to the courts of criminal jurisdiction

All these duties are subject to the overriding consideration that first and foremost the police surgeon shall bear in mind the welfare and general well-being of the patient."
This may involve refusing to examine a child if the child was distressed.

7.6 He said he had on occasions been called by paediatricians in the Cleveland area to give a second opinion as to the diagnosis of sexual abuse. He believed he enjoyed a good working relationship with other medical practitioners in the county as well as paediatricians. Dr Oo informed us that Dr Irvine was prompt and co-operative. Dr Irvine's evidence indicated his view that he had considerable influence over the other police surgeons in the Cleveland area. He had not considered that there was a need for guidelines for the examination of child victims of sexual abuse. In his experience he considered that there had always been agreement with other doctors involved.

Experience of Child Sexual Abuse

7.7 He saw about 161 children in just over 2 years on suspicion of sexual abuse and made 58 positive findings, 17 of which were of anal abuse. He had seen the children because there had been either a complaint from the child or suspicion from parent, school teacher or others:

"In essence therefore I was asked to carry out an examination in order to corroborate evidence of suspicion that was already present. Until this year I have never experienced a case in which a child had gone to hospital for some entirely unrelated condition and was then diagnosed as having been sexually abused."

7.8 He was concerned about the diagnosis of sexual abuse in the absence of complaint or suspicion and felt that it was a dangerous way to proceed given the current state of knowledge.

Area Review Committee Working Party

7.9 In February 1986 he was invited to attend the ARC working party. He had been invited on a previous occasion in 1985 and had consulted the Assistant Chief Constable Mr Smith who asked him not to attend. According to his evidence up to that time he had not been consulted by the police as to the medical aspects of the discussions in the ARC working party. At the meeting they discussed the roles of paediatrician and police surgeon. His feeling at the end of that meeting was that they accepted that they had a joint role to play:

"I saw the police surgeon's role as assisting in the investigation side of the abuse with the paediatrician having the interest in the ongoing care of the child."

7.10 When they discussed the venue for examination of a child victim he pointed out that the hospital was not always the best place for examination, in particular those children who had been assaulted by an outsider and might well prefer to be examined in a doctor's surgery rather than undergo the experience of going to hospital. However in cases of assault within the family:

"I felt then and I feel now that the involvement of a paediatrician is important and we would carry that out within the hospital usually." [see chapter 3]

First Meeting with Dr Higgs

7.11 The first occasion he met Dr Higgs was at the Middlesbrough General Hospital at the examination of the six year old child referred to in the previous chapter. He went to assist Dr Longwill in the forensic aspect of a police surgeon's duties. Since there were two doctors present he did not for the sake of the child attend the examination but commented that an "examination by committee" was taking place.

7.12 On the 10th March, Inspector Whitfield telephoned him and told him he was concerned about the case of this child, in the light of the diagnosis of re-abuse by Dr Higgs at a time when the alleged perpetrator of the first abuse could not have been responsible. He was asked by the Inspector to examine the child. One of the reasons for an examination by him:

"was to either be able to confirm or refute the diagnosis to them" (the police).

Dr Irvine agreed to do so but said that they would need the consent of Dr Higgs. After Inspector Whitfield approached Dr Higgs unsuccessfully for permission, according to the police and Dr Irvine, Dr Irvine then telephoned Dr Higgs. He said:

"Dr Higgs was very firm that she did not consider a further examination was necessary....... She asked me what was wrong with her diagnosis. I expressed my reservations about her diagnosis being based solely on the presence of reflex anal dilatation. She was rather abrupt and told me she had no doubt at all that reflex anal dilatation was in itself indicative of sexual abuse and she refused to allow me to examine the child."

He saw her as inflexible and immovable. Dr Irvine had obtained his information as to the basis of her diagnosis from her statement to the Police after her examination of the child on the 17th February. At the request of the Police Dr Irvine attended the case conference on the 11th March at which Dr Higgs was also present. According to Dr Irvine both he and Inspector Whitfield asked Dr Higgs if the police surgeon might examine the child, Dr Higgs refused and said it would be a further abuse of the child. She provided him with two slides taken the previous day. Dr Irvine told her that he was concerned about a diagnosis being based purely on the presence of reflex anal dilatation, and that she was reading too much into the paper by Dr Wynne and Dr Hobbs to imply that it was a specific sign of abuse:

"I attempted to caution her on continuing to make a diagnosis which in my experience was not safe, however she refused to listen to me and was dismissive of my views".

In his view her attitude was:

"Basically that reflex anal dilatation was a sign of child sexual abuse and occurred for no other reason."

This was the first case where there was a disagreement over the medical diagnosis, and was the beginning of the antipathy between them. From this moment the two doctors were on a collision course.

Dr Irvine Seeks Advice from Dr Roberts

7.13 From Dr Roberts we learnt that it was soon after this meeting in March that Dr Irvine first consulted her. She was asked about the nature of his telephone call:

"He was very concerned about the diagnoses that were being made in Cleveland and he was wanting to discuss with me, because he knew that I had a lot of experience, my views about the significance of various medical findings; really to pick my brains and to chew over the problem and to try to find out what the truth really was."

Although Dr Irvine did not refer to it at all in his evidence, from the evidence of Dr Roberts, it is obvious Dr Irvine was from March very much influenced by her perspective of the issue.

7.14 After consulting Dr Roberts it is clear that he had formed the firm view that the anal dilatation test "was a new and unreliable form of diagnosis" and he gave firm and conclusive advice to the Police on the diagnosis. In various conversations with police officers he told us:

"I expressed my concern about the diagnosis being made on the basis of this single physical sign in almost all the cases."

7.15 His emphasis upon the "diagnosis based solely on the presence of reflex anal dilatation" did not take into account other physical signs observed in many cases by Dr Higgs. His passionate conviction that in the abstract the test was invalid and dangerous led him in his evidence to some exaggeration of his own experience of the matter. Although he was justified in his view that a diagnosis of child sexual abuse should not be based upon the sign alone, he went to the other extreme of outright rejection of the test for any purpose.

7.16 During April he was hearing murmurings from the Police and he was aware of the enormous influx of children into the Middlesbrough General Hospital during May. He attended the meeting in Stockton chaired by Chief Superintendent Scott on the 8th May and expressed his view of the medical evidence. In conversation with Detective Superintendent White after that meeting he was "violently opposed" to the diagnosis, and no doubt expressed a similar view in his advice to the Assistant Chief Constable Mr Smith on the 29th May. The police acted upon his advice to treat her diagnosis with caution. [see chapter 6]

Dr Irvine Examines Dr Higgs' Patients

7.17 The first time Dr Irvine actually examined children diagnosed by Dr Higgs as sexually abused, (as far as the Inquiry has been made aware), was a family on the 27th May, the day after Dr Higgs had seen them. He examined all 3 children and found no signs of sexual abuse, vaginal or anal.

7.18 The examinations of the 3 children and his findings confirmed (if it was indeed necessary), Dr Irvine's very strongly held views about Dr Higgs' diagnostic techniques. He told us that he honestly believed that Dr Higgs, by the use of a faulty diagnostic test, was wrongly removing unabused children from their innocent parents and breaking up families and homes.

Meeting 28th May

7.19 He attended the special meeting on the following day in a determined mood. Dr Irvine told us that when the discussion turned to medical examination the view of Dr Higgs and Mrs Richardson was that there was no role for the police surgeon in the examination of child victims of sexual abuse in the future and by implication:

"as I was the one dissenting voice they would get rid of me and thereby be able to wage their war against the abuse they believed to be in existence unopposed."

7.20 He said he was "extremely frustrated" but did not lose his temper however:

"The temperature of the meeting itself increased with the passage of time."

7.21 His suggestion on the 28th May was recorded by Inspector Makepeace that Dr Higgs was:

"one of only three doctors or so in the country whose clinical practice and interpretation is at variance with the vast majority of medical opinion."

This was obviously incorrect and misled the police. He was also prepared to say that Dr Higgs was incompetent because she relied on the new and unreliable diagnosis:

"in the absence of other findings and in her failure to look for other corroborative evidence."

7.22 This meeting reinforced Dr Irvine's views about Dr Higgs, and his advice to the Police was contained within the memorandum from Superintendent White circulated throughout the Force [see chapter 6].

Opposition to Diagnosis

7.23 He was aware of the numbers of children taken from their homes and became increasingly concerned that what was happening was a grave injustice to them and their families. He considered whether there were any steps he could take to try to restrain Dr Higgs continuing to diagnose sexual abuse by this method. He felt powerless to stop it. He did not go to see either Dr Higgs or Dr Wyatt to discuss the issue with them or to find common ground. He did not go to the District Health Authority or to the Northern Regional Health Authority. As far as we are aware from the evidence he did not discuss the problem officially with the Family Practitioners' Medical Health Committee. He was not aware of nor party to the efforts of others to try to resolve the problem. We were surprised to hear from him that he was unaware at the end of June of the existence of the Second Opinion Panel or the Regional Reference group. (He was however to take part in joint examinations with the latter from July.)

Television and Media Appearances

7.24 He decided to bring the matter before a wider audience and elected to enter the public debate. He was approached by Tyne Tees Television on several occasions, and took part in a television interview on the 26th June:

"I did not come to the decision to say yes lightly. I thought about it very carefully. I had become very concerned about the grave injustices that I saw taking place in Cleveland. On the one hand I had the advice that one never makes a public criticism of a colleague, and I bore that in mind. But at the end of the day my concern and anxiety about the grave injustices bore heaviest on my conscience and I agreed at their request to make a statement."

He had spoken to Mr Smith about going on television and asked him for his opinion:

"He suggested that I should consider it with some caution."

At the television interview he was asked:
"You're categorically stating that she (ie Dr Higgs) was wrong?"

Dr Irvine replied:

"Absolutely. There was no evidence of abuse on those children."

7.25 Having got into the public debate he was both unwise and indiscreet to engage in specific comments on the diagnosis of a colleague in respect of a particular family, more especially since those children were by then wards of court. He also gave one or more press interviews and was extensively reported in the newspapers.

7.26 He did not stop to consider the impact on others of what he was saying.

"My great concern was trying to get this whole thing stopped......I was genuinely and desperately upset."

His involvement in the public debate became more and more highly charged and it undoubtedly contributed to the dispute between the Police and the social workers.

Involvement with Mr Stuart Bell MP

7.27 Mr Bell telephoned him and went to see him in his home on the 28th June and informed him that he was raising the matter in the House of Commons the following week. Mr Bell discussed the situation with him.

Regional Reference Group and Second Opinions on Behalf of Partents

7.28 As a result of the enormous difficulties experienced during the middle part of 1987 and the consequential referrals for second opinions, Dr Irvine found himself from the beginning of July engaged in a number of joint examinations for the purpose of second opinions. He saw some children at the request of parents with Dr Clarke, a police surgeon from Liverpool, and others with Dr McCowan, a paediatrician from Northallerton. He saw at least 10 children in conjunction with paediatricians from the Regional Reference Group.

Approach to Examination of Children

7.29 The police very much admired and spoke warmly of his kindly approach to children. It was the opinion of Mr Makepeace, who had known Dr Irvine for a number of years, that he was "one of the best police surgeons ever" and excellent with young children, "he had a gift". However, during the joint examinations with members on the Regional Reference Group some paediatricians expressed concern as to his abrupt and, in their view, insensitive approach to the examination of children.

His View on Anal Dilatation

7.30 Dr Irvine's committed view point and emotional need to disprove the diagnosis of anal abuse supported by the test of anal dilatation has made an objective evaluation of the evidence he gave on medical aspects difficult.

It was his stated belief:

"that abuse has not taken place in the great majority of these children."

Throughout the main part of his oral evidence he was strongly of the view that anal dilatation may appear in normal healthy children and in children who had been chronically constipated. He told us that he had seen it from time to time, (two or three times a year), in children passing through his surgery. He had not seen any cases of anal abuse in his own practice. At one time he said he had from time to time carried out the test on his patients, but when pressed indicated that before March of 1987 he did not specifically carry out the buttock separation test, but:

"on examination of the anus in children I have seen it reflexly dilate."

Asked what he would do next if he saw signs of anal dilatation accompanied by fissures he said:

"In one of my normal patients who was otherwise fit and well and healthy, I would not go any further........I would not actually do anything about it. Mere reflex dilatation on its own without any other signs and without a complaint or allegation would not necessarily make me suspect anything other than it could be normal."

7.31 A number of reports written by him as police surgeon over the period were provided to the Inquiry. There was only one case in which he found significant anal dilatation and in that case there were other signs which led him to consider abuse. There was no case in which he found significant anal dilatation and no other signs. In the other cases he referred to the absence of anal dilatation. He had found evidence of anal abuse in the absence of the sign. He pointed out that it was quite common to be unable to find abnormal findings, but that this was not inconsistent with many allegations, such as touching.

7.32 On the third day of his evidence having no doubt reflected overnight he changed his view and said:

"The one thing I would like to clarify is that, although I do not consider anal dilatation in itself to be diagnostic of anal abuse, as I have quite positively stated, I do accept that it is an indicator to look for further things. What I have disagreed with, is the term "strongly suspicious". It is a situation that has never arisen, but if I did find it I would act in the same way as I do with other children where I find signs of sexual abuse".

In those circumstances he told us he would consult with a paediatrician.

7.33 In this part of his evidence relating to the anal dilatation test he gave a very confused and confusing account of his practice and of his thinking on the subject. It is doubtful whether he did do the test before 1987 or actually saw anal dilatation. It is also doubtful whether he has been testing children in his surgery to look for this physical sign; if he had done so in the manner he first indicated to the Inquiry, it might have given rise to some concern.

7.34 His final evidence on the subject when he said that: "it is a situation which has never arisen", raises the suspicion that his experience of the phenomenon was extremely limited.

His View on Digital Examinations

7.35 Like Dr Roberts he would not generally diagnose anal abuse without performing a digital examination.:

"I consider it an essential part of the examination before a diagnosis of anal abuse having taken place is made....... I feel that I would never positively make a diagnosis without carrying out an internal examination." Although he performed a digital examination on many children during the course of the Inquiry it was not clear either from his oral or written evidence that any useful information was gained. In no child was the sphincter severely damaged so that it had no tone and could not contract or resist a dilating finger.

7.36 He pointed out, quite correctly, that if he was to give evidence in court he must perform the examination as he considered appropriate, and that if in his view, that included an anal digital examination, then he had to perform that examination.

General Comments

7.37 The issue of child sexual abuse presents difficult problems for all professionals involved in its detection and aftercare. Dr Irvine is an efficient and conscientious police surgeon who tried his best to face these difficulties and got out of his depth. He found himself placed in the position of medical adviser to the Cleveland Constabulary, and did nothing to extricate himself. His strongly held views and emotional behaviour did not help a situation which required a calm, cool and dispassionate evaluation of the problems. Unfortunately his views were strongly reinforced and to some extent formed by his early conversations with Dr Roberts, who was far from neutral on the issues concerned (see chapter 11). The firm approach of Dr Higgs was met by an emotional response of equal strength from him.

7.38 He occasionally expressed his opinions without all the available information and in ignorance of the wider issues of child sexual abuse. He did not appear to have advised the police to seek an outside and independent medical opinion. On the contrary he encouraged them in their stand. He bears a measure of responsibility for the troubled relationships between the Police and the Social Services Department, and the lack of balance in some of the media coverage.

7.39 Dr Irvine is not alone in finding the problem of child sexual abuse within the family deeply distressing nor in his concern that families should not be falsely accused. However, on the evidence presented he appears to have adopted a position where his examination was unlikely to support an allegation or complaint and he often implied that negative findings refuted it. He rejected out of hand clinical symptoms and signs that other doctors considered significant; furthermore he became emotionally and personally involved in a way that compromised his professional position.

Dr Beeby

7.40 The other police surgeon to our knowledge who examined children in the Cleveland crisis was Dr Beeby. He qualified in 1977 and has been Divisional Police Surgeon for the Langbaurgh Division since 1983. He is the other police surgeon in Cleveland with some experience of child sexual abuse cases.

7.41 He examined the three children referred to earlier in somewhat unusual circumstances, on the 24th May. He found no signs of abuse on any of the three children.

7.42 From June 1987 he carried out 12 joint examinations with paediatricians in the area. He does not appear to have been a focus of controversy during the crisis, although he clearly followed the line of his Senior Police Surgeon, but without the same degree of emotional involvement.

CHAPTER 8

Health Services in Cleveland

Introduction to the Health Services in Cleveland

Relationship between the Department of Health and Social Security (DHSS), Regional Health Authorities and District Health Authorities

8.1.1 Regional and District Health Authorities in England and Wales are corporate bodies deriving their functions from the Secretary of State for Social Services, and are the main agents through which the Secretary of State is able to discharge his statutory responsibilities as set out in the National Health Service Act 1977.

8.1.2 They also have some executive responsibilities, among them the allocation of resources to District Health Authorities, monitoring the performance of District Health Authorities, and the appointment of consultant medical staff in the Region.

8.1.3 Regional Health Authorities monitor District Health Authorities formally through an annual review involving Chairmen, General Managers and relevant officers of the respective authorities. There is also much informal monitoring through regular contact between Chairmen and Officers.

8.1.4 District Health Authorities are responsible for providing Hospital and Community Health Services to the public, with the exception of family practitioner services.

The Northern Regional Health Authority—General Background and Deployment of Clinical Resources

8.1.5 There are 16 District Health Authorities in the geographical area covered by the Northern Region of which three, South Tees, North Tees and Hartlepool are equal to the geographical areas covered by Cleveland County Council and the Cleveland Constabulary (see appendix M).

8.1.6 The Chairman of Northern Region is Professor Sir Bernard Tomlinson, the Regional Medical Officer is Dr Liam Donaldson, the Regional General Manager is Mr Douglas Hague. Dr Edwin Pugh is a specialist in Community Medicine at the Region.

8.1.7 In the three Districts mentioned in paragraph 5 are the 3 hospitals with paediatric wards with which the Inquiry has been concerned. They are Middlesbrough General Hospital in South Tees District Health Authority, North Tees General Hospital in North Tees District, and Hartlepool General Hospital in Hartlepool District. The Assessors and I visited these Hospitals.

8.1.8 At Middlesbrough General there are 4 consultant paediatricians, Dr Grant, appointed in 1966, Dr Wyatt appointed in 1983, Dr Morrell appointed in 1985 and Dr Higgs appointed in June 1986. At North Tees there are 2 consultant paediatricians, Dr Oo, appointed in 1970 and Dr Dias appointed in 1974. At Hartlepool there are 2 consultant paediatricians, Dr Nirmal, appointed in 1978 and Dr Symon, appointed in April of 1987. Prior to Dr Symon's appointment the second consultant was a Dr Welch, who has since retired.

8.1.9 There is no consultant community paediatrician as such in Cleveland, although the North Tees District Health Authority does have a Community Child Health Department headed by a senior clinical medical officer—see page 155.

8.1.10 The Region has no responsibility for and no control over general practitioners in the area—that is the responsibility of the local Family Practitioners' Committee—see page 156.

Relationship between Regional Health Authority and Consultant Medical Staff

8.1.11 Consultant medical staff working in hospitals other than teaching hospitals are contractually responsible to the Regional Health Authority. There is no teaching hospital in Cleveland, and so all the consultants there have contracts held by the Northern Region.

8.1.12 Consultant contracts do not define the work to be undertaken. This is done through a job description which is first prepared in draft by the District Health Authority and finalised by the Regional Health Authority prior to the post being advertised.

8.1.13 The job description covers the duties of the post and working relationships within the district and usually includes, where appropriate, a weekly provisional timetable of duties including locations. Posts are advertised as being within the speciality concerned (such as paediatrics) but sometimes there is mention of a special interest within the title of the post. This does not in any way preclude the consultant engaging in other special interests which he or she may develop over the years. Professor Sir Bernard Tomlinson stated in his evidence:

"How they deal with their responsibilities is very much an individual matter. The Regional and District Health Authorities look to the consultants to fulfil their contracts in terms of giving unstintingly of their time and skill to care fully for their patients, but their 'style' is inevitably and rightly individual and the details of their clinical practice do not come within the purview of Health Authorities unless difficulties arise. Titles or job description do not, and must not, restrict clinicians in the development of additional expertise or new techniques within their speciality, whether or not such extensions of practice are within their written commitments. Provided they cover their essential and defined responsibilities effectively, development of other skills and interests is to be applauded."

Involvement of the Northern Region in the Crisis

8.1.14 The region became involved as the employers of Dr Higgs and Dr Wyatt and their involvement is examined in some detail at page 114.

8.2 District Health Authorities

South Tees District Health Authority

8.2.1 South Tees District Health Authority covers an area south of the Tees, including Middlesbrough, in and around which all major hospital services are based. Paediatric services are currently based on wards 9 & 10 of Middlesbrough General Hospital in buildings which are over 90 years old. It is anticipated that they will move to new purpose built premises at the South Cleveland Hospital in the mid 1990s.

8.2.2 The Chairman of the South Tees District Health Authority is Mrs Collins. Mr Donaldson is the District General Manager. Dr Drury is the Unit General Manager of Middlesbrough General Hospital. Mr Mitchell, the Office Services Manager at Middlesbrough General Hospital acted as Unit General Manager while Dr Drury was on leave from 9 June to 22 June 1987. Mrs Chambers was the Administrative Nursing Officer for the Medical and Paediatric Unit of South Tees.

8.2.3 The South Tees District Health Authority has two full time Nursing Officers (Child Protection) who have responsibility for child abuse in the community; Mrs Roach has responsibility for Middlesbrough and Mrs Dunn for Langbaurgh. They are the Designated Officers for the county wide committee which oversees the management of child abuse procedures, established by the Area Review Committee in 1976. On the formation of the Joint Child Abuse Committee (see chapter 3) they both became members and Mrs Dunn served on the working party redrafting the Procedures Manual. They also play leading roles in the District based subgroups of the Joint Child Abuse Committee. Mrs Dunn and Mrs Roach were the first point of contact for community nurses suspecting child abuse and provide liaison between the statutory and voluntary agencies involved in services to children. They attend initial child abuse case conferences and review meetings. They provide advice to staff throughout the District.

8.2.4 Both Mrs Roach and Mrs Dunn have since 1985 been actively engaged in lectures, talks and seminars as well as training sessions for various disciplines on the subject of child abuse and child sexual abuse.

Involvement of South Tees District Health Authority in the Crisis

8.2.5 South Tees Distict Health Authority were involved in the crisis as the majority of the cases diagnosed as being sexually abused by Dr Higgs and Dr Wyatt were admitted to Middlesbrough General Hospital. Their involvement is consequently dealt with in some detail at page 120.

8.3 North Tees District Health Authority

8.3.1 North Tees District Health Authority covers an area north of the Tees, including Stockton. All hospital services are concentrated on the North Tees General Hospital in Stockton which is a modern District General Hospital. Paediatric services are provided within two wards with a total of 44 beds, with associated out-patient facilities. It is the District policy to admit children to the paediatric wards even though they may be under the care of other specialists.

8.3.2 The paediatric service is predominantly run by two consultant paediatricians, Dr Oo and Dr Dias, and Dr Higgs and Dr Grant also have one session a week respectively.

8.3.3 In addition there is a comprehensive Community Child Health Service which includes health visitors, school nurses and clinical medical officers.

8.3.4 A Principal Clinical Psychologist is employed by North Tees. Mrs Heather Bacon works with children and gives therapy to children in child abuse cases. She is the only Child Psychologist working in this field in the whole of Cleveland.

8.3.5 Two consultant Child Psychiatrists, Dr Chisholm and Dr Wignarajah, work from North Tees in the Department of Child and Family Psychiatry. This is a sub-regional unit which serves the whole county. Dr Chisholm concentrates on referrals from North Tees and Hartlepool while Dr Wignarajah concentrates on South Tees.

8.3.6 The District General Manager during the period of the crisis had moved on to another part of the country by the time we came to hear evidence. The former District Medical Officer died in April 1987. The Inquiry heard evidence from Mr Anthony Beckwith, the Service Review and Development Manager of the District.

Involvement of North Tees in the Crisis

8.3.7 The involvement of North Tees can be divided into three main areas.

8.3.8 Firstly, there were a number of cases of suspected sexual abuse referred to North Tees during the period of the crisis which were subsequently brought to the attention of this Inquiry. A number of these were cases transferred from Middlesbrough General Hospital during June.

8.3.9 Secondly, two consultant psychiatrists based at North Tees had a limited role in the crisis and had seen a few of the children involved in the Inquiry [see page 153].

8.3.10 Thirdly, Mrs Bacon, the Clinical Psychologist, became involved in some of the cases which were referred from the North Tees District. [see page 154].

North Tees involvement in cases before the Inquiry

8.3.11 The number of referrals in North Tees for cases of suspected sexual abuse were much less than in South Tees during 1987. According to a schedule produced by Dr Oo some 37 children were admitted to the hospital for cases of suspected sexual abuse from 1 January to 31 July.

8.3.12 Of those 37 children 6 were transferred from Middlesbrough General Hospital. This came about when in mid-June the then District General Manager was approached by the Unit General Manager of Middlesbrough General Hospital with a request to transfer a number of children from Middlesbrough General to North Tees. It was agreed that North Tees would take a maximum of six children.

8.3.13 Thereafter on the 13 June six children were transferred, one family of three, one family of two and a single child. Two children stayed five and six days, three stayed for 18 days and one stayed for 40 days.

8.3.14 We heard evidence from Dr Oo as to the procedures which were followed in the North Tees district for cases of child sexual abuse. He told the Inquiry that he followed the procedures laid down in the ARC 1984 guidelines, with some slight modifications for sexual abuse which was not covered in the guidelines. In such cases, Dr Oo told us, that it was his policy to undertake a joint examination of the child with the senior police surgeon (Dr Irvine), in order to avoid repeated examinations and to exchange information and knowledge. We have not heard any evidence from either Dr Oo or Dr Irvine that this arrangement was anything other than satisfactory.

8.3.15 Children seen by Dr Oo were referred by Accident & Emergency, General Practitioners, Health Visitors or School Teachers and also from the Social Services Department or the Police Community Relations Department. Referrals other than from A&E were seen in an outpatient clinic. If the case was doubtful or the abuser was known to be outside the family then the child was not necessarily admitted to hospital. Dr Oo referred all children to the Clinical Psychologist and, depending on her opinion, the Social Services Department were informed if appropriate, a case conference initiated and further management planned.

8.3.16 It was not the general policy of Dr Oo to ask that a place of safety order be taken out—in only four of Dr Oo's cases in 1987 were such orders taken. In these four cases we were told that the children in question either had a definite history of sexual abuse or there was cause for concern for their well-being which had already brought about an admission to hospital. Dr Oo commented:

"Sexual abuse is rarely life-threatening and if the abuser appears to be outside the family, I will allow the child to go home with the agreement of the Social Services Department and refer the child to the Child Psychologist. Later we would then involve the Social Services Department."

8.3.17 The Inquiry did not hear any evidence to suggest that the this system was working other than in a satisfactory manner. We did hear evidence of problems of referral from the Clinical Psychologist to the Child Psychiatrists.

8.4 Hartlepool

8.4.1 While other parts of Cleveland were suffering a crisis of referrals in 1987, in Hartlepool numbers remained steadily low. Hartlepool District Health Authority was not separately represented at the Inquiry.

8.4.2 We were told by Mr Curtis, The District General Manager of Hartlepool District Health Authority, in a letter to the Inquiry that Hartlepool is a very close knit community with a generally static population.

8.4.3 Child health care is monitored within the community by the community nursing staff, social workers, nursery and school teachers and general practitioners. The general monitoring by the various agencies ensures that individual families where problems exist, or are likely to arise, are identified so that appropriate measures may be taken in order to ensure that an individual child's development is not adversely affected.

8.4.4 He told the Inquiry that the benefit of a close knit community is that there is little anonymity on the part of anyone living in Hartlepool. Not only are the relevant agencies able to identify families where problems might arise, but the families themselves also know of the role played by the various agencies and are aware of the help and support available, and the degree of co-operation between the various agencies. The Inquiry was told that this is the view held by the medical and nursing staff of the Authority.

8.4.5 With regard to the incidence of child abuse in Hartlepool, Mr Curtis told us that he thought the level of child abuse cases detected in Hartlepool was not markedly different from that of other parts of the County. The difference lies between those child abuse cases which are separately diagnosed as ones of sexual abuse or physical abuse. He advised caution in making statistical comparisons due to the small numbers involved.

8.4.6 Dr Nirmal told us that the consultant paediatricians in Hartlepool, Dr Symon and herself, did not have special expertise in child sexual abuse, and had very few such cases referred to them. We understand that in Hartlepool cases of child sexual abuse were frequently dealt with by police surgeons. The consultants began in 1987 to attend the JCAC on an alternate basis. When in any doubt in a particular case as to whether the abuse was not purely physical, but also involved sexual abuse, they sought a second opinion from Dr Steiner in Newcastle.

8.4.7 The Assessors and I visited various agencies in Hartlepool during the Inquiry. We saw something of the informal, helpful and co-operative relationship that existed between the Police, Social Services and other agencies. We were impressed with the sensible and pragmatic way of working together without professional rivalry getting in the way of the best interests of the child in a situation where there appeared to be no undue pressure on the agencies involved

8.5 Involvement of Northern Regional Health Authority

Involvement of the Regional Health Authority in Events Leading up to the Crisis

Appointment of Dr Higgs

8.5.1 A new post in consultant paediatrics was created in 1986 to which Dr Higgs was appointed in June to take effect from the 1st January 1987. The Region considered at the time that it was a good appointment to make in 1986. In their closing submission to the Inquiry they state:

"The District and the Region were getting a neonatologist whose special interest in the general paediatric field was in the familial, social and preventative aspects of paediatrics. This was a bonus in that the South Tees population contains many communities, which are amongst the most 'deprived' in the Northern Region. In addition, Dr Higgs showed an interest in the roles of other professions and agencies (as evidenced by her early contact with the Social Services Department to ask for policy documents). Such an awareness of the importance of other disciplines in health care is not always a feature of traditional medical practice and it is something which is striven for in modern undergraduate and postgraduate training schemes. The fact that Dr Higgs had voluntarily sought and obtained a formal attachment, during training, to a Child Psychiatry Department, is further evidence of her potential."

Dr Higgs' Timetable

8.5.2 Dr Higgs' job description was agreed with the South Tees Health Authority who supplied the final draft which included a provisional timetable. The post was designated as one with special interest in neo-natalology and the timetable included four neonatal sessions a week.

8.5.3 A few weeks after Dr Higgs was in post Mr Donaldson, the General Manager of South Tees Health Authority wrote on the 16th February to Dr Donaldson of Northern Regional Health Authority in the following terms:

"It has been brought to my attention that Dr Higgs who was appointed as consultant paediatrician with a special interest in neonatalology is widening her activities considerably into the child abuse and social services areas. This may be a very desirable development and should be considered as such, but as this is a somewhat sensitive area, I think it would be desirable if you could get an agreed timetable from Dr Higgs which would be the basis for discussion."

8.5.4 This was seen to be a somewhat unusual request. Dr Pugh replied on behalf of the Northern Regional Health Authority. He first consulted Dr Higgs by telephone and asked about her interest and involvement in social paediatrics. Dr Higgs expressed her regret that the matter had not been handled within South Tees District, without recourse to Regional level. She said she was in the course of establishing a regular pattern of work in a new post and would be happy to discuss it with Mr Donaldson and that this particular aspect of her work was interspersed throughout her routine activities and could not be isolated as a separate entity. Dr Pugh was reassured that she was fulfilling her contractual commitment to neonatal paediatrics. He understood from Dr Higgs that she would contact Mr Donaldson about her timetable. Dr Pugh followed up his telephone call with a formal letter on the 9th March requesting a timetable. He wrote:

"As manager of the District he (Mr Donaldson) wishes to have a timetable of your activities with special emphasis on quantification of time dedicated to neonatal intensive care, general paediatric workload and social paediatrics e.g. child abuse etc. You will remember that your job description was for a consultant paediatrician with special interest in neonatal intensive care. I would be grateful if you could forward me a timetable of your weekly service activities."

Dr Pugh did not receive a reply nor a timetable from Dr Higgs.

8.5.5 Dr Pugh replied to Mr Donaldson on the 25th February:

"I have subsequently spoken to Dr Higgs regarding her activities in these fields. Middlesbrough as you know has considerable problems within the field of child abuse and social deprivation and children. Dr Higgs does not have any formal time tabling of her activities in these areas. Indeed problems relating to social deprivation and child abuse can occur at any time and will be interspersed throughout all her routine activities."

In the third paragraph he added:

"You obviously have reservations regarding the sensitive area of social services and child abuse. Could I ask you to expand why an agreed timetable is necessary and what the the discussion would be should such a timetable be available."

He had no reply from Mr Donaldson to that request.

8.5.6 A few weeks later Mr Donaldson telephoned Dr Pugh to indicate his desire to obtain a timetable to quantify the time spent by Dr Higgs in neonatal medicine. He had gained the impression that she was becoming increasingly involved in social paediatrics and he wished to confirm this was not at the expense of her contractual commitment to neonatal medicine. No reference was made by Mr Donaldson at that time to child sexual abuse.

8.5.7 On the 8th June Dr Pugh received another letter from Mr Donaldson reminding him of their telephone discussion some months before on the timetable and adding:

"we agreed that at some stage you would be asking Dr Higgs for a copy of her timetable so we could clarify whether in fact Dr Higgs was carrying out the duties for which she was appointed."

He asked for the timetable and said:

"Local subjective evidence at the moment would increasingly indicate an apparent interest in social medicine."

We were not told and still do not know why Mr Donaldson did not telephone Dr Higgs and speak to her himself.

8.5.8 Northern Regional Health Authority was unaware at that time of the upsurge of child sexual abuse in Cleveland and of the crisis which was developing.

8.5.9 Dr Pugh wrote to Dr Higgs to ask her to confirm whether her provisional timetable in her job description reflected her work pattern and pointed out that he had no reply to his letter to her of the 9th March. He also wrote to Mr Donaldson saying he had rather assumed that she would have been in touch with Mr Donaldson direct and that he had written to her again. He pointed out that under the provisional timetable in the job description she was scheduled to perform four sessions weekly in the neonatal unit. Mr Donaldson replied on the 3rd July:

"I presume that other events have overtaken Dr Higgs' preparation of a timetable".

8.5.10 Two matters emerged relevant to this interchange over Dr Higgs' timetable. The first was the efforts of the District and the Community Health Council to obtain a priority in neonatology for the new consultant's duties. The second was a presentation considered by others present to be somewhat intemperate by Dr Higgs and Dr Wyatt on the 21st September 1986 to the District Medical Advisory Committee, based upon a paper signed by Dr Higgs, Dr Morrell and Dr Wyatt, entitled "Skimping on the Care of the Newborn". This paper also appeared as part of a widely circulated letter to the District General Manager was entitled 'Asset stripping in the Paediatric Services'. The two doctors put forward the view at the meeting that six additional consultant paediatricians should be appointed. Although not yet in post, nor yet a consultant, Dr Higgs played a prominent part at the meeting which at one stage according to the chairman of the committee, Mr Martin, became acrimonious. Mr Martin told the Inquiry in written evidence that some senior doctors were offended.

8.5.11 Early in 1987, Mr Martin, encouraged by Dr Deirdre Devlin, a Senior Clinical Medical Officer in the Community Child Health Service, discussed with Mr Donaldson the scope of Dr Higgs' duties and what duties she was in fact carrying out. Dr Devlin apparently commented that:

"although Dr Higgs was being appointed as a consultant in paediatrics with a special interest in neo-natology, Dr Devlin had heard more about Dr Higgs' interest in child abuse"

Dr Devlin had also commented to Mr Martin after a meeting of a Committee in early January of which both she and Dr Higgs were members that:

"Dr Higgs intended having clinics in the community".

8.5.12 Mr Martin was sufficiently disturbed by these conversations with Dr Devlin that he discussed with Mr Donaldson the scope of Dr Higgs' duties and what duties she was in fact carrying out. As a consequence of this discussion Mr Donaldson wrote the letter of the 16th February.

8.5.13 There has been no evidence whatsoever before the Inquiry to show that Dr Higgs at any time neglected her duties in the neonatal field. On the contrary, evidence presented to the Inquiry suggests that Dr Higgs performed such duties efficiently and conscientiously and there was never any criticism of them. Dr Higgs said that she had not drawn up her timetable at the time she was asked about it by Dr Pugh; she told him she was in the course of establishing a regular pattern of work in a new post and said she would be happy to discuss it with Mr Donaldson. She did not reply to Dr Pugh's letter because she felt she had done so in the telephone conversation. Mr Donaldson did not get in touch with her and she did not consider the matter further until she received the letter from Dr Pugh in June which was during the crisis and she had no time to reply.

8.5.14 Dr Higgs throughout the entire period appears to have had the support of Dr Grant and Dr Morrell, the other two consultant paediatricians in the District. According to Professor Sir Bernard Tomlinson, Dr Morrell praised the general paediatric work of Dr Higgs and Dr Wyatt and said that he had learnt a great deal about child abuse and child sexual abuse particularily from Dr Higgs. He referred patients to her and placed great reliance on her judgement. He knew that both she and Dr Wyatt were working very long hours but their general work was getting conscientiously done. Dr Grant told Sir Bernard she had no doubt about the capabilities of Dr Higgs and Dr Wyatt.

The Complaints

8.5.15 The events in Cleveland first came to the attention of the Region on the 16th June, with a telephone call from Mr Donaldson, saying that he had received complaints about Dr Higgs and Dr Wyatt. The complaints alleged that they examined children on the wards late at night without parental permission and that they had examined children for sexual abuse who had been admitted for other conditions. Dr Donaldson indicated that the complaints had to be taken seriously and they agreed to meet and discuss them next morning. Dr Donaldson sought advice on parental consent from a senior consultant paediatrician in the area.

Second Opinion Panel

8.5.16 On the 17th June Mr Donaldson described the complaints and the increase in the number of cases of sexually abused children together with the practical difficulties on the Ward. He sought advice on the question of consent. Mr Donaldson also sought help to deal with the request from the Director of Social Services for a second medical opinion on some of the children believed to have been sexually abused. The idea of the Second Opinion Panel was conceived and an approach was made to Professor Kolvin at Newcastle. It was decided to use people from both within and outside the Region, and at an early stage it was thought that a member of the Leeds paediatric group should be included as they were known to have particular expertise within that field. Dr Donaldson did recognise that the inclusion of Dr Wynne might cause some difficulty as she had given second opinions on some of Dr Higgs' cases and had in some instances aroused parents' anger [see chapter 11]. It was decided nevertheless that it was important to have a balanced panel of experts and it was felt that the Leeds paediatricians had been in the forefront of published work in the phenomenon of child sexual abuse. It was decided that no one who had already seen a child would again be asked to pass an opinion on that child. In setting up the Independent Panel the Region was concerned to help to resolve the position of existing children and their families. The establishment of such a panel was, according to the Region, without precedent.

Involvement of Mr Hague

8.5.17 The Regional General Manager, Mr Hague was also involved in the discussions and decided all the complaints should be dealt with at regional level.

Involvement of Professor Sir Bernard Tomlinson

8.5.18 On his return to Newcastle on the 21st June, the Chairman of the Health Authority, Professor Sir Bernard Tomlinson, became closely involved in the crisis and together with Dr Donaldson and Mr Hague kept in close touch with the events in Cleveland both by telephone and by a number of visits to Middlesbrough. They pursued a "strongly interventionist and high profile policy" which they saw as going far beyond the region's normal strategic role. They believed it was essential and that it had been fully justified by the subsequent march of events.

In Touch with DHSS

8.5.19 The Regional Officers were in touch with the Medical Officers of the Department of Health and Social Security and spent considerable time dealing with the composition and setting up of the Second Opinion Panel. [see page 118]

Evaluation of Clinical Practice of Dr Higgs and Dr Wyatt

8.5.20 The Regional Officers were immediately anxious to investigate whether the clinical practice of the two paediatricians was within the bounds of acceptable medical practice. They asked Drs Higgs and Wyatt to Regional Headquarters on the 23rd June. The meeting was held in the evening and took 4 hours. The two doctors set out at length their methods, views, and the validity of the diagnoses they were making. They did not respond to individual allegations asking for time to consider them and to seek legal advice.

They gave a general assurance that it was not their normal practice to examine children without parental permission. The first batch of complaints were given to the two doctors and they were asked for their written comments as soon as possible.

8.5.21 The Regional Officers investigated the consultants' training and experience in child sexual abuse. They challenged forcefully, at times fiercely, the two consultants to explain the points that were put to them. Both Professor Sir Bernard Tomlinson and Dr Donaldson agreed that both Dr Higgs and Dr Wyatt had answered questions and argued consistently and logically. They could not conclude on the basis of the evidence before them alone that there was a prima facie case for suspending the consultants pending serious disciplinary action on grounds of professional incompetence or professional misconduct. They concluded:

"Both paediatricians were held in regard in paediatric circles. They were fully convinced of their methodology and the correctness of their diagnoses and were aware of the effect on families but were dedicated to and convinced of their duty to protect the child above all else."

The complaints clearly had to be answered but in their view there was no evidence of clinical incompetence.

8.5.22 The two doctors were told that it was the intention to set up a Second Opinion Panel. They were reluctant to agree to it but the Regional Officers were firm and said they would be proceeding with it.

8.5.23 A later meeting of the Regional Health Authority concluded that:

"The decision that there was no case on the basis of the present evidence, for suspending the two consultants because of suspected professional incompetence or professional misconduct was correct."

Maintaining Public Confidence

8.5.24 On 25th June Dr Donaldson telephoned Dr Wyatt to tell him that he was writing to him and Dr Higgs informing them "you are required not to undertake any examinations to look for signs of sexual abuse in children without parental knowledge and permission except in circumstances where a court order removes the necessity for such permission."

Dr Wyatt raised objections but was persuaded by Dr Donaldson that this was an exceptional situation, and he agreed, saying that he would inform Dr Higgs.

Meeting with Doctors and their Legal Advisers

8.5.25 Members of the Regional Health Authority met with the two doctors and their legal advisers on Friday 26 June to consider the approach to handling the complaints. Before the two doctors arrived the Regional Health Authority members discussed the importance of maintaining public confidence in the service, and it was felt that a mechanism had to be established to enable the service to continue so that new cases coming in were handled in such a way that diagnoses were not challenged and children did not become the subject of legal wrangling and controversy. When the two doctors arrived they agreed to answer the complaints as urgently as possible. The Regional Health Authority were told that Cleveland County Council had instituted wardship proceedings in respect of some of the children involved. The County Council were to meet their legal advisers and Dr Higgs and Dr Wyatt were invited to attend. The Regional Health Authority thought that it might be helpful if Mr Hague and Dr Donaldson were also to take part. In the event although Mr Hague and Dr Donaldson travelled to York to take part in the meeting they did not have an opportunity to do so.

8.5.26 At a meeting on Sunday 28th June, Professor Aynsley-Green, Dr Donaldson, Professor Sir Bernard Tomlinson, Professor Kolvin and Dr Hans Steiner, considered the problem of restoring public confidence in the Independent Panel, the integrity of which had been challenged by Members of Parliament and others because of the participation of Dr Wynne. They thought that the Panel was still the best way of resolving the situation of "existing" parents and their families. It was agreed that Dr Donaldson, Professor Sir Bernard Tomlinson and Professor Kolvin would speak to the Press and would produce a detailed statement of the method of working of the Panel to be provided to the Courts hearing the wardship cases.

Agreement to Set up Regional Reference Group

8.5.27 It was also agreed to establish a mechanism for all new cases to be seen by a second paediatrician from within the Region, as well as, wherever possible, a child psychiatrist. Again, there was no precedent for such a group, which was to be known as the Regional Reference Group. The Region pointed out in evidence that in normal circumstances, clinical judgement is not controlled by the Region. In the unusual situation in Cleveland in June 1987, the Region took steps to limit the clinical freedom of all South Tees paediatricians, with their consent, by setting up the Regional Reference Group [see page 119].

Response to Media Pressure

8.5.28 A Press Conference took place on 29th June and the Independent Panel and the Regional Reference Group were discussed with the media. Dr Donaldson felt that the press conference did offer a good deal of reassurance to the public but also commented:

"the service was not allowed to remain free from further outspoken comment".

8.5.29 On the 30th June, the Chairman, Dr Donaldson, the Regional Nursing Officer and Mr Hague visited South Tees District. They met Dr Grant, Dr Morrell, the Chairman and Officers of South Tees. They visited the new Child Resource Centre.

8.5.30 On the 1st July they received the request from the Minister for Health for a report on the situation as a matter of urgency. That report was compiled by Dr Donaldson in only two days and has been provided to the Inquiry.

8.5.31 Dr Donaldson was approached in the attempts by Mr Walton and Mr Smith to resolve the JCAC guidelines on medical examinations [see chapter 3]. In view of the recent setting up of the Regional Reference Group for new cases he was hesitant about the greater involvement of the police surgeons. He was also aware that relationships between certain police surgeons and paediatricians in Cleveland had not been good. In conversation with Mr Walton of the Social Services Department he expressed considerable reservations about the new guidelines being rushed through so quickly without further discussion. The new guidelines were also briefly discussed with officials from the DHSS.

8.5.32 Dr Donaldson told us that early in July some pressure was put on him to disclose the results of the Regional Reference Group's examination of three children who had been diagnosed by Dr Wyatt during the previous weekend. As a result of this approach Dr Donaldson was in touch with the President of the General Medical Council and with the British Medical Association, seeking advice on issues of disclosure and confidentiality. Throughout this time, which covered the Parliamentary Debate on 9 July, the Region was in frequent contact with the DHSS.

8.5.33 On Monday 13 July Dr Higgs and Dr Wyatt were invited to the Regional Health Authority prior to a meeting with senior officers from other agencies. The workings of the Regional Reference Group were discussed and the doctors expressed some reservations. They were asked by the Region if they would like to withdraw from clinical practice in order to concentrate on legal proceedings but they did not wish to do so.

8.5.34 Professor Sir Bernard Tomlinson, Dr Donaldson and Mr Hague then had a meeting with the Chief Constable, the Chief Executive of Cleveland, the Chairman of South Tees, Mr Bishop and Mr Michie of the NSPCC. The purpose of the meeting was to review the situation and to see if the Regional Health Authority needed to take any further action or could assist any of the other agencies. The Social Services Department put forward the opinion that the Regional Reference Group should be disbanded in view of the setting up of the Child Resource Centre and in the interests of avoiding the need for children to have more than one examination. The Region felt that this course of action would lead to a deterioration in public confidence and would be a disaster. However, they did agree that they would give further thought to the future of the Regional Reference Group. Dr Donaldson commented on the meeting:

"it struck me very clearly that the roles of the two main agencies (Social Services Department and Police) were essentially different. The Police wished to see if there was sufficient evidence and decide on the need to prosecute, the Social Services Department might still have to act to protect the child even if there was insufficient evidence to prosecute."

8.5.35 Throughout this period Dr Donaldson was repeatedly telephoned and involved in individual cases, in contact with the media and representatives of other agencies such as Mr Bishop and for a time he was unable to engage in any work other than that arising from Cleveland.

8.5.36 During this period cases were continuing to cause public controversy. Dr Donaldson was in frequent contact with the doctors on the Regional Reference Group who were seeking advice on individual cases. On Saturday 19 July, Dr Donaldson warned Dr Higgs over the telephone that it was particularly important for her to be aware of the wider implications of her clinical work in the present climate.

8.5.37 By this time the Inquiry had been announced and Dr Donaldson was devoting most of his time to preparing evidence for the Region.

8.5.38 There was an exchange of correspondence between Dr Donaldson and Mr Donaldson regarding the possible suspension of the two doctors. Mr Donaldson initially wrote to Dr Donaldson on 21st July, requesting that action be taken against the two doctors in order to restore public confidence in the paediatric service in Middlesbrough:

"as you have been unable in practice to limit the adverse effect of Dr Higgs and Dr Wyatt's actions, I must formally ask that you consider the suspension of both consultants and in particular Dr Higgs".

8.5.39 Dr Donaldson delayed replying until 4th September, when he said:

"I am pleased that you have been reassured by the involvement of the Regional Reference Group and I would reiterate that despite the considerable logistic difficulties of operating such an arrangement, I believe it has been of great value in maintaining public confidence in the Service".

8.5.40 With regard to the matter of suspension, Dr Donaldson commented:

"We felt...that without prima facie evidence of professional incompetence or professional misconduct this was not a step which could be taken."

8.5.41 On 21st September Mr Donaldson replied to the effect that as the two doctors had been relieved of their clinical duties because of their involvement with the Inquiry, the changed circumstances had removed the need for suspension. He wrote:

"Previously, I was extremely concerned at the situation that then existed and I am pleased that you and your colleagues found a tactful and effective way of handling this issue."

British Paediatric Association

8.5.42 The President and Secretary of the British Paediatric Association visited Newcastle on 22nd July 1987 at the request of Professor Sir Bernard Tomlinson. They met Regional Officers and Dr Higgs and Dr Wyatt. They wrote to the Region on 27th July giving advice—see medical chapter and appendix

Comments on Northern Region during the Crisis

8.5.43 The response of the Northern Regional Health Authority was immediate and effective and designed as far as possible to allay public disquiet and try to restore confidence in the Paediatric Service.

8.5.44 The setting up of both the Independent Panel and the Regional Reference Group was timely, innovative, and for the most part effective.

8.5.45 Their investigation of the role played by the doctors in the crisis appears to us to have been thorough and, on the information available, it is unlikely that they could have done very much more.

8.5.46 Throughout the crisis they appear to have been at pains to be of assistance to other agencies, and did not hesitate to become involved in meeting them and trying to work out a solution to the evolving situation.

8.5.47 The presentation of evidence to the Inquiry was very well prepared and most helpful. We are grateful both to Professor Sir Bernard Tomlinson and Dr Donaldson for their valuable contributions.

8.6 Independent Panel and Regional Reference Group

A. Independent Second Opinion Panel

8.6.1 This was set up in June in response to a request by Mr Bishop to the Health Authorities to make arrangements for the clinical assessment of children diagnosed by Dr Higgs and Dr Wyatt as having been sexually abused. The intention was for an Independent Panel of consultants to provide second opinions in a number of cases where the diagnosis was in dispute.

8.6.2 After much discussion Professor Kolvin, Professor of Child Psychiatry, University of Newcastle, agreed to chair a panel of experts with an equal mix of paediatricians and child psychiatrists, each having a special knowledge and experience of child sexual abuse, drawn from both within and outside the

Northern Region. A paediatrician and a child psychiatrist conducted their enquiries and examinations together. Prospective members of the Panel met and discussed the general approach they should take, although no specific directives were made by the Region as to how they should proceed. The paediatrician would lead on the history and examination in relation to evidence of physical disorder, and the child psychiatrist in relation to emotional disturbance.

Method of Working

8.6.3 Two members of the Panel were allocated by Professor Kolvin to each child and family, and care was taken to ensure that any member of the Panel who had already seen the child or family did not take part in that exercise. The consultations involved a scrutiny of all available medical and Social Services records and were undertaken jointly in a manner agreed between the two doctors, taking into account the comfort and the best interests of the child. The choice of venue depended on the preferences and needs of the individuals concerned and specialist facilities and resources at Newcastle were laid at their disposal. Parents and current foster parents or others acting in loco parentis were interviewed and there was close collaboration with a key social worker. In addition an experienced children's nurse was made available to the Panel and a standard method was devised for collecting and collating the information.

Outcome of Investigations

8.6.4 The Panel saw a total of 29 children from 12 families, of which:

— In the cases of 12 children who had been diagnosed as having been sexually abused the diagnosis of sexual abuse was confirmed by the Panel;

— In 4 cases the initial diagnosis was sexual abuse and the Panel did not confirm it

— In the cases of 6 children who had been diagnosed as being sexually abused the Panel considered the medical signs sufficient to have merited further investigation;

— 7 siblings were examined and the original diagnosis by the paediatricians that no sexual abuse had occured was supported by the Panel.

8.6.5 Of the 12 families 8 were previously known to Social Services. In 6 families the diagnosis of the index child was made by Dr Higgs, and in 3 families by Dr Wyatt.

8.6.6 There are dangers in interpreting the analysis above simply at face value. It is important to bear in mind this was a selected group of children and they were examined by the Panel at a time considerably later than the original examinations.

Problems

8.6.7 A number of problems arose in the working of the Panel.

(i) Children were seen only with their parents' consent. 4 sets of parents whose cases were causing the Social Services concern did not give consent; 3 did not reply to the Social Services' request for permission; while 4 children were made wards of court and for that reason the Panel did not examine them. Some parents were reluctant to give permission to the Panel for two reasons. They and/or their legal advisers preferred to obtain second opinions from doctors of their choice. There was also public criticism made by Mr Stuart Bell MP and others about the independence and integrity of the Panel which made their work more difficult. Mr Bell in particular had voiced public criticisms about Dr Wynne being on the Panel. A Press Conference was held in order to allay public fears.

(ii) The involvement of a child psychiatrist was unusual, and in some children the need for further psychiatric care was identified which was not immediately available.

B. Regional Reference Group

8.6.8 The Regional Reference Group was established at the end of June 1987 to provide second opinions on all new cases of suspected child sexual abuse detected by consultant paediatricans in the South Tees Health District. The intention was that all new cases would be seen by a second paediatrician from within the Region. A joint examination with the police surgeon would be undertaken if possible, and it was also suggested that cases might be discussed with a child psychiatrist, following the arrangement for the

Independent Panel. At the same time it was noted that problems might be anticipated due to the difficulties of getting a child psychiatrist quickly and the length of time a psychiatric assessment might take. The setting up of the Reference Group was announced at the Press Conference of 29th June.

Purpose

8.6.9 The purpose behind the Reference Group was to provide a second opinion on the diagnosis of all the local paediatricians. It also helped paediatricians in South Tees when they were faced with children whom they feared were sexually abused, and yet they knew that in the growing crisis their clinical assessment might not be accepted by either the Social Services, Police or Courts. Dr Donaldson asked that the consultants who gave second opinions would keep him informed as to how the new arrangements were working.

Outcome of Investigations

8.6.10 The Reference Group initially consisted of 4 paediatricians and 2 psychiatrists with 2 more paediatricians being recruited later. It saw 22 children from 12 families, 8 of which were previously known to the Social Services for problems other than child sexual abuse. The initial diagnosis of child sexual abuse was made in 4 families by Dr Higgs and in 5 by Dr Wyatt. The Reference Group findings can be summarised as follows:

— In 7 children where sexual abuse had been diagnosed by the clinician, the diagnosis was confirmed;

— In 4 children were sexual abuse had been diagnosed the diagnosis was not confirmed but there was case for concern and further investigations

— In 3 siblings originally found not to have been sexually abused the Reference Group supported the finding;

— In 8 children the referring clinician's original diagnosis of sexual abuse was not confirmed.

As with the findings of the Independent Panel, there are dangers in interpreting the analysis simply at face value.

Problems with the Running of the Reference Group

8.6.11 The Regional Reference Group was set up as a matter of urgency and it created an unique arrangement in providing an automatic second opinion in each case. There were bound to be difficulties in operating such an arrangement. Problems which arose can be divided between the practical and the conceptual.

Practical Problems

8.6.12 The practical problems can be summarised thus:

(i) Where sexual abuse was suspected the need to have a second opinion was viewed as urgent. The doctors who were required to give the second opinion were expected to travel to South Tees Health District very quickly. They had great difficulty in rearranging their own practices in order to be available. The psychiatrists never managed to do so and never attended an examination.

(ii) The members of the Reference Group were invited to perform their joint examination with police surgeons who were often not known to them; whose precise role was not clear to them; and whose manner of examination proved in some cases to be unacceptable. The friction thus caused in some cases detracted from advantages which might otherwise have arisen from a joint examination.

(iii) The physical accommodation available in Middlesbrough General Hospital is limited and some visiting paediatricians expressed the view that it was unsuitable for the evaluation of children and families where the possibility of child sexual abuse was being considered

Conceptual Difficulties

8.6.13 In addition there were inherent in the arrangements a number of conceptual difficulties, some of which were foreseen by the Northern Region, but which made the Regional Reference Group less effective.

(i) Among members of the Reference Group were paediatricians without much clinical experience in child sexual abuse. Individuality of style and approach, differing views as to the weight of findings and the response to those findings created conflict and difficulties.

119

(ii) Some members of the Reference Group felt that they were expected to confirm findings by the paediatrician who made the original diagnosis, and the consequential pressures created problems when they stated alternative views. Dr Higgs and Dr Wyatt argued when members disagreed with their findings and questioned the experience and approach of some of the Reference Group. In other situations where a clinician might seek a second opinion he or she would do so when there was uncertainty as to the significance of the diagnosis or because he had not the facilities or skill to deal with it. In Cleveland the referring paediatricians involved were confident of their diagnoses, and where the second opinion differed from their own found themselves in the difficult position of having to be responsible for a patient and to act upon a contrary diagnosis made by a doctor acting at the behest of the Northern Region and without the continuing care of the child.

(iii) The Social Services Department were placed in a similar position. When the paediatricians agreed then it confirmed the medical diagnosis but when they disagreed the dilemma of the Social Services Department was made more acute. How were they to act in accordance with their statutory responsibilities?

(iv) Transmission of confidential medical information to the media about some cases created an additional difficulty. It is not known whether these disclosures had been made with the permission of parents or others on behalf of the children, but the permission of Reference Group paediatricians was not given according to evidence placed before the Inquiry. This kind of revelation added to the difficulty of operating the new mechanism.

8.6.14 In short, the Regional Reference Group had value as an emergency measure in unusual circumstances, but had many disadvantages and would not appear to be a practical mechanism in the long term. It served to create many more difficulties than had been envisaged when it was first established, and in many ways presented more problems than the Independent Panel. When any Health Authority finds itself having to consider setting up a similar mechanism it is essential that a method of working is agreed between all participating clinicians beforehand and it must be ensured that there should be no firm diagnosis until after the Reference Group consultants have examined the children. From the experience in Cleveland, this is not, however a mechanism we would recommend.

Other Second Opinions

8.6.15 A number of doctors were asked to give second opinions on cases diagnosed as being sexually abused by Dr Higgs. These included Dr Clayden, Mr Heald and a number of Police Surgeons including Dr Roberts, Dr Paul and Dr Clarke. The police surgeons overwhelmingly found that there was no medical evidence for sexual abuse having occurred. In some wardship cases the evidence of the police surgeons was preferred to Dr Higgs and Dr Wyatt, while in others that of Dr Higgs and Dr Wyatt was relied upon.

8.7 Involvement of South Tees District Health Authority

8.7.1 During 1984 in the South Tees District professionals were becoming increasingly aware of the existence of child sexual abuse and in particular the need for improved training. The District Health Authority had appointed in mid 1987 a Health Visitor (Child Abuse) part-time to supplement the work of the two specialist Nursing Officers by concentrating on the preventative and educational aspects of this field of work.

Response to Child Abuse Prior to the Crisis

8.7.2 The ARC considered the need to identify sexual abuse as a distinct category for the purposes of registration. (See chapter 3).

8.7.3 In December 1984, a small group was set up by the(Nursing Officers) Designated Officers' forum to examine a discussion paper produced by the NSPCC relating to their Child Protection Team. The group subsequently reported back emphasising the need for recognition of child sexual abuse as a specific category of abuse, and that the ARC needed to receive advice on appropriate guidelines for work in this area.

8.7.4 In May 1985, Mrs Dunn was concerned about the arrangements in the area for combatting child sexual abuse and discussed with Mrs Roach and the District Health Education Officer the possibility of preventing child sexual abuse by some form of educational means. They decided to hold a meeting to which a wide range of people would be invited. This group included representatives from Social Services Training, Education and the NSPCC. They addressed four key issues:—

— What was being done locally about the problem of child sexual abuse

— The resources available locally

— Future action to be taken by the Group

— What response is needed locally.

At the time there were some but very few local initiatives.

Child Sexual Abuse Training Co-ordinating Group

8.7.5 Mrs Dunn and Mrs Roach decided to set up a child sexual abuse training co-ordinating group and arranged the first meeting in mid-June 1985 with the hope of a much wider representation, including Police, General Practitioners, Psychiatrists, Psychologists, Community Medicine and Education. The response was disappointing possibly due to other factors. Various proposals were made and a progress report presented to a (Nursing Officers) Designated Officers, meeting in September 1985. The reaction was not encouraging and the group decided to continue to meet and to try to make progress on their own initiative.

8.7.6 Mrs Roach said that it was quite difficult to interest people in the subject of child sexual abuse:

"I think because it is such a difficult subject anyway and it was still very much in its infancy...."

In her evidence Mrs Dunn told us about these training sessions and the problems some professional have coping with child sexual abuse, she said:

"Somehow sexual abuse touches a part of the individual which perhaps physical abuse does not. Most of us can see how we could quite easily hit a child in a moment of stress.....and emotional abuse again I think we can all understand the damage that is done by it ....sexual abuse has an effect on the person which is an individual response depending on perhaps your own knowledge, your own background experience, and some people find it extremely difficult even to listen to us talking about it. I have sometimes to go back to a professional group. I have been asked to go back to repeat the training I have given because they were so distressed, and really shut off because they found it so painful. So I think it does affect people differently than hearing about physical abuse, and so I think it needs much more training in the feelings attached to dealing with sexual abuse".

8.7.7 They in time extended their membership and distributed a questionnaire to training agencies of the groups who might encounter the victims of child sexual abuse in their work.

8.7.8 They received responses from 25 groups. The answers showed that most of the organisations recognised the need to train their workers and most would find a support group useful.

8.7.9 The group reported to the JCAC on its first meeting in 1987. Mrs Roach said:— "We actually sent the package, this paper, to the JCAC to have it taken forward......It has not gone forward".

General Managers' Involvement

8.7.10 Following the Jasmine Beckford Inquiry, Mr Donaldson asked the then acting Community Unit General Manager, Mr Whitley for a report on the management of child abuse within the District. In his reply, Mr Whitley included a report from Mrs Dunn and Mrs Roach dated 31st January 1986. They drew attention to a general increase in the identification of child abuse generally and child sexual abuse in particular. The figures showed an approximate increase of 40% in cases from 1984. They stated:— "Liaison with Social Services has improved greatly...The same can be said of the Police Community Relations Department". The Designated Officers agreed:— "That if procedures are followed rigorously the system in Cleveland works well".

8.7.11 The report went on to say:

"In response to the build up of information and media publicity on child sexual abuse, we felt that a multi-disciplinary approach would be most useful in training staff. This is a learning situation for us all and we have set up a child abuse training co-ordinating group to look at ways of sharing training and improving the level of experience and expertise amongst field workers. This has developed into sessions in Junior Schools as an attempt to prevent sexual assaults".

They were also providing regular training sessions on wards 9 and 10 of Middlesbrough General Hospital.

8.7.12 They listed a number of areas of concern including the need for more regular supervision of health visitors in child abuse cases, training and updating of health visiting staff, and that general practitioners should attend all case conferences which rarely happened.

8.7.13 Mr Whitley added:— "By employing two Nursing Officers with a specific remit in relation to child abuse, this Authority recognises the importance of this issue and has a resource to liaise with all agencies concerned once abuse is identified, and also to lead the front line staff in identifying child abuse".

8.7.14 In discussion there was some concern expressed that hospital clinicians were not picking up child abuse and that "the degree of commitment by the three paediatricians varied considerably".

8.7.15 A follow-up report received by Mr Donaldson on 9th June 1987, referred to the appointment of the part-time Health Visitor, and spoke of the possibility of appointing a Designated Doctor (child abuse) to specialise in child abuse work. The report stated that: "Epidemiological work and preventative actions were identified as aspects requiring significantly more attention in relation to the development of a more positive strategy for dealing with child abuse".

8.7.16 Throughout 1986 both Nursing Officers reported increased demands on their time, with cases of child sexual abuse being a notable feature.

8.7.17 A number of training sessions were held in the District for other professionals in 1986 and 1987.

Appointment of Dr Higgs

8.7.18 Mr Donaldson was concerned as to the overall increases in the volume of admissions that might result from the appointment of a new and active paediatrician, Dr Higgs, taking up post on 1 January 1987.

8.7.19 In February Mr Martin, Chairman of the Medical Advisory Committee drew to the attention of Mr Donaldson that Dr Higgs, appointed with a special interest in neonatology was widening considerably her activities into child abuse and social medicine. That in itself did not trouble Mr Donaldson; what he was troubled about was that she might be diverted from neonatology which was her prime responsibility. Consequently, at the suggestion of Mr Martin he wrote to the Regional Medical Officer. (See page 113)

Paediatric Wards Early 1987

8.7.20 During the early months of 1987 the paediatric wards in Middlesbrough General Hospital were heavily occupied for an unusually long period of time because of chest infections and consequently the facilities were under very heavy pressure. Following this, on 16th March senior nurses wrote to their Nursing Manager, Mrs Chambers expressing their concern about staff shortages and particularly the deplorable conditions and poor facilities for parents. They also expressed their "grave concern for the safety of the children in our care".

8.7.21 Prior to 30th April 1987 the admission of children to the paediatric wards with suspicion of sexual abuse was very small. Their admission caused no significant problem to the paediatric service. Nurses felt that they were able to cope with them.

The Crisis

8.7.22 The influx of cases over the first week of May could not have been anticipated by the management of South Tees nor for that matter was it by Dr Higgs and Dr Wyatt. It was sudden and took them all by surprise.

Photographs

8.7.23 The crisis came to the attention of Dr Drury because the wards were full and there was a request for clinical photography to be provided out of hours. The unit had its own clinical photographer but he is not generally available outside normal working hours nor at weekends. Detective Superintendent White told Dr Drury that the police photographer would only take photographs when the Police themselves were proceeding with investigations.

Admissions

8.7.24 The May children also included the siblings of children diagnosed as sexually abused. There were being brought onto the ward and a number of similar diagnoses being made. The numbers themselves at that time were not so large that the hospital could not cope, but they were appearing on the ward bypassing the usual admission procedures.

8.7.25 This caused certain problems for the nursing staff who needed to have on their nursing records information such as which people were or were not allowed to visit children and also when it was permissible to allow children to be removed from the ward. Parents were also coming to the hospital seeking their children and the nursing staff did not know initially whether the parents were or were not allowed to collect their children (see page 126).

Social Services and the Unit Manager

8.7.26 Dr Drury believed there was a communication problem with Social Services and that the hospital staff were not receiving all the relevant information. As a result, during the first week of May, Dr Drury spoke to Mr Walton on the telephone about poor communications from Social Services.

8.7.27 It was agreed:

(i) that social workers must liaise with the nursing staff at all times;

(ii) that the nurses must know the status of the children on the ward as to whether place of safety orders had been made and generally who had custody and control of the children in question;

(iii) that the social workers must report to the nursing staff when coming onto the ward and leaving the ward.

8.7.28 Mr Walton implemented these arrangements and thereafter, Dr Drury told us, there was a significant improvements in communications.

Dr Higgs and the Unit Manager

8.7.29 On the 7th May, Dr Drury was told of the high number of admissions since the beginning of the month. He obtained a report from Mrs Dunn and informed the Chairman of South Tees District Health Authority.

8.7.30 Dr Drury then received a telephone call from Dr Higgs who asked him why he was involved. He explained his position as Unit General Manager. In evidence he commented:

"New consultants often/sometimes have not had a great deal of personal experience in dealing with hospital management. At that time I did not know what Dr Higgs' previous experience had been, and therefore it was a possibility that she was not particularly au fait with how hospitals were run; and particularly in my instance, as I was a doctor, that might have been confusing".

8.7.31 He felt it was important to see her not only to deal with these matters generally but the problem relating to 'communication' in particular. He felt that it was essential for a consultant who has developed a particular expertise or interest in their subject to ensure that the nursing staff were fully aware of that particular interest so that they were able in their turn to make their own arrangements as to patients' assessment and plan the care of the patient accordingly. He wished to stress the importance of new developments being discussed with management. He arranged to see Dr Higgs on the 14th May.

8.7.32 On the 14th May, Dr Drury met Dr Higgs for 4 hours. He described the meeting as difficult at first:

"I think Dr Higgs at that time, certainly for the first part, was defining for herself what the role of a General Manager was, perhaps what I could contribute even; what my understanding of the present situation was, and that would lead her to challenge what I said. But I think it has to be admitted it was difficult going to begin with. However, the meeting certainly ended very amicably, and at the end of the meeting I felt I had actually got to know Dr Higgs a little".

8.7.33 Dr Drury did, however, manage to discuss other matters, and stressed a number of points to her:

(i) that she was a key figure, that she had expertise that others may lack and that she should provide leadership;

(ii) that the nurses would need to be trained to deal with the situation, and he asked that Dr Higgs produce local guidelines;

(iii) that the nurses were somewhat sceptical and there was a need to allay their suspicions, for there to be proper communications, and for them to know and be aware of correct procedures;

(iv) that the position of the parents needed to be considered.

Dr Higgs in a forthright manner expressed her concern for children and we were told that for some three hours she took a somewhat semantic approach as to exactly what he meant by any word or phrase. During the last half hour of their discussion he said that she became more communicative and acknowledged these points. She agreed to consult with the nursing staff and promised to meet Mrs Chambers and Mrs Moore. Dr Drury told her of his meeting with Mr White and asked her if it was correct that there was some disagreement with Dr Irvine and she agreed that there was and they had different approaches to diagnosis. In an attempt, as he said, to help matters, he asked whether there would not be some benefit in having one medical examination at which both she and Dr Irvine were present. She said that there were practical difficulties and that he was not always available.

8.7.34 Mr Donaldson met Mrs Dunn on the 19th May and was briefed that there was a sharp increase in referrals from the Eston area, almost equally of physical and sexual abuse and these were being detected by Dr Higgs. Mrs Dunn advised him that Dr Higgs was only finding what was there and they could expect a steady increase.

Mrs Dunn's view of the Medical Diagnosis of Child Sexual Abuse

8.7.35 Mrs Dunn told us in evidence that she knew of the medical controversy within the field of sexual abuse after she attended a seminar at which Dr Wynne appeared at the end of 1986. She had also seen the articles in the Lancet and read an article in the Observer about Dr Wynne's work.

8.7.36 She described her reaction thus:

"I just accepted that this was good news for sexually abused children I think. When I first read the article I thought that this was good news, this is going to make it easier for people to diagnosis sexual abuse. But then, of course, I read the rejoinder saying that there were lots of other differential diagnosis they thought which might give these signs. I did also have knowledge from attendance at an International Conference in Australia last year when I was asked to give a paper there. I heard other papers delivered and there was one paper which was mentioned—I did not hear it—where they spoke to the difficulty of diagnosis from certain signs".

8.7.37 At the conference in Australia Mrs Dunn gave a paper on her role as a specialist nursing officer and about the preventative work she was doing.

8.7.38 She described to us the process by which she became increasingly aware of the full implications of the diagnosis:—

"What I was trying to say was that I had thought I had accepted that there must be a large number of sexually abused children in the community, but, when faced with the facts coming from the hospital, I , too, found myself in a position of denial for a while and actually had to work my way through the feelings and then realise that actually this was possibly a sign of what was there to be found".

8.7.39 She further commented:

"I think, having read what Dr Wynne had said, and having heard her speak, and seeing what was happening in Leeds, it was not a surprise, particularly once I had adjusted to the idea of what it meant in numbers".

Extra Accommodation

8.7.40 On 19th May, the same day that Mr Donaldson had met Mrs Dunn, Dr Higgs spoke to him about needing more beds for abuse cases. Mr Donaldson considered with his staff the potential need for extra accommodation.

Meeting on 1 June

8.7.41 As a result of this request for extra accommodation, Mr Donaldson got in touch with Mr Bishop to arrange a meeting to discuss the situation. This took place on the 1st June. (see Chapter 4). Mr Donaldson attended with Dr Drury, the new District Medical Officer Dr Ramaiah on the first day of his appointment and Dr Higgs. Mrs Richardson attended with Mr Bishop. Dr Higgs and Mr Bishop expressed their conviction that there was a lot of undiscovered sexual abuse in the community. They agreed to proceed on a South Tees rather than a Cleveland basis initially. Mr Bishop would meet with the Chief Constable to try to get the Police involved at an early stage—preferably at an initial clinical examination. Mr Bishop would report the increased level of detection to his Committee. A small group would be set up to deal with short-term co-ordination if any further peak in admissions occurred and to improve liaison. Dr Higgs and Mrs Richardson would produce a report seeking to produce accurate data and to quantify the likely level and make specific proposals to the two authorities. At this meeting neither Dr Higgs nor Mrs Richardson alerted the others to a situation of emergency or that the diagnosis was controversial.

8.7.42 The report was never in fact written. It would have been very helpful to have had such a report quickly.

JCAC Working Party Meeting 1 June

8.7.43 The working party meeting chaired by Mrs Richardson and attended by Mrs Dunn also met on lst June. Mrs Dunn told us in evidence:

"I think most of us were preaching caution with the actions at the time, and that really we would have appreciated it if there had been a gap between the diagnosis or the notification of signs and the actual action which had to be taken. I think most of us would have appreciated it if we could have got some system whereby we could then have stopped and shared information a little. I was never consulted and asked about the Health Visitor's knowledge of the background of families, this sort of thing which would have helped to give a balance to what turned out to be one sign of abuse. This has been the unfortunate thing which other people will have identified, that we got hung up on a medical diagnosis when it was really only a small part of the picture of abuse".

It does not, however, appear that her words of caution were put to the working party.

Nursing Support

8.7.44 According to Dr Drury's deputy Mr Mitchell, during the second week of June there were occasional 'mumblings' from senior nursing staff about the number of children on the wards suspected of being sexually abused, and he discussed the situation with Mrs Chambers. She told us they had "little choice but to continue to provide what amounted to hotel accommodation for children under place of safety or care orders occasioned by suspicion of sexual abuse".

Numbers

8.7.45 On the l0th June, Mr Mitchell received an urgent telephone call from Dr Wyatt stating that he needed more beds in his unit as he was having to send children to other wards and to other hospitals.

8.7.46 The critical weekend was that of the 12/13th June with the admission of 20 children to the Middlesbrough General Hospital. The events which took place about midnight or later led to the complaints of two nurses about Dr Higgs and Dr Wyatt.

8.7.47 On Monday 15th June about 9.30am Mr Mitchell received a telephone call from Mr Urch, Secretary to the South Tees Community Health Council. Mr Urch said he had received a telephone inquiry from the Police concerning child sexual abuse over the weekend.

8.7.48 About 10.00am, Mr Mitchell was told by Mr Crown who had been the on-call Administrator over the weekend that Mrs Chambers wanted to see him to explain about the events over the weekend. Mrs Chambers explained to him her great concern over the activities of Dr Higgs and Dr Wyatt in particular, and about the whole child sexual abuse situation. She gave him the statements from the nurses.

8.7.49 Mr Mitchell immediately informed Dr Drury by telephone of the admission of another 20 children over that previous weekend and that there were statements from two nurses making complaints about Drs Higgs and Wyatt.

Nurses

8.7.50 The Inquiry received written and oral evidence from a number of nurses from the paediatric wards of Middlesbrough General Hospital. We found their evidence valuable in that it gave us an insight into how the crisis was affecting a group of professionals who had to cope with some of the worst effects of the crisis when it was at its peak, and were unable to do anything to change the situation. It became apparent that some nurses were angry at what was happening and took the unusual step of complaining to the Region about the practice of the two consultants Drs Higgs and Wyatt.

8.7.51 Mrs Chambers told us that before Dr Higgs joined Middlesbrough General Hospital on 1st January she had been told that Dr Higgs had a special interest in child sexual abuse, although Mrs Chambers told us that she had no reason to think Dr Higgs would concentrate on this rather than any of her other duties.

Admission Procedures

8.7.52 The normal way in which children are admitted to Hospital, according to Dr Drury, is for them to be referred by their general practitioner or to be brought directly by parents to the Accident and Emergency Department. In such instances proper admissions procedures are followed. The same procedure would apply to admissions of children to the wards through the paediatric admission room. Children who had been suspected of sexual abuse might be brought directly to the paediatric admission room by social workers. During this period the proper admission procedures were not being observed and some children were examined for whom no admission documents had been prepared. Mrs Chambers received a number of complaints from nurses, either communicated directly or through ward sisters.

8.7.53 A ward sister, Mrs Hornby summarised the situation to us as follows:

"I feel that the standard of communication was quite poor really. The consultants very rarely came back to the ward to speak to the parents or the children once the diagnosis had been made, and this caused a lot of problems to the nursing staff being unable to give vital information to the parents as to what was to happen".

Mrs Chaplin, a state registered sick childrens' nurse commented:

"We felt that the parents relied upon the nursing staff to give them information as to what was happening to their children, and in actual fact we did not know what was happening".

Mrs Morrison a ward sister told us that this led to further difficulties for the nurses: "Some of the parents became abusive, when for example they asked for information which the nursing staff were unable to provide".

8.7.54 Mrs Chambers told the nurses on the wards that when they received notification that a place of safety order was being invoked they were to ask had the parents been told about it, did they understand what it meant, and were they allowed access.

8.7.55 The nurses were not sure as to whether or not they were able to make a full nursing assessment of the children and what questions they were allowed to ask because of the sensitive nature of the diagnosis. They did not receive any instructions from the consultants about the children and said they were unable to draw up care plans for the child, as they would for normal admissions. Such care plans would contain details of normal daily living activities, what problems had brought the child to hospital and what nursing needs the child had. We do not entirely understand why the nurses were unable to draw up normal nursing records for children despite the lack of communication from doctors and social workers. In early May, Mrs Chambers instructed that all children should have care plans.

12/13th June

8.7.56 On the 12th June Sister Chaytor made a report of an incident in which it was alleged that between 11pm and 1am Drs Higgs and Wyatt wanted to wake up a child who had not been admitted for sexual abuse in order to provide a control to compare the abused children. The nurses were upset at this incident and the fact that anal and vaginal examinations were taking place late at night. Nurses complained that whenever the two doctors diagnosed abuse they were 'elated'. Dr Wyatt told the Inquiry:

"I was certainly not 'elated' either at that time or at any other time when I found signs consistent with child sexual abuse . However, as a consultant paediatrician, I am bound to feel professional satisfaction when I find evidence which helps explain the child's condition and I can only think that any professional satisfaction which I showed may have been interpreted as 'elation'."

The doctors examined four children, one admitted by Dr Wyatt for failure to thrive, another was examined at Dr Higgs' request, a further two at the request of nurses who had noticed anal abnormalities. With regard to waking up children in order to examine them, Dr Higgs told the Inquiry that it was sometimes necessary, though to the best of her recollection she only woke up one child on the 12th June. This was at the request of Dr Wyatt and involved a child who had been admitted very underweight and with a history of vomiting. Of the nurses' criticisms, Dr Higgs said:

"I did not realise how upset they were on the night. I mean the nurses were helping us to examine the children who were examined. I was not aware of their distress about that and was very surprised to hear of their criticisms subsequently."

The doctors were going to examine a fifth child but did not do so because he and his mother were asleep.

Mrs Chaytor collected statements from the nurses and conveyed them to Mr Mitchell and Mr Donaldson. Mrs Chambers told Mr Horner who was Acting Chief Nursing Officer. He talked to the nurses in the week following the 16th June.

8.7.57 On 14th June Mrs Chambers spoke to Dr Higgs about the nursing establishment. Dr Higgs suggested that Mrs Chambers "get more nurses", but as Mrs Chambers said: "We have no more nurses to give". Mrs Chambers further said: "Dr Higgs seemed not to understand that the nursing budget is a finite amount".

8.7.58 The meeting was inconclusive. In order to provide a short term solution nurses were taken away from other wards to assist on the paediatric ward.

8.7.59 Another problem experienced by the nurses in June were the large numbers of healthy children on the ward together with sick children. Mrs Morrison told us:

"The children, those referred for sexual abuse, appeared normal healthy children. Some of them were abusive and destructive on the ward, probably through boredom. This caused great problems for the nursing staff...It was very difficult for us to nurse the children who were ill on the ward. Some of these children needed peace and quiet and intensive nursing, which it was difficult to provide with so many children to occupy".

8.7.60 The ward was ill-equipped to contain the presence of these active, lively children with no specific illness who were, in some cases, difficult to control. This created havoc. Overcrowding made matters worse, with parents and children sleeping on camp beds as there was not sufficient space, and there were only two lavatories which we were told got into a "disgusting state", making working conditions for the nurses increasingly more difficult.

8.7.61 We heard that children were taken from Middlesbrough General Hospital to Leeds by social workers without the nurses being informed. In one case after a wardship decision in the High Court there was a failure of communication between social workers and the hospital of decisions taken in court in Leeds. Parents came on to the ward demanding their children back. When the nurses asked the duty social worker, she did not know what had happened. Mrs Morrison commented:— "I just felt it was polite if they could have let us know". The social worker concerned had made unsuccessful efforts to inform the hospital.

8.7.62 Mrs Dunn found that during the crisis in May and June communication between the nursing staff and herself deteriorated. On one occasion a ward sister would not speak to her on the telephone. She felt it was the frustration of not having the information.

"I went straight to the hospital and talked to the staff then personally face to face. They expressed a lot of anger and frustration....I think I was more concerned about distress. Some of the sisters looked as if they had not been sleeping very well and really looked quite ill. I was really very upset about their emotional state. I felt they were really being put under a great deal of pressure. They were not so much angry as just asking why didn't somebody speak to them, why didn't somebody tell them what was going on?".

She went on to say:

"The feelings attached to this whole crisis began to be feelings of helplessness. I think this was one of the most difficult things to deal with, that as professionals who had been feeling that they were fairly competent, suddenly we just felt helpless in the face of this crisis which rolled on and rolled over us all".

8.7.63 Mrs Dunn discussed it with Dr Higgs, who said she was finding what there was to be found. Mrs Dunn and Mrs Roach made some recommendations in writing to give to Dr Drury.

8.7.64 Some nurses felt that Drs Higgs and Wyatt were not helpful in teaching them how to deal with parents and children who had been diagnosed as sexually abused. This was seen as another area where communication between doctors and nurses was lacking.

127

8.7.65 It is not generally for paediatricians to teach nurses but we would suggest it is their responsibility to tell nurses how they wish their patients to be cared for. This lack of communication is to be deprecated and much of the confusion and distress could have been averted if the doctors had been able to tell the nurses why the children who had been diagnosed as sexually abused were on the ward, on what basis they were there and how they should be cared for. The doctors should have been more sensitive to the extent to which nursing resources and the physical environment in which nurses were working were stretched to the limit during the time of the crisis. Nurses felt aggrieved and that they were working in the dark.

8.7.66 Social workers should also have realised the additional burdens they were placing upon the nurses. Senior managers from the Health and Social Service Authorities should together have worked out a way of informing and assisting the nurses, bearing in mind that they were being asked to cope with an unfamiliar problem on a scale which made their normal work considerably more difficult.

8.7.67 The efforts made by Mr Donaldson, Mr Mitchell, Dr Drury and Mr Walton undoubtedly helped the situation in June. By July the crisis was beginning to ease up.

Reallocation of Children

8.7.68 An orthopaedic surgeon, Mr Hooley, spoke to Mr Mitchell about his concern over a number of children placed in his orthopaedic wards. Some were not physically ill and were causing some disturbance on his ward and he said that one small child was in traction in an adult bed and this was totally unsatisfactory.

8.7.69 The childrens' wards were full to overflowing and children were being transferred to other wards in the hospital and some had been transferred to North Tees General Hospital.

Pressure on Nurses

8.7.70 The nursing staff of the childrens' wards were under severe and constant pressure and close to breaking point. This pressure, combined with great concern on the part of senior nursing staff about the activities of Drs Higgs and Wyatt was undoubedly making the care of those physically ill children on the wards extremely difficult.

Media

8.7.71 The media interest in the situation caused problems for the nurses and added to the pressure on them. (See page 168)

8.7.72 Mr Stuart Bell MP visited the hospital on six occasions during the week from the 19th June. Some nurses were critical of him. (see page 167)

8.7.73 Overall, the nurses felt that some of their needs were overlooked, and they felt this deeply. No-one, either fellow professionals or parents or other members of the public seemed to have paid sufficient attention to the effect their activities were having on the nurses.

Management Response

8.7.74 Mr Donaldson met the two consultants. He sought to convince himself that they were "within the ethical and legal limits" and they sought to convince him how imperative it was to unearth abuse and of the consequent long-term damage to the child. In the course of the conversation Dr Wyatt told Mr Donaldson that he had radically changed his clinical practice about a month previously having seen what Dr Higgs was doing and that he now thought this was the most important aspect of child health.

8.7.75 On the same day Mr Donaldson spoke to Mr Bishop about the changed position and Mr Bishop asked whether second medical opinions could be arranged. Mr Donaldson investigated the nurses complaints. He took legal advice and met Dr Donaldson to discuss them. Mr Donaldson raised with Dr Donaldson the possibility of obtaining a credible alternative clinical opinion.

8.7.76 Later that day Mr Donaldson saw Mr Bishop and they reviewed the position as regards the high numbers the previous weekend. Mr Bishop's immediate concern was that he had run out of childrens homes and foster families and could not move the children then in Middlesbrough General Hospital. He asked if there was any accommodation and Mr Donaldson offered a spare ward at Hemlington Hospital. Mr Donaldson told Mr Bishop that they would arrange second opinions as soon as possible.

Response to Parents

8.7.77 On the 18th June in Ward 9 there was a confrontation between Dr Wyatt and parents of some of the children still being detained in hospital since the weekend because Social Services could not move them. Dr Wyatt was harangued by a group of parents and he called the Police, who remained for a while on the ward. Mr Mitchell pointed out that neither Dr Higgs nor Dr Wyatt had got in touch with him.

8.7.78 Mr Mitchell visited Ward 9 about 2.15pm to find a number of parents in a distressed and angry state and two Police Officers, whose presence seemed to be controlling the situation. He asked the parents to accompany him to the Administration Building where he could listen to their complaints. That also removed them from the vicinity of the paediatric department. About 12 members of families accompanied him to Dr Drury's office. He provided tea and coffee and explained the complaints procedure to them.

8.7.79 The main complaint of the parents at this time was that until then no one had taken time to listen to them. Some totally disbelieved the accusation of sexual abuse, others were very upset and wondering who could possibly have done this to their children.

8.7.80 Mr Mitchell and Mrs Chambers discussed these problems with Dr Drury and explained that distressed parents were starting to complain about what was happening to them and their children.

8.7.81 Mr Donaldson had a long talk with Dr Wyatt and Dr Higgs joined them. Mr Donaldson said he could not accept the present situation and would have to do something radical to reduce the tension, perhaps closing the wards for further admissions until Social Services could get the children out. He said he did not want to do anything as crude as that and could they ease back on admissions for 4 or 5 days to reduce the tension. The discussion digressed but essentially they maintained that if they came across sexual abuse they had to do something about it and they could not shirk their duty. Mr Donaldson was doubtful that he had made sufficient impact upon them.

Medical Advisory Committee

8.7.82 Mr Donaldson rang the Chairman of the Medical Advisory Committee and agreed that a panel of senior doctors should see the two paediatricians in the morning.

8.7.83 The next morning three senior consultants from the area met Drs Higgs and Wyatt at Middlesbrough General Hospital. The three consultants were Dr Williams, past Chairman of the Medical Executive Committee, Dr Mehta, Secretary of the Medical Executive Committee and Dr Bramble, Chairman of the Senior Medical Staff Committee.

8.7.84 According to Dr Williams "the purpose of this interview was to try to ensure that the activities of Dr Wyatt and Dr Higgs concerning the examination of children in the childrens' wards and clinics for evidence of sexual abuse were carried out in strictly ethical manner".

8.7.85 Dr Mehta explained to the Doctors that this was an informal meeting and no specific incidents were to be discussed. She said that there had been complaints and the three of them had been asked by the District General Manager to speak to them to discover their views of what they were doing in relation to diagnosing children suspected of having been sexually abused. She hoped that in all cases requiring consent this had been obtained. She said that they wanted reassurance that the doctors' behaviour had been proper at all times.

8.7.86 That reassurance was given without reservation. The tenor of their reply was that they had discovered that many more children were being sexually abused than had previously been suspected and that they had been and were working in close liaison with Social Services.

8.7.87 The senior consultants were assured that the examinations of children had been carried out in a strictly ethical manner. They expressed their concern about the method of referral and were assured that all cases had been properly referred to them.

8.7.88 According to Dr Williams:

"They stated repeatedly that in all their actions the interests of the children were their main consideration and that they were not influenced by any ulterior motive... Both Dr Wyatt and Dr Higgs appeared to be in control of themselves and quite confident. During the whole interview it was clear that Dr Wyatt was the dominant of the two paediatricians and it was he who did most of the answering and talking".

8.7.89 The senior consultants discussed the meeting afterwards. Dr Mehta felt the matter was so important and so urgent that Mr Donaldson should be advised to inform the Regional Health Authority immediately, which he had already done.

Alternative Arrangements

8.7.90 On the 20th June Mr Donaldson met Mr Bishop and Mr Walton and the two paediatricians to discuss what steps needed to be taken to ease the accommodation situation. Dr Wyatt had plans of ward extensions which he seemed to think would cost a few hundred thousand pounds and would be built in a few weeks. Both paediatricians were adamant the children should not go to Hemlington.

8.7.91 On the 22nd June, on his return from holiday, Dr Drury asked to see Dr Higgs and Dr Wyatt. He asked them to prepare guidelines for the nurses. These were previously requested from Dr Higgs and had not been provided. They also discussed the facilities at Hemlington Hospital. Dr Higgs told us: "We felt this would be inappropriate because it would make assessment and support even more difficult, both for the professionals and the families". After that briefing meetings were held on a daily basis, including all the senior managers and frequently Mrs Chambers.

Media

8.7.92 Press interest on Tuesday 23rd June was intense. Dr Drury issued a press statement and gave interviews. He worked very closely with Dr Steiner in Newcastle to provide facilities for the work of the Second Opinion Panel which was set up on the 23rd June.

Resource Centre

8.7.93 Discussions went ahead as to how to relieve the strain of otherwise healthy children on the ward. A special meeting was held on the 24th June in the Hospital by Dr Drury which included Mrs Richardson and Miss Glassbrook.

8.7.94 As a temporary measure the Orthopaedic Teaching Centre in the grounds of the Hospital was made available as that building most closely met the need outlined by Miss Glassbrook. The Centre was vacated and made ready in two working days and on Monday 29th July it was opened. From 9.00am to 4.00pm each day the children were taken from the ward to the Centre, relieving the pressure on the ward and allowing the special needs of those children and their parents to be met.

8.7.95 The nursing staff continued to express concern regarding proper admission procedures of children and on the 8th July Dr Drury drew up and issued a form to ensure the proper documentation of further admissions. In July, Sister Hornby adapted the nursing card index.

Specific Problems over Medical Records

8.7.96 At the end of June with the knowledge that further investigation of individual complaints would require access to case notes, Dr Drury decided to recover all the case notes relevant to the issue. It became apparent that only about 50% of the notes were in the records library.

8.7.97 On the 25th June Dr Higgs and Dr Wyatt delivered immediately about 70 sets of case notes, and they were reminded of the need to supply the photographs. On the same day, the District Health Authority started receiving requests from solicitors for case notes. Thereafter, the Administrative Staff of the Hospital made strenuous efforts to recover the missing files writing increasingly anxious requests to other hospitals and to the two doctors concerned. The last set of case notes appeared on 7th September. Dr Drury did not know if he had obtained all medical records as he had no agreement at that time (September) as to the total number of names. In most cases the notes related to children who had been discharged from hospital.

South Tees Conclusions

8.7.98 The District Authority was faced with a very difficult situation in May and June. It came upon them unawares and could not indeed have been forecast by anyone. They did their best to react to the crisis and contained large numbers of children in three separate periods. It was not until the influx during the middle of June that they were overwhelmed and had to seek the assistance of North Tees General who took a small number of children.

8.7.99 Nurses provided the necessary care in the absence of any real understanding as to their function. The presence of apparently, healthy even if abused children on a paediatric ward devoted to the care of sick children disturbed and distressed them. The Hospital is antiquated and the facilities for parents to stay on the ward are inadequate in any event. The crisis created pressure upon such facilities and added to the many problems the nurses had to face.

8.7.100 It was greatly to the credit of the District Authority that they deprived the Orthopaedic Teaching Centre of their premises and provided them at very short notice for the Middlesbrough Child Resource Centre. This was of enormous assistance to the Social Service Department and also relieved the pressure on the paediatric wards, (particularily ward 9), during the daytime.

8.8 DR HIGGS

Previous experience

8.8.1 Dr Higgs qualified in 1974 from the University of Adelaide Medical School. She moved to the United Kingdom in 1977. She is married with 5 children.

8.8.2 She has specialised in paediatrics throughout her medical career and between 1979 and 1986 was based in Newcastle. In 1979 she joined a research programme into cot deaths at the University of Newcastle Medical School. She then took part in the Riverside project, which involved staffing clinics, schools and nurseries in a deprived area of Newcastle with University medical staff. Thereafter she was working in various hospitals in the Newcastle area, and developed her two interests of neonatal intensive care and child abuse. She spent 6 months working in general paediatrics under the late Dr Christine Cooper, a leading authority in child abuse and a powerful advocate for better services for 'damaged children' and their families and in touch with the American experience of child sexual abuse. She learnt from Dr Cooper of the need to place the child within a legal framework. She said:—" By that I think is meant it can be very difficult for families to accept that possibly their care of the child is not optimum for the child and that one needs to have some control and authority over the situation to help the parents to adjust and change in order to appropriately parent their child or children."

The improvement in parenting had to take place within the time limits of the child.

8.8.3 She had a two year attachment to the Child Psychiatry Unit in Newcastle, which was her first contact with children suffering from the effects of sexual abuse and referred for psychiatric treatment for that reason.

8.8.4 She was appointed first assistant (senior registrar) to Dr Hey at the Neonatal Intensive Care Unit in Newcastle in 1985.

Attending Seminars on Child Sexual Abuse

8.8.5 In 1983 she attended a two day conference on child sexual abuse at the Northumbria Police Headquarters. In June 1986, Dr Cooper invited her to accompany her to a conference in Leeds on child sexual abuse arranged by BASPCAN. It was the first time she heard Dr Wynne lecture and saw her slides. This lecture made a great impression on her:—

"I think I realised for the first time the numbers of children that could be involved in this problem, the importance of the medical examination. The general feeling was that there were not many findings, that the doctors did have a role, really quite a small role to play. I think what was impressive about the Leeds conference is that there were doctors who had been working in this field, who had had a number of years' experience, had children with physical findings that were actually then able to be related to histories from the child of abuse and also admissions by perpetrators."

8.8.6 Dr Hobbs and Dr Wynne believed that child buggery was more common than was previously suspected; that it might be the cause of a variety of problems from vaginal discharge to sexualized behaviour and that it might be detected by physical examination of the anus. It was suggested that it was not uncommon within the context of other forms of child abuse, non-accidental injury, failure to thrive and emotional deprivation:

"It was acknowledged that what they were describing was new."

She did not recall that it was controversial.

First Diagnosis of Anal Abuse

8.8.7 A month later, on the 16th July, 1986, in the absence of the consultant on holiday she was asked, as acting senior registrar,to see in Newcastle, a Cleveland family, who were patients of Dr Wyatt and had been referred to the Fleming Family Assessment Unit. The two girls had recently been taken into the care of the Cleveland County Council after a history of failure to thrive, inadequate parenting and one of the children had been referred to Dr Wyatt with a number of bruises which were thought to be non-accidental. She said:

"Because one of the findings made by Dr Wynne and given at the Leeds conference was that approximately 25% of children who were physically abused were also sexually abused, I felt that it was appropriate for me to examine the bottoms and genitalia of both children of the family."

In the case of one child not quite 3, she saw for the first time the signs of "reflex relaxation and anal dilatation":

"It was quite a striking finding. I had not seen it before."

She telephoned Dr Wynne at Leeds and received confirmation that:—"The appearance which I described was consistent with sexual abuse." She also telephoned a woman police doctor Dr Ellis Fraser and asked her to examine the child for a second opinion. The family were admitted to the assessment centre a few days later; the father was admitted to another hospital for a day or two with gastro-enteritis, and on the 22nd July Dr Higgs examined the child again and:— "the finding was still there." On the following day, 23rd July, Dr Fraser found no abnormal signs on examination of the child but formed the opinion that sexual abuse was likely and informed the parents. According to Dr Higgs, as a result of the child complaining about a sore bottom and referring to her 'Daddy', she examined her 2 days later on the 25th July and again saw 'reflex relaxation and anal dilatation'. Dr Fraser examined later that morning and on this occasion confirmed Dr Higgs' findings. The parents were arrested.

8.8.8 Dr Higgs was asked for her explanation for the presence of the sign on one day , then not apparent on later examination, and then returning after a few more days:—

"My concern was then, and still is, that the child had probably been abused in hospital. Although that sounds preposterous, the way the ward is laid out is there are cubicles for the families; parents have free access to their children; there is certainly opportunity for privacy. This problem has been described as one of compulsive behaviour disorder in people who carry out sexual abuse. I did not have any other explanation for it. The child was not constipated, which is another slight possibility. There was no other explanation for the disappearance and the return of the sign."

Fifteen months later at the Inquiry she still felt that the only plausible explanation was that the little girl had been previously abused and reabused in hospital. Asked if she had any doubt that it was right, she said:— "I do not have any other explanation for it."

8.8.9 Dr Higgs saw fluctuations in the sign of anal dilatation whereby it disappeared and reappeared days or weeks later in this child, her sister and two or three other children in Middlesbrough during 1987, and the diagnosis made by Dr Higgs on each occasion was further sexual abuse.

Application for Post of Consultant

8.8.10 She was interviewed for the post in South Tees in June 1986 and at the interview:—"I discussed all my interests, that of wishing to continue to work as a general paediatrician with a special interest in neonatology, and also in child abuse and parenting problems." She was offered the job and it was deferred to the 1st January 1987 to enable her to complete some research in Newcastle.

Contact with Other Professionals Before Taking up Post

8.8.11 Dr Higgs first met Mrs Richardson and Mrs Marjorie Dunn at BAPSCAN meetings in 1986. After being offered the post of consultant in Middlesbrough she got in touch with Mrs Richardson as Child Abuse Consultant:—"to obtain information on available resources in the area and any statistics she could give me on child abuse. It is possible that I rang Mrs Dunn first and she then referred me to Mrs Richardson for this information."

8.8.12 Before taking up her appointment she was also a signatory with Dr Wyatt of a letter expressed in strong terms about the lack of paediatric resources in the area. [see page 113]

In Post

8.8.13 After her arrival in Middlesbrough she had her office and her secretary in the Middlesbrough Maternity Hospital and also attended Middlesbrough General Hospital and the North Tees Hospital. Dr Higgs' duties included the neonatal unit at the Maternity Hospital and general paediatrics at the other two hospitals. No criticism has been made of her duties in the neonatal unit and general paediatrics.

Contacts with Other Professionals after Arrival

8.8.14 Child abuse was one of her special interests and she felt that contact with the Social Services Department, which she saw as important, should be through the Child Abuse Consultant. She however made a visit to see Mr Bishop and Mr Walton to introduce herself soon after her arrival in January. Even before that she had met with Mrs Dunn and Mrs Roach, a meeting arranged by Mrs Dunn who was aware of her interest in child abuse. The purpose of the meeting was to discuss co-operation in the child and family health service. Dr Higgs recalled agreeing to a suggestion from Mrs Dunn that it would be helpful if Health Visitors could approach her direct for advice on problem families. In her membership of the JCAC she came in contact with other professionals engaged in this field, such as the Education Department, NSPCC, Nursing Officers, Health Visitors, Probation Service and the Police. Dr Morrell and she arranged with Dr Hensall, the Senior Clinical Medical Officer in the Community Service a regular forum for doctors working with children to meet and discuss an integrated approach to Child Health Services in the South Tees District.

8.8.15 In March she drew together professionals of different disciplines involved in sexual abuse of children into a group they called the Cleveland Sex Abuse Group and they held their first meeting in April. This group did not include the Police.

8.8.16 She did not see child abuse in general and child sexual abuse in particular as a specialist area of paediatrics but as part of general paediatrics and an important factor in child health generally.

Comments on Dr Higgs

8.8.17 Letters about Dr Higgs have been provided to the Inquiry referring to her competence and her approach to her work. Nurses have written:—"We have seen in her the same level of care, compassion and dedication as always shown by Dr Wyatt."...."She cares very deeply about child health problems in Cleveland." ......"My observations have shown her to be a caring person who has great affection for the children.".....'Dr Higgs is an extremely dedicated and a very caring person for her patients and families." The public have written: "please Dr Higgs keep fighting for those children"...."I would like you to know how much I admire and support you in your work" ....."I just want to say keep on doing what you believe is right, keep on trying to stop child abuse"

8.8.18 From the evidence given to the Inquiry it was clear that Dr Higgs had a warm relationship with children many of whom became very fond of her. We watched a video recording of an interview with two children and whatever may be the criticisms of Dr Higgs in other aspects, we were very impressed by her handling of those children.

First Case of Anal Abuse in Cleveland

8.8.19 The first child in whom Dr Higgs saw the sign of anal dilatation in Middlesbrough was the little girl of 6 referred to several times previously. Dr Higgs first examined her in February with the Woman Police Surgeon Dr Longwill. On the 10th March on a routine check-up she saw the sign again and diagnosed further anal abuse. As a result of the police being informed, both Detective Inspector Whitfield and Dr Irvine telephoned her that evening.

8.8.20 According to Dr Higgs, Dr Irvine telephoned to ask her permission to examine the child before the second examination on the 10th March. She told us:—"Since a police surgeon had jointly examined the child with me already, taken specimens and provided a statement to the Police, I did say that I did not consider a further examination appropriate, particularly since the child had begun disclosure work." It was clear to us that the purpose of Dr Irvine's telephone call was to ask to re-examine the child in the light of a diagnosis of reabuse. Dr Higgs said that the question of a second opinion came up at the case conference the following day, but she did not recall a direct request at the case conference either by the Police representative or by Dr Irvine for an examination by him. She understood Dr Irvine to be disagreeing with her that the anal signs could be due to sexual abuse but agreeing with her that the genital bruising could be consistent with sexual abuse. She said that she would not have refused a request for a second opinion in the circumstances. She did not remember Dr Irvine attempting to caution her about her views. We are satisfied from the evidence that the police request on that occasion for a second opinion from Dr Irvine was refused by her.

8.8.21 She seemed both in her written and oral evidence unaware of the feelings of others and their response to this case. It was a feature which also became apparent during other aspects of her evidence.

This child was only the second one in whom Dr Higgs had ever seen anal dilatation. She did however diagnose sexual abuse on each occasion that it appeared on that child in the absence, as she agreed, of full knowledge of the sign's ability to fluctuate, the likelihood of its recurrence or why it should recur. She assumed in that child that on each of the 4 occasions the reason must be further sexual abuse, even in the foster home in June. She did not appear to have stopped to ask whether there could be an alternative explanation and whether reabuse on each occasion was credible.

8.8.22 She did not consider telephoning the Police to ask for a police surgeon to take forensic samples or take them herself, although she diagnosed reabuse on the 10th March and further abuse on the 16th March.

8.8.23 She did not know until much later that this child was suffering from a skin complaint, *lichen planus et atrophicus*, which can produce changes which may be confused with child sexual abuse.

8.8.24 This 6 year old girl was photographed in all 6 times. Asked about this Dr Higgs said:—"Yes , it was over a period of about four and a half months. (She) was a little bit embarassed at times to have it done. .....She was a bit embarassed about the examination but agreed to my request. There was no force or coercion. She certainly was at times embarrassed about having that done."

Early Cases of Anal Abuse

8.8.25 Also during February a child was referred to her suffering from encopresis (soiling). She observed the sign of anal dilatation, but the child was under the care of a child psychiatrist and Dr Higgs took no independent action.

8.8.26 The next case of anal dilatation in which she diagnosed that the children had been sexually abused was the family of three children on the 19th and 20th March. Prior to the arrival of the two year old at hospital with acute constipation,there were no alerting signs of suspicion of sexual abuse, nor were there any such signs in the two siblings. By the end of April she had seen the sign of anal dilatation in children of 4 families, the first family in Newcastle in the summer of 1986, then three families in February and March 1987.

Rise in Numbers in May

8.8.27 The numbers increased dramatically from the beginning of May. She was asked:—

"Do you have any explanation for the substantial rise in numbers from April onwards as compared with before that time?"

"I had seen I think three families before the end of April and at the end of April was reviewing children who at that time were fostered, and signs were found in those children of sexual abuse which led to the examination, not only of the natural children of the foster parents, but also a number of other children that had been associated with that family. Having looked at quite a large number of children over a short period of time, I think I became increasingly confident about the findings."

"Why was your confidence increasing?"

"Well, the earlier children that I had seen in the year had subsequent to examination, made disclosures of abuse which seemed to confirm the view that those findings were valid to be acting on."

Dr Wynne had confirmed her diagnoses in the three children in March and subsequently other diagnoses of hers and of Dr Wyatt.

8.8.28 The children seen by her in Newcastle had been placed in a foster home in Cleveland. In October 1986, Dr Higgs had visited them there and was complimentary about the care the children were receiving. She saw them in outpatient clinic in February 1987 and again on the 30th April. On that occasion in April she found anal signs and diagnosed further sexual abuse. She does not appear to have taken into account the way in which the foster parents cared for the two little girls and that she had examined them twice previously in the foster home with no anxiety.

8.8.29 Although the foster family brought in a large number of children over the first week of May, there were also other children seen in her out-patient clinic and admitted to the ward. This increase in referrals of children from different sources occurring during the same short period in early May did not cause her to stand back and question the diagnosis she arrived at from the signs.

134

8.8.30 She arranged for the abused children to be admitted immediately to hospital and retained for observation. It was for instance a joint decision between her and the social workers that a one parent family should remain on the ward although she agreed in evidence that there appeared to have been no need for them to do so. According to the Second Opinion Panel it had caused unnecessary stress to an already anxious mother. The children in that case were not on place of safety orders. This was also a period of considerable overcrowding in the ward itself.

8.8.31 Throughout May she diagnosed as sexually abused a considerable number of children and the rate of admissions to the Middlesbrough General Hospital rose steeply.

Meeting of the 28th May

8.8.32 She was not a member of the working party chaired by Mrs Richardson and was not involved in any of the discussions over the redrafting of the guidelines. She was invited by Mrs Richardson to attend the meeting on the 28th May and gave the Inquiry her account of it. She told us that she and Mrs Richardson did not discuss the role of the police surgeon before the meeting. She was aware of Dr Irvine's views on the anal findings, but she did not appreciate until the meeting how strong his views were. She did not see that she and Dr Irvine were going to have very much interaction. "It seems crazy with hindsight now, but at the time I did not realise that it (anal dilatation) was going to cause clearly the problem that it has caused, or part of the problem that it has become." "I had not heard from other doctors that there was a great difference of opinion about it and I felt he was, I suppose out on a limb is one way of putting it."

8.8.33 When the meeting moved to discuss medical aspects of child sexual abuse Dr Higgs said:—"This part of the meeting never really got off the ground because Dr Irvine launched into a personal attack on me. His comments were directed towards my reliance on Drs Wynne and Hobbs who he considered to be totally wrong." Dr Irvine said that she:—"kept reinforcing how she had uncovered a massive problem of sexual abuse in Cleveland that in the past had been missed by everyone." Dr Higgs said that she tried to defuse the situation but Dr Irvine did not respond. She recalled:—" One of the police officers commenting that Dr Irvine had been seeing anal dilatation for years and that it was a normal finding." She did not think that she would have used the word 'controversial' about the technique. She would have said:—"That it was a technique that had recently started to be applied to children." She did not see it as controversial. Dr Higgs was prepared to have another meeting to try and resolve the conflict of medical opinion. She told us that she recognised the difficulty into which it put the Police.

8.8.34 After the meeting she went with Mrs Richardson to see Mr Walton and Mr Hughes. At that time Dr Higgs said she knew about Dr Roberts, but did not realise that her views were widely held. She learnt of Dr Paul's views after reading the article written by him and provided to her by Dr Irvine at the meeting.:—"But it seemed to me that it was more an expression of his own opinion rather than an objective presentation of clinical data and analysis of medical literature. I was not aware of Dr Clayden's letter to the Lancet. [see chapter 11] The result was that although I re-examined my own position, it did not lead me to conclude that there existed a sufficiently strong body of contrary opinion for my views on the physical signs of sexual abuse to be considered ill-founded." She discussed with Mrs Richardson on the telephone that evening, the risk to children, the problem that the differences of professional opinion caused, and learnt from Mrs Richardson that a memorandum would be issued. She was concerned about two matters in particular, the protection of the child from further abuse and the fear that the child might be silenced.

Better Facilities

8.8.35 During June the rate of referrals and the numbers of children diagnosed as sexually abused, (both by her and by Dr Wyatt) rose and increasing numbers of children were admitted to Middlesbrough General Hospital. By the middle of June the resources both of Social Services and Middlesbrough General Hospital became exhausted. Her response to the crisis was to seek increased resources. She asked Mr Bishop for more social workers and better facilities. At her request there was a meeting at the Middlesbrough General Hospital on the 20th June to see if more accommodation could be made available at the hospital. She and Dr Wyatt attended to express their strong opposition to the opening of a ward at Hemlington Hospital for children suspected of having been sexually abused.:—"We felt this would be inappropriate because it would make assessment and support even more difficult, both for the professionals and the families."

8.8.36 During July she continued to diagnose cases of sexual abuse. The numbers of children diagnosed as sexually abused were less. By this time both the Second Opinion Panel and the Regional Reference Group were giving second opinions. There was by then enormous public concern and media exposure over the whole subject. Dr Donaldson told us Dr Higgs became frustrated and said to him on a number of occasions in July that the 'needs of the children' were being lost sight of in the present controversy.

8.8.37 From the end of July she was freed from clinical duties in order to concentrate on preparation for the evidence she was giving in numerous court proceedings, and the evidence for the Inquiry. She had not returned to practice by the time the Inquiry completed the evidence in January 1988, but we were told that she would be taking up an appointment in March in Newcastle concentrating upon neonatology.

Checks and Balances

8.8.38 During the period January to July, Dr Higgs was given the opportunity on numerous occasions to consider some of the consequences of the way in which she dealt with cases of child sexual abuse and the effect upon children, parents, Health Services, social workers and Police. She was asked to think about various aspects in different ways, but all spelt caution. These conversations were in three contexts:

1 **Asking her to look at the management of the children and scarcity of resources**

   — Dr Drury asked her on the 14th May to look at priorities even within children. He commented that she refused to discuss priorities and stressed her concern for children. [see page 123]

   — Mr Bishop in early June told both Dr Higgs and Dr Wyatt of the strain on other services of uncovering so much abuse and wondered if there was any way they could reduce the rate of diagnosis to enable Social Services to provide proper services for children and families. The response of the doctors was that this was not professionally acceptable to them and this was a major new development which needed from the other services a suitable initiative.

   — Mr Donaldson on the 18th June, after the confrontation between parents and Dr Wyatt, asked both doctors if they could ease back on admissions for four or five days to reduce the tension and they told him:—"If they came across sexual abuse they had to do something about it and they could not shirk their duty".

   — Mr Urch of the Community Health Council in his conversation with Dr Higgs told her of the effect on the wards and asked her to hold back.

   — Dr Wynne in a telephone conversation during the crisis advised Dr Higgs to exercise some caution.

   — Both the Regional representatives and Professor Forfar, President of the British Paediatric Association, raised words of caution referred below in their discussions with the two doctors.

2 **The acceptability of the diagnosis was questioned both by fellow medical practitioners and by laymen**

   — Dr Irvine questioned the diagnosis first on the 10th March and the 11th March. He made his view very plain on the 28th May and produced an article by Dr Paul in support of his own opinion. The existence of medical dispute over the diagnosis was clear. [see chapter 11]

   — At the same meeting Detective Superintendent White expressed the considerable reservations of the Police and said that they were going to view her diagnoses with caution.

   — Dr Drury on the 14th May told Dr Higgs of his meeting with Detective Superintendent White and asked if if there was some disagreement with the senior police surgeon and she told him that there was and that they had different approaches to diagnosis.

   — On the 1st June Mr Bishop at the lunchtime meeting told us that he cross-examined Dr Higgs on the medical diagnosis and the basis for it. He said Dr Higgs told them:—"I felt confident about the diagnoses that I made."

   — At the meeting with Professor Sir Bernard Tomlinson and Dr Donaldson on the 23rd June there was prolonged discussion on the validity of the diagnoses. Dr Higgs told them that she only made the diagnosis when she could find no other medical explanation for the signs and they appeared to be consistent with child sexual abuse. She said that she had made considerable efforts to feel competent to diagnose this condition and felt few others working in this area were yet at that stage.

- At the end of June Dr Donaldson wrote to both doctors asking them not to examine children for evidence of sexual abuse without parental knowledge and consent.

- Dr Donaldson told Dr Higgs in July that it was particularily important for her to be aware of the wider implications of her clinical work in the present climate.

- The doctors called in by the parents to provide second opinions began to see children in the latter part of June. The views of Dr Roberts were however available in the letter pages of the Lancet and she and other doctors from different parts of England had been questioning the basis of the diagnosis of the Leeds team since the previous November (1986).

3 Ethical Considerations

- South Tees District Health Authority invited three senior consultants to interview the two doctors to try to ensure that the activities of the two doctors concerning the examination of children were carried out in a strictly ethical manner. This interview was held on the 19th June.

- On the 23rd June the Northern Region's representatives considered the question of ethics at their meeting with the two doctors.

- On the 22nd July The Chairman and Secretary of the British Paediatric Association discussed with the two doctors their practice.

These occasions set out above required Dr Higgs to consider her practice and to justify her actions. She continued to have to do so throughout the summer in the Juvenile Court and the High Court and in November in her long evidence to the Inquiry. From her evidence she gave us a clear impression of calm certainty and unshakeable conviction about the correctness of the diagnoses made by her during the entire period of the crisis. She gave little indication of any change of attitude to the approach to and management of this problem. However, allowances have got to be made for the difficulty of a witness who had not finished giving evidence in wardship proceedings and had not yet been involved as a potential defendant in projected civil litigation. Nevertheless, in the light of all that had gone before, we found this to be a matter of some concern.

8.8.39 Dr Higgs in her evidence to the Inquiry expressed her approach to and opinion on a number of matters which are summarised below:

1 Second Opinions

The obtaining of second opinions was one of the matters of criticism by some parents.

Dr Higgs told us that she regularly discussed cases with paediatric colleagues in the area such as Dr Wyatt, Dr Morrell, Dr Oo and Dr McCowan. She and Dr Wyatt made a practice of examining and confirming each others' diagnosis. She also discussed with colleagues at Newcastle as well as Dr Wynne and Dr Hobbs at Leeds. She did not particularily choose Dr Wynne. Dr Hobbs would also have been a choice but was not available on the occasions she needed a second opinion in Leeds:—

"I chose her because both she and Dr Hobbs are doctors that have been dealing with this problem for quite a while. They have, I think, a vast experience and I think are certainly the most experienced paediatricians who have knowledge of this problem. Leeds is close by. As with any other situation in which you ask a second opinion, you ask someone whose opinion you respect that you know has a great deal of knowledge about the subject or about the problem." All the cases referred by her to Dr Wynne were confirmed by Dr Wynne as signs of sexual abuse. Where the signs were reasonably clear she did not think a second opinion entirely necessary. "Since the question of whether or not a child has been sexually abused cannot, except in gross cases, be finally determined by means of a medical examination of the child and since the result of a contrary medical opinion would be to preclude such a full assessment, I was opposed to such second opinions when parents asked me to arrange them."

2 Regional Reference Group

Dr Higgs was involved in some of the examinations arranged through the Northern Regional Health Authority. She was concerned that the doctors involved in giving second opinions were disagreeing with her diagnosis without the clinical responsibility for the continuing care of the child who was her patient. She felt that they were 'blocking' the further assessment of her patient. In her view some of the paediatricians had less experience of child sexual abuse than she had. She did not agree with the suggestions for alternative management of the children examined (not strictly within the Reference Group doctors' responsibility). She clearly found it difficult to accept their opinion when it differed from hers.

3 Working with Police Surgeons

Dr Higgs told the Inquiry that she had carried out joint examinations with police surgeons other than Dr Irvine in Cleveland and encountered no difficulty in doing so. We heard from Dr Ellis Fraser of the good working relations with the women police doctors in Dr Higgs' previous post in Newcastle.

Dr Higgs said she did not forbid police surgeons to examine children in whom she had found signs of sexual abuse. According to her the only police surgeon who approached her to request a second examination was Dr Irvine. From the information available to the Inquiry, that appears to be correct. All the occasions complained about related to Dr Irvine.

She was told in several specific cases by a social worker that there was a request for a second examination by a police surgeon.:—"In each case the social worker expressed the view that he or she did not think a further examination either appropriate or in the child's best interests; I agreed with this view as in each case the request for a further examination was some time after the original examination." We know this not to be correct in the case of the child seen in February and rediagnosed twice in March. In the other cases her influence clearly carried a great deal of weight with social workers, and she gave us the clear impression that she did not want the senior police surgeon to examine these children. This was no doubt for a number of reasons including their open disagreement, his strongly worded objection to her method of diagnosis, and his requirement for a digital examination in order to assess the presence or absence of anal abuse. [see chapter 11]

Relationship with Nursing Staff

8.8.40 She was accustomed to taking part in the training of nursing staff in her previous hospitals and found on her arrival in Middlesbrough that there was no current programme of weekly clinical meetings attended by junior medical and nursing staff. She organised lunchtime meetings, and on occasions showed video recordings on the subject of sexual abuse and provided copies of a booklet which was shown to the Inquiry.

8.8.41 As a result of the large numbers of children admitted to the wards she was not able to prepare the ward staff, (nurses and doctors) to care for children who had been subject to sexual abuse nor to cope with parents who were facing the allegation. She was aware of the difficulties that the ward staff were facing in dealing with these children, but did not have sufficient time herself to counsel those on the ward team with problems and there was no-one close who could.

8.8.42 In her evidence she did not appear to have appreciated sufficiently the importance of the suggestions that Dr Drury was making on the 14th May,[see page 123]that she was a key figure; that she had expertise and should provide leadership; that in particular she should provide local guidelines to help the nurses cope with a new problem. Although she agreed to meet nursing officers, despite several attempts she did not manage to do so; on each occasion she was either late or did not arrive at all. She said:—"It was an extremely busy time." From her evidence we gained the impression that she was unaware of the importance of seeing the nursing officers or of the marked distress and general upset of the nursing staff whom she was not carrying with her. In evidence she recognised that she might not have fully appreciated the pressure under which they were all working. Her response to the pressure on the nurses was to ask for more nursing staff to be provided. She tried to make herself available to nursing staff who wanted to discuss cases and we gained the impression that she felt she had done all she could and that she had been successful in forming a good relationship with the nursing staff.

She was taken aback by the criticisms of some nurses to the Inquiry.

Keeping Medical Records

8.8.43 The rapid processing and unusual admission procedures meant that medical and nursing documentation was not as thorough as it should have been.

8.8.44 She felt the need to keep some sensitive information such as case conference notes and records, photographic slides, and information from parents and from children in her office rather than in the medical notes which were much more accessible. She adopted the same practice in cases of physical and emotional abuse. It was pointed out to her that a significant disclosure made to her by one child in June did not come to light until the court proceedings in August. She believed that she had passed the information on either to the Police or Social Services. But the only record available indicates the reverse. No mention of that information was in the medical notes.

Supervising Discharge Summaries/Informing GPs

8.8.45 She was not aware at the time that discharge summaries were not always going out. This was the responsibility of the junior staff . They were incomplete and on one occasion at least incorrect. General practitioners were not kept as well informed as they might have been, or they needed to be if they were to provide support to the family. She agreed in evidence that she should have kept the general practitioners better informed.

Division of Responsibilities with Social Services Department

8.8.46 In her view it was the responsibility of the doctor to give the diagnosis and the subsequent management was a multi-disciplinary matter, and not within her sphere of responsibility. After a diagnosis of sexual abuse she alerted Social Services. She said:—

"If I had not reached that opinion, that I thought a child was being sexually abused, I would not have notified the Social Services Department." .... "I would say that I thought a child was being sexually abused. I think it is very difficult to say that it definitely has. You cannot say that 100%"

She indicated to the Inquiry that she had nothing to do with the subsequent management of the children who were her patients, but she continued to take an interest in how Social Services did deal with them. In one case history there was a note in July in the social worker's file that Dr Higgs was very angry that the child had gone home as "she feels that he has been sexually abused and how do I stop it happening again?" Dr Higgs according to the note accused the social worker of taking unilateral action. Dr Higgs said in evidence:—

"I certainly was angry because this was a very worrying little boy who I felt had gone back into an unknown environment and certainly was at further risk of sexual abuse because that had not been explored further."

Understanding of Place of Safety Orders

8.8.47 This emphasis on the separation of the child from the parents was for two major reasons, the protection of the child from further abuse and the need to engage in 'disclosure work' interviews with the child. She saw the control of the situation to be by means of place of safety orders, and told us:—"I would say that I think this child has been sexually abused from what I have found. ..... I felt that having raised the question of sexual abuse that the children should be admitted to a neutral environment such as the hospital for further assessment." This step would protect the child from further abuse and also avoid "the possibility of silencing the child".

8.8.48 Dr Higgs agreed that she was adopting a management model used in physical abuse cases. She told us that on most occasions the place of safety orders were obtained without reference to her, but on notifying the Social Services Department she would give her recommendation. She explained that she would say if a parent was so angry or upset she thought the child might be removed from hospital and in those cases she anticipated that a place of safety order would be obtained. She never queried the obtaining of place of safety order with any social worker. We know from the evidence of the Emergency Duty Team that place of safety orders were asked for by both doctors.

8.8.49 On one occasion at the request of a social worker, she went along to describe to the Magistrate the findings and concerns about the children.

8.8.50 Asked about the obtaining of place of safety orders and care orders she said:—"I think because it is such a difficult problem, that the professionals involved do need to have control of the situation, and if parental co-operation was not there, then that would be an appropriate situation."

Approach to Disclosure Work

8.8.51 Both she and Dr Wyatt saw the interviews with the children after medical diagnosis as crucial. They told Dr Donaldson that they regarded disclosure as the 'gold standard'. It clearly to them was the most important element of the fuller assessment. Dr Higgs was considerably reinforced in her confidence in the physical signs by the 'disclosures' she understood were being obtained from children in the early part of the year.

She was asked:—"Would you think it right, as a result of a diagnosis by you, that the people interviewing the children should start from the assumption that it has happened and look to get the child to be able, by facilitation, to disclose what has happened". She replied:—

"I think that is a reasonable starting point, although once work with a child starts, I would expect other professionals would start forming their own views about the children in the families and again, ideally that would be where there should be several meetings of the various professionals involved to look at how things are progressing and to try and make decisions as you go along."

"How do you yourself think that those who would give the broader assessment should act? Should they be relying upon your diagnosis or should they be starting from scratch?"

"I do not give my opinion lightly, and I would want that to be regarded as an important factor. I find it hard to say start from a clean slate, put that to one side."

She expressed an opinion in writing for the court in one case:—

"I think it is unsafe for these children obviously to be released from care until a full assessment, including continuing disclosure work has been undertaken. I think disclosure work in this situation requires a period of separation from the parents."

Her view of the importance of 'disclosure work' led her to see the need to deny or restrict access to the parents.

8.8.52 She took part in a disclosure session which was recorded on video in one case with each of the two elder children. In other cases she had conversations with the children concerned after she had made the diagnosis of sexual abuse and kept separate notes of the conversations.

Attendance at Case Conferences

8.8.53 She took the view that case conferences were very important. At the time she felt it important to attend them and give the information verbally, and explain the relevance of the medical findings. As time went on she found it very difficult to attend particularly when she became very busy. She tried to give a verbal report to someone who would be attending, such as a social worker, but that was not possible if she was prevented at the last moment. In evidence she saw the need to put the information on paper, but would prefer to attend and give it verbally. She gave the impression from her evidence that she did not appreciate the difficulties caused to other professionals by the lack of medical evidence at a case conference on sexual abuse where action has been taken by Social Services, such as a place of safety order based on her medical diagnosis.

Relationships with Parents

8.8.54 She explained to the Inquiry her philosophy and her practice:—

"My practice has been, and I think will continue to be, that I am actually quite straightforward and honest with the parents."...... "I believe that I have always been as supportive and sympathetic as possible in breaking the news of my opinion to the parents concerned, though in view of its gravity I appreciate that no amount of sympathy or support will avoid the inevitable distress."

She explained the difficulties of not informing the parents of her diagnosis since they might jump to other conclusions. If the child was to be admitted to the ward the parents would always have to be given a reason. Where an appropriate alternative to the diagnosis of sexual abuse existed she would give it as the reason for admission, in order to allow more time to deal with the problem. She pointed out the difficulties of the social workers being over-stretched and not being available and the consequential delay in informing the parents. She was asked:—

"Would it not have been perfectly easy for you to have said, in ordinary language, 'This is only a differential diagnosis. It may be suggestive of sexual abuse but, on the other hand, it may be suggestive of other things and we will just have to look into it more thoroughly before we reach any conclusions?"

"That might have been a gentler way of dealing with it but at the time that I raised it with the parents, I had reached my opinion about the likely diagnosis in the children and gave them my honest opinion.

"The problem was that for you it was not a differential diagnosis. It was a conclusive diagnosis."

"If it had been a differential diagnosis, I may not have raised the issue of sexual abuse with them. It was only when I was as clear in my own mind as I could be about the diagnosis that I raised it with the parents."

8.8.55 This practice of immediate communication to the parents of a firm and unequivocal diagnosis created difficulties for both Social Services and the Police, a situation which she appears neither to have understood nor to have reflected upon.

Medical Examination of Siblings

8.8.56 "Another important consideration in the equation was the necessity to examine any siblings of the index child. I took the view that siblings were potentially at risk of abuse and needed to be examined as quickly as possible, preferably before the abuser had a chance to reinforce a threat not to tell." The risk was that if the child or siblings were silenced,:—"information that is quite important to further assessment and working with the children and families or whatever can be seriously hampered and delayed and may never get off the ground if you do not have as much information as you can obtain".

8.8.57 While she believed it important to examine siblings as soon as possible, her busy programme and wide responsibilities resulted in her often arriving late, and working late in the evening after the children's bed-time. This was a cause of understandable complaint by parents.

Relationship with the Police

8.8.58 She told us that her relations with the Police in her previous post in Newcastle were satisfactory and we have no reason to think otherwise.

Statements to the Police

8.8.59 She was accustomed to a police officer visiting her at the hospital and taking a statement. When the pressure of work made her unavailable to police officers who made appointments, she was very slow at responding to their requirement for a written statement. As she said it was not high on her list of priorities. Although Dr Higgs did not consider the provision of reports for legal purposes as her highest priority, in matters concerning children, the preparation of a medical report may be crucial to the police investigation and other court proceedings. We would suggest that if a doctor does not understand the importance of the report for the Police then he or she should leave the recognition and management of child sexual abuse to others. Dr Higgs told us that she had no experience of criminal proceedings nor of giving evidence in a criminal court and did not appear to have put her mind to the difficulties that she had created over non-production of her statements both to the police and to social workers. She recognised the advantages of police involvement at an early stage in view of the need to consider a prosecution, and accepted that she should have established a pattern of working with the Police early on , particularly as regards the provision of statements.

Forensic Evidence

8.8.60 She indicated to the Inquiry that she was prepared to take the forensic samples herself where appropriate. We were told she did so on at least one occasion. There were however at least three children who showed signs of renewed anal dilatation while resident in hospital, in the case of each of whom she considered that the child had been reabused in hospital. She did not notify the Police or suggest taking forensic samples in any of them. She had no explanation for this.

Diagnosis of Sexual Abuse

8.8.61 She answered the suggestion that she might have been guilty of over-zealously seeking out cases of sexual abuse:—

"That is obviously quite untrue. The children in which I thought there were signs of sexual abuse I felt were children that needed to be examined in that way for a variety of reasons, as well as having referrals from other agencies such as social workers. I certainly was not seeking out sexual abuse or screening children for the problem. I looked at children in whom I thought that was appropriate. .....I am not saying that I was not looking for it. I certainly was looking in children where I thought sexual abuse was a differential diagnosis of their presenting problem,... ......if children present to me and I find evidence of sexual abuse then I cannot ignore it. The numbers are very worrying I agree... I think the sign itself is a very important sign. I believe it is a good indicator of sexual abuse and that is the diagnosis that we need to look into very carefully."

She was asked; "Have you ever seen anal dilatation of a significant degree in a child and not diagnosed sexual abuse?''....."No, I do not think so."

8.8.62 It had not been her practice to reach a finding of sexual abuse unless she had been satisfied in her own mind that there was no reasonable alternative explanation for any signs which she had found.

"My knowledge of the possible causes of reflex relaxation and anal dilatation, particularly in conjunction with other physical findings, is that I have only seen data to present sexual abuse as a cause for that. I have certainly seen other opinions, but not any data to substantiate other opinions. You have to keep an open mind about it. As yet there is no data to support another view, so you practise your medicine with what information you have available."

8.8.63 Asked about cases where it might be preferable to take the minimum action possible while the case was being investigated further, she said that "it depended on the firmness of your view as to whether sexual abuse had taken place. Certainly in some cases I would think that would be appropriate." She put a lot of weight on her findings in the overall assessment otherwise she would not have raised the cause for concern. "I considered the assessment not only to be looking for corroborative evidence but also to assess the child in the family to see what sorts of further steps needed to be taken."

"I do not consider that I acted other than correctly in reaching diagnoses of child sexual abuse as I did. As a paediatrician, my duty is to the child who is my patient. Although I recognise the seriousness of expressing a medical opinion which may lead to a child being removed from home to a place of safety, having reached the view that there was no other reasonable explanation of the pattern of physical signs which I found in the light of the history available, it would have been wrong for me not to have arranged the admission to hospital of that child for further assessment."

She was asked:—"Do you recognise that there have been any diagnoses made by you that can properly be described as false positives?"

"I do not think so. The reason I say that is that a number of children I do not think have been fully evaluated and fully assessed and there remains a question mark over those but, with increasing information about the children that I have seen and diagnosed, it strengthens my view about the importance and relevance of the diagnosis that was made."

Her Present View

8.8.64 She was asked about her present view:—"What is your view about whether these particular physical signs are relevant to the finding or diagnosis of child sexual abuse?" She said:

"I still feel that they are very relevant and, if anything, I think the further literature that I have read has strengthened that view rather than made me conclude that it was not a valid view. ......I think I feel very strongly now that there should be a very rapid broadening of the assessment when a doctor does find signs in a child that he or she thinks are consistent with sexual abuse.......rather than there being many medical examinations of children, that the assessment should be much broader and much quicker initially...."

Medical Examination

8.8.65 She was asked how she examined the children, a matter of complaint by some parents. She told us:—

"I think it is important to carry out a full general examination of children."

"Dr Cooper always said that it is important to examine children, if you are looking for signs of sexual abuse, in the knee-elbow position, and she particularily recommended that."

When she parted the buttocks she did not apply undue pressure. She told us:—

"You actually see the sphincter relax and open up. It is quite a distinctive thing that you can see. It is very difficult to miss if it is happening. .... In my view it is an abnormal sign .... What you actually see is the anal orifice relaxing and opening up in front of you, and what you are visualising is the relaxation of the sphincter that normally keeps the anal orifice tightly closed." She said that the child needed to be relaxed and co-operative in order to see the sign.

Fluctuating Signs

8.8.66 There were 10 cases or so on the schedule provided by the paediatricians where she recorded on different dates markedly different degrees of opening of the anal orifice. Asked her explanation for it, she said:—

"I am not sure that I have a clear explanation for a fluctuation in the size of opening. It is something that

I have had to think about quite a lot and discuss and one of the possibilities is that, if the opening is less and then becomes worse, there may have been reabuse. Another explanation may be that possibly the child is in a different state of relaxation. Even if the child is not very co-operative on examination or it is a small child wriggling, you do still see reflex relaxation and anal dilatation, although the degree may be different. It is something that I need to continue to think about and worry about........ My difficulty is that I am not sure how the sign of reflex anal dilatation resolves ...... One of the possibilities is—and I think it is the most worrying one—that when dilatation does become worse, there has been reabuse and that needs to be looked into."

8.8.67 On one occasion the sign was seen by her and Dr Wyatt at 12.00 noon and 4 hours later it was not there. She was asked:—"Does an increase in dilatation always involve the inference that there has been reabuse or only sometimes?"

"It depends really on other circumstances. Certainly that would be something that I would consider: that there has been reabuse. I do not think enough is known about how reflex anal dilatation resolves but one of the causes of increased dilatation could be reabuse. .... It is not known whether it is related to the length or frequency of abuse and I think that is something that would be helpful to try and elicit."

"In considering reabuse of the same child, have you put your mind to whether it was a continuation of the sign of the original abuse or clearly reabuse?"

"It is something I have thought about quite hard and I thought it was reabuse. It is something I discussed with Dr Wynne and in her experience, if the dilatation becomes less over a period of time and disappears, that is the normal way that the sign resolves, but I do not know the absolute answer to that. ...... I do not have another explanation for it as yet."

8.8.68 In the child first seen in February she accepted in evidence the possibility that the sign could on occasions be more obvious than others without there being reabuse. In every case of fluctuation of the sign she diagnosed further anal abuse.

Consent/Photographs

8.8.69 She was criticised by some parents for examining and photographing children without the consent of their parents. She told us that she did not examine or have photographs taken without the consent of parents or the child, if old enough. On two occasions a child objected and she examined later with the child's consent. If the child was brought to hospital by parents or on a place of safety order and examined later it was her practice to infer consent.

Children Who Benefitted

8.8.70 In making comments and expressing criticisms of Dr Higgs' practice, we accept that she did recognise sexual abuse in some children to their considerable benefit. [see page 152].

General Comments

8.8.71 There is plenty of evidence that Dr Higgs is a caring, competent, hard-working doctor, with a particular expertise in the care of children. She was aware that sexual abuse of children occurred and that until recently it had passed largely undetected. She believed that paediatricians had a responsibility to right this wrong and that the majority of her professional colleagues were not engaged in looking for evidence of sexual abuse in their care of children.

8.8.72 The physical signs of buggery highlighted by Dr Wynne and Dr Hobbs in 1986 suggested a way by which the children might be identified. Her confidence in the reliability of the sign of anal dilatation was increased by her taking the prudent step at an early stage of obtaining a second opinion from Dr Wynne, who agreed with her diagnosis on each occasion. She also relied upon the 'disclosures' said to have been obtained from children she had diagnosed. Once she had what she saw as satisfactory confirmation from those sources together with the agreement of some paediatric colleagues, she moved confidently forward.

8.8.73 She and Dr Wyatt gave each other great support in this field. She relied thereafter upon the anal dilatation test as diagnostic rather than raising suspicion and requiring further investigation. It was only rarely that she relied exclusively upon anal dilatation as the only physical sign. There is no doubt however that she relied heavily upon the sign in support of her diagnosis.

8.8.74 Her method of diagnosis, followed also by Dr Wyatt, was to exclude other factors and come to the conclusion there was no cause other than sexual abuse. This elimination of other factors did not allow for the boundaries of present knowledge and the possibility of the unknown. In the current state of knowledge she was unwise to come to a firm conclusion rather than a strong suspicion on physical signs alone. As a recently appointed consultant venturing into a new field, at a time when the work of Hobbs/Wynne had not been widely affirmed her reliance upon the physical signs alone and the anal dilatation test in particular was premature. To give a firm diagnosis of sexual abuse without other grounds of suspicion, no prior allegation or complaint by adult or child and no social family history was to risk the upheaval of the family and the child without the assurance that the diagnosis would be substantiated. She lacked appreciation of the importance of the forensic element of her work, and the need to justify her conclusions at case conferences, care proceedings and/or in the criminal courts.

8.8.75 From the evidence before the Inquiry we are satisfied that she did not examine children for sexual abuse other than on occasions when in her professional judgment there were grounds to do so. Further we have in general no reason to question the accuracy of her clinical observations. It was the certainty of the conclusions drawn from the findings which was open to criticism. She was prepared to reach a conclusion upon sexual abuse and give an unequivocal diagnosis without giving an opportunity for others such as social workers to obtain a wider assesssment of the family. She herself admitted the child to the hospital and then expected the social worker to obtain a place of safety order.

8.8.76 This form of management of the problem was due to a number of factors:

— In her experience of physical abuse a place of safety order was the likely consequence of the medical diagnosis and she treated sexual abuse in the same way. Her training and inclination led her to the view that families overburdened by social difficulties needed control for their future management which she understood was provided by a place of safety order;

— She also saw the need for a place of safety order for the sake of the child to protect from continued abuse, and believed strongly in the element of compulsive behaviour of abusers suggested in some textbooks. She was also much influenced by the concept of 'disclosure work' the results of which she accepted without question and which she saw as the 'gold standard'. If disclosure was to take place it required a period for the child away from the parent, thereby necessitating removal of the child from home and the denial or restriction of access by the parents. This also applied to siblings who might be silenced. She also saw the result of those interviews as confirmation of her diagnoses, rather than an independent assessment.

8.8.77 The diagnosis was her sole responsibility; the admission to the ward of the hospital was at her direction. Other than retaining the child on the ward for a limited period her responsibility except to advise, came to an end. There were however three matters which contributed to the total reliance of Social Services upon her judgment and gave her diagnosis added authority which was disproportionate.

— First she met in Mrs Richardson someone who shared her outlook and believed equally fervently that there was a great deal of undetected sexual abuse and they were finding it. Mrs Richardson had great influence in her capacity of Child Abuse Consultant and in her personality over other social workers at all levels.

— Secondly, Dr Higgs ought to have appreciated the effect upon social workers with their statutory duty to protect the child of such a firm and unequivocal diagnosis of serious sexual abuse. She encouraged them in their approach to her diagnosis and recommended the taking out of place of safety orders and the children remaining isolated from the family. This does not excuse the social workers who had their own independent judgement to exercise, but it is understandable why they did not do so.

— Thirdly the memorandum of Mr Bishop effectively underlined Dr Higgs' view of the management of these cases.

8.8.78 Her enthusiasm and authority placed her in the position of professional leadership. It is easy with hindsight to see how the situation began and developed. What is less easy for us to understand is how Dr Higgs let it go on. It only came to an end when others installed and operated mechanisms which precluded her taking action on her own. Her view that she was discovering abuse which was 'there to be found' never faltered during the months of May and June and while abuse of some children did come to light the numbers admitted got out of control.

8.8.79 The numbers of children diagnosed by her or by Dr Wyatt in outpatient clinics sometimes on a single day never appears to have given her pause for thought.

8.8.80 She showed an inability to understand the point of view of others or appreciate their difficulties during the crisis. There was from time to time a marked lack of communication with other professionals trying to cope with the problems which arose, such as the nurses. Her obvious ability to deal with children and empathy with them did not extend to their parents.

8.8.81 Both she and Dr Wyatt saw opposition as the denial of those who could not recognise and acknowledge the problem which existed. In as Dr Wyatt called it "managing the denial" both of them ignored or overlooked wise advice from others they might have heeded, including Dr Wynne. Their belief in the validity of the conclusions from the physical signs led them into over confidence in the diagnosis.

8.8.82 In many cases the result of her diagnosis caused unnecessary distress to children and their families; in some it caused yet further moves for children already upset and whose lives had been disrupted. This leads us to the reflection that some of those children suffered harm after they were removed from home whatever may or may not have happened to them previously.

8.8.83 She did not recognise the place of priorities and the inadequacy of the resources in Cleveland to meet the crisis. If intervention was to take place on the scale implied by her practice she shared with others a responsibility to ensure that the resources necessary to meet the needs of the children were available. This included not only suitable accommodation, but also skilled social workers and a sufficient reserve of experienced foster parents for their care. She had a responsibility to recognise that situation and to take it into account for the sake of the children she was caring for.

8.8.84 In assessing and criticising her part in the events last year we have in mind that she alone did not create the crisis. She was one among many professionals and shares with others the responsibility for what happened. To place it all upon her is to distort reality, and an unjust over-simplification of the complex issues which arose in Cleveland.

8.9 Dr Wyatt

Background

8.9.1 Dr Wyatt is 38, married with 3 children. He qualified in 1973. Early in his medical training he developed an interest in paediatrics and has considerable experience of children from deprived and disadvantaged backgrounds. He had previously worked in the University Department of Paediatrics in Southampton. His first consultant position in August 1983 was with the South Tees Health Authority based on the Middlesbrough General Hospital. He has had special experience in burns, oncology and neo-natology. He assumed an enormous work-load in South Tees and tackled it with energy, determination and enthusiasm. His duties were such that he took out-patient clinics most days of the week and almost always started his ward rounds in the evening, sometimes late, continuing to the early hours of the morning on occasions.

8.9.2 Before and during the Inquiry many letters have been received indicating the high regard many nurses and parents have for the care and concern he has always displayed in his work with children. The letters speak of his care and compassion, and his constant concern to reassure both parents and children, as well as his expertise. Mr Urch, Secretary to the South Tees Community Health Council told us:

"The commitment to those most in need, the genuine care and ability to involve the child and a very underprivileged mother was laudable and very, very welcome."

Mr Urch went on to say:

"...the people in the community liked him, almost loved him. He worked in a position which was pleasing, particularly to mothers on the poor end of the scale, that you often had people arguing that the doctor had never listened to them like this."

He has emerged as a dedicated, conscientious, extremely hard-working doctor, caring and considerate with children and parents. He started a cystic fibrosis clinic, and one for handicapped children. He described his approach to paediatrics as follows:

"If I have a "particular" paediatric interest it is in the general health of children, rather than in any specialised corner of paediatic medicine. Broadly speaking, rather than simply responding to acute disease, I try to encourage general good health in children and prevent decline in health."

He was acutely aware of the special needs of children in an area so deprived as Middlesbrough, commenting that:

"Middlesbrough was a very demanding environment where the existence for many children was a hard one."

8.9.3 Even at the height of the crisis during May and June the children seen and diagnosed by him to have been sexually abused were only a small number of the children seen by him week by week. He averaged 75 outpatients a week. Everything he did he tackled with enthusiasm and a somewhat single-minded approach. We were also told by Mr Urch, that soon after his arrival Dr Wyatt caused a degree of upset among medical officers working in the community. As far as the Inquiry can ascertain from Mr Urch's evidence, which was at times somewhat opaque as to detail, the objections centred mainly around the way in which Dr Wyatt wished to carry out initiatives in the community led by him but presented in such a way that he did not carry with him doctors already working in the community. Mr Urch further suggested that Dr Wyatt's single minded dedication might have made him unpopular with professionals:

"He would work all hours but this is the thing that would upset other people. It did not endear him to them."

8.9.4 In September 1986 he was the principal author and one of the signatories with Dr Higgs to a widely circulated letter expressed in strong terms deploring the lack of paediatric resources in the area and outlining a plan for a unit like that of Dr Steiner in Newcastle. Such aims were laudable but their presentation was unrealistic and somewhat naive in their disregard for the realities of practical constraint and met with an indignant response from Mr Donaldson.

Previous Experience of Sexual Abuse

8.9.5 Prior to 1987 his knowledge and experience of child abuse was limited and of child sexual abuse minimal. The first case of sexual abuse he saw in Middlesbrough was 2 months or so after his arrival in 1983. The child was a baby of 6 weeks with a vulval tear. He saw the injury as a case of non-accidental injury and was surprised when the Police informed him that the father had admitted to a sudden sexual urge and had sexually abused the child. His perception at that time was that child sexual abuse was a form of non-accidental injury.

Contact With Dr Higgs

8.9.6 Before Dr Higgs' arrival in Middlesbrough he knew of her from Dr Morrell and he was aware of her special interest in social deprivation and child health. On an occasion when she visited the paediatric ward at Middlesbrough in March 1986 he took the opportunity to consult her over two of his patients.

His First View of Anal Dilatation

8.9.7 After Dr Higgs took up her appointment, although he was senior to her, he deferred to her greater experience in child abuse and in particular to her knowledge of child sexual abuse. He first examined a child with her for suspicion of sexual abuse in late March. Dr Higgs called him in and it was the first time that he observed the sign of anal dilatation. The sight of it obviously affected him deeply. In evidence he described what he saw.

"The child is in the knee-elbow position; the buttocks are parted; the anus is apparent and as one watches it the anal canal opens from the outside inwards, and this proceeds for some time, until the proximal end of the anal canal is open and you can look into the rectum."

He started to include the test in examining certain children about whom he had a long term concern.

Dr Wyatt's First Diagnosis of Sexual Abuse

8.9.8 On the 7th April he saw a little girl and as a result of his concern about bruises on her body including a bruise on the mons pubis, he asked to see other children in the family. He examined one of the siblings, did the test, and he saw for the first time in one of his patients the signs of anal dilatation. He concluded that the child had been sexually abused and informed Social Services.

146

New Perception of Problems

8.9.9 Several of his patients about whom he had concern due to their failure to thrive were seen by Dr Higgs during May and diagnosed to have been sexually abused. The diagnosis of sexual abuse in one family was a significant milestone in his growing perception of the problem. There was no association with non-accidental injury. He had known the children for 2 to 3 years and had tried to deal with their problems. They were seen by Dr Higgs who made a diagnosis of sexual abuse and sent them to Dr Wynne at Leeds for another opinion. Both those paediatricians observed anal dilatation and other signs considered to be consistent with anal penetration.

8.9.10 Dr Wyatt told us that the diagnosis in respect of this family caused him great concern because he realised he had been looking after the children for some time and had missed the true diagnosis. He told us that it was a part of the continuous process of self questioning he was going through. At the beginning of May there were two further cases. The health visitor referred to him a family he had been looking after for some time because of failure to thrive. On this occasion on examining the two children he diagnosed sexual abuse and his diagnosis was confirmed by Dr Higgs. The children were subsequently placed with foster parents where Dr Wyatt told us they subsequently thrived. On the same day he saw a child in out-patients for review and examined the child, found signs consistent with sexual abuse which were confirmed by Dr Higgs. He told us:

"I realised I had been trying to help this child and her family for 2 or 3 years without discovering the problem."

These children were all diagnosed during the first 'wave' of admissions in the first week of May.

Growing Confidence of Dr Higgs' Diagnosis

8.9.11 He was aware that Dr Higgs was becoming increasingly convinced that the physical signs of anal dilatation were reliable indicators of possible sexual abuse. Cases of his and of Dr Higgs sent to Dr Wynne at Leeds were confirmed. He saw Dr Wynne as an acknowledged expert in this field. Various 'disclosures' were made by children which were seen by him and Dr Higgs as further confirmation of the physical signs. Dr Wyatt was increasingly impressed with the work of Dr Higgs which she discussed with him from time to time. He said that he was satisfied that her practice was being tested and confirmed from case to case. She was clearly a competent, caring and thoughtful doctor. He was encouraged to trust her abilities and advice in a field new to him.

Relevance of the Signs

8.9.12 He discussed the relevance of the signs with Dr Higgs. She told him that she knew of no other explanation for this sign and that this view was supported by the only properly researched paper by Hobbs and Wynne in October 1986. He formed the view that:

"In the absence of a visible stool in the anal canal, and following reflex relaxation, I know of no other cause to explain this sign other than sexual abuse. I realised that I had been consistently missing obvious signs of sexual abuse, and hence that I had not been offering the children the care they deserved. This was sufficient impetus to me to make me determined to improve my own diagnostic skills and awareness in this area and to try and cure this weakness in my clinical practice as a general paediatrician. I felt that I was not doing my best for the children and that I had better correct that".

Change of Practice

8.9.13 He told Mr Donaldson in June that he had radically changed his clinical practice about a month previously, having seen what Dr Higgs was doing, and that he now thought this was the most important aspect of child health. In July he told Professor Sir Bernard Tomlinson and Dr Donaldson that he had learned from Dr Higgs and:—"admitted that until six months previously he did not know how to recognise the problem."

Increase in Numbers

8.9.14 In his written evidence he dealt with the sudden upsurge of cases in May:

"There are perhaps several factors which gave rise to the increase in May and June of this year in the numbers of children being diagnosed in Cleveland as suffering from sexual abuse. The main reason is that, with the appointment of Dr. Higgs, there was a consultant with the experience, commitment and time to consider and investigate the problem of child sexual abuse thoroughly and to teach others about it. As from May, once I was convinced of the importance of the problem and once I had learned the diagnostic techniques, a second consultant was, in appropriate cases, considering sexual abuse as a differential diagnosis. To some extent, there was also a "backlog" of previously undiagnosed cases and many of our initial cases were children who had previously been referred to the hospital on many occasions and in respect of whom concern was raised at much the same time. Furthermore, once the interest of initially Dr Higgs and then myself about child sexual abuse became known, I suspect that possible cases tended to be referred to us rather than to other consultants and this again increased the numbers which we diagnosed."

Responses to the Crisis

8.9.15 In early June he went with Dr Higgs to call upon Mr Bishop. They refused to see anyone else. Mr Bishop said that Dr Wyatt told him that during this early period of crisis he had spent a proportion of his time seeking "to manage the denial." Presumably this visit to Mr Bishop was part of that activity.

8.9.16 On the 10th June he made an 'urgent' telephone call to Mr Mitchell, standing in for the Unit General Manager of North Tees, saying that he needed more beds in his unit as he was having to send children to other wards and other hospitals. He attempted to restrict visiting on the ward by parents of children admitted as sexually abused to half an hour a day, in his enthusiasm for the principle of 'disclosure work'.

8.9.17 On the 20th June he and Dr Higgs met Mr Donaldson and Mr Bishop to discuss what steps needed to be taken to ease the accommodation situation, and in particular to discuss the proposal to use Hemlington Hospital to accommodate children who had been diagnosed as being sexually abused. Dr Wyatt produced a drawing for an extension to ward 9 which he appeared to think could be built in a few weeks, and expressed disappointment that Mr Donaldson did not appear to consider the idea viable.

Leading Role

8.9.18 Once Dr Wyatt was convinced of the significance of the anal dilatation test he took a leading role in the detection of sexual abuse. His energy and enthusiasm was fuelled by his belief that he had previously failed some of his patients. During June he did not stop to consider the wisdom of admitting large numbers of children over the same period.

Large Numbers

8.9.19 On the 5th /6th June he diagnosed 9 children as sexually abused, with signs of anal interference. The diagnoses were confirmed by Dr Higgs and he admitted them to the ward. It was also on the 5th June that he saw a boy who was at a special school and diagnosed anal abuse, since confirmed by the judgment in the wardship proceedings. After hearing descriptions of the behaviour of boys at the school and diagnosing abuse in other boys at the school, Dr Wyatt offered with another paediatrician to examine all the children. Although this offer was considered unnecessary and indeed somewhat over-enthusiastic at the time and was rejected by the Education Authority, the total number of children involved was not likely to have exceeded 30. Other children had suspicious signs, and the suggestion was not as over-zealous as it first appeared to be, or as was reported in some sections of the media. Nevertheless it was more appropriate to be dealt with by the Education Department than by him.

8.9.20 During June he as well as Dr Higgs diagnosed considerable numbers of children as sexually abused and admitted them to the wards of Middlesbrough General Hospital. He did not seem aware of the effect upon the nurses of the volume of admissions and the problems of coping with the children in hospital. He does not seem to have stopped to consider the wisdom or the need to admit children of families with long-standing problems known to Social Services on an emergency basis to the ward.

18th June

8.9.21 On the morning of the 18th June Dr Wyatt was called out of his Cystic Fibrosis Clinic to Ward 9 where angry parents were causing problems for the nurses on the ward. Dr Wyatt vacated his day unit facilities to provide accommodation for two social workers to talk to the parents. However, this was not sufficient to bring about calm and Dr Wyatt called the Police. This did not appear to have any effect. Dr Wyatt persuaded parents to leave the ward but the children, in many cases encouraged by their parents, continued to be excited and to run around, "making the nurses' job almost impossible." Dr Wyatt remained with the parents and was eventually joined by some policemen. The parents constantly asked him questions about their children, but Dr Wyatt retained professional dignity in the midst of increasing chaos and insisted that he had to protect the confidentiality of his patients. He offered to discuss cases individually away from the group but this did not satisfy the parents. Some parents left to go to the offices of the Evening Gazette and others went with Mr Mitchell.

Checks and Balances

8.9.22 He, like Dr Higgs, was given the opportunity by others to consider the acceptability of his diagnoses and the effect upon other services.

— At the meeting with Mr Bishop in early June he heard Mr Bishop ask for some reduction in the rate of diagnosis.

— He expressed his view to Mr Donaldson who asked for restraint on the 18th June.

— At the meeting with the three senior consultants, referred to in the chapters on South Tees and Dr Higgs, Dr Wyatt played a prominent part according to Dr Williams, who told us that:

"during the whole of the interview it was clear that Dr Wyatt was the dominant of the two paediatricians and it was he who did most of the answering and talking."

8.9.23 It would appear that he was acting here in his role as consultant with the greater seniority and as a professional who was seriously concerned with the health problems of the children of Middlesbrough. In much of the evidence and in the media Dr Higgs has appeared as the more dominant personality, but the dedication, single-minded enthusiasm and determination of Dr Wyatt was a considerable factor at this time and they supported each other in their work in the field of child sexual abuse.

He also attended the meetings with the representatives of Northern Regional Health Authority and met Professor Forfar.

July

8.9.24 He continued his clinical duties during July and was freed from them at the end of the month in order to concentrate on preparing evidence for legal proceedings and for the Inquiry. He also had not returned to practice at the close of the Inquiry, but was due to do so in Middlesbrough General Hospital in March of 1988.

8.9.25 Dr Wyatt in his evidence to the Inquiry expressed his approach to and opinion on a number of matters which are summarised below.

Second Opinions

8.9.26 He frequently involved Dr Higgs in order to share his clinical experience and build an expertise in this relatively new and expanding area of paediatric practice, and saw nothing unusual in discussing cases with a colleague. In his view a second opinion from a doctor who had no responsibility for the patient was not generally in the interests of the child. In one case, he told parents of a child of 3 and a half, that since he and Dr Higgs had given independent opinions, it was not in the interests of the child to have a further second opinion. He took the view that the parents were at liberty to seek an alternative consultant opinion through their general practitioner and he would not have interfered with that. Asked if he was doing his best to discourage it he said:

"I was not doing my best to discourage it; I was doing my best to respond to the denial that was clearly evident..... She was denying that the diagnosis was correct."

He said that it was not a good idea to have a second opinion:

"Because I am trying to look after the child."

When asked why it should not be in the child's interests to establish whether that child should be removed from its mother or father he replied:

"Because I have diagnosed signs consistent with child sex abuse; I have reported that to the Social Services; the child is taken into a place of safety. That was the situation when discussion arose as to a second opinion."

While Dr Wyatt agreed that the medical diagnosis could only be a beginning to a wider investigation, he considered that his clinical findings were not open to question and that the further investigations by other agencies should seek to gather information to support the diagnosis and consider the future management of the child. He was certain of his medical diagnosis. Such confidence was misplaced.

Regional Reference Group

8.9.27 He was very concerned about the imposition of second opinions by the Region in cases where he had made a diagnosis of sexual abuse, although he had agreed, albeit reluctantly, to the scheme. He found difficulty in accepting the working of the Regional Reference Group.

8.9.28 One consultant after giving a second opinion wrote in a letter that he well understood the dilemma Dr Wyatt was in with that child:

"I think it all rests on what size the mesh in the safety net should be. He has a much narrower mesh than I do and I would not like to say which of us is right. He comes over as an extremely caring doctor who is prepared to put his neck on the block for what he sees are the best interests of his patients."

8.9.29 Another consultant was concerned at the pressure put on him throughout the visit to agree with Dr Wyatt and Dr Higgs. He took the view that the findings did not warrant the diagnostic label of sexual abuse. They disagreed with him stating that in their opinion the findings were absolutely certain and typical of anal abuse. He said that Dr Wyatt showed a marked and not entirely rational emotional reaction towards the failure of the consultant to support fully his diagnosis. He felt it might partly due to the stress of the current situation in South Tees, but also to a considerable and disturbing extent to a conviction that no alternative diagnosis or management procedure could be considered.

Disclosure Work and Place of Safety Orders

8.9.30 The need for disclosure work was a powerful factor in his mind for taking a place of safety order. It was necessary for 'disclosure work' to remove the child and retain him in hospital. He also saw 'disclosure work' as the 'gold standard'. His approach to place of safety orders was, like Dr Higgs, conditioned by his experience of physical abuse cases and the need to take steps for the immediate protection of the child concerned. When asked if he would expect a child to be removed upon the medical examination alone in the majority of cases, he replied:

"In the cases that I have experience of, yes. The physical signs that I acted on are consistent, in my view with child sex abuse, and at the moment it is my view that those children need protection."

8.9.31 The evidence given by members of the Emergency Duty Team in the Chapter on Social Services underlines his approach to place of safety orders and his insistence on the obtaining of the orders even late at night and after children had been allowed home. [see 4–94] His general attitude to the problem can be illustrated by a case history where he agreed that he attended the case conference and opposed a plan by social workers for the child concerned to return home and the father to leave. He felt that the proposed protection plan presented opportunities for possible collusion by the mother with the father and:

"the only way forward as far as I could see, was to seek further information in the form of disclosure." In that case he was envisaging 'disclosure work' with a three and a half year old girl starting from the premise that she had been sexually abused. He told us:

"In that particular instance I thought disclosure work was very important".

In the same way as Dr Higgs, he became involved in the subsequent management of the children and had a considerable influence over events in some cases.

Knowledge of the Medical Controversy

8.9.32 He was aware that there was local opposition from Dr Irvine to the diagnosis but he was not aware of the wider dispute. He did not read the Hobbs/Wynne paper until June nor the correspondence in the Lancet. When he had read it he did not consider the letter from Dr Clayden was relevant. He read rather more in preparation for the wardship hearings in which he was to give evidence than he had previously. Until a late stage in the crisis the sum of his knowledge of anal dilatation came from demonstrations by Dr Higgs and his own recent practical experience.

Police

8.9.33 On the whole he does not appear to have been the focus for the police concern over the controversial diagnosis and there was little evidence adduced to the Inquiry by the Police about Dr Wyatt.

He showed photographs to police officers on one occasion to assist as he saw it in the context of further understanding of sexual abuse.

Case Conferences

8.9.34 He agreed that his attendance at case conferences was not good. That was also obvious from case conference notes shown to the Inquiry.

Medical Notes

8.9.35 In one case he examined the child on a Friday evening and did not find time to write up the notes until 2 days later. This was the subject of considerable criticism by the Judge in the wardship proceedings. While he probably regarded the notes he was making in other cases as sufficient for his own use in managing his patients it is unfortunate that he did not take steps to inform himself of the purpose to which they would be put and the crucial part they might play in court proceedings.

Photographs

8.9.36 He had photographs taken as an accurate record for the purpose of court proceedings such as care proceedings and as part of the medical notes. He also considered that they would form a useful library for teaching purposes.

Telling the Parents

8.9.37 Dr Wyatt told us in evidence:

"I regard it as a very serious matter to suggest that a paediatrician should not give to the parent his honest opinion, once he is sure of it, as to the nature of the child's problem. I think it is deceitful and potentially destructive of the relationship between consultant and parent, which ought to be based on trust and a common interest in the welfare of the child, to be less than open and honest with the parent on the subject of the child's condition. I would find it very difficult to carry on trying to help both parent and child, which I would hope to do one way or another in all cases including cases of child sexual abuse, if I were not honest with the parent about the nature of the problem. It would have been to act in a manner which was foreign to me not to discuss with parents my diagnosis of child sexual abuse as soon as I was sure of it."

"I think it has an effect on me and it can be very upsetting for everybody, but I still feel that there is an obligation professionally for me to account myself to the parent who is responsible for the child."

8.9.38 It seems clear from the evidence that his diagnosis based on the clinical signs was given to the parents as soon as he had completed examination of the child in clear and unequivocal terms and before any discussion with social workers or further investigations were carried out. In the context of child sexual abuse this practice was unwise.

Siblings

8.9.39 Dr Wyatt, like Dr Higgs, followed the practice of bringing in the siblings of a child diagnosed as being sexually abused. This practice was carried out with particular regard for the protection of the children, lest they be silenced or threatened. However little thought was given to the effect of having large numbers of healthy children on the ward.

Medical Examination

8.9.40 He did not examine the ano-genital region routinely and did not raise immediate cause for concern if there was in his view no evidence or no strong evidence of sexual abuse. He generally examined the genitalia where there was an abnormal anus. Following the practice of other paediatricians, he did not carry out a digital examination.

8.9.41 He considered physical signs to be very important.:—" There is no other explanation that I know for the physical signs of reflex anal dilatation. (It) is really consistent only with child sexual abuse on the present state of knowledge. There is a real possibility that in future other causes may be found for reflex anal dilatation....... I feel no less persuaded by the validity of the physical signs in association with child sexual abuse. I accept that there may be other causes demonstrated in the future. I know of no others at the moment."

8.9.42 He disagreed with Professor Kolvin that signs were rarely unequivocally diagnostic.

"When I see those physical signs, as I have in these children, I am reasonably certain—not certain; I am reasonably convinced that there has been child sex abuse."

He was asked if he regarded it as unsafe to make a diagnosis of child sexual abuse on the physical findings alone until it became clear that reflex anal dilatation is associated only with child sexual abuse. He replied:

"I do not agree with that approach. I accept that a working diagnosis, an opinion by a consultant, does not imply certainty, but I cannot, in dealing with individual children, ignore the responsibility that I have to each of them."

8.9.43 He did not pass on any reservation to social workers because as a consultant paediatrician he had to take responsibility for his opinion. He had acted in almost all cases of anal dilatation. He saw the purpose of the wider assessment for management of the child.

He was asked:—"It is not for diagnosis, is it?"

"Not at the moment, because we have not got evidence that there is a wide differential diagnosis on the physical signs."

He thought that the fluctuating signs of dilatation depended on whether the child was relaxed.

He felt there were instances:—"where I have not acted where I could have acted."

The Future

8.9.44 At the time that he gave evidence to the Inquiry he was both convinced and committed to his approach to the problem and felt that he could not ignore his responsibility to the children.

Children Who Benefited

8.9.45 In making comments and in criticisms of Dr Wyatt as with Dr Higgs, we do not overlook that his diagnosis was correct in respect of some children and his intervention to the benefit of the child concerned. In one case ("Parental Anger" Page 30) in his judgement the Judge said there was:

"so much evidence to support the finding that these children had been sexually abused" that it was not necessary to "debate" the respective merits or the views of Dr Wyatt supported by Dr Higgs and Dr Steiner on the one hand and Dr Clarke and Dr Paul on the other, who from slides and photographs of the genitalia and documents in the case came to the conclusion that there was no medical evidence of sexual assault on either child."

The Judge went on to say that:

"Dr Wyatt and Dr Higgs may well consider it unfortunate that in one instance in which whatever their merits from a medical point of view their conclusions were proved to be correct, they did not receive the same publicity as was given to them when they were judged to be wrong...it must not be forgotten that it was due to the initiative of Dr Higgs that the sordid and unhappy history of these children was brought to light."

Comments

8.9.46 Dr Wyatt is a dedicated doctor totally and single-mindedly committed to the care of his patients. The arrival of Dr Higgs at the beginning of 1987 opened his eyes to the problem of child sexual abuse and its place in the differential diagnosis of children with medical problems. He felt genuine and strongly that he had been failing some of his patients and resolved, with all the considerable enthusiasm he displayed towards his work, to modify his practice. He was not inhibited by his lack of experience. In the same way as Dr Higgs he eliminated other possible causes, made a diagnosis of sexual abuse and did not allow for the present limited state of knowledge. He accepted the sign of anal dilatation with enthusiasm and acted upon it on almost every occasion when it was present.

8.9.47 Once convinced of the validity of the diagnosis he took a leading role in the detection of children considered by him as having been sexually abused, and in their admission to hospital. In the space of three months he admitted over 43 children on a diagnosis of sexual abuse. This he arranged without any thought for the consequences, the strain upon resources, human, physical and financial. His belief that extensions to wards could be built very quickly was an example of lack of forethought and commonsense. He became emotionally involved in and committed to his diagnosis in respect of the children under his care.

8.9.48 He did not see the need for a full social work assessment before making a firm diagnosis of sexual abuse.

8.9.49 He shared with Dr Higgs the beliefs in the need for the place of safety order, the removal of the children from home and the restriction or denial of access to parents in the cause of 'disclosure work.'

8.9.50 The volume of admissions did not give him any cause to reconsider his practice. He was deaf to words of caution or appeals for restraint. The pressure of the work had a marked effect upon his approach to parents which was commented upon by some parents as very different from his previous caring attitude to them. There can be no doubt that during May, June and the early part of July both doctors were grossly overworked.

8.9.51 Dr Wyatt did not make any independent inquiries or read any medical literature on the subject until a late stage in the crisis.

8.9.52 Many of the comments made about Dr Higgs at pages 143–145 apply equally to him. He, too, shares a responsibility for the crisis. But as with Dr Higgs it would an unjust over-simplication to place the whole burden of the crisis upon the shoulders of Dr Higgs and him. There were many other contributing factors to the crisis.

8.10 Junior Medical Staff

8.10.1 The Inquiry heard evidence from Dr Alison Steele, Registrar in the Paediatric Department of Middlesbrough General Hospital. She described the work of the Department and we gained an impression of how busy it was—Dr Steele told us that she worked on call every second night, and averaged 104 hours a week.

8.10.2 Dr Steele described the effect on the unit of a bronchitis epidemic at Christmas 1986, when admissions were averaging 100 a week. In addition the antiquated buildings had to be evacuated when asbestos was found in the roof.

8.10.3 The situation at the height of the crisis once again imposed gruelling workloads on medical and nursing staff, which the inadequate facilities made even more difficult. Dr Steele said that a number of the children who had been diagnosed as being sexually abused also had behaviour problems, and their language and behaviour caused offence to a number of other patients and parents.

8.10.4 Dr Steele gave us a valuable picture of the way in which physical and human resources were stretched during the crisis.

8.11 Child Psychiatric and Psychological Services in Cleveland

Child Psychiatrists

8.11.1 The Department of Child and Adolescent Psychiatry is a hospital based service at North Tees and it was the practice at the time of the crisis only to accept referrals through medical channels or through the Courts. Referrals were not accepted directly from Mrs Bacon, the Clinical Psychologist employed by North Tees District. It had been necessary for her to obtain the general practitioner's consent or referral by the school medical officer or police surgeon.

8.11.2 The techniques used by Dr Chisholm did not include family group therapy and he expressed himself unhappy with some of the approaches and techniques used in disclosure work. He believed that the psychiatrist ought to have a therapeutic rather than a diagnostic role in cases of child sexual abuse. Dr Wignarajah was concerned about the separation of children who were suspected to have been subject to sexual abuse from their parents. He expressed particular concern about one boy who was moved to three separate sets of foster parents. With this difference in attitude, it seems likely that the Department of Child and Adolescent Psychiatry was not in a position to offer Mrs Bacon the kind of professional support she was in need of during the crisis.

8.11.3 This failure of support during the crisis is now recognised and we are told that the Psychiatrists and Clinical Psychologist are meeting from time to time and have come to an understanding about referrals in the future on the basis that the general practitioner is to be informed of each referral. Nonetheless, from our impressions of the evidence to the Inquiry we formed the view that there was a considerable difference of approach between psychiatrists and psychologists; these differences remain to be resolved. We were told that paediatricians elected to refer several children to the child psychiatrist in Darlington.

Mrs Heather Bacon

8.11.4 Mrs Heather Bacon was appointed a Principal Grade Psychologist (child and family) by the North Tees District Health Authority in 1985. She came to North Tees from Bradford where she had worked for 5 years as a member of a psychiatric multi-disciplinary team. She developed an interest in child abuse and had attended various courses on work with sexually abused children as well as a training workshop at Great Ormond Street Hospital for Sick Children.

8.11.5 In North Tees she was based in a community setting with the bulk of her referrals from primary health care, from health visitors, general practitioners and social workers. She received some referrals from paediatricians, particularily Dr Oo. She saw herself as clinically autonomous in her practice and largely independent. The majority of her time was spent in clinical work, usually with families sometimes with individual children of all ages. She normally held regular clinics at health centres and worked at Social Services family premises. In the area of child abuse she worked closely with members of the local social work team.

She made various attempts to forge close links with the Child Psychiatric Services in the area but they appear to have foundered over difficulties such as referral arrangements and differences of view about the general approach and style of working.

8.11.6 Both Mrs Bacon and the members of the North Tees Social Work Team were committed to a model of intervention based on family therapy techniques. All had received some training in this method of approach. Mrs Bacon described the primary aim as:

"to break the taboo of secrecy, to help adult perpetrators towards taking responsibility, to assess the stance of the mother, and begin to identify areas of family disfunction. The aim for work with an individual child is to establish a trusting and honest relationship with the child when the child may be able to share his experience so that his understanding of what has happened can be established leading to helping with this."

She had a strong commitment to help individual children through the use of professional skill and experience. She saw all her work in terms of the therapeutic value it had for the child and the family.

8.11.7 The expectations of the Health Authority in making her appointment were not made clear to us. The lack of clarity on the part of her employers about her role and the difficulties with which she was faced in trying to establish sensible working arrangements with colleagues seemed to us to leave Mrs Bacon not only independent as she chose to describe it, but also isolated and unsupported in the complex work she undertook.

8.11.8 During 1987 she found herself taking part in interviews with children diagnosed as having been sexually abused. She had previously had referred to her only children with problems which required treatment. In one case, which she said was the most difficult she had ever had to deal with, she was presented with a medical diagnosis of sexual abuse on three children which she had no reason to doubt. She was considerably criticised during the Inquiry for her style of interview of the two elder children which was based on the assumption that they had been abused and probably by their father. These interviews persisted over several weeks and caused distress to the children and their parents. Mrs Bacon agreed in evidence to the Inquiry that if the presumption of abuse made from the original medical diagnosis was called into question then the application of the interview techniques used to secure a disclosure from the children and acceptance that the parent was an abuser was inappropriate.

8.11.9 Her emphasis on the importance to be attached to the achievement of what she saw as therapeutic goals clouded her perception of the role of the clinical psychologist in the process of evaluating the likelihood of abuse having taken place. There was a failure to separate the evaluative phase in work with a child and his family from the therapeutic phase. While expressing no criticism of family therapy, the experience in this and other cases before the Inquiry leads us to the view that practitioners should be cautious about the use of family therapy techniques in the evaluative phase of a child sexual abuse referral. [see chapter 12]

8.11.10. The criticisms of Mrs Bacon related to this one case. The Inquiry was able to see from video-recordings of interviews that she has a kindly, sensitive approach to children. Other witnesses paid tribute to the high qualities which they perceived in her professional work.

8.12 Community Child Health Service in Cleveland

8.12.1 A team of doctors, nurses and health visitors are employed by the South Tees District Health Authority who are separate from the hospital services and who work in the community in child health.

8.12.2 The Inquiry heard evidence from the Rev Dr Ian Guy who is a Registered general practitioner and non-stipendiary priest. He was employed by South Tees Health Authority as a Senior Clinical Medical Officer in the community child health service until 31st August 1987.

8.12.3 Dr Guy's work included counselling of sexually abused children and teenagers who had sexually abused other children. He had no direct involvement with specific cases which had come before the Inquiry but gave evidence about the procedures followed by community medical and nursing staff and the part that the Health Authority has played in the Joint Child Abuse Committee.

Role of Medical Staff Based in the Community

8.12.4 Dr Guy told us that community child health doctors may come across abused children during their routine examinations of school children and in the course of their work in child health clinics. On occasions teachers, community nurses and social workers may discuss children about whom they are concerned with the community doctors informally.

8.12.5 Community doctors followed the 1984 ARC guidelines, until they were changed in July 1987. He told us the 1984 guidelines advised community doctors to refer all cases of child abuse to the family doctor, but in practice doctors often found it more practicable to make a direct referral to a consultant paediatrician. He said that they would normally discuss the case with the consultant by telephone first.

The District Health Authority's Involvement with the Joint Child Abuse Committee

8.12.6 Dr Guy told us that he was a member of JCAC along with two other representatives from the authority, Mrs Roach, and Mrs Dunn. Two consultants working in South Tees are also members, Mr P Brackenbury, Consultant in Accident and Emergency and Dr Higgs.

8.12.7 He told us that the two Nursing Officers play an important role in contributing to the work of the JCAC. This was partly the result of their being Chairman of the Langbaurgh and Middlesbrough sub-groups of the JCAC. They are the main link between Health Authority and other agencies in the day to day operation of procedural guidelines produced by the committee.

Liaison between Community and Hospital Services

8.12.8 Dr Guy said that the two Nursing Officers act as channels for the exchange of information about abused children between hospital and community nurses. All nursing staff, community and hospital, are obliged to inform the Nursing Officers about abused children using procedures set out in the ARC 1984 guildlines. Also the Nursing Officers monitor the records of children who attend the Accident and Emergency Departments in order to check patterns of attendance which might indicate child abuse.

8.12.9 We were told in evidence that there was some resentment among the community doctors at attempts by Dr Wyatt to work in the community. This is referred to in 8.9.3.

8.13 General Practitioners

Background

8.13.1 General practitioners play a key role in the National Health Service. They are responsible for the primary care of the members of the community. Not only do they possess detailed knowledge of their patients and their families, their background and the environment in which they live and work, but they also act as a link between them and other parts of the Health Service.

8.13.2 The planning and administration of general medical services is the responsibility of Family Practitioner Committees of which (we were told) there are 90 in England. They are independent of the Regional Health Authority.

Role of Family Doctor

8.13.3 The family doctor is not expected to give treatment involving special skills or experience outside the scope of his training and practice, and if a 'second opinion' is required from a specialist in a particular field, he will refer his patient elsewhere and often to hospital.

8.13.4 We heard evidence from Dr John Canning who was secretary of the Cleveland Local Medical Committee. We also heard evidence from a local general practitioner as to his involvement in a particular case who told us of some of the dilemmas faced by general practitioners.

Cleveland Local Medical Committee

8.13.5 The Local Medical Committee is separate from the Family Practitioner Committee but encompasses the same area, that is the County of Cleveland. The committee consists of 28 elected general practitioners from nine constituencies in Cleveland, three representative of senior hospital medical staff, one for each of the Health Districts in Cleveland, one family medical health practitioner, the district medical officer for the three districts, and there is provision for the co-option of seven other medical practitioners.

The 28 general practitioners are elected from a total of approximately 265 general practitioners in Cleveland.

On the 26 May 1987 the committee were asked to nominate suitable members to sit on the Joint Child Abuse Committee.

Complaints by General Practitioners

8.13.6 Dr Canning said that he had not had any formal complaints from doctors. Doctors to whom he had spoken informally made one repeated complaint, the lack of communication between the consultants and general practitioners. In some cases there was no communication at all. General practitioners had not been informed when the diagnosis of child sexual abuse had been made. Parents were arriving at surgeries and doctors did not know what was going on, which made life difficult when dealing with parents. Dr Canning explained that general practitioners would have normally expected a prompt letter from hospital consultants and then follow-up letters, depending on what had been found.

8.13.7 He told us of specific examples related to his Committee by members which exemplified this lack of communication between the general practitioners and the hospital and the difficulties experienced by general practitioners during 1987. A general practitioner was criticised by parents for referring a child patient to hospital for a medical condition, who was subsequently diagnosed as sexually abused. The general practitioner was unaware that this had happened since he had had no communication from the hospital. One general practitioner had difficulty in seeing his patient in hospital because the child was the subject of a place of safety order. The ward sister had initially refused permission. That ward sister had previously allowed a general practitioner to see another child patient and had been told that this should not have happened.

8.13.8 Dr Canning also told us that if the consultant had contact with the general practitioner immediately after the first physical examination had been carried out, the general practitioner might have been able to offer useful background information about the parents. The general practitioners' primary concern is that of the child but as family doctors they are concerned with the whole family. He said that it was usual for a general practitioner to see a child on a more regular basis than they would an adult. A child was usually seen by a general practitioner with the mother. This enabled the general practitioner to gain a fair degree of knowledge of the family and their background. This knowledge should have been drawn upon by consultants in making a diagnosis of sexual abuse.

Mr Stuart Bell MP

8.13.9 The subject of child abuse was referred to at the July meeting of the Local Medical Committee in connection with the statement from Mr Stuart Bell MP to the effect that no parent should take his/her child to Middlesbrough General Hospital without first seeking legal advice. Dr Canning raised this after discussion with the Chairman of the Committee and had, with his consent, written to Mr Bell expressing concern that the Committee had not been consulted about a matter relating to the provision of care by general practitioners.

GPs' Role in Child Sexual Abuse

8.13.10 Dr Canning told us that there was some confusion amongst general practitioners as to the best way to deal with problems arising from cases of child sexual abuse. Accordingly he felt it would be appropriate to have guidelines for dealing with such cases. He suggested that the Joint Child Abuse Committee should have provided guidelines and these should have been considered by the Local Medical Committee.

Case Conferences

8.13.11 Dr Canning told us that there is a general problem for general practitioners of attendance at case conferences, in that they are usually organised at very short notice, and general practitioners may have previous commitments. He referred us to an article in the British Medical Journal, supporting the view that the general practitioner is in a good position to know the family circumstances in addition to processing essential medical knowledge and therefore it is crucial to the efficient operation of case conferences that general practitioners attend. If the general practitioner is unable to attend the information might be relayed either through the Chairman or through a member of the primary health care team who is able to attend, usually the health visitor.

Experience of a Local General Practitioner

8.13.12 In private session we heard evidence from a general practitioner to a Cleveland family whose children were diagnosed as sexually abused. This doctor referred a child suffering from acute constipation to Dr Higgs at Middlesbrough General Hospital. The child was diagnosed as having been sexually abused. The next day the two siblings were taken to the hospital and also diagnosed as sexually abused.

8.13.13 This doctor told us that this was his first case of child sexual abuse and he outlined to the Inquiry some of the difficulties he encountered as a general practitioner in dealing with it. He told us that he was both a friend of the family and their general practitioner.

When a place of safety order was obtained for the child he knew nothing of what it meant. He told us "I was not at all certain during the duration of the place of safety order what part I as a general practitioner could play. The children were obviously ostensibly in the care of Social Services, but it was my understanding that the parents still maintained parental rights and what these rights were I was not sure, and I was certainly very unclear to my own role as a general practitioner and how to perform that role". He felt that there should be information circulated to general practitioners explaining the implications of place of safety orders, who has custody or control, what are the parents rights and what powers a general practitioner has with such a child specifically in connection with obtaining a second opinion.

8.13.14 After the diagnosis of sexual abuse was made by a consultant paediatrician, the parents wished to obtain an independent second opinion, whilst their child was in hospital. He told us that Dr Higgs opposed a second opinion and this created a difficult situation.

8.13.15 He felt there were no clear guidelines on the clinical care of his patients whilst subject to the place of safety order. He felt that there should be guidelines particularily to advise as to the right of a general practitioner either at the request of the parents or of his own volition to seek a second opinion. It was not clear to him what right he or the parents had to refer the child to a different consultant and from whom permission was required. He pointed out that this situation is more complicated when the clinical problem such as chronic constipation is related to the initial diagnosis of anal sexual abuse. Further if a second opinion is requested does the first consultant have:—"the right or privilege to intercept a doctor invited for further opinion", particularly when the child is in the care of social services through a place of safety order or care order. He wanted to know if a second opinion was obtained who should be responsible for ongoing patient management and suggested it should be the general practitioner.

8.13.16 The doctor told us that the Social Services' action caused considerable distress to the parents and as their general practitioner he had to deal with this. He said he was not kept informed by Social Services of their strategy and he considered that where Social Services are dealing with a family in circumstances such that they might reasonably anticipate that stress will be caused to that family they ought to keep the general practitioner fully informed as to what is going on so that he can provide support and provide appropriate management to the extended family. He told us "Even a general practitioner who has little contact with a particular family and deals with them remotely is seen as a central figure by the parents. In a situation where there is a conflict of interest or where, for example, Social Services are dealing with the parents in one way, the paediatricians in another, the general practitioner becomes a kind of port of call to go to for help. I think in this instance I felt that the general practitioner's role was being seriously threatened by not knowing which way to head, not knowing how to organise this. Certainly what I have not said is that I have had to provide a great deal of general counselling and support for these parents. It struck me half way through that because of the way the whole case was developing, if either parent required any psychological back-up, the usual avenues were closed. It was not appropriate for them to see social services, partly because they were already involved in a different capacity. They were afraid if they saw a psychiatrist or clinical psychologist or someone else in the National Health Service their records would not be safe and I believe this is so, because it is possible for records to go from one Department to the other in a hospital. So actually providing counselling and support service for parents becomes the primary service of the general practitioner who gets stuck in this "cogmesh" of who is doing what". He considered there should be an early appointment of a key social worker who should establish immediate liaison with the family practitioner who should be informed as soon as possible of thedates of case conferences.

8.13.17 He also told us that where a parent is suspected of having been the instigator of sexual abuse it becomes difficult for him/her to be referred for support counselling to Social Services or clinical psychology services as these agencies are invariably involved in work with the child. He feels there should be guidelines as to whether a section of these services is able to provide independent support.

8.13.18 He had no contact with two of the children of the family involved because they were placed in separate foster homes, outside his catchment area. He felt that in the interests of the feelings of the children and also because of the importance of continuity of care, wherever possible children should be brought by Social Services to see their regular doctor.

Role of the General Practitioner in the Crisis

8.13.19 Overall, we were presented with very little evidence as to the role of local general practitioners in the crisis, with the exception of those general practitioners who were also police surgeons. There can be no doubt from the evidence presented that a diagnosis of sexual abuse will have repercussions for the general practitioners looking after a family where it is diagnosed. General practitioners would benefit from some guidance in cases of suspected sexual abuse. We endorse Dr Canning's suggestion that general practitioners should have more training in sexual abuse. We also stress the importance of the role of general practitioner at case conferences.

CHAPTER 9

Reactions to the Crisis

9.1 Community Health Council

9.1.1 Mr Urch, the Secretary to the South Tees Community Health Council gave evidence on its behalf and told us that Community Health Councils were established under the National Health Service (Reorganisation) Act 1973, Section 1, to be the 'consumer watchdog' of the District Health Authorities (DHAs), and to represent the views and interests of the consumers of the DHA's services—ie hospital inpatients and outpatients. The Community Health Council is funded through the Regional Health Authority to whom it reports annually.

Early Community Health Council Interest in Paediatric Services in Cleveland

9.1.2 He said that the Community Health Council had for some years been concerned that a paediatric speciality should be established to match the needs of the children in the District. Expectation was high when Dr Wyatt took up post in 1983:

"The first appointment of Dr Wyatt was welcomed and everybody was excited; a young, new consultant, committed to care in the community was with us; it was the beginning of a better era. It soon became obvious to many people that the manner in which he managed his practice, his work, offended many other disciplines. Our hopes were tempered by the attitude and atmosphere engendered about him, by the way he was going about his work."

9.1.3 Mr Urch told the Inquiry that although Dr Wyatt was well regarded by the community, other professionals found him difficult to work with, having more time for his patients than for his fellow professionals. This led to the inclusion in the 1986 Community Health Council report of a passage which read:

"Multidisciplinary commitment to child health is essential and an integrated service can only be achieved by inter-unit activity and therefore managerial accountability is of paramount importance and requires there to be no artificial distinction between professional and managerial issues".

9.1.4 Mr Urch first came into contact with Dr Higgs on the 2nd October 1986, in connection with a particular family who had made a complaint to the Community Health Council.

9.1.5 Mr Urch also described a meeting with Dr Wyatt and Dr Higgs on the 2nd October 1986 concerning the setting up of a paediatric unit in South Tees; during which they made proposals what Mr Urch put forward as "dreams" for a paediatric service in South Tees, dreams which, if fulfilled would have given the doctors "the most wonderful paediatric empire in England".

Meeting of 12 May

9.1.6 At a meeting of the Community Health Council on 12th May 1987 Mr Bishop was questioned about the dramatically increasing numbers of referrals for child abuse. Members of the Community Health Council expressed concern at acute hospital beds being used for children who were suspected of being abused when they were aware of a lot of pressure on those beds already.

9.1.7 Mr Urch then got in touch Mr Donaldson, to voice the Community Health Council's concerns:

"what was the legitimate role of the clinician, was it being properly pursued, and what were we to do with all the fit young children galloping around in acute hospital wards in which the desperately ill children would have had to be nursed if admitted."

Mr Donaldson told Mr Urch that once a place of safety order had been taken out it was Social Services' responsibility to look after the children.

9.1.8 Mr Urch then got in touch with Mr Bishop who confirmed that as long as consultants diagnosed child sexual abuse then Social Services would have to act.

9.1.9 After speaking to the Clerk of the Justices, Mr Cooke, Mr Urch spoke to a senior police officer, a conversation which Mr Urch found to be helpful, as he was told that:

"pending further instructions from the Chief Constable to divisional commanders, unsubstantiated evidence from Dr Higgs will not be a matter for investigation."

9.1.10 Following this conversation, Mr Urch felt it was time to "have another go" at Social Services, this time through Mr Walton. He got exactly the same response as he had from Mr Bishop. Mr Urch was very vague in his evidence about dates, but these conversations were taking place in late May—early June.

9.1.11 Mr Urch told of seeing in June "5,6, or 7 families" who visited his office following a diagnosis of sexual abuse of children and of receiving telephone calls from about "20 others" whom he referred to the Parents Support Group. He was getting messages that something was very wrong on the paediatric wards in Middlesbrough General Hospital:

"we had members everwhere within the District and they came back with --- well, it was beginning to be the talk of the district. No matter where you went or who you met, people had something to say about it, they had an opinion".

The concern was beginning to focus on the activities of the two paediatricians, and Mr Urch told us he was becoming increasingly aware of the difficulties in managing the activities of the two doctors:

"the Community Health Council's major concern was that here were two paediatricians creating a situation which nobody felt they could do anything about stopping; everyone accepted that there was chaos. Certainly there were fit and well children running around that hospital ward. It was like hellzapoppin' land."

9.1.12 In mid June Mr Urch telephoned Dr Higgs.Mr Urch said his discussion lasted about an hour. He saw himself under extreme pressure at this time but denied that he had become caught up in the strength of feeling of parents. In describing the meeting he said:

"I suppose (I was).....basic and aggressive. It is true, I was, but it was to produce some response from this cool, calm, unruffled lady; some response to show that she cared, that she understood......"

and later he said:

"We must have talked for an hour and I was I suppose rude....but she never lost her temper, she did not raise her voice. There was nothing I could do to persuade her that what she claimed, which was basically that having made a diagnosis I have no alternative. What flows from there is not my concern. She expressed concern that there was no support for the parents or for the extended family".

Mr Urch said he was becoming increasingly upset at having to deal with so many members of the public, and in questioning Dr Higgs' methods of working, particularly in looking for signs of sexual abuse in children who were presenting with unrelated conditions, he called her all the names he could lay his hands to. The fact that she remained calm incensed Mr Urch further. When asked as to what he hoped to achieve from the meeting he replied:

"If we split that long conversation into two halves, the first half was an endeavour for her to respond to the needs of everybody involved and to recognise that it was her initial response which was causing this situation with which nobody in the council could cope and could she not co-operate with them in bringing it to an end."

9.1.13 In summing up the purpose of the Community Health Council's submission to the Inquiry, Mr Urch said that the Community Health Council felt there was now a need:

"to re-establish the credibility of paediatrics, where it is most needed, and that is not going to be easy."

Comments

9.1.15 In his evidence Mr Urch was emotional and somewhat intemperate. He was upset and he told the Inquiry how he and others felt about the situation. He was in a difficult position, without any direct managerial role, but feeling that he had to do something. His experience reflected the anxieties, bewilderment and helplessness of lay and professional people over the situation on the hospital wards at Middlesbrough General Hospital.

9.2 **Reaction by or on Behalf of Parents**

9.2.1 The growing distress, anger and frustration of the parents found expression on the weekend of the 18th June. The parents of three children diagnosed early in 1987 as having been sexually abused, described trying unsuccessfully for 2-3 months to obtain information about any national support group for parents but on the 16th June they made contact with the organisation Parents Against Injustice (PAIN). The Director, Mrs Susan Amphlett, later visited Cleveland and subsequently gave evidence to the Inquiry.

9.2.2 A day later, the 17th June, the Rev Michael Wright met another couple whose three children had been diagnosed four days earlier as sexually abused. As a result of some intense activity in the days that immediately followed, he helped to form the Cleveland Parents Support Group representing 33 families. Both couples mentioned above joined this group.

The Reverend Michael Wright

9.2.3 The Rev Michael Wright is employed by the Cleveland Social Services and manages a unit caring for elderly, mentally infirm people. He is also part-time priest-in-charge of St Cuthbert's Church of England parish in Middlesbrough. He told the Inquiry that when he was first contacted he visited the home of the couple concerned and then went to Mr John Urch. Mr Urch told him of a small group of parents who were meeting together and later the Rev Michael Wright was invited to attend a meeting of this group. At this meeting on 18th June, comprising 8 couples, it was decided to publicise the existence of the group and a letter was prepared for publication which the Rev Michael Wright first read to his Bishop and then took to the Director of Social Services. The letter was published in the local Evening Gazette and as a result the Cleveland Parents Support Group was formed and the Rev Michael Wright became its coordinator.

9.2.4 The Rev Michael Wright also gave evidence of a later meeting, on the 22nd June, with Mr Bishop at which he outlined to Mr Bishop the main points of concern of the parents. He said that at this meeting Mr Bishop suggested he was treating all the parents as being innocent but he explained this was not the case and he could identify at least three categories of parents as:—

    1 A small group who accepted that their children had been abused and were grateful for the diagnosis.

    2 A small group who did not believe the diagnosis and could not work out where, when or by whom the abuse had taken place, but nevertheless accepted that the doctors must be correct in their diagnosis. These parents became suspicious of their family, friends and neighbours.

    3 The largest group were those who believed there had been a misdiagnosis, there being nothing to substantiate the medical diagnosis.

9.2.5 It was suggested to the Rev Michael Wright by Mr Bishop that there was a fourth category, those whose children had been abused and the parents did not accept it and he was asked to what extent he had looked critically at this point. He replied "I have not tried in depth to look critically. I have not seen that as my role", and when it was put to him that he would be unwise to disregard the possibility that some of the parents in the group were abusers, he said "Yes. That is something that has weighed with me".

9.2.6 The media were already involved and giving some publicity to events in Cleveland but their interest increased with the publication of the Rev Michael Wright's letter and he appeared on Tyne Tees Television on 19th June. As a result a number of parents got in touch with him. This was also the date that Mr Stuart Bell MP became aware of what was happening, visited Middlesbrough General Hospital and saw parents there (see 9.3).

9.2.7 On Sunday 21st June, the Rev Michael Wright invited to his home Mr Stuart Bell MP and Mr Tim Devlin MP where they met the parents of three families.

9.2.8 By Monday 22nd June, media interest was intense and national and the parents of one family recorded "Went to the.....Hotel—was on Tyne Tees Television. Didn't say anything. All in the national news now, papers as well". At a meeting of the Parents Support Group that evening national and local press were present but were excluded by the Rev Michael Wright. An article prepared by the Rev Michael Wright was published in the Guardian newspaper on 29th June.

Mrs Amphlett

9.2.9 On the 12th July, Mrs Amphlett, Director of Parents Against Injustice (PAIN) visited Cleveland and met some of the parents. Mrs Amphlett in her evidence to the Inquiry stressed several points arising from her meetings; she said:

— There was not sufficient emphasis on the child within the family setting. Until child abuse was established the emphasis on our society should be on the protection and preservation of family life.

— There was a need to protect children from misguided and over-zealous professionals.

— A full assessment of the family was necessary, and a more major parental involvement in investigation and decision-making.

— It was important that parents attend case conferences and have the opportunity to correct misconceptions.

9.2.10 She felt that:—"Social workers need to retain a degree of independence from the medical opinion. They are the people who are able to go into the home environment, which in our opinion is the most valuable information about that child. If the diagnosis is not conclusive, and until they learn to accept, or to realise, that their opinion is equally as important as the medical opinion, then there are going to be many more children taken into care who should not be taken into care."

9.2.11 Further points she made were:

— In many cases parents were not interviewed by social workers.

— Parents had more confidence in police interviewing than in social workers.

— Parents did not want to subject their children to unnecessary medical examinations but it was important that they should have the right to a second medical opinion.

— Parents felt powerless with social workers. She suggested the provision of a code of practice.

— Many solicitors were inexperienced in child care law and parents consequently did not get the best advice.

— The effect of A v. Liverpool City Council was very unjust to parents. [see chapter 16]

— To remove children on the test of the balance of probabilities was an infringement of civil liberties.

Mrs Amphlett also asked the Inquiry to hear evidence from an expert from the United States, Dr Underwager, whose evidence is referred to in chapter 12 Listening to the Child.

9.2.12 The Cleveland Parents Support Group acted as a central guiding agency for the parents who were members of it. The Rev Michael Wright acted as public spokesman and met and discussed the issues being raised by parents with a number of people. He also arranged special church services and pastoral and spiritual care and counselling for parents. Through the Group parents were encouraged to formulate their complaints and to direct them to the appropriate person or body and to prepare a standard form of submission to the Inquiry. At the time of the sitting of the Inquiry the Group remained in being, meeting at least once a week.

9.3 Members of Parliament

9.3.1 The Inquiry received representations from Members of Parliament from constitutencies both within the Cleveland area and outside. We heard from three local MPs, Mr Stuart Bell [Middlesbrough], Mr Frank Cook [Stockton North], and Mr Tim Devlin [Stockton South]. We also heard from Mrs Claire Short MP and Mr Alan Meale M.P. and from Mrs Virginia Bottomley MP.

9.3.2 We were grateful to have received their contributions and took them into account in our deliberations. We have also taken into account the discussions in the House of Commons on the 29th June, 9th July and 16th July as recorded in Hansard.

Mr Frank Cook MP

9.3.3 Mr Cook brought to our attention a case which underlined the problems of adults abused as children who disclose the abuse at a later stage. He provided the Inquiry with a considerable volume of evidence on the subject and in particular he emphasised the need, as he saw it, for agencies to operate in a statutorily determined and properly defined framework.

9.3.3 Mr Cook referred to two Early Day Motions he had put down in the House of Commons seeking a Royal Commission to receive evidence to establish the true scale of child sexual abuse and to make proposals designed specifically to ensure such a framework. He had some knowledge of the Scottish system for child protection and he thought it would be helpful for the Inquiry to look at this system.

9.3.4 He told the Inquiry of a discussion he and Dr Mowlem, Member for Redcar, had with the Minister of State for Health, and of a meeting he had with Mr Bell, MP in which he expressed his disagreement with some of the public statements made by Mr Bell because he felt they were not contributing to the real issue of child welfare. He said that he and some of his colleagues had disassociated themselves from Mr Bell's public statements.

Mr Tim Devlin MP

9.3.6 The Inquiry received written representations from Mr Devlin about some of his constituents. There were 5 families of 10 children. All of them with the exception of one family were considered in the Inquiry. The one exception arose from access proceedings. Two families were also on Mr Bell's list to the Minister. One family was never the subject of a place of safety order or any court proceedings but had been connected with a foster family. The other family was dealt with in wardship and the children dewarded and sent home at the end of July.

9.3.7 Mr Devlin also asked us to consider 4 general matters of concern:—

— late night investigations of children

— the automatic removal of children with little investigation

— the diagnoses of Dr Higgs and Dr Wyatt

— the rise in referrals of child sexual abuse to the Social Services Department.

All these matters we have covered elsewhere in the report.

Mr Stuart Bell MP

9.3.8 Mr Bell is the Member for Middlesbrough and is also a member of the Bar. He was instrumental in bringing the problems in Cleveland to the notice of the House of Commons and played a significant role in the later stages of the crisis. He provided to the Minister a detailed 'dossier' and gave evidence to the Inquiry.

Sequence of Events

9.3.9 In his evidence he told the Inquiry that he first became aware of complaints from parents whose children had been diagnosed as having been sexually abused and had been detained in Middlesbrough General Hospital on Friday the 19th June. That evening he visited the hospital where he saw some parents and also Mr Ian Donaldson, the District manager of the South Tees Health Authority. He returned to the hospital on the Saturday and in all he made 6 visits to the hospital. Over that weekend and during the next week Mr Bell spoke several times with Mr Bishop, mainly on the telephone. He attended a meeting of more parents at the home of the Rev Michael Wright, had discussions with other Members of Parliament whose constituencies lay in Cleveland, with the Leader of the County Council, the General Manager of Northern Region Health Authority and local councillors. He interviewed and took "case notes" from parents and he became caught up in the media attention being devoted to Cleveland.

9.3.10 In the course of his activities in Cleveland Mr Bell decided that the events in the County needed to to be brought to the attention of the House of Commons. He attempted to raise it in an Adjournment Debate on the Queen's Speech, and on the 26th June he discussed the situation with the Minister of State for Health, Mr Tony Newton, MP.

9.3.11 It was also on the 26th June, according to Mr Bell, that as a result of seeing Dr Irvine on television during the early evening, he first became aware of the diagnostic technique of Dr Higgs and that it was being challenged by the senior police surgeon, and that, according to Dr Irvine, the Police had not been able to play a full part in the investigation of child sexual abuse.

9.3.12 Later that evening Tyne Tees TV carried the story of the magistrates who refused a care order on three children alleged to have been sexually abused. In the light of that decision Mr Bell called for the suspension of the two doctors. He also publicly praised Dr Irvine and called him a 'man of courage'.

9.3.13 Even later that evening Mr Bell appeared on a television programme 'Nightline' in which Mr Bishop also took part.

9.3.14 Over the weekend Mr Bell got in touch with and went to see Dr Irvine at his home.

9.3.15 In anticipation of making a speech in the House of Commons on the 29th June Mr Bell spoke to Mr Ord, the Deputy Chief Constable, and asked about child sexual abuse guidelines and to confirm that they had not been operative. He telephoned him again and read to him the Private Notice Question he was about to lay in the House of Commons. According to Mr Bell, Mr Ord said that he could not deny any of the facts in his statement. Mr Ord did however suggest to him that the statement was a 'bit strong'.

9.3.16 On the same day in the House of Commons, Mr Bell put down the Private Notice Question asking the Minister of State for Health if he would make a statement on the recent increase in the number of cases of alleged child abuse in Cleveland Health Authority area and the Minister responded by saying that investigations were in hand and a report awaited from the Regional Health Authority. On the 6th July Mr Bell gave a press conference.

9.3.17 On the 7th July Mr Bell delivered a file containing his observations and the results of his inquiries to the Minister and on the 9th July Mr Newton announced in a statement to the House of Commons the setting up of a Statutory Inquiry.

9.3.18 After the start of the Inquiry Mr Bell continued to take a close interest in the problems; continued to make a number of public statements; and attended the Inquiry hearings on many occasions.

Mr Bell's Reactions to the Crisis

9.3.19 Mr Bell became deeply involved in the crisis and the perspective of the parents. He told the Inquiry that his anxiety was to "break the circuit" which he saw as a diagnosis being made of alleged child sex abuse, followed by a social worker applying for a place of safety order and a JP who signed such an order in his own home. He suggested to Mr Bishop that he should seek a court injunction to achieve a "breaking of the circuit". Early in his involvement he saw the Social Services Department as taking a neutral position and that Mr Bishop was being very helpful. He felt that he was working with 'someone who was obviously at the sharp end'. He was informed by Mr Bishop of the proposal to have a Second Opinion Panel and discussed it with Northern Regional Health Authority. Initially he gave public support to it.

9.3.20 Mr Bell was most concerned at the statement by Dr Irvine on television that the Police had been excluded from investigations into sexual abuse. During the course of the 'Nightline' programme, later that evening he changed his mind mind about Mr Bishop and the Social Services Department and no longer saw them as neutral. During the programme Mr Bishop was asked whether he supported the paediatrician or the police surgeon. According to Mr Bell, Mr Bishop made it clear that he had no alternative but to act on the diagnosis of the the paediatrician although he said he would take into account the view of the police surgeon. Mr Bell said:—"Now I understood that in fact he was partisan." He felt that the Social Services Department was a willing and co-operative participant in the events.

9.3.21 Mr Bell was also concerned to find that the three children referred to at 9.3.12 had not been reunited with their parents after the magistrates court hearing; but that the Cleveland County Council had made them wards of court. He said he was astonished to learn that Dr Wynne was to be one of the members of the second opinion panel and made a public statement thereafter about his lack of confidence in the panel.

Mr Bell's Allegations and Criticisms

9.3.22 From his statements in the House of Commons, his documentary submissions and his evidence to the Inquiry, the major allegations and complaints put forward by Mr Bell may be summarised as follows:—

1. There had been a fundamental attack on family life, disrupting the lives of people, including children, because:—

   (a) children attending hospital for routine injuries and ailments were subjected to examination for sexual abuse;

   (b) that children were being found to have been sexually abused solely upon a diagnosis of reflex anal dilatation;

(c) such diagnosis was followed automatically by a place of safety order obtained from a magistrate at home;

(d) in dealing with these matters social workers adopted an attitude of insensitivity and a lack of compassion towards the parents;

2. That Cleveland Social Services were 'empire building', thereby acquiring substantial additional financial resources and that in the course of this exercise:—

(a) elected representatives at a Joint Child Abuse Consultative Committee meeting on the 16th June were misinformed;

(b) at a meeting of the Social Services Committee on the 25th June the request for additional resouces was supported by Councillors who were not entitled to the detailed information they appeared to have;

3. That the Police were obstructed

(a) because Dr Higgs and Mrs Richardson colluded and conspired to keep the Police out of allegations of sexual abuse

(b) by the refusal of the doctors and the social workers to allow the police surgeons to examine the children.

9.3.22 Response to this Criticism

1. Fundamental Attack on Family Life

1.(a). The Inquiry was satisfied from the evidence presented that there was no routine screening for sexual abuse. In each instance of a child attending hospital for 'routine injuries and ailments' there were grounds in the professional judgment of the examining consultant for the investigation of the child for the possibility of sexual abuse.

1.(b). Although in the opinion of the Inquiry the sign of 'reflex anal dilatation' was given undue weight by the paediatricians' medical examinations in only 18 cases out of 121 cases was it the sole physical sign and in no case was it the sole ground for the diagnosis.

1.(c). Prior to the 29th May there was no automatic application for a place of safety order, although they were applied for in many cases. After the 29th May in the Middlesbrough area, Eston and Langbaurgh, as a result of the memorandum signed by Mr Bishop, that appears to be correct. As far as the Inquiry has been able to ascertain all applications for place of safety orders were granted. Mr Bell suggested that the Council was 'very cleverly' seeking orders from large numbers of magistrates so that none realised the extent of what was going on. The place of safety orders have been looked at by the Inquiry and we are entirely satisfied that this allegation is unfounded.

1.(d). Mr Bell suggested in his evidence that:—"Social Services have a lack of compassion, a lack of sensitivity, a lack of respect for people and a lack of a sense of social justice." For the reasons set out in the chapter on Social Services, and in our conclusions, we do not consider that this is either an accurate or fair description of the approach of the Department or of individual social workers. Certainly in some instances there was a lack of sensitivity. Social workers were however, during the two months of the crisis, unsure of their ground; overwhelmed by the weight of numbers; and primarily motivated by a concern to protect children from further abuse. We are satisfied that they acted with the highest motives, and that any inappropriate actions taken were the result of a directive which required them to seek a place of safety order in each case, a practice which we criticise elsewhere.

The Inquiry is satisfied that there was disruption of the lives of people, with serious consequences to the children and families concerned but we are equally satisfied that at no time was there an intention to make a fundamental attack on family life. That was not the attitude, and from the evidence of numerous Cleveland social workers we are satisfied never would be the attitude, of any of them nor of the Social Services Department.

2. Empire Building

2.(a). From the evidence supplied to the Inquiry, at the meeting of the Joint Child Abuse Consultative Committee on the 16th June there were officers present from the Police and Social Services Department among others. They were Mr Walton, Mrs Richardson, and Superintendent Saunders. Mr Bishop, the Director of Social Services was not present. Neither the Police nor the Social Service representatives chose to expose to the elected members the differences between them. On the contrary the elected members were told without any dissent from any other agency of the good co-ordination between the County Council and outside agencies. We are satisfied that the elected members were not informed of the true situation; but we are also satisfied that in the light of the Police part in this lack of candour it was no more than the misguided efforts of officers of two agencies not to 'wash their dirty linen in public'.

2.(b). Mr Bell told the Inquiry that he did not believe that Mr Bishop had anything to do with the provision of detailed information to Councillors who according to Mr Bell were not entitled to that information. It seemed to be his view that only the Chairman of the Social Services Committee was entitled to receive detailed information and briefing from the Director and senior staff. Other than to place these matters on record we have no information about this allegation which is outside our terms of reference.

From the evidence presented to us we were satisfied that Mr Bishop appeared to be acting in good faith in asking for additional resources to meet the enormous increase in referrals. Beyond that opinion, again it was our view that this allegation was outside our terms of reference.

3 Collusion and Conspiracy

3(a) These allegations have been made by Mr Bell throughout the Inquiry and in evidence of the 71st day he said:—" My view of this is that there was a clear conspiracy on behalf of people in this area to the detriment of my constituents. The conspiracy had at its heart Dr Marietta Higgs, Dr Wyatt, Mrs Sue Richardson and I believe that Mr Bishop either knew fully what was going on or he did not know fully but he should take full responsibility for the actions of his Department."

We carefully considered the positions of Dr Higgs, Dr Wyatt and Mrs Richardson and these allegations. There is no evidence whatsoever of any collusion or conspiracy between them. The most that can be said is that with others in the area they shared a common view that there was a great deal of undetected sexual abuse and that they had to 'manage the denial' of others in bringing such abuse to light and in trying to meet the needs of abused children in Cleveland. The correctness of that shared perception and the subsequent management is dealt with exhaustively in other parts of this report.

3(b) We are satisfied that in some cases there was a refusal to allow the police surgeon to examine the child concerned.

In the first case in March, we can see no justification by Dr Higgs for that refusal. The social workers in that case were placed in some difficulty by her approach. In subsequent cases there was a marked reluctance even before the issue of the memorandum on the 29th May, by Dr Higgs and some social workers to permit the senior police surgeon to examine children. That reluctance was largely connected with the outspoken and vehement opposition displayed by Dr Irvine to Dr Higgs' methods of diagnosis and it contributed to the worsening state of relations between the social workers and the Police. The Police accepted the view of Dr Irvine. They acknowledged in evidence that the chances of finding forensic evidence were slim and that their request for the senior police surgeon to examine was largely to counter the diagnosis of the paediatrician. From March onwards therefore the medical diagnosis was unlikely to be free from dispute and the medical evidence unlikely to satisfy a criminal court. However this did not preclude or prevent other inquiries and from the police files we are satisfied that the Police did investigate these allegations, although there were delays in certain cases. Their inability to detect an offender or to proceed was related to the absence of other evidence rather than the dispute over medical evidence. We do not consider that the police were in fact obstructed in their investigations.

Mr Bell's Case File

9.3.23 The Inquiry was provided with the information sent to the Minister on the 6th July by Mr Bell. Mr Bell provided case notes to the Minister in respect of a total of 19 children from 11 families. In addition other children were referred to during the Inquiry in whom Mr Bell had taken a particular interest, another 3 or 4 families which we considered. The families concerned fell into 3 groups.

1. Families where the police surgeon, Dr Irvine was asked by the Police to carry out a second examination and according to the Police and Dr Irvine, that request was refused. There were 8 children from 5 families. We have not investigated all in depth but it was broadly true that the senior police surgeon, at the request of the Police, asked to examine these children and was refused. In the case of one family, the Police insisted and he did eventually examine the children. No other police surgeon asked to examine children and no other police surgeon was refused.

2. The second group presented to the Minister related to complaints by families over the removal of their children and their subsequent management. There were 11 children from 6 families. 9 of them became wards of court. All 9 wards returned home to their parents by order of the court. We had evidence of children being removed from home on a diagnosis of sexual abuse and subsequently returned home, after the medical diagnosis either was not accepted by the court or was not pursued by the Social Services Department. We did not have 'overwhelming evidence of children going in for routine complaints and being diagnosed for alleged sexual abuse.'

Not all the information given to Mr Bell by parents was accurate and some was misleading. In the case of one child, the father's complaint of injustice was countered by the child's clear description of the abuse she said he did to her. The mother of that child did not know of the father's previous convictions and sentences for sexual offences on children. One family complained of a routine visit to hospital for the treatment of threadworms, when the medical notes set out inappropriate sexual behaviour at school and the referral to hospital by the senior medical officer. A three year old girl was referred to hospital with a vaginal discharge and found on forensic tests to have contracted gonorrhoea. A relative was found to be the culprit. Another child was found to have anal warts and the second opinion panel having taken the advice of a venereologist, formed the opinion that they had not been sexually transmitted; but it was a reasonable ground for suspicion.

3. The third group were two families where action had been taken by the Social Services Department on cases previously known to them. One of them was in wardship where there was concern about the risk of future harm to children. We received some evidence from senior social workers in respect of both families.

In the first case the criticisms of Mr Bell were acknowledged and accepted by the Social Services Department. In the second family from subsequent wardship proceedings the actions of the Social Services Department in removing the child appear to have been justified.

Critics of Mr Bell

9.3.24 Mr Bell told us that he received overwhelming support from his constituents and from many people throughout the country who wrote to him in support. On the other hand, some were critical of what he said and did.

Nurses

9.3.25 Nurses were upset and complained to the Inquiry that:

(a) he failed to inform the sister that he was present on the ward on more than one occasion;

(b) he was asked to leave the ward on one occasion and did not; this was denied by Mr Bell;

(c) he was conducting 'constituency surgeries' in a room off the ward in cramped conditions and thereby monopolising the only room available for parents to sit and smoke. We saw the facilities at the hospital and they are in any event out of date, cramped and inadequate for the needs of the children and families who use them. We could visualise the difficulties that must have been created by his visits.

(d) he wrote a letter which appeared to give parents permission to visit their child, who was in the interim care of the Council, on the ward.

(e) Mr Bell said on television that he would not allow his 5 year old son to go to Middlesbrough General Hospital for treatment. We formed the view that this was an emotional response to the crisis. [For a graph showing admissions to Middlesbrough General Hospital see appendix D]

Northern Regional Health Authority

9.3.26 In a prepared statement the Northern Regional Health Authority accused him of inflaming public opinion and jeopardising the proper functioning of the paediatric services in Cleveland.

Social Services Department

9.3.27 The Social Services Department found his attitude unhelpful. He clearly became emotionally involved in the cases of individual families and took their side. Social workers were upset that:

(a) He did not visit the Social Services Department's offices.

(b) He did not listen to their point of view or try to understand their difficulties. They were his constituents too.

(c). He did not check with the Social Services Department the accuracy of any facts given to him by parents.

Mr Bell said that there was no reason to speak to Mr Bishop or other social workers since from the beginning of July the matter was in the public arena.

(d). He never made available to Mr Bishop or the County Council the 'dossier' that he provided to the Minister and to the Inquiry.

(e). In their opinion Mr Bell undermined attempts at a solution to the problem by calling into question the integrity of the Second Opinion Panel. He suggested in his evidence that the only second opinion Mr Bishop wanted was Dr Wynne. We are satisfied from the evidence before us that having initiated the request for a second opinion process, from 15th June Mr Bishop was engaged both with the District Health Authority and subsequently with the Regional Health Authority in finding a suitable formula for providing second opinions and that he had nothing whatever to do with the choice of Dr Wynne as one of the consultants chosen to work in pairs.

(f). He criticised Social Services for not working within agreed guidelines. His remarks were made in ignorance of the fact that there were no formally agreed guidelines for dealing with sexual abuse until July 1987. [see chapter 3].

Mr Bell's Influence on Public Opinion

9.3.28 He talked of social workers 'looking for child fodder'. He compared the situation in Cleveland with the Salem witch trials. These were some of the intemperate and inflammatory remarks made on television or to the newspaper reporters which had a part in exacerbating an already very difficult and sensitive situation. The problem needed to be investigated and it was entirely proper in our view that the effect upon children and their families should be widely known and publicised. We share his concern at the removal of children from their homes without a full and careful assessment other than in cases of concern as to physical harm. We recognise the need of a Member of Parliament to represent the interests of his constituents. The crisis however had arrived at a point where commonsense, moderation and some degree of calm was needed.

9.3.29 Mr Bell agreed in his evidence that there was no further evidence upon which he was relying to support allegations such as conspiracy and collusion, and empire building. He recognised that he did not have all the facts and argued that his role was to put forward the complaints of his constituents and the perceptions of the parents.

9.3.30 We were sad that he was unable, in the light of the further knowledge that he clearly had, to withdraw or modify allegations which could not be substantiated.

9.4 The Media

Introduction

9.4.1 The media has played an important role in the Cleveland crisis at all stages. At the end of June 1987 various elements of the media brought the crisis to the attention of the wider public, by means of television, radio and the newspapers, locally and nationally. They presented the issue before the Inquiry sat. They exhaustively covered the public hearings of the Inquiry itself. Some, although not most, newspapers have kept the Cleveland scene in the public eye between the close of the Inquiry and the publication of the report. The role of the media on the Cleveland crisis is not yet complete. They will no doubt comment on the report and thereafter. They have the last word.

9.4.2 Their importance in the recognition of the crisis, the enhancing of some aspects of the problems rather than others, the effect they have had upon those directly involved in Cleveland and upon the wider public has led the Inquiry to venture upon some comments both about their role and their relationship with the Inquiry.

9.4.3 Sexual abuse presents particular problems for everyone and the media, reporters, commentators, editors cannot be immune from their own feelings and prejudices. The Inquiry was reminded to 'be aware of your own biases'. There is the added element of 'voyeurism' spoken of by Dr Cameron, which affects both the public and those who provide the information and the stories to the public. All this leads inevitably and naturally to viewpoints, moral stands, on occasions to campaigns on one side or another.

Before the Inquiry

9.4.4 By the time the media became aware of the Cleveland story there were already local campaigns in being, Mr Bell MP, Dr Irvine, the parents and the Rev Michael Wright. The press of course had a responsibility to cover the story and it was a story which justified and indeed required to be reported.

9.4.5 There were however other campaigns, some local, some national, and Cleveland has been the battlefield in which the viewpoints of national groups and individuals have been fought out. The media has responded to some of these and given prominence to the opinions of various protagonists. Some of these battles have also been fought within the confines of the evidence presented to the Inquiry and to some extent reported by the press.

9.4.6 The effect of the Press generally, was to underline and increase the importance of the story. The media assisted Mr Bell in his efforts to place the crisis in the public domain.

9.4.7 Another factor was almost inevitably an element of selectivity which in time may become distortion. The comprehensive coverage by the media was for many understandable reasons, to some extent one-sided.

9.4.8 There is a danger of the media, even by accurate reporting, assisting in a degree of hysteria among the public, both locally and nationally; for instance was it safe to take a child who needed medical attention to be seen by a paediatrician at Middlesbrough General Hospital, or would the child be removed from the parent with an allegation of sexual abuse. The media then became a factor in the continuance of the crisis.

Difficulties Experienced

9.4.9 Some of the press created difficulties at the Middlesbrough General Hospital for the nurses carrying out their duties in the paediatric wards. The nurses complained that interviews were taking place on or near the wards. At least one journalist employed an extreme subterfuge to obtain information at the hospital, by dressing up as a nurse to gain admission to the wards. We were told that the entrance to ward 9 was constantly blocked making it difficult not only for nurses but also for ambulance, medical and catering staff.

9.4.10 The social workers involved in the crisis found the press attention very difficult to manage and were under considerable pressure. Social workers have a responsibility to protect the privacy of the people they serve; in this instance the children and their families and they were not in a position to respond to press criticism. Mr David Jones, Secretary of the British Association of Social Workers told us:—"a lot of us social workers have considerable sympathy for our colleagues in Cleveland who have been subjected, I think, in many quarters, from the press, and to some extent from Mr Bell, from quite intolerable pressure of constant statements and questioning of their work, even when the courts have looked at matters. And it would make it, I would say, almost impossible for social workers to exercise their judgements consistently in that context. In as far as the local Social Services Department has continued to discharge its responsibilities to people in Middlesbrough and in Cleveland, it owes a lot of credit to those who continue through these very difficult times, not only at the moment, but in our experience, it will now last some years into the future".

9.4.11 Senior officers of the Health Authorities and of the principal agencies found themselves devoting a major amount of time dealing with the press.

9.4.12 At the hearing of one interim care application 17 journalists packed a small court.

At the Inquiry

9.4.12 The Inquiry took a decision not to permit television cameras or photographs during the hearings, but permitted a television and photographic session immediately before the preliminary hearing on the 4th August. There were 74 days of hearing and of those on 8 days evidence were given in private. The evidence was heard in public for all or part of the day with the press present and able to report it. There were only two reasons for part of the hearings being in private :

— to protect the children in circumstances which required details which might identify them.

— to protect the parents who gave evidence and thus not to identify their children.

9.4.13 At the preliminary hearing on the 4th August it was stressed that no-one was on trial and that it would be helpful if the Inquiry could be conducted without sensational headlines or any form of additional emotional pressure on individuals. There was a particular request to preserve as far as possible the anonymity of the children concerned and consequently their parents. Mr Justice Hollis made an order permitting the use in the Inquiry of information in wardship proceedings upon the basis that nothing was done to identify the wards. Further orders were made by other Judges in later wardship proceedings to give the Inquiry the right to consider further cases.

9.4.14 Another area of concern referred to by me at the preliminary hearing was the interviewing or reporting the remarks of those who were likely to be or to have been witnesses at the Inquiry, and I said:—"There is a considerable risk of misunderstanding if witnesses give interviews dealing with matters covered by their evidence and reports of those interviews appear to suggest that different accounts have been given on different occasions."

9.4.15 Both at the preliminary hearing and on subsequent occasions I referred to occasions when in public session there might be reference to matters which it was in no-one's interest to be reported or discussed outside the Inquiry chamber, or which if so reported or discussed would serve only to bring grief to individuals. I repeated a: "plea for sensitivity and that those charged with the responsibility of reporting the proceedings of the Inquiry should at all times exercise great care and circumspection in doing so."

9.4.16 There were particular problems which arose during the Inquiry. It was necessary to refer, sometimes in detail to children, their family histories, schools, and on occasions intimate details of their ano-genital region. Children were naturally not named in public but were referred to by letters of the alphabet. We became aware that the press knew the identity of some of the children.

9.4.17 The members of the press who regularly attended the hearings were thanked both during and at the end of the Inquiry for the responsible way in which they reported the daily evidence. The regular reporters were excellent in their response to the requests not to identify children and the general desire to protect the children concerned from any publicity. In the main, the press scrupulously observed the requests that I made and did not report the lapses from confidentiality which from time to time occurred. Their restraint and forbearance served to expose the occasions when newspapers and television fell below this high standard.

9.4.17 An added complication was the hearings of wardship cases with all the requirements of confidentiality side by side with the Inquiry sometimes dealing with the same child. This presented everyone with difficulties in the conduct of the Inquiry and for the press in their proper task of reporting proceedings held in public. Since some of the wardship cases remained to be heard after the Inquiry concluded its hearing of evidence and submissions at the end of January, to have waited for the conclusion of the wardship cases would however have put back the start of the Inquiry until at least March or April 1988.

Between Inquiry Hearings and Publication of the Report

9.4.18 On the final day of the Inquiry I indicated that:—"it would be unhelpful and might indeed be prejudicial to the Assessors and to myself if interviews with witnesses or comments on the quality of their evidence were to appear in print or on the airwaves before my report is published." I asked the press not to make it more difficult for us. I asked those with an interest in the Inquiry not to go public. I pointed out that they would have the last word and asked that they should not say it before I reported. I said:—"It is my job with the assistance of the Assessors to evaluate the evidence, the documentation and everything that has gone on, and it is the job of no-one else until I have reported."

With a few notable exceptions the witnesses and the press have responded magnificently to the final request of the Inquiry.

General Comments

9.4.19 The powers of this Inquiry as in others were limited to a decision whether to hear evidence in public or in private. There was no power in the Inquiry to regulate in any way the approach of the media to the participants in the Inquiry outside the premises or general coverage of the proceedings.

9.4.20 There was therefore a real need to initiate and preserve good relations with the press; for that, an efficient and likeable press officer was indispensible. We were extremely grateful to John Park for the excellent and agreeable way in which he handled the Chairman, Assessors and members of the media present in Middlesbrough.

9.4.21 In a highly charged Inquiry of great public interest and consequently newsworthy, we do not consider that the Chairman should have any powers to regulate the press. Such a recommendation would be entirely outside the way in which Inquiries are conducted, and on the whole we have seen no reason to support any such curbs upon the provision of information to the public. Requests by the Inquiry would seem to us to be generally more appropriate. During the period of the hearings requests were adequate. But the lack of 'muscle' does, however, lay upon the media generally and editors in particular, the responsibility to observe moderation and have an awareness that the impact of the reporting on television, radio or in the newspapers, can have a disproportionate influence upon those caught up in such a crisis, and may create uncertainty, confusion, and injustice.

9.4.22 Such a responsibility has not been recognised in certain quarters and in this delicate and sensitive field where the welfare of children requires to be remembered, it was from time to time obviously overlooked.

CHAPTER 10

Legal processes in Cleveland

10.1 The legal processes and the courts were not immune from the crisis in Cleveland. The jurisdiction of the courts was invoked in various ways: by application for place of safety orders, for care orders, and in wardship. There was considerable pressure upon the resources of the Juvenile Court only alleviated by recourse to the use of the wardship jurisdiction in the High Court with the result of moving the point of pressure elsewhere.

10.2 The legislation which provides the framework for child protection is considered in chapter 16. In this chapter we look at the effect of the crisis upon the legal services in Cleveland.

Explanation of legal terms

10.3 *A place of safety order* is designed to give emergency protection to a child who is considered to be at risk by a single magistrate who generally makes the order. The application is usually made by a social worker, NSPCC official, or police officer. Neither parent or child is informed in advance and the child upon granting the order maybe taken to a place of safety for up to 28 days. The Local Authority if applicant has less control over the child than under the provisions of an interim care order.

10.4 *A care order* is applied for by a Local Authority who has under the child care legislation the duty to intervene in the normal responsibilities of parenthood in certain circumstances. There is a complex legal framework which sets out the grounds for intervention which include a belief that a child is being ill-treated or neglected or that his/her proper development is impaired and that he/she is not receiving adequate care or control from the parents. If the Local Authority believes one of these grounds to exist it has a duty to bring the matter before the Juvenile Court who will decide if the ground is made out and whether the child is in need of care or control which he/she is unlikely to receive unless an order is made. If both parts are proved the usual orders made are either supervision or an order committing the child to the care of the Local Authority. While the case for hearing is being prepared a child can be kept in the care of the Local Authority for a limited period under an *interim care order.*

10.5 *Wardship* is an application to the High Court based on the ancient parental duties of the State towards its children, its procedure regulated by statute. It was the alternative forum to the Juvenile Court in care proceedings in Cleveland.

Place of safety orders

10.6 The initial route to the Juvenile Court was by way of place of safety orders. Between 1st January and 31st July 1987, 276 place of safety orders were applied for by social workers under the powers granted in s. 28 of the Children and Young persons Act 1969. These place of safety orders were not identified by the grounds upon which they were applied for and it is not possible to say exactly how many were in respect of allegations that the child concerned had been sexually abused. But 125 children between those dates were diagnosed as sexually abused by 4 paediatricians and 91 of them were the subject of such orders. All but one application appears to have been made ex parte, that is to say without the parent present, and none appears to have been refused. Within the total of 276 there was more than one order in respect of the same child.

10.7 The Social Services Department operated a highly interventionist policy in the use of place of safety orders. The effect of their general approach to the use of these orders was accentuated by the memorandum of the 29th May issued by Mr Bishop, directing social workers to apply for them on receiving a diagnosis of child sexual abuse from a paediatrician. Further a trend away from applications for the maximum 28 days to periods not exceeding 7 days as advocated in their manual was not maintained in 1987 and was specifically reversed in early June for reasons set out below. Mr Bishop himself was in favour of a limit of 7 days.

10.8 Before the crisis period of May/June and before the 29th May memorandum a number of place of safety orders in cases of diagnosis of sexual abuse were applied for and granted for 28 days. The reason for the longer order was not so much the need to protect the child as the need perceived by social workers to have sufficient time to engage in 'disclosure work' with the child.

10.9 Of the 276 orders were applied for out of hours by the Emergency Duty Team. The majority of the orders were likely to have been granted during the day. We learnt however that of those 227, 174 were heard by a single magistrate at home, during the hours of court sittings, despite a clear understanding between the Clerk to the Justices and the Social Services Department that social workers would make these applications in the first instance to the full court. We heard of no difficulties encountered in attending court to make such an application. Although the Juvenile Court usually sat 3 mornings a week, in June there was a complement of 72 Juvenile magistrates on the panel and other courts were sitting during the week. We were told that Teesside was one of the busiest areas in the country.

Interim Care Orders

10.10 During early June the numbers of interim care orders applied for dramatically increased. On Monday 8th June there were 45 applications for interim care orders waiting to be heard. This increase in the workload led the Clerk to the Justices, Mr Cooke, to talk to one of the Court Liaison Officers, Mr Morris to discuss the implications for resources and to ask for a meeting with the Director of Social Services. In the evidence to the Inquiry there was some difference of recollection as to what was said between Mr Cooke and Mr Morris. Mr Morris went away with the impression that Mr Cooke was suggesting that Social Services should apply for 28 day orders to ease the strain on the courts, and he then advised the Emergency Duty Team to apply for 28 day orders. This they did for a brief period,and the effect can be seen in figures between the 15th to 17th June when 16 out of 17 applications were for 28 days. However the Middlesbrough Child Resource Centre opened at the end of June; the Second Opinion Panel and the Regional Reference Group began to examine children and the numbers of place of safety orders fell equally dramatically.

10.11 On the 11th June Mr Cooke met Mr Bishop to discuss with him a particular interim application which from his point of view was being most unusually opposed by the parents. They had been denied access to their three children. Mr Cooke tried to suggest to Mr Bishop that Social Services should allow supervised access to the children, but Mr Bishop was advised by the social worker in charge of the case that there should be no access. Over the next few days according to Mr Cooke applications for interim care orders under s.28(6)[Children and Young Persons Act 1969]:—"were coming thick and fast and with little notice and taking precedence as emergency applications (which they were) over other cases that had been in the lists weeks and even months earlier, much to the chagrin of the parties and their representatives in those cases."

Level of Concern

10.12 The level of concern in the Juvenile Court was sufficient for the Chairman of the Juvenile Panel, Mr Davies, to pay Mr Bishop a visit with Mr Cooke on the 15th June, in order to make Mr Bishop aware according to Mr Cooke of:—"the disruptive effect that these applications were having on the work of the Juvenile Courts." By this time the case referred to above had already occupied two full days on an interim application, with a Saturday set aside for it, and including hotly disputed medical evidence .

10.13 Mr Davies said that there were three matters of special concern to magistrates receiving the applications.

1 The effect on the courts of applications which were increasing in volume and complexity. There was great concern about the backlog of cases and the delay to the regular work of the courts.

2 Prior to 1987 it was not the practice of the Social Services Department to refuse access to parents on the obtaining of a place of safety order and this approach was known to the Bench. Mr Morris told us that in the past access was almost invariably granted and denial was a marked change of policy. The requirement of separation of child from parents during 'disclosure work', which might take weeks or months was a new development. Mr Davies said that the denial of access on a place of safety order or on an interim care order was recognised by the magistrates as a most serious deprivation for parents and children and knowledge that it was now a common practice was a matter of deep concern. The reasons for denying access in particular circumstances was known to the magistrates but there was unease that access might be denied too readily.

3 The conflict of medical evidence was also of great concern. Mr Davies told us that:—"It was the first time in my experience that Teesside magistrates had been invited to assess the quality of conflicting medical evidence provided by experts in child abuse." Mr Cooke said that his magistrates were not used to dealing with that sort of thing. On that occasion Mr Cooke specifically made the suggestion that 28 day place of safety orders might be applied for to relieve congestion in the courts. This was a somewhat unusual reason for making an order for that period of time. However it is clear from the

evidence of Mr Cooke that he did not influence in any way the discretion of the magistrates in the period they should grant. He does appear to have had some influence over the period applied for by social workers.

Over the whole period January to July of the 276 orders granted for all reasons, 105 were for 28 days, 48 for 7 days or less.

10.14 The suggestion of Mr Bell MP that social workers were spreading the applications round the Magistrates in order that they should not know what was going on was not borne out by the evidence and figures we received. Looking at the 174 orders granted at home by a single magistrate. it is clear that the magistrates most often asked are those nearest to the area office concerned, or retired and therefore likely to be at home. Magistrates living further away and out at work were not approached at all or rarely.

10.15 In July at the suggestion of the Chairman of the panel Mr Cooke sent out to all members of the panel a reminder about applications for place of safety orders, including applications during court hours, the granting of applications and the interim hearing under s.28(6)[Children and Young Persons Act 1969]. Nothing was said about access by children to their parents.

Records of Place of Safety Orders.

10.16 One reason for the uncertainty about the number of place of safety orders was the absence of complete records or of accurate record keeping. Social Services had difficulty in giving figures to the Inquiry. The Juvenile Court was unable to do so at all. It was not the practice of single magistrates granting the orders to inform the Clerk that they had done so. The Clerk expected that copies of orders would be sent to him and kept a file for that pupose. In practice it did not happen, a matter of which the Clerk was unaware until the crisis arose. In evidence he found the number of orders granted "astonishing" and said he thought he had about 50 or 60 but had not counted them. He told us:—"I am not aware of any statutory authority that requires me to keep a record of place of safety orders." He did not know of the Home Office Circular 25 of 1986 which reminded Clerks of the need to make appropriate arrangements to ensure the recording of adjudications arising from applications for place of safety orders. He also told us that he was intending to do something about the situation. At the time he gave evidence on the 13th October he had not made any arrangements to have up to date information on the orders granted. He felt he had more important things to consider in view of the crisis.

10.17 The consequences of this lack of knowledge and failure to comply with the Home Office Circular became obvious in early June with the listing of large numbers of interim care applications for hearing on the expiry of the place of safety orders.

Understanding of the use of/need for the order

10.18 There was general uncertainty expressed to the Inquiry about the use and powers of a place of safety order. The nurses did not know how to deal with parents wishing to see their children on a ward when an order had been obtained. Paediatricians appear not to have understood its purpose. Dr Higgs suggested to Mr Morris that a 28 day order should be sought on one group of children in order to enable 'disclosure work' to be undertaken. A family practitioner asked for guidance as to the effect of an order obtained on one of his patients. There was a difference of opinion among social workers as to its meaning and the extent of control it gave them over the child. Some described it as a grey area. At least one social worker candidly told us that she thought it was a kind of interim care order. Mrs Richardson believed in a structured and authoritarian approach to families where sexual abuse was alleged and saw the place of safety order as the method by which control was gained over that family. It is likely that she would have expressed that view to other social workers. Certainly some of them believed it entitled them to have the child further medically examined and to refuse to allow the parents to have the child examined by doctors of their choice. They believed that they had the right to refuse access or restrict access to parents under the order.

Refusal/Restriction of Access

10.19 The refusal or restriction of access to the parents caused great distress, much resentment and created great difficulties. Since the purpose of it was to engage in 'disclosure work' with the child to confirm the sexual abuse, there was no possibility of compromise over the type of access which might otherwise have been agreed. There was for the parents no recourse to the courts either under the place of safety order or under the interim care order [Save under Section 12B Child Care Act 1980]. It had a dramatic effect upon the degree of dispute, the opposition to the interim care applications and consequently upon the resources of the Juvenile Court. It was a major ground of complaint addressed to the Inquiry by parents.

Pressure on the Juvenile Courts

10.20 In early June the effect of granting the large number of place of safety orders began to be felt in the Courts. The 45 applications for interim orders was an extreme example of it. This was an unprecedented number and the difficulties of the situation were accentuated by the contesting of the interim applications, some of which then took from one day to several days to try. The first of these, already referred to, posed a problem previously unknown to the magistrates who were not accustomed to disputed medical evidence from experts. This was resolved by recourse to wardship proceedings with the agreement of all concerned. The difficulties faced by the Juvenile Court in hearing interim applications with only partial information on matters which were both complex and contentious highlights a problem which is likely to increase.

10.21 In general two or three Juvenile Courts sat on three mornings a week. During the crisis in June there were between 14 to 17 courts sitting in a week and volunteer magistrates were being sought in great numbers to man the Courts. Sitting on Saturdays was proposed. By the end of June most of the contested matters had, with the agreement of the Director and of the parents' solicitors, become wardship applications. Mr Cooke said this decision was received with delight and the pressure was off the Juvenile Court.

Wardship

10.22 The pressure moved from the Juvenile Court to the High Court. The District Registrar had an increased volume of work through the District Registry and he dealt with many of the wardship cases which during the next few months were settled by the agreement of the County Council and the parents. In all those cases the children went home, some with supervision orders and conditions. The Registrar referred other cases to the Judges for hearing. In July Mr Justice Hollis heard a number of cases in Leeds, two of which were fully contested. In each of those there was considerable medical evidence which set out the controversy within the medical profession. Mr Justice Hollis released cases waiting to be heard to Circuit Judges sitting as High Court Judges. From August until the following May 1988, the wardship cases relating to these children were tried in the High Court of the Family Division either by High Court Judges or by Circuit Judges sitting as High Court Judges, or Deputy High Court Judges, in Middlesbrough, Leeds, and Newcastle. As far as we are able to ascertain all but three of the wardship cases relating to children caught up in the crisis have now been heard.

10.23 The first cases were started in the High Court in June and the most recent were heard in May 1988. One of the remaining cases is listed for July. The problems in that case are now unconnected with sexual abuse but relate to long-standing difficulties in the family. A second case is a dispute between parents in which the Local Authority has intervened. In the third case there was an interim care order with leave to the County Council to return the child to live with the parents last July and no further steps have been taken in the proceedings. This was in fact quite a speedy disposal of the list of cases in the circumstances. The first few were heard very quickly—children made wards in June and cases heard by the end of July. There were however difficulties in getting some cases heard, due to a number of factors.

Cleveland County Council

10.24 Cleveland County Council was a party in every case. It was not generally possible for cases to be heard at the same time by different Judges. Even if the Inquiry in which the Council was represented on a daily basis had not been running, there would no doubt have been great difficulties in these complicated circumstances in having two or more applications heard at the same time. With their responsibilities to the Inquiry it was clearly impossible. As it was the Council was stretched almost to the limit to comply with all the demands upon them from the Courts and from the Inquiry.

Medical Evidence

10.25 The availability of Dr Higgs and Dr Wyatt was another problem. Either or both of them were in every case. They were also represented at and providing lengthy written and oral evidence to the Inquiry.

Medical experts were called by the Council and by the parents, some of whom were not available at certain times. Others had to fit in the court hearings and their attendance at the Inquiry.

Guardians ad litem

10.26 Another factor was the availability of guardians ad litem. The Official Solicitor was not invited to represent any individual children. Guardians were appointed from the panel in the wardship cases and that also created difficulties. In one case according to Mr Justice Sheldon in his judgment given on the 20th April, 1988, place of safety orders were granted in respect of children in April 1987. They were thereafter in the care of the Council and made wards of court. It was not until October 1987 that a guardian was appointed from the panel by the Registrar. The guardian made it clear that she was unable to start her investigations for several weeks, and in fact did not start until the 22nd December. She applied for Legal Aid on the 4th January 1988 which was not granted until the 29th March . She applied for psychiatric examination of the children in April and this was refused by Mr Justice Sheldon solely on the ground of the delay it would cause to the hearing. The case was eventually heard in May 1988. [for further comments on wardship see chapter 16]

Cleveland County Council Legal Services.

10.27 The County Secretary's Department is responsible for the provision of legal services, which includes advice and legal representation in court in child care cases. In practice, ever since its inception as an Authority in 1974, the Council has been represented in the Juvenile Court and in the preparation and presentation of legal reports in matrimonial proceedings by Court Liaison Officers employed within the Social Services Department.

10.28 In Cleveland decisions to initiate legal proceedings in respect of children who have been abused or are thought to be at risk are formally delegated to Social Services Area Offices. The extent to which those responsibilities were exercised independently of case conferences was unclear. From the evidence before the Inquiry it appears that Area Officers invariably followed the recommendations of case conferences.

Court Liaison Officers

10.29 None of the Court Liaison Officers was qualified either as a barrister or as a solicitor, though one at least had a law degree; some were qualified social workers; all were experienced at appearing before the Juvenile Court in care proceedings. They handled routine child care cases including preparation of cases for court and represented the Council in court. We were told that from time to time, Court Liaison Officers consulted one of the County solicitors, in cases of complexity or for a legal opinion on how to proceed. They had frequent discussions on cases and matters of procedure. Despite this close contact between the Departments, the Legal Division of the Council appears to have played a limited role in the crisis. There is no evidence that they were ever consulted over any of the problems which arose in 1987 before the cases went to the High Court. They do not appear to have been consulted on the interpretation of a place of safety order; whether access could be denied the parents; whether a parent could be refused a second medical opinion.

Case Conferences

10.30 We were told that solicitors from the Legal Division provide advice at case conferences on invitation.In fact, the presence of a member of that Department at a case conference was extremely rare. From the records before the Inquiry, a solicitor from the County Secretary's Department seems to have been present at three of the 175 case conferences held between April and June 1987 in Cleveland. Given the complexity of many of the cases considered and the implication of the matters under discussion for children, parents and the Authority, this struck us a serious shortcoming in the arrangements adopted in Cleveland for the management of child abuse.

As far as we are aware no member of the Legal Division was invited to attend any meetings of the JCAC.

The Crisis

10.31 The crisis of numbers began in the first few days in May in the case of the foster family and the associated children brought in to hospital and into the care of the Council. The Social Services Department instructed private solicitors. It was not until late June that the Legal Division took over the conduct of those cases.

10.32 In the large number of cases that were referred during the rest of May and even more so in early June, it was necessary to consider whether, in taking the series of steps the issue of a place of safety order, the removal of the children and the application for a care order, there was sufficient evidence to prove the necessary criteria in the Juvenile Court. The Legal Division does not appear to have been consulted. In particular, after the early part of June when everyone must have been aware of the depth of medical controversy, no-one, especially Mr Morris appears to have sought legal advice as to the effect the medical controversy might have on the care applications. The question should then have been asked—ought the children to be moved from their homes if Social Services was to be in difficulties in proving the allegations in the courts. If they could not and the children were sent home, (as the majority of them were eventually), were they acting in the best interests of the children in removing them in the first place? No-one seems to have put their minds to this problem and the consequences for the children in their care. During the period of the crisis, particularily when the dispute over medical evidence became known, objective legal advice on the probabilities of the outcome of each case would have been invaluable and the seeking of it prudent.

Other advice received

10.33 In a number of cases Court Liaison Officers attended case conferences. There was no evidence that they sought to test or weigh the evidence upon which the proceedings were to be instituted. The Social Services Department appears to have relied very heavily upon the advice of Mr Morris, one of their senior Court Liaison Officers. Mr Morris had been a practising social worker since 1968. He had obtained an LLB, obviously took a keen interest in the law, and was a founder member of the legal section of British Agencies for Adoption and Fostering. He was not however qualified either as a barrister or as a solicitor. He was responsible for the legal sections in the 1986 social work manual issued by Social Services for the guidance of their social workers.

On one occasion he spent some time with Dr Higgs discussing the outcome of her medical examination in a particular case, in which the parents, guardian ad litem, and Local Authority were all involved in seeking further medical examinations of the children which did not appear to be either helpful to the children, their medical treatment or be likely greatly to assist the Court. They were medically examined 6 times. He does not appear to have advised on that aspect of this case.

10.34 In spite of the increased scale of referrals the basic arrangements for the consideration and initiation of care proceedings continued to be dealt with on the basis of accepted practice. Whilst the Court Officers may have sought advice on individual cases there was no indication that they thought themselves out of depth in the complexity of the cases they were being asked to initiate. It was not until the third week of June that solicitors from the Legal Division became directly involved and advised proceedings by way of wardship rather than care proceedings. Parents and their representatives had become frustrated at the difficulties of proceeding in the Juvenile Court. Parental access to children was being controlled by the Social Services through the use of interim care orders. Delays in the appointment of guardians commonly delayed a full hearing of the proceedings for several months. Against this background the hearings for an interim order had become increasingly contentious and prolonged.

10.35 Mr Morris gave advice on access and on medical second opinions on the 19th June at a Child Abuse Group meeting. He told us that he gave the Child Abuse Group 'clear and categoric' advice to allow second opinions. It was the first time that he was asked to advise on whether access could be denied. The notes of the meeting of the 22nd June show that where parental co-operation as to no access was not forthcoming an interim care order should be sought.

Use of Wardship by the County Council.

10.36 Before 1987 Cleveland County Council did not invoke the wardship jurisdiction on a frequent basis. In 1984 they issued 8 wardship applications, 13 in 1985 and 18 in 1986. According to Mr Morris this was a combination of the good relations they had with tne Juvenile Court and their inexperience in the High Court. Wardship was however extensively used in 1987 for several reasons: initially to relieve the pressure on the Juvenile Courts and to cope with the frustration of parents and their legal advisers at the slow progress of their cases through the Juvenile Courts, and thereafter because of the complexity particularily with the considerable volume of disputed medical evidence. In one case referred to by Mr Bell, MP, the Juvenile Bench refused to make a care order in respect of some children, and the Local Authority unable to appeal against that decision, made the children wards of court.

10.37 The Legal Division in written evidence to the Inquiry gave some details of the way in which the wardship jurisdiction was invoked, by a mixture of legal representation from the County Council, and the instruction of private solicitors by parents who were on occasions plaintiffs in the originating summonses. This required the Local Authority to agree not to take a point of jurisdiction which would otherwise have prevented the parents' applications. In the case of the foster family which arose in May, the Social Services Department instructed independent solicitors, but later in June the Legal Division took those cases over. Prior to 26th June, instructions to issue wardship proceedings were accepted from Social Services Area Officers and the senior Court Liaison Officer. After that date such proceedings required the specific confirmation of the Director or Senior Assistant Director.

Termination of access under interim care orders.

10.38 In many cases during 1987 both before and during the crisis in order to facilitate disclosure work with the children and to do so without the pressure social workers felt would be imposed by the parents on the child, particularily by the supected abuser, the Council sought to restrict and in some cases to refuse access to either or both parents. Social workers were advised by Mr Morris that if they thought it necessary to suspend access for a period (generally for the purpose of 'disclosure work'), they should serve upon the parent a notice under s.12B of the Child Care Act 1980 terminating the access of the parent to that child. This somewhat draconian procedure was advised by Mr Morris as a result of a Divisional Court decision of Mr Justice Wood (v. Bolton Metropolitan Borough Council ex parte B [1985] F.L.R. 343). This notice was served on several parents, while the children were subject to interim care orders. Understandably the parents were extremely upset by the apparent finality of the notice before their case had even been heard. We heard no evidence to suggest that parents were given any written or oral explanation of the purpose of the procedure which was to enable them to appeal in the Magistrates' Court against the refusal of access. The effect of the notices on parents was to increase the anguish and fuel their opposition to the course pursued by the Council.

Guardians ad Litem.

10.39 In Cleveland the Guardian ad Litem Panel was administered by a senior member of Social Services, Mr Hughes, the Child Care Consultant. He gave evidence about the difficulties which he encountered in the management of the panel well before the crisis arose. Mr Bishop, Mr Morris and Mr Cooke also gave evidence about problems with guardians ad litem.

Availability of Guardians.

10.40 The major difficulty we heard about related to finding sufficient guardians for the volume of cases in which they were appointed by the courts.

10.41 Cleveland has a population of over half a million. The panel was set up in 1984 in accordance with the 1983 Regulations. The policy of the County Council was to operate a reciprocal arrangement with neighbouring counties. Soon after its inception, North Yorkshire withdrew from the arrangement. Durham, with its much smaller population was unable to provide sufficient guardians ad litem for the needs of a much larger area, with a greater demand for the services of guardians. This placed an enormous strain upon the arrangement, and it became clear during the Inquiry that the duty upon the Local Authority to ensure that the number of persons appointed to the panel was sufficient had been discharged with the greatest difficulty by Cleveland and that there had been a chronic shortage; there simply were not enough guardians available.

10.42 The backlog of cases in 1986 and early 1987 even before the crisis caused some rethinking and negotiations were underway to recruit other guardians including independent social workers. From the latter part of 1986 the panel began to be hybrid.

Delays

10.43 The shortage was not however cured. The Inquiry heard evidence that even before the number of cases reached crisis proportions in June 1987, there was commonly a delay of two to three months or more between the making of the order for appointment of a guardian and the case being allocated to a nominated person. In July the delay was approximately 14 weeks. Early in 1987 the waiting list for guardians was 60 and the delay was at least 3 months. In the middle of July guardians were required to be nominated for 82 waiting child cases. This delay before nomination has to be added to the period a guardian may take to investigate and report in any individual case. According to Mr Cooke:—"more often than not it takes 6 months or more from the return date before a case is finally disposed of." This was before the crisis took over.

10.44 For a variety of reasons the appointment of guardians to act for children was during the crisis the cause of considerable delays. The delays in the Juvenile Court were a matter of considerable concern to the parents waiting for the cases to be heard and no doubt, subsequently in the wardship proceedings. The first reason was non-availability to which we have already referred. The inability to find sufficient guardians in cases which clearly merited the child being allocated a guardian was a major delaying factor both in the Juvenile and in the High Court. Guardians notified that they were nominated were on occasions unable to take up their duties for weeks or months. In the High Court, where they were appointed in wardship cases of suspected sexual abuse during 1987, they were not appointed in accordance with the Guardian ad Litem and Boarding Out Regulations which do not apply to wardship. The consequence of that was a requirement for the guardian to apply for Legal Aid to represent the child. In one example the Legal Aid Committee took 3 months to grant the application. The guardian him/herself has no right to remuneration in the High Court as we understand Cleveland guardians discovered.

Independence.

10.45 We received evidence from those who acted as guardians in Cleveland as well as elsewhere and they spoke with one voice in expressing their dissatisfaction with the existing arrangements for managing the panel and the impression of lack of independence from the Social Services Department who in almost every case will be the applicant for a care order in the case in which the guardian is representing the child. There were in our view both apparent and real problems as to genuine independence and impartiality.

10.46 Apparent reasons included the fact that in Cleveland the administrator of the panel wrote on Cleveland County Council Social Services Department writing paper. On occasions parents of the child the subject of the application received letters with that heading.

10.47 More fundamental is the administration of the panel by a member of the Social Services Department of the Local Authority, the applicant in the proceedings. Guardians told us that they were understandably anxious to be accepted as independent of the Local Authority. But with appointment, administration and remuneration by the Council, they recognised how difficult it was for parents to accept that. One Cleveland guardian told us that families on occasion regarded the guardian as another arm of the Social Services Department.

10.48 This regrettably, was on occasions the view also of social workers and of case conferences. We saw examples of case conference recommendations that the guardian nominated be:—"experienced in disclosure work," (thus prejudging whether disclosure work was desirable and needed to be carried out.) Case conferences sought the appointment of named guardians, and in the foster family case in early May, at the planning meeting on the 3rd May on two associated families which the guardian of one group of children attended, it was agreed that if possible she should be the guardian of the other family.

10.49 There is a major difficulty for guardians, according to the evidence, in being appointed by the Local Authority and having the duty to disagree with and even on occasions to criticise actions and decisions of the very Council who appointed them. The conflict is obvious.

Independence of the Administrator of the Panel.

10.50 Mr Hughes indicated to us that the administration of the panel presented difficulties of a conflict of loyalties. He said he had felt concern about the role of administrator for some time. He felt he could not have any consultation with, nor could he give any guidance to individual guardians who have been nominated. In his view that might create a conflict of interest as the cases might be those which as Child Care Adviser he might have been involved in advising the Department on the action to be taken. In fact the day to day running of the panel and nomination of guardians was delegated to a clerk. He did have, if he chose to use it, influence over the appointment of guardians, but because of his dual role he did his best to keep out of it. He was aware of occasions when case conferences recommended specific names; his attention would be drawn to it. He would usually ask why they wanted a named person. He did recall on one occasion appointing as guardian someone recommended by the case conference. We were entirely satisfied that Mr Hughes carried out his duties with scrupulous impartiality and integrity.

Duties of Guardian ad litem

10.51 It became clear to us during the Inquiry and from looking at case conference notes and Social Services files that on occasions guardians attended case conferences, occasionally planning meetings and that in both instances they played a full and involved part in the discussions. These guardians were not acting as observers.

10.52 Some guardians during the crisis saw it as part of their duty to engage in 'disclosure work' with the children to whom they had been allocated. One or two were appointed for that purpose. Some guardians spent an enormous amount of time with the individual families, in one instance 80 to 100 hours. One guardian visited the children weekly over a considerable period. The children grew to look forward to her visits, but her role in their lives ceased at the end of the proceedings.

10.53 We were told during the course of the Inquiry that Cleveland County Council had come to an arrangement with the Children's Society, a voluntary child care agency of national standing, to manage their Guardian ad Litem Panel in future. This enabled improvements to be made to the provision of the guardian ad litem service to the Teesside Juvenile Court and we were glad to hear that the backlog of outstanding work had been completely cleared.

PART TWO

RESPONSE TO CHILD SEXUAL ABUSE
(EXPERT EVIDENCE)

Part 2

CHAPTER 11

Medical Examination and Assessment

Clinical Examination and Assessment

Introduction

11.1 The Inquiry received evidence from a number of medical practitioners of different specialities about medical examination and diagnosis of children believed to have been sexually abused. Some evidence related to individual children from Cleveland, other evidence was of a general nature. It is not the function of the Inquiry to evaluate the accuracy of any diagnosis nor to resolve conflicting evidence nor to assess whether an individual child was or was not sexually abused.

11.2 Child sexual abuse describes aberrant adult behaviour; it causes physical and emotional damage to the child. Thus it is the cause of the child's symptoms and signs and in that limited sense child sexual abuse is the diagnosis of the child's problem. So, while recognising that it is not an accurate description, the term 'diagnosis' has been used throughout the course of the Inquiry to describe the conclusions reached from the symptoms and signs.

No physical signs of sexual abuse

11.3 We were reminded that in many cases of sexual abuse there may be no physical damage and therefore no symptoms and signs arising from that damage.

11.4 In non-intrusive acts and even in some intrusive acts, such as oral intercourse, no physical damage occurs; even some acts of buggery leave no trace directly relating to the act, although there may be other evidence, for example, bruising due to how the child was held. Dr Wynne told us that:—"there may be no abnormal signs in penetrative anal abuse." Dr Raine Roberts in the preamble to medical reports on 14 Cleveland children said:—"I would emphasise that gross sexual abuse of a child can occur without it being possible to find medical evidence of abuse."

Medical Descriptions

11.5 According to Dr Paul (1986) "Penile penetration of the vagina and/or anus is a common form of sexual abuse," in children. Such assaults are likely to cause damage and leave marks. The Inquiry was presented with a volume of evidence as to the significance of the symptoms and signs of damage and the inferences to be drawn from each and from the accumulation of them. This evidence was presented both in general terms, and in examples from clinical notes, photographs and slides provided to the Inquiry in respect of individual children. We thought it would be helpful to refer to certain signs the importance of which was exhaustively canvassed in evidence and about which there are both conflicting views and some measure of agreement. In the medical evidence we sought as we have sought elsewhere to find the points of agreement and the middle ground in areas which at first sight seemed irreconcilable. In this Report we do express some comments about the helpfulness and the objectivity of some of the medical witnesses which inevitably affected our minds in the assessment of the value of the particular evidence given. We realised in this Inquiry the truth of the quotation:—"the complex forces which can affect judgment and action in dealing with emotionally powerful material," and that it applied to some degree to some witnesses caught up in this Inquiry even from outside the area who became themselves involved in the outcome.

11.6 One problem which beset the Inquiry and provided ammunition for cross-examination was the lack of agreed medical terms to describe the signs observed. In the charged atmosphere of the disputed hearings in the courts, differing uses of the same words are likely to confuse the medical and legal professions. This problem was recognised by a number of witnesses who agreed that it was important to be careful to use consistent language and medical terms which might find acceptance from all sides. It is a topic which urgently requires the attention of the medical profession.

11.7 Not only were there differences in the words used to describe what was seen, but we had the feeling that on some occasions at least medical practitioners examining within a short period of each other either did not see or did not elicit the same clinical signs. For the purposes of this report it was not necessary to explore the problem any further, but it is likely to present difficulties in the future.

11.8 It is essential that there is clear and widely recognised standard nomenclature in general use by all medical practitioners engaged in examining, recording, advising and giving evidence in any type of court proceedings concerned with child sexual abuse.

11.9 Genital abuse in girls

* Examination of the female genitalia

We were told that it is easier to examine the child while she is lying on her back with her legs apart. If the child is anxious, it has been recommended that the child lies between her mother's legs with her mother's arms around her. The child lies with legs apart and heels close together.

* Inspection

The method of inspection was suggested as follows. Skin damage is noted first without touching, with the labia together, and then with the labia separated with the first finger and thumb of the left hand (right handed examiner) and again any damage , bleeding or swelling noted. Dr Bamford where possible got the child to do this herself. The hymen would then be in view and the size of the opening can be assessed. Dr Wynne recommended the use of an auroscope without the speculum, for this provides a light source and magnifies 3 or 4 times. Some examiners measure it, in anterior and posterior diameter with a short ruler, others use glass rods (see below) and note any defects in the edge.

* Glass rods

The purpose of this procedure, which involves inserting a glass rod into the opening of the vagina, is to display the hymenal edge and try to estimate the size of the opening.

The Inquiry was told of two techniques; the first using Glaister rods, which were circular spheres of various sizes on a glass handle. The smallest size was 7mm which made them unsuitable for smaller children. Dr Ellis Fraser had rods fashioned for her own use; they were of uniform diameter with a smooth rounded end and of varying sizes (3, 5, 7 mm). The rod is inserted and the edge of the hymen is then more easily seen as it lies upon it. Dr Roberts used Glaister rods and was very dismissive of the usefulness of Dr Ellis Fraser's version. Dr Higgs and Dr Wyatt used the same version as Dr Ellis Fraser, from whom Dr Higgs learnt the technique. Dr Irving and Dr Beeby used neither.

* Digital examination

Digital examination of the pelvis via the vagina, usually with two fingers is an essential part of most obstetric and gynaecological examinations. However all witnesses were agreed that it is not the practice to attempt a digital examination, even with the little finger in pre-pubertal girls. In a child suspected of being sexually assaulted, the investigation is not likely to find anything of value; it would upset most children (if it did not it would be a cause for concern) and it may cause damage. To our knowledge, it was not the practice of any doctor who gave evidence to attempt it.

* Colposcopy

The use of an instrument that provides light and magnification in the investigation of girls in whom sexual abuse is suspected has been introduced in the USA. We were told that with this instrument (colposcope) signs of injury to the hymen and vagina which had not previously been detected, were found. It was not however used by any of the doctors in Cleveland or who gave evidence to the Inquiry.

* The Structure of the female genitalia

The labial folds close to cover the opening of the drainage tube from the bladder (the urethra) and the opening of the vagina. Across the opening of the vagina is the hymen, a thin membrane with a small central aperture. The inner edge may be smooth or irregular, thin or rounded. The size of the opening may vary with position, and it can stretch without tearing. If it tears it is said not to heal, and therefore scars are not seen, only a defect in the edge remains. If it is fully stretched, it breaks, it may bleed and then it shrinks away.

An absent hymen does not necessarily indicate digital or penile penetration. However in the female the genitalia prior to puberty are as under-developed as those of the male. The vagina is small; the hymenal opening may be difficult to find. The organs grow comparatively little from birth until puberty so there is

184

little increase in the size of the hymenal aperture. The onset of puberty varies widely; 95% of girls begin between 9 and 13 years.

* Signs of genital abuse

The only finding that would leave little or no doubt of sexual penetration would be the presence of semen or other material (blood, hair), foreign to the child in the vagina. Venereal disease also demands some explanation. Signs which suggest sexual assault are those of damage to the labia, hymen, and vagina for which there is no alternative explanation.

* Damage to skin

Weight of varying degree was put by experts who gave evidence on the finding of a reddened, bruised or smooth skin around the introitus to the vagina. Intracrural intercourse might produce such changes, but so might rubbing for other reasons.

Swelling and reddening of the more delicate skin lining the labia was said to be perhaps of more significance and may heal with scars and fibrous bands. The latter may be so extensive as to cause fusion of the labia; evidence that this might be so was presented to the Inquiry but it was not said to occur in any of the Cleveland children.

* Damaged hymen

Tears in the hymen with raw bleeding edges indicate recent damage of which attempting vaginal penetration is one explanation. A wide open vaginal opening with little or no hymen left is generally an abnormal finding in a pre-pubertal girl. We were told that the hymenal opening is small perhaps 2-3 mm in a small child. There was some disagreement in the evidence as to the range of size which would cause concern; the upper end of the normal range, that is to say at which concern might be expressed, was said by some to be 5mm up to 7 years and 7 mm up to puberty. According to Professor Dewhurst, Professor of Obstetrics and Gynaecology (in his textbook on the Gynaecology of Childhood and Adolescence):—"The central orifice, which averaged 4mm in diameter at birth, is rarely more than 5mm in diameter when a child is five years of age....The phase of gradual growth of the genitalia starts for most girls when they are between seven and nine years of age." The hymenal orifice:—"will measure 7 mm or more in diameter by the time a reaction to estrogen stimulation is grossly visible...... During the premenarchial phase of accelerated genital growth the orifice averages 10mm in diameter".

Knowledge of the behaviour of the hymen in pre-pubertal girls after it has been stretched is less certain. One view we were given was that once it has disappeared it can never return.Another view is that it can be stretched (dilated), and leave the vaginal orifice appearing open only to return to some extent when attempts at penetration stop. It may be a matter of degree.

* Vaginal damage

Penile penetration of a pre-pubertal girl is likely to be painful to both abuser and the child; force would be necessary and tears of the vaginal wall are probable. Insertion of fingers or other objects is more difficult to detect. Forceful stretching of the vaginal opening is likely to tear the skin immediately behind the opening and between it and the anus (posterior fourchette). Scars in this area were reported in some Cleveland children.

A vaginal bleed after suspected assault would probably justify examination under anaesthesia with a view to identifying the cause, and if there had been a vaginal tear, its extent. We heard of one such event in Cleveland.

Evidence of genital abuse in Cleveland

11.10 The evidence centred mainly on redness and swelling in some, and scars, tears in the hymen and a wide hymenal opening in others. The signs recorded by Dr Higgs and Dr Wyatt were in the main confirmed by Dr Wynne in those children she examined, but not by Dr Irvine, Dr Paul, Dr Roberts and others in the children they saw. Dr Roberts was unhappy to accept that a widely open hymen (10 mm) was 'indicative of' or 'consistent with' sexual abuse. She felt that the normal values currently used were suspect. She based her comments on her general experience whilst working as a family doctor (where she agreed that she had few opportunities to examine the genitalia of pre-pubertal girls) as a police surgeon, and as Director of the Manchester Rape Centre where she examined many, mainly pubescent, girls in whom rape was suspected.

11.11 Professor Dewhurst presented evidence to the Inquiry that an orifice greater than 7 mm in a pre-pubertal girl would be exceptional, but was not able to see any abnormality in photographs and slides shown to him of open vaginas. He pointed out the difficulties of such assessment made from photographs. Other experts shown the same photographs considered the open vaginas to be grossly abnormal.

Conclusion: Genital Abuse

11.12 From the evidence presented to the Inquiry we formed the following conclusions with which the weight of the evidence was in agreement.

The absence of evidence of damage does not exclude intracrural intercourse or fondling. An intact hymen less than 5 mm in diameter makes penile penetration highly unlikely in any girl, pubescent or otherwise. Penile penetration is likely to cause pain and tears in girls before puberty. Adults pushing other things into the vagina of young girls for sexual gratification may obviously cause damage depending on their size, but they may not. If the assault had occurred in the previous 3 days, collecting forensic evidence should be a mandatory part of the examination; if there is any grounds to suspect infection, particularily if there is a vaginal discharge, tests for sexually transmitted diseases are essential. The finding of evidence of recent injury (tears) or old injury (scars) are consistent with sexual abuse and in the absence of any other credible explanation are suggestive of it.

Anal abuse

Examination

11.13 It is appropriate for a doctor to examine the anal canal in a wide variety of medical conditions many of which are not associated with local symptoms like irritation, soreness, pain, rectal bleeding and problems with defaecation.

11.14 The examination is usually performed with the patient lying on his or her left side with the knees drawn up to the chest. However a better view may be obtained with the patient kneeling in the knee elbow position. There was some criticism of the knee elbow position, principally from the police surgeons' protocol to the Standing Medical Advisory Committee. However in the New Police Surgeon it is said:—"the knee elbow position has many advantages." Dr Christine Cooper trained her students to examine in that position and the preponderance of expert opinion given in evidence was that either position was suitable; but the left lateral position allows the child more privacy. The age of the patient, compliance and preferences as well as the medical indications will influence which position is appropriate.

11.15 The examination has three stages:—inspection, palpation and digital examination.

* Inspection

The Inquiry was told that to inspect the perineal area the buttocks are gently separated. Damage and disease of the anal verge and surrounding skin are noted. The signs may include redness, swelling, breaks in the skin, skin tags, bruises, bleeding, pigmentation etc.

* Buttock separation

To inspect the anus the buttocks have to be separated. The normal response to buttock separation is for the external anal sphincter to contract tightly and then relax to its previous tonal position. It stays closed. The Inquiry was told by Dr Bamford that the external sphincter can be held tightly closed for 9-12 seconds only; others claimed longer periods, up to 30 seconds. Thus on buttock separation, the external sphincter can only hold the orifice of the anal canal tightly closed for a brief period. After that time it relaxes and then if the anal canal muscles are weak or over-stretched or have lost their normal tone the anal canal may open. That is what is called reflex anal dilatation or reflex relaxation and anal dilatation. If the child interprets the buttock separation as an indication to defaecate then the canal will open and a stool will appear. This is obviously normal and must not be misinterpreted.

The separation of the buttocks only becomes a 'test' when the doctor specifically waits to see if the opening of the anal canal occurs. It is not, we are told, the usual practice to do so, thus the current uncertainty in the medical profession as to whether it may be a normal phenomenon or may occur in certain disorders.

* Palpation

This will include gently pressing the skin around the anal verge to roll back the skin to see if a fissure is present. It was Dr Ellis Fraser's practice to palpate gently and press the external sphincter to test its tone.

* Digital examination

In rectal examination a gloved finger is inserted through the anal canal. It is an essential part of clinical examination in a variety of illnesses and is often done to detect swellings of such structures as the rectum, prostate, bladder, uterus and ovaries which lie within the pelvis. The finger is advanced through the anal canal, often as far as it is possible and tolerable. Digital examination is less commonly performed to examine the anal canal itself.

There was a difference of opinion as to the need to perform a digital examination on a child suspected of having been anally abused.

* Proctoscopy

This involves inserting instruments (proctoscopes or sigmoidoscopes) through the anal canal which allow the observation of the lining of the rectum and anal canal. Such examinations are commonly performed by surgeons, particularily ano-rectal surgeons. If a child has bleeding from the rectum, and the lining is thought to be torn, then proctoscopy under anaesthesia would be the appropriate investigation. This situation did not arise in Cleveland in the first 6 months of 1987. Proctoscopy is practised as part of the examination of children suspected of anal abuse in some places in the USA. Mr Heald advocated its use in the UK if anal abuse was suspected. It was not clear to the Inquiry what he expected to find. In his opinion, anal abuse was exceedingly rare; he had seen very few cases in many years of practice as a consultant proctologist in Basingstoke. As the benefits of the investigation were unclear to us, and as the risk of anaesthesia is self-evident, we formed the view that proctoscopy should probably only be performed for the clinical indication whatever the suspected cause.

Medical terms describing the anal region

11.16 Because there was some confusion as to the interpretation of signs of anal abuse we have listed most of the terms used and what in general they were used to describe.

* Fissure—is a break in the lining of the anal canal, usually extending from inside the canal to the anal verge and travelling vertically to the verge. Cracks in the skin surrounding the anus which might be due to scratching from threadworms or eczema are not included. A fissure is an open lesion; it may well bleed. Most authorities and experts agreed that when fissures heal they leave a scar which may be detected.

* Skin tag—is a mound of skin on the anal verge which may be associated with or have resulted from a fissure.

* Anal verge defect—On some photographs discussed in the Inquiry there were apparent crevices in the anal verge; these some experts considered to be obviously abnormal and called fissures, whereas others dismissed them as normal. Dr Higgs and Dr Wyatt described them as fissuring. As there is uncertainty as to their origin, the term 'fissuring' appears to be unsafe to use. An anal verge defect describes an indentation covered with skin in the anal verge, without a break in the skin lining or bleeding. It may or may not indicate that the anal verge has been previously stretched or torn.

* Anal canal folds—Defects must not be confused, as some seem to have been done from photographs, with folds in the lining of the anal canal which can be seen as it opens. For those doctors who have not seen the anal canal open on buttock separation, (which is likely to be a large number of doctors), we are told that the appearance of the anal skin folds may come as a surprise.

* Prominent veins—Veins cluster under the surface lining at various levels in the anal canal. The upper rings of veins when congested and chronically dilated form haemorroids. These are not relevant to anal abuse in children. Lower more superficial complexes of veins lie under the skin around and in the anal verge. It is dilation of those veins which can be seen as discolouration which some experts consider may be caused by the trauma of habitual anal penetration.

* Skin changes—With rubbing, the skin thickens and may crack (lichenification); it may darken (pigmentation); and these changes around the anal opening may result in a rounding and smoothness of the anal verge.

* *Funnelled*—This word has been used to describe the anus as deeply set, as though at the end of a funnel, due, some have speculated, to the loss of surrounding fat. Others use the word to mean a funnel shaped anal canal with the external sphincter stretched and open and the internal sphincter less so; it is a fixed state. Others use it to describe the dynamic opening of the external before the internal sphincter. Drs Wyatt and Higgs used 'funnelled' to describe the shape of the partially opened anal canal and 'funnelling' to describe the dynamic process. We do not describe the approach to a deep set anus as a 'funnelled anus' whatever its shape. We use it to describe a fixed funnel shaped partially opened anal canal.

* *Tyre sign*—In some situations it would appear that the external sphincter may be stretched or retracted to reveal the lower border of the internal sphincter, so that the indentation between the lower border of the internal sphincter and external sphincter which can be felt on digital palpatation of the normal anal canal can be seen. However it was clear from published reports that the tyre sign was also used to describe general swelling of the anal verge—a more acute and transient phenonomen. The two can and should be distinguished in any report. In those children who had this sign in Cleveland it was not possible from the records to determine what was seen.

* *An open anal canal*—The anal canal may on inspection be partially or completely open, a dilated anus. This may be because the sphincters are weak and lax. The sphincters may, however, be weak and lax in tone and yet keep the anus closed. If the anus is open due to poor muscle tone or loss of nervous control, the lining may invert and give a rolled appearance to the anal verge—a patulous anus. Very rarely, the anal and rectal lining will turn itself inside out like a sock; this is a rectal prolapse. In none of the children in this Inquiry was a patulous anus or prolapsed rectum observed. If the anal canal is open, or dilated it is in the same state.

* *An opening anal canal—Anal dilatation*

In this report 'anal dilatation' is the description generally used when the anus opens on inspection. The initials RAD, reflex anal dilatation, and RR, reflex relaxation have been avoided, although they were commonly used in evidence presented to the Inquiry.

* *The anal canal and defaecation*

The anal canal is the last segment of the digestive system; it controls the evacuation of the waste.

In adults it is 3 to 4 cm in length. It is held closed by two concentric muscles. The internal sphincter works automatically and like all other muscles that line the bowel, it is not under voluntary control. The external sphincter surrounds the internal sphincter and extends to the immediate opening, the anus, and is responsible for the folds in the skin in the anal verge. This muscle can be contracted at will. Both muscles are in a constant state of contraction or tone.

The bowel empties when the faeces (stool) enter the rectum which is that part of the bowel immediately above the anal canal. This stimulates a contraction wave in the rectal wall which propels the stool to the anal canal which in response, relaxes its tone and opens. (The recto-anal reflex.)

As the stool enters the anal canal it passes over the junction between the lining of the bowel (the mucosa) and the skin. This smooth skin normally lies in folds in the closed canal and is very sensitive and it is from sensations in this skin that an individual becomes aware of the need to defaecate. Babies would then automatically allow the stool to pass through. As small children learn to interpret the sensations, they begin to gain control. On becoming aware of the advancing stool, the individual can contract the external sphincter tighter until the propulsive wave passes off, and the stool is then stored in the rectum until more arrives and further waves occur. A propulsive wave may be initiated by straining. Thus the sequence in evacuation is first the internal sphincter and then the external sphincter opens and the stool is extruded.

Signs of anal abuse

11.17 Textbooks of forensic medicine contain graphic descriptions of the damage caused by a single traumatic episode of buggery. They include bleeding from tears in the lining of the rectum, anal canal, and the skin of the anal verge; bruises on the perineum and a lax sphincter, so stretched and torn, that the anal canal is open, (dilated) and continence is not possible.

11.18 The signs of habitual anal abuse were a central issue in the Inquiry. We were directed to certain textbooks of forensic medicine as to the signs to be found in the passive homosexual. For example, in "The Essentials of Forensic Medicine" Polson quotes Fatteh (1962) who wrote:—"It is an interesting inspection finding that the sphincter, ready to receive the examining finger, reflexly dilates and presents a central hole.''(BMJ Feb 17, 1962) That was in response to a letter from Dr Gancz (BMJ Jan 27 1962) referring to the same phenonomen.

11.19 Professor Goligher (in Surgery of the Anus, Rectum and Colon, 1984 5th Ed.) refers to four findings which should alert to the likelihood of homosexuality—1. the presence of anal warts, 2. diminished anal sphincter tone, 3. he refers to Feigen (1964):—"in which palpation of the perianal region leads to contraction and subsequent relaxation of the sphincters." 4. the 'O' sign, the ability voluntarily to maintain the anus in a dilated condition. He went on to say that he had never elicited the third or fourth:—"but if they were present they would certainly make me think seriously of the possibility of homosexuality."

11.20 In Taylor's Principles and Practice of Medical Jurisprudence Dr Paul, an often quoted authority, states:—"A useful guide to a patient's habituation to anal intercourse is the 'lateral buttock traction test'....... Patients who are well used to anal penetration react to the gentle lateral traction by a relaxation of the anal sphincter......It is no more than a possible guide to the diagnosis" and other possibilities are set out. In a later paper (1986), he asserts a 'positive' test on buttock separation is only significant if a triad of signs is also present. This triad is 1.:—"Thickness of the anal verge skins with reduction or obliteration of the anal verge skin folds. 2. Increased elasticity of the anal sphincter muscles allowing the introduction of three or more examining fingers with ease. 3. Reduction in the power of the anal sphincter muscles to contract with reduction of the power of the 'anal grip'.

11.21 Many of the forensic textbooks show illustrations of the damage caused by anal abuse of children. The anal signs of abuse were brought forcibly to professional and public attention by an article in Lancet in 1986 by Drs Hobbs and Wynne entitled 'Buggery in Childhood—a common syndrome in child abuse'. In the summary they state:—"In 27 children, disclosure of abuse by the child or perpetrator (most commonly the father) was recorded. Anal findings on inspection included fissures, dilatation and reflex dilatation, loss of sphincter, shortening and eversion of the anal canal, external venous congestion, and generally reddening and thickening of the perianal tissues." They state: "Diagnosis of buggery is made from the history, physical findings, and associated evidence—particularily behaviour in the child's play. Of greatest importance is a clear history given by the child of interference with his bottom."

Interpretation of anal signs

11.22 Experts differed in the weight they placed on particular signs. Public attention, directed by the media, centred on the single sign of anal dilatation. Dr Higgs and Dr Irvine were opposed in their views as to its significance. This sign is therefore considered separately and at length at page 190. There was also conflict on the importance of performing a digital examination to assess the tone and strength of the anal sphincter. Again Dr Higgs and Dr Irvine held opposing views. This issue is also considered separately at page 192.

11.23 It was accepted that anal abuse may cause a range of signs, from surface skin damage, fissures, defects of anal verge, to severe lacerations, but that in our present state of knowledge, none of these in themselves, or in various clusters, establish with reasonable certainty that anal abuse has occurred. All are, or may be, open to alternative explanations. All, singularly and in various combinations were seen in the children in Cleveland in whom child sexual abuse was suspected.

11.24 From the evidence presented to the Inquiry it was generally agreed that certain findings carry more weight than others.

1. The presence of semen in the rectum of a child is to be regarded as strong evidence of sexual abuse. Lubricants, hairs or similar evidence are of importance.

2. The finding of an infection which is transmitted by sexual contact (e.g. gonorrhoea) is to be regarded as evidence of sexual abuse. Anal warts may be sexually transmitted and if they are found the possibility of sexual abuse should be considered.

3. Tears, bruises, bleeding around the anus and in the anal canal, in the absence of a reasonable explanation, as with other evidence of non-accidental injury, are grounds for grave suspicion that abuse has occurred, though the inference that it was sexual abuse does not necessarily follow.

4. Breaks in the anal verge, causing fissures, scars or defects are a matter of concern. A large hard stool, which has had to be forced out can stretch and tear the skin: such tears are, we were told, vertical to the anal verge, and if caused by a downward moving stool are usually at 12 o'clock, (at

the front edge) and usually single. It was argued that fissures caused by pushing things into the anal canal occurred at the points of a star and were often multiple, and that the tear was worse on the outside, whilst fissures caused by downward forces were broader and deeper at the upper end. Insufficient is known about the frequency and causes of anal fissures. On the present knowledge multiple fissures would appear to be grounds for concern, irrespective of previous bowel history. It was suggested to the Inquiry that pushing up other things such as suppositories or enemas, might cause similar damage. Such activities are not uncommon in paediatric practice and we were given no evidence that damage causing fissures was a generally known hazard.

5. Damage to the skin and anal margin resulting in redness, swelling, cracking of the skin could be due to a variety of skin disorders, like eczema, to scratching, or to lack of attention to cleanliness. Soiling and soreness are seen in neglected children. These findings would not appear in themselves to be sufficient to raise the suspicion of abuse.

6. Likewise chronic skin changes with thickening of the skin, (lichenification) and pigmentation whilst they should be noted and the possible causes sought should not of themselves on the current state of knowledge raise the suspicion of abuse.

7. Anal skin tags often occur at the outward end of a fissure caused by pushing something out of the anal canal. It is not known whether they are all, or, the majority are caused in this way. They would not appear in themselves to be grounds for suspicion.

Dilated anus

11.25 Normally the anal canal is closed, and remains closed on carrying out of normal activities which separate the buttocks, such as sitting or kneeling. An open anal canal is abnormal, even a slight opening would result in incontinence of wind and liquids with staining. It can occur if the muscles or their nerve supply is damaged. In the absence of any other detectable cause an open anal canal in a fixed position is a ground for concern.

Anal dilatation

11.26 Anal Dilatation is the phenomenon which has caught the imagination of the media, but it is not as was often said a *recent* discovery by Dr Wynne and Dr Hobbs. The sign is as follows: when the buttocks are separated, the external sphincter and then the internal sphincter open so that the observer can see through the anal canal into the rectum. The anal sphincters are controlled in part automatically, in part by learned subconscious behaviour, and in part consciously; all in a very complex system not altogether understood by the experts. The controlling mechanism will change with age and will be influenced by levels of awareness and local sensations. Some passive partners in homosexual relationships are said to be able to open their anal canals in anticipation (the 'O' sign). In many children subject to anal abuse, Hobbs and Wynne (1986) found that the anal canal opened on buttock separation. Sometimes it opened and shut, (winking); sometimes it opened and stayed open so that the observer could look into the rectum. In some of the photographs of the children in the Inquiry, the pink lining of the rectal mucosa could be seen through the anal canal.

11.27 Dr Higgs and Dr Wyatt used the term reflex relaxation to describe the opening of the external sphincter and anal dilatation for the opening of the internal sphincter and thus the whole of the anal canal. Dr Bamford did not consider it to be a reflex. Mr Heald thought it might be a consequence of perineal stimulation provoking a recto-anal reflex with anal dilatation, but then it might be expected that the opening of the internal sphincter would precede the opening of the external sphincter. Dr Clayden suggested:—"it may be a combination of a learned response to avoid pain with a reflex inhibition associated with severe anxiety".

11.28 It is not known whether it occurs in normal individuals, whether it occurs in certain physiological states, (it has been described in anaesthetized patients) and whether it occurs in certain disease states. It is *not* common medical knowledge that the anal canal will dilate on buttock separation, nor does it usually occur in normal children, according to the evidence placed before the Inquiry. As it is found in many children who have been sexually abused it was concluded by some to be a sign of sexual abuse. Although most experts agreed that anal dilatation may follow anal abuse, there was considerable disagreement as to the other circumstances in which it might occur.

* *A normal phenomenon* In evidence to the Inquiry, Dr Irvine, Dr Roberts and Mr Heald all said that they had seen anal dilatation in children they believed to be normal. On cross-examination, it became clear that the numbers were few, and their confidence that anal abuse had not occurred rested on their perception of the family. It is of great importance to establish whether or not they are correct. Clearly it does not happen in all children, or indeed in many children; but it might happen in a few children. Such studies would be very difficult; they may present ethical problems; yet such information would be of great value.

* *Forceful separation of the buttocks* we were told that in some children, particularily in the left lateral position, firm pressure has to be used to separate the buttocks in order to obtain a clear view of the anus. It was suggested, particularily by Dr Roberts that forceful separation of the buttocks might have the effect of triggering off the opening of the anal canal, but she gave no reason for this. Dr Higgs had tried it on her own children and found that it did not. We also received other evidence that it is not possible in neurologically normal children to open the anal canal by forcibly separating the buttocks. Finger pressure close to the anal margin is used to roll the skin of the anal verge outwards in order to display fissures. Again it will not of itself open the anal canal. If it stimulates recto-anal reflex, as Mr Heald surmised then it might. But it is not the force of the finger pressure which opens the canal.

* *In Constipation* Constipation means different things to different people. It is commonly used to mean difficulty with defaecation, and it is implied that the stool is hard and the bowel is emptied infrequently. A hard stool, forced out, may damage the skin lining of the anal canal; the force may cause the surrounding veins to distend. The stool itself may be small and lumpy. One form of treatment is to give a medicine which makes the stool bulkier.

In some infants and young children, however, who continue to resist defaecation by contracting the external sphincter, the rectum becomes distended with faecal masses which when ultimately evacuated may well exceed the size of an erect male penis. Such a stool may tear the sensitive skin lining the anal canal causing a painful fissure which may in turn cause the internal sphincter to tighten (to go into spasm) which further aggravates the problem. The question is whether constipation of this degree could cause anal dilatation. Dr Wynne and Dr Morrell gave evidence that they had looked at many constipated children and had not seen it. This was the view of Dr Higgs and Dr Wyatt. Others believed that constipation might; they included Dr Irvine and Dr Roberts but their argument was of a theoretical nature.

* *In Megacolon* If constipation is very prolonged in children, the rectum can become permanently distended with hard impacted faeces (megacolon or megarectum) and then it cannot be corrected by the simple remedies for constipation. Dr Clayden, a consultant paediatrician from London is an expert in this disorder. He considered that anal dilatation might occur with buttock separation if megacolon were present. In this condition the internal sphincter is over-stretched and not responding properly and the external sphincter itself cannot avoid liquid soiling, (spurious diarrhoea). It is far more than simple constipation. It is clearly important if anal dilatation is observed to determine whether or not the rectum and lower colon is overloaded with faeces. We were told that the faecal masses can usually be palpated abdominally; they may also be observed up the opened anal canal; if there is doubt there may need to be a digital examination. According to Dr Clayden, after defaecation, if there was not chronic constipation and retention of some faeces he would expect the anal dilatation to cease.

One of the treatments for this chronic condition is to stretch the anal sphincter under anaesthesia by forcing in four fingers (sphincter dilatation). Mr Heald said that after sphincter dilatation the sphincters remained lax, for three or four weeks, but it was difficult to test and therefore he could not be certain. Dr Clayden said that little or no change could be detected after the procedure. The operation is only performed on children with a long-term serious problem with defaecation and the anal canal is not normal to begin with.

It would appear that the sign of anal dilatation should be viewed with some caution in cases of chronic constipation.

* *Other possible causes of anal dilatation* Other possible causes of anal dilatation were suggested by various witnesses. Dr Roberts suggested the presence of threadworms. Dr Ellis Fraser said that in her experience there might be slight opening from threadworms but not comparable to wide opening generally referred to. Dr Bamford considered that threadworms were not relevant to the sign. Dr Dias suggested bronchodilator medicines, but there was no other evidence in support of that proposition. Dr Clayden said that theoretically anxiety or fear might cause the opening. The possibility of fear as the cause was canvassed in a judgment of Judge Hall in one wardship case. There was however no evidence of that before the Inquiry.

191

The size of the opening at the end of the test may vary with the state of the child, being larger when the child is more relaxed, and smaller when the child is tense. It could well vary with the position of the muscular diaphragm which supports the pelvic contents. In view of such factors, until more is known, it would be unwise to put too much reliability on the extent of the opening.

* Views of the Two Associations

11.29 The Association of Police Surgeons in their protocol to the Standing Medical Advisory Committee referred to the buttock separation test and said:—"If, within half a minute, the anus positively dilates for two or three seconds then reflex anal dilatation can be said to occur and while not pathognomic of sexual abuse it should certainly give rise to strong suspicion that sexual abuse has occurred and other signs and symptoms searched for. Taken on its own, it is not sufficient proof." Their President, Dr Jenkins in evidence to the Inquiry supported that statement. By a letter addressed to the Inquiry at the end of November, and after both Dr Irvine and Dr Raine Roberts had given evidence, Dr de la Haye Davies the Secretary of the Association asked the Inquiry to accept a rewording of the passage quoted above, to read:—

"While not pathognomic of sexual abuse, it should give rise to suspicion that sexual abuse may have occurred."

Dr Appleyard on behalf of the British Paediatric Association said that anal dilatation raises:—"a significant area of anxiety that should be followed through. One cannot ignore such a sign".

* Assessing Anal Sphincter tone by digital examination

The open anal canal, or the opening anal canal may both indicate a stretched or weakened anal sphincter, but on the other hand they may not. In the diagnosis of anal abuse some medical experts, in the main police surgeons, relied on a more direct assessment of anal sphincter tone. They attempted to assess the tone by digital examination and the sphincter power by asking a child to grip the finger tightly. The child of course has to understand what is being requested, to be able to do it and to be prepared to do it. Its value in young children must be limited which raises the doubt as to the usefulness of the triad recommended by Dr Paul.

There was a wide difference of opinion as to the value of attempting to assess sphincter tone by seeing how far the anal canal could be stretched. In the main, paediatricians, (Drs Higgs, Wyatt, Morell, Oo, Wynne, Hobbs, Clayden, Bamford, Appleyard) considered it was unnecessary and of doubtful value. The police surgeons considered it was an important and necessary part of the examination. Dr Clayden, who was described to the Inquiry as having unique specialist knowledge and experience of disorders of defaecation in children, considered it was not possible to assess sphincter tone by digital examination. Furthermore the view was expressed that as the indication was suspected sexual abuse, a digital examination by a stranger, albeit a doctor, was particularily inappropriate. No paediatrician who gave evidence, written or oral, performed a digital examination as a routine part of the examination for sexual abuse.

By contrast, Dr Irvine and Dr Roberts considered that it was an essential part of their investigation; that anal abuse could not be diagnosed without it; and that not to perform a digital examination bordered on the negligent. It was also the practice of Dr Jenkins, to perform digital examinations. However, the advice in the protocol of which we were given a copy described the the need for a digital examination as 'controversial'. In the same letter referred to above this was corrected to:—"This is a controversial subject to some people. Council was unanimous that there is no controversy among police surgeons ... about the need for digital examinations. ....the controversy is between police surgeons and some other groups of doctors (e.g. some paediatricians)." It was not the practice however of the Northumbria Women Police Doctors according to Dr Ellis Fraser. It does not appear to have been Dr Roberts' routine in the examination of all the children referred to her after an allegation of sexual abuse but only those in which anal abuse was alleged.

Dr Jenkins told us that he would not do a digital examination unless he had seen the sign and fissures were present. In any event he would not do such an examination if there were fresh tears because it would be painful.

Various techniques of assessing sphincter tone were described. Dr Irvine inserted his first finger and invited the child to squeeze. Dr Jenkins inserted first his little finger and advanced it, then a larger finger, then the thumb and perhaps two fingers if the anal canal accepted them easily. Dr Paul, whose writings were provided to the Inquiry, recommended in the case of adults inserting three fingers and spreading them

192

if possible to demonstrate the damaged sphincters. It is uncertain if he recommended the insertion of three fingers in the case of young children. Dr Roberts on the other hand inserted only the tip of her little finger.

In none of the Cleveland children examined by police surgeons, Drs Irvine, Beeby, Roberts, Paul and Clarke, whose reports were before the Inquiry, was a weak or damaged sphincter considered to be present. In conclusion, the value of digital examination in anal abuse of children remains a matter of medical controversy.

* Recovery

The next vexed question is how long it takes for the damage caused by anal abuse to repair itself. Children recover with remarkable speed, their skin heals with more facility than adults, so skin lesions like cuts, bruises and abrasions will disappear in days. But skin thickening and pigmentation will take weeks at least before it reverts to normal. Fissures too can heal quickly but may leave a scar. The precise nature of anal verge defects appears unknown; on general grounds they may be expected to remain.

Witnesses expressed varying opinions as to how long the anal dilatation would take to recover and it will obviously vary with the severity and duration of anal abuse if that is the cause. Dr Higgs said: "My difficulty is that I am not sure how the sign of reflex anal dilatation resolves...I think we need to look at the resolution of this sign carefully." Dr Wynne who probably has more experience than anyone else, and who has followed up many of the children in whom she found the sign thought that it had usually disappeared more quickly but it also could persist for months.

* Eliciting the anal signs

Whilst there were clear differences of opinion about the interpretation of physical signs, there was also uncertainty as to whether the signs were present or not. This would seem to depend not only on the experience and skill of the observer but also the length of time since the injury, if abuse is thought to be the cause. Furthermore the disappearance of the signs when the child was separated from the possible perpetrator added weight in the minds of some doctors to the evidence that abuse had occurred.

In some children in Cleveland the anal canal opened more widely on some occasions than others. In a small group of children the sign fluctuated from time to time; it appeared, disappeared and reappeared in one child four times over several months. It was believed by Dr Higgs and Dr Wyatt and had at one time according to them been believed by Dr Wynne that it signalled on each occasion fresh anal abuse. From the bulk of the evidence that is unlikely always to be the case.

There were occasions when Dr Higgs and Dr Wyatt elicited anal dilatation at a time when Dr Irvine and Dr Beeby did not. Likewise Drs Paul, Roberts and Clarke did not to our knowledge demonstrate anal dilatation in any child they examined in Cleveland.

Various explanations were suggested for this position. Dr Wyatt considered that it depended to a large extent upon the state of relaxation of the child; the length of time the examiner may have waited, the way in which the buttocks were separated.

According to the evidence of Dr Roberts, in Cleveland she never found evidence of anal abuse or the sign of anal dilatation. If anal opening is a normal finding in some individuals it might be expected to persist; it was never however elicited in children examined at the parents' request.

General Conclusions on Anal Dilatation

11.30 We are satisfied from the evidence that the consensus is that the sign of anal dilatation is abnormal and suspicious and requires further investigation. It is not in itself evidence of anal abuse.

In considering generally physical signs on a suspicion of sexual abuse, we endorse the observation in 'Some Principles of Good Practice':—"Abnormal physical signs are rarely unequivocally diagnostic with the exception of the presence of semen or blood of a different group to that of the child."

In a Hobbs/Wynne paper which formed part of their presentation [see page 198] they said:—"The specific forensic examination must take place in the context of the whole child examination which in turn forms part of the assessment of the family as a whole." It is important at all times to have that advice in mind.

Aspects of the Medical Examination

Consents to medical examination

Parents

11.31 Concern and indeed anger has been expressed during the Inquiry by parents about medical examinations carried out on their children. The major issue raised and given wide publicity by the media was the example of a child presenting at hospital for a medical problem unconnected with any allegation of sexual abuse; the child being examined by a paediatrician and diagnosed as sexually abused. The inference drawn by parents and the media has been routine screening for sexual abuse. We are entirely satisfied that there has been at no time routine screening of sexual abuse and that the paediatricians in Cleveland have only examined children when in their professional judgment there was cause to do so.

With the help of a considerable body of medical opinion and the comments of other individuals and bodies we have extracted the following views. In doing so we do not wish to stray unnecessarily into the realms of medical ethics nor the patient/doctor relationship. But it seems helpful to us to restate views widely held with which we agree.

  i. When a parent takes a child to be seen by a doctor, the parent must be assumed to imply a consent to all examinations of the child, considered necessary in the clinical judgment of the doctor.

  ii. If a child presents to any doctor with any potential medical problem which alerts the doctor to the need to examine any part of the body, it is his duty to do that examination, and failure to do so might expose him to serious criticism.

  iii. In many cases, particularly young children at for instance a health clinic an examination of the child would be expected to include a visual examination of all parts of the body. Failure of a child to thrive for instance, would require a doctor to make a thorough and comprehensive examination.

  iv. Where a child presents with particular problems in the ano-genital region, such as urinary tract infections or constipation there must obviously be a specific examination of that part of the body.

  v. On admission to hospital it is the practice to examine the whole child which would seem entirely appropriate. Any necessary examinations of the child while an in-patient in hospital would be assumed upon the parent consenting to the child's admission to hospital.

  vi. Where a child presents with a suspicion of physical or sexual abuse a complete examination of the child is necessary for a number of reasons, including the immediate health and welfare of the child, the assessment whether the suspicion is supported by medical evidence and the careful recording of all relevant signs including bruises, lacerations, tears for later court proceedings.

  vii. General anaesthetics, or surgery would require specific consent.

  viii. Routine complete examinations of children including the ano-genital region, outside the above examples would not appear to be the practice nor would it appear an appropriate one.

11.32 In all these instances parental consent should be sought, but in many it would be implied. In children suspected of being sexually or indeed physically abused, the parent clearly should be asked for consent to examine, but not to examine one part of the child. Paediatricians would usually require to make a full medical assessment of the child in either eventuality and were parents to give consent to examination of the ears, nose and throat, chest and abdomen but not below this would seem unworkable and unsuitable. In any event evidence was given by several paediatricians that many children find examination of the ears more upsetting than visual inspection of the anus.

11.33 In cases of suspected physical or sexual abuse situations do arise when a parent does not give consent. This is a grey area which we deal with in chapter 16. The proposed emergency protection order would clarify the right of others to require the medical examination to take place. Nothing should however detract from the need of a doctor to put the health, welfare and safety of the child first.

The consent to be given by the parent is informed consent.

11.34 It has caused us some concern as to the extent to which parents always understand the purpose of the examination by a police surgeon instructed as he is by the Police to examine, and to look for forensic evidence such as in suitable cases, the taking of swabs. In the Cleveland crisis this problem largely did not arise since the police surgeon was, no doubt to the knowledge of the family, likely to find no anal abuse.

11.35 For many if not the majority of children said to have been sexually abused, there is no health problem requiring treatment and the doctor called in has no medical duty of care for the child beyond the examination. The purpose of the examination is to assist the protecting agencies or the parents. There is a danger, in the present climate of opinion, that the informed consent of the parent may not be forthcoming for a police surgeon's examination or a second opinion other than one called for by the parents. This may be at a stage when others such as the Social Services Department may not have armed themselves with the appropriate authority of an interim care order and may not wish to take that action at that stage. Child sexual abuse requires professionals to act in the best interests of a child which may not be in the best interests of the parents. Medical examination is a clear example of this difficulty. The issue of parental consent to medical examination on suspicion of sexual abuse is one which under present arrangements is difficult to resolve.

We refer to the special position of a ward of court in chapter 16.

Consent by child to examination

11.36 The Childrens' Legal Centre in their written submission to the Inquiry expressed views about the need to obtain the consent of the child to medical examination, and referred to the decision of the House of Lords in Gillick v. West Norfolk A.H.A. [1986] A.C.112. Lord Scarman in his speech at page 188 said:—"Save where statute otherwise provides, a minor's capacity to make his or her own decision depends upon the minor having sufficient understanding and intelligence to make the decision."

11.37 One child in Cleveland told the Official Solicitor that she was misled as to the purpose of the examination. Samantha in her story, see Child Abuse chapter, who was 16 was not consulted. (This was in 1985).

11.38 However the suggestion of the Childrens' Legal Centre that children often underwent medical examinations of an "intimate internal and often distressing and painful nature", was not generally borne out in the evidence, nor in the discussions the Official Solicitor had with some of the children. Complaint was made of the use of glass rods and of digital examination. Some children found the examinations embarrassing or upsetting; others were less concerned about them.

11.39 We were impressed by the advice given, particularly by Dr Bamford, as to the way in which the child even a young child can be involved in the actual examination so as to reduce the need for the doctor to touch the child, even in the taking of swabs for forensic purposes.

11.40 One most important element must be the approach of the doctor examining any child, the consideration, kindness, explanation of the steps being taken. But in addition with the older child of appropriate age and understanding his/her consent should also be obtained. According to Dr Wynne, teenagers sometimes refuse, but usually come back on another occasion for the examination.

Place of examination

11.41 Where the child is examined initially appeared to cause some difficulty. As is set out in the chapter on the ARC, the Police originally saw no objection to the medical examination of a child in a suitably furnished room in a police station. There is now unanimity according to the evidence before the Inquiry that the police station is not a suitable place for the medical examination of a child.

11.42 Medical examinations of children believed to have been sexually abused within the family circle were generally considered in the evidence to be best carried out in a hospital where suitable facilities are set aside for the purpose. Dr Wynne would however prefer a house which could be used for a number of purposes including medical examinations, in preference to a hospital.

11.43 Various doctors, mainly some of the police surgeons, saw the advantages of the family practitioner's surgery for a sexual assault outside the family, which would avoid the necessity of the child going to hospital.

The flexibility of the venue according to the circumstances was advocated.

Who should carry out the examination

11.44 This question presented major problems in Cleveland both during 1987 and for several years previous, according to the deliberations of the ARC working party.

A number of views were expressed, but the medical experts were unanimous on a number of matters.

a. Any doctor engaged in this difficult and delicate field must have some specific training to the extent that he/she is likely to be involved.

b. The doctor must have the right approach to and sympathy for children, and the right approach to the problems involved.

c. The doctor must be prepared to take the forensic samples needed in certain cases.

d. The doctor must be prepared to attend case conferences whenever possible.

e. The doctor must be prepared and experienced in providing evidence to and giving evidence in court proceedings, criminal, juvenile court and other civil courts.

Dr Roberts gave us some very helpful advice about the training of suitable doctors and the need for a list of doctors in each area with suitable qualifications to be called on in suspected sexual abuse cases.

Number of examinations—Second Opinions

11.45 A matter which has greatly concerned us in relation to the children in the Cleveland crisis has been the number of examinations by different doctors of the same child. There is a danger that such examinations take place more for the purpose of providing information for the adults than for the advantage of the child. One family was examined by three paediatricians and four police surgeons; another family was examined by four paediatricians and two police surgeons. There are many other instances. This criticism is not intended to discourage all necessary examinations and repeat examinations of a child undergoing treatment or routine check-ups by the doctors having the care and responsibility for that child. The examinations to which we refer were not principally in that category. These repeated examinations were made for the purpose of confirming or refuting a diagnosis of sexual abuse and in some instances in Cleveland they got out of hand. Many of those who gave evidence, including Dr Higgs and Dr Wyatt deplored this trend.

11.46 When an allegation of sexual abuse has been made, clearly there are many different organisations and individuals who have a legitimate interest in the outcome of the medical examination and may wish for a doctor of their choice to confirm or to refute the original diagnosis.

11.47 There is a natural desire of parents in particular, faced with these most serious allegations of sexual abuse, to have second opinions. Dr Appleyard said that it was long-established medical practice that parents are entitled to a second opinion. The Police may want their own police surgeon; the Local Authority has its statutory duty towards the child; the guardian ad litem has a duty to the child and to the court.

11.48 A distinction should be drawn between the consultation between consultants in a hospital where the first doctor seeks the guidance and expertise of a colleague, and formal second opinions. The first is normal practice and it would be good manners and proper to inform the parents but within the hospital would not be a situation requiring their consent since the doctor caring for the child is acting for the child and the parents. This may require a joint examination or a second examination within the hospital. The second position is the arranged second opinion for whatever purpose, and may include numerous examinations for the benefit of different groups.

11.49 One difficulty is to bring the number of examinations within reasonable limits. It is only in wardship proceedings that the court has control over the medical examinations of a child who is a ward of court.

11.50 There is also the knowledge since the court hearings of the last 12 months both in Cleveland and elsewhere that some doctors have a particular viewpoint and the danger that one side will go to Dr A and the other side to Dr B. The strength of feelings engendered by sexual abuse has not passed by the medical profession and the loss of professional objectivity can be detected both in those engaged in "an inexorable quest for sexual trauma in all suspected cases'' (Dr Zeitlin, Lancet Oct 10, 1987) and those seeking to refute the medical diagnosis. In most of these cases the child is not the patient of the examining doctor, and in many of them will not become the patient. The result may be, it has been suggested, that the repeated examinations themselves may become an abuse of the child. Dr Bamford suggested that there was a danger that the child might be sexualised.

11.51 Another problem of the examination by a doctor in these circumstances is the degree of expertise. With some doctors called in for second opinions Dr Higgs and Dr Wyatt felt with some justification that however distinguished they might be, they had little practical knowledge of the presenting problem. From the evidence presented to the Inquiry much of it was of a somewhat academic quality and many of the experts had little first-hand clinical experience of the aspects seen and described by Dr Higgs and Dr Wyatt. For instance in many years of experience Mr Heald had seen very few cases of anal abuse in his area of the country.

11.52 The Northern Regional Health Authority provided an emergency service in their Second Opinion Panel and also on a short term basis the referral to the Regional Reference Group [see chapter 8]. They gave a much-needed and invaluable support to the community in a time of crisis but for the reasons set out in that chapter neither arrangement should be considered as a long-term model.

11.53 Various suggestions were made for ways in which to cut down the number of medical examinations. At the present time the medical examination is assuming a disproportionate importance in the assessment of whether sexual abuse has occurred. While the emphasis remains on medical findings it is difficult to achieve this satisfactorily.

11.54 Joint examinations by paediatrician and police surgeon have been advocated. This appears to work well in certain cases in Manchester between Dr Bamford and Dr Raine Roberts, according to Dr Bamford in acute cases, and in Tower Hamlets. It is also the practice of Dr Oo with either Dr Irvine or another police surgeon at North Tees General Hospital. Dr Wynne however indicated that it had caused difficulties both in Leeds and Bradford, and that a trial period in Bradford had been halted.

This is a most difficult problem and some suggestions are put forward in part 3 of the report.

Informing the parents

11.55 Dr Higgs and Dr Wyatt considered it their duty immediately to share with the parents their views on the possibility of the diagnosis of child sexual abuse as soon as they had reached it. This was before consultation with the Police or Social Services, or any wider assessment of the family. The difficulties to which this approach led are set out in the various chapters in part 1 of this report.

11.56 Dr Cameron warned of the dangers of the sole professional making the diagnosis of sexual abuse in isolation with all the burden that that decision entails. Dr Wynne said:—''You must not get isolated in a field like that.'' She went on to say:—''I think one of the difficulties is that when a professional first starts seeing children who have been sexually abused, it is very upsetting. I do not know whether people have talked through what it is like being a professional seeing a child of three who has been anally abused. When we started in Leeds not only were we upset and continue to be upset, but I think it makes you very anxious. .....The way anxiety affects me is that I become more cautious and I am less likely to diagnose child abuse.''

She felt they had become extremely cautious and that was not necessarily in the children's best interests. ''When we first started we were somewhat more precipitate.''

In Archives of Disease in Childhood, (1987, 62, 1188) Bentovim et al. sets out advice on telling parents of the diagnosis.

If the proposals set out in part 3 are acceptable this situation in its stark setting would not arise.

Recording the findings—written and photographic and confidentiality

11.57 Some Principles of Good Practice recommended:—''There is no substitute for accurate detailed accounts and diagrams of the physical appearances in the medical records and an appropriate pro forma can be very effective.''

11.58 We were told of the great importance of the doctor examining a child, where there is raised suspicion of sexual abuse, making very careful notes of all aspects and recording the negative findings as well as the positive findings. This includes, where appropriate, the recording of the taking of the forensic swabs and the swabs for sexually transmitted diseases. A number of the witnesses had devised forms which they filled in while examining the child; some of these were helpfully provided to the Inquiry. Dr Margaret Lynch provided to the Inquiry a particularily useful pro forma used in her area of London which we have set in full in the appendices. [see appendix F]

11.59 Some Principles of Good Practice state:—"photography is desirable as a record in itself and because it may reduce the need for subsequent examinations. ....It should be borne in mind that photography on separate or subsequent occasions constitutes further examinations of the child."

11.60 There was criticism during 1987 at the use of photography and the Police were particularily unhappy at its use. Dr Higgs told us of one child who was embarassed at repeated photography. But there was general approval of the use of photographs as part of the clinical record among medical practitioners and with the proviso in the quotation above as to the frequency, there appears to be no reason to object to the practice, with the appropriate consents.

11.61 In normal circumstances medical records of a patient are confidential and their disclosure to others would require the consent of the patient. This would not apply where the disclosure was to be to other medical practitioners involved in the patient's clinical management, and other health care professionals also involved in the patient's care and in confidence. In cases where sexual abuse of a child is suspected, it is likely that many of the patients would be too young to give consent to the disclosure of their medical records to other agencies having a need to investigate, such as police and social workers. If the sexual abuse is suspected within the family, the consent of the parent of the patient cannot be assumed to be forthcoming in every case. It is vital to share that information in a multi-disciplinary context where the level of suspicion has reached the necessary threshold. The welfare of the child then requires its disclosure to a wider audience.
'Some Principles of Good Practice' point out that that parents need to appreciate that there may be wider sharing of information between professionals from many disciplines. They add the reminder that doctors must realise this.
"The doctor has to reconcile the extent to which confidentiality can be maintained, in the face of the best interests of the child. In practice, the best interests of the child come first even though this may conflict with the best interests of the parent". They added that when the child is a patient, parents cannot expect to be accorded the benefits of confidentiality. It must be made clear that all relevant information given by them to the doctor concerning the assessments may need to be shared among the professionals working on the case. It was a recommendation of the General Medical Council in 1987: "On the recommendations of the Standards Committee the Council in November, 1987 expressed the view that, if a doctor has reason for believing that a child is being physically or sexually abused, not only is it permissible for the doctor to disclose information to a third party but it is a duty of the doctor to do so".

Evidence of Certain Experts

Dr Wynne—11.62

Dr Raine Roberts—11.63

Dr Jenkins and the Police Surgeons Association—11.64

Dr Appleyard and Professor Forfar and the British Paediatric Association—11.65.

Dr Wynne and the Leeds presentation

11.62 The Inquiry accepted an invitation to see a presentation by Dr Hobbs and Dr Wynne of their work. We were told that this presentation has been shown at a number of seminars attended by medical and social work professionals.

There were four speakers, Dr Hobbs, Dr Wynne, both consultant paediatricians at separate hospitals in Leeds; Dr Hanks, principal clinical psychologist in psychotherapy and family therapy; and Mrs McMurray, Co-ordinator in Child Abuse for Leeds Social Services Department. For reasons of time, we did not allow the opportunity for cross-examination of all the speakers, although they were willing to give evidence. We invited Dr Wynne only to give evidence. We were provided with very interesting data evaluating the results of the work done at Leeds, some of it not published, and some of it is therefore included in the appendices [appendix L]. One of the features of the work of the Leeds team which came across from the presentation was the multi-disciplinary framework in which it is carried out. In this chapter we will concentrate only on the medical aspects, while wider multi-disciplinary context will be dealt with in chapter 14. It should always be borne in mind that the Leeds team were not medical practitioners working in isolation from other professionals.

The views of other medical practitioners about the work of the Leeds paediatricians have been aired in the correspondance columns of and several articles in the Lancet and Archives of Disease in Childhood. We have been provided with copies of them. Those views, many of them expressed at the Inquiry, range from the support of the Northumbria Police Women (Dr Ellis Fraser) to the condemnation by Dr Roberts. [see page 200] Dr Bamford said of the Hobbs/Wynne work:—"I think they have made a contribution and their papers in the Lancet described the appearances of children in which there have clearly been sexual abuse. .... I do not think that there has been a proper scientific evaluation of the alternatives." There were times during the medical evidence when it seemed to the Inquiry that the professional dispute over the diagnosis and research of the Leeds team was being fought out in the arena of Cleveland.

The work of the Hobbs/Wynne team however very much influenced the events in Cleveland, both for the two paediatricians concerned and for the Social Services Department, in a number of ways.

1. Both Dr Higgs and Mrs Richardson, among others, had heard members of the Leeds team speak on several occasions, and Dr Higgs' first sight of anal dilatation was a month after hearing Dr Wynne for the first time.

2. Dr Wynne was asked by Dr Higgs to give a second opinion on the clinical findings on 10 children in 5 families. In none of these cases did she take any sort of history and was not expected to do so. We are told that the examinations were very brief and her conclusions were unequivocal. She saw for instance a family of three children in March. In respect of the youngest her opinion was:—"Chronic sexual abuse. These signs are consistent with repeated anal penetration over a prolonged period." Her opinion of the middle child was "sexual abuse, with a dilated vagina consistent with digital or partial penile penetration and a markedly abnormal anus." The opinion on the eldest child was:—"sexual abuse. The signs are consistent with chronic anal abuse with penetration." In each of the other cases she confirmed the diagnosis of sexual abuse.

In evidence she said that it was not for her to tell a colleague the way to make a wider assessment of the probabilities of sexual abuse. She seems not to have appreciated the weight that was and would inevitably be attached by a recently appointed consultant in a new field to the professional opinion of a more experienced and respected colleague. Dr Higgs was confirmed in her professional opinion that these were unequivocal signs of sexual abuse and there was no need for further evaluation of the families concerned nor consideration of any alternative possibility.

3. Great reliance was placed by the Social Services Department upon her confirmation of the diagnoses by Dr Higgs in the case of the foster family at the beginning of May. The Director had required a second opinion and the Social Services Department felt secure in the diagnoses of Dr Higgs supported as they were up to the hilt by Dr Wynne. Her support in those cases confirmed the accuracy of the diagnostic techniques, the reliability of the signs observed and added weight to the reliance upon the medical diagnosis alone in subsequent sexual abuse cases.

Dr Wynne in her very helpful evidence candidly explained that she had herself become more cautious, and she urged caution in her evidence. She had come through a phase when she took more immediate action. In order not to overload the system she now put controls in at the diagnostic stage. From her own experience she tried to give good advice to Dr Higgs, and attempted to advise her to proceed slowly, without success.

Dr Roberts

11.63 Dr. Roberts is a general practiner and police surgeon in Manchester and also Clinical Director of the new Sexual Assault Referral Centre set up with the assistance of Dr Bamford at St Mary's Hospital. She is consulted by local paediatricians and social workers on cases of suspected child sexual abuse in the Manchester area.

She told us in her evidence that in 1986 she saw 160 children in Manchester referred to her with suspicion of sexual abuse. Her involvement in the field of child sexual abuse both nationally and in Cleveland made her an important witness to the Inquiry in a number of ways.

She disagreed with the findings of Drs Hobbs and Wynne and wrote a letter published in the Lancet, (21st November 1986) disagreeing with the Wynne/Hobbs paper. She told us that she had received a number of communications from consultant paediatricians agreeing with what she had said. In her lectures and in discussion at medical meetings after this time she expressed concern about the interpretation of anal findings, and so by the time of the Cleveland crisis she already had strongly held views. Her disagreement was based on her own experience.

She said that prior to October 1986:—"My experience of children who have been anally abused, which did go back over a number of years, had not generally included children who had got anal dilatation." Her experience of diagnosing anal abuse was therefore rather limited. She told us:—"I did not see many children who had been buggered." She had seen positive medical signs of anal abuse in about 14 children since the beginning of 1985.

Upon reading the Wynne/Hobbs article she was prepared to consider anal dilatation might be a significant finding even though she had not observed it in children where she had made a diagnosis of anal abuse. She further explained:—"In October 1986 the controversial article in the Lancet was published and only a fortnight later I saw a 4 year old child at the request of the Greater Manchester Police." On examination she saw the following signs:—"the anal area appeared to be sore and that there was reflex anal dilatation." She formed the view that the findings were consistent with the anus having been penetrated and informed the police. She discovered later that the child had repeatedly suffered from threadworms and often had an itchy bottom. From the subsequent investigations carried out by the social workers it was unlikely that sexual abuse had taken place. Dr Roberts told us she believed an account by the grandmother was malicious. This case made her change her mind with regard to the reliability of anal dilatation. She told us: "I took it (anal dilatation) on board and got egg on my face.......This case prompted me to write my letter to the Lancet disputing the opinions given by Drs Hobbs and Wynne in their article......How can you make the diagnosis without gently feeling inside the anus?"

She was being presented with a diagnosis and diagnostic technique that she had not previously considered in her practice. Either she had been missing a great number of cases over the years or the work of Dr Wynne and Dr Hobbs was not reliable. Dr Roberts came to the latter conclusion.

She expressed to Dr Irvine her firm view as to the unreliability of the sign of anal dilatation, when he consulted her in March, presumably soon after the case conference on the 11th March. She was strongly opposed to:—"the teaching of Dr Hobbs and Dr Wynne" and its application by Dr Higgs and Dr Wyatt. Later she said of Dr Higgs and Dr Wyatt:—"They appear to have followed uncritically some of the teaching of the Leeds paediatricians on the subject of anal abuse, but have gone further in that in many cases they have made a firm diagnosis on the basis of one inadequate examination, without considering other factors."

She was involved in Cleveland as one of the expert witnesses on behalf of the parents. By the time she gave evidence to the Inquiry she had examined or commented on other doctors' examination of 39 children from 20 families at the request of Cleveland parents between June and November 1987. She and Dr Paul on one day examined 14 children in twelve and a half hours. She said:—"I do not think that I found signs of anal abuse in any of them."

She found signs of sexual abuse other than anal abuse in some and in others there was "cause for concern". She pointed out that in many of her reports she did not say that there was no evidence of sexual abuse but that there was no medical evidence. We were somewhat concerned that in some cases she examined, non-physical indications of a worrying nature were masked by strongly expressed comments in the reports provided to the parents for court proceedings that there was no medical evidence of abuse. These non-physical findings were however described in a later summary provided by her to the Inquiry as matters which raised concern.

The language of these reports was frequently couched in expressions of absolute certainty, such as:—"No medical evidence of sexual abuse whatsoever" and "It is not possible to make a diagnosis that a child has been sexually abused merely by a visual inspection of the anus. This is purely the view of a small number of paediatricians and is not accepted by most doctors".

She agreed in evidence that the way one particular report was framed might have given an inadequate picture of concern to the Juvenile Court receiving it.

The impression we gained was, that in her belief that the sign was unreliable and that the paediatricians concerned both in Leeds and in Cleveland were in error, she provided to the courts clinical signs as she observed them, but may have given a somewhat partial impression in reports on at least some of these children. The presentation of her reports both written and oral took her outside the role of impartial expert witness traditionally required of police surgeons. Clearly there are dangers to the Police Service and the legal system as a whole of such a development.

Dr Roberts' view on anal dilatation and digital examination

11.64 She said of the test that it was not new.:—"I think it is something that has always been observed. I have observed it over the years and noted it. It is usually not regarded as being particularily significant." She had however been carrying out the test only for the last 18 months. In the present controversy she also said she did the test very carefully:—"Any child where the anus does open, I think one has to be slightly suspicious." She qualified it by saying:

"Interested rather than suspicious......My view now is that it is an odd and bizarre phenomenon which does not really seem to have much significance. It is in a lot of other children as well. I do not believe it does indicate sexual abuse".

She was of the view that digital examination of a child was necessary. "I would not make a firm diagnosis except in the presence of serious injury, without feeling it necessary to do a digital examination." She would only only have considered the possibility of anal abuse if the sphincter was lax on digital examination .

She was also of the view that no paediatrician could give a proper diagnosis of anal abuse unless there were obvious signs of acute injury without such an examination. In her opinion the evidence would be incomplete and the diagnosis incompetent.

Dr Roberts' criticisms of Dr Higgs and Dr Wyatt

11.65 Her criticisms of the diagnoses and examinations of the two Cleveland doctors were supported by Dr Clarke and Dr Paul who examined some children. Her criticisms were couched in strong and emotive language including strong personal criticisms of Dr Higgs. She asserted that the paediatricians were insensitive in their examinations, and referred to a number of children held screaming by two nurses behind locked doors. From the evidence before the Inquiry one instance identified was a gross exaggeration of the facts and the other which came from an account given by a friend of the mother not present at the examination does not appear to be true. In her written evidence she told us:—"The child cannot distinguish between an assault carried out in a hospital room by a stranger (a doctor) and a similar experience elsewhere. I am concerned that some children will suffer lasting harm as a result of being subjected to examinations involving the use of force. Paediatricians pride themselves in caring for the whole child and patronise the police surgeon, and yet some are prepared to countenance, or even commit, outrageous sexual assault of children in the hospital which has occurred in some cases in Cleveland."

She did not withdraw these remarks at the Inquiry. They were not borne out by the investigations by the Official Solicitor of the children whom he represented.

Concluding Remarks

11.66 Dr Roberts' evidence to us contained some very helpful advice about the training of police surgeons in a multi-disciplinary context which is a true reflection of her invaluable experience and which we have carefully considered.

She has great experience in examining both women and children suspected of being the victims of rape and other sexual assaults, including sexual abuse in the family. She said herself, however that her experience of diagnosing anal abuse was slight.

In her evidence on anal abuse, she appeared to have become associated with the cause of the parents and was unable to provide us with the cool, detached and considered testimony the Inquiry might have expected of the expert, particularly a police surgeon.

Counsel to the Inquiry advised us in his closing submission that the evidence of Dr Roberts proved to be: "extremely and unnecessarily critical and contentious...far from passing to planes of increasing authority and moderation it became more and more passionate in character and thus perhaps of less value...We will not be urging you for a moment to adopt or accept her views, because we seek to stress throughout the vital importance of striving for middle ground, and obviously Dr Roberts does not stand on middle ground in regard to this issue."

This assessment with which we agree is a matter of regret.

Dr Jenkins—Police Surgeons Association

11.67 Dr Jenkins was current President of the Police Surgeons Association of Great Britain. He gave evidence on behalf of the Association; provided the Inquiry with the protocol of the Association to the Standing Medical Advisory Council, and the agreed joint statement of the joint working party of the Association of Police Surgeons and the British Paediatric Association. He also gave us some very helpful evidence from his own wider experience in East London referred to in chapter 14.

The police surgeons firmly believe that they have an important role to play in the detection of child sexual abuse. One element of this is their experience in gathering forensic evidence. Another important element is their willingness to go to court and to give evidence and their experience in doing so, an experience not necessarily shared by other medical practitioners. Dr Jenkins also pointed out the role of liaison between the Police, the Medical Profession and the Social Services.

Nevertheless the Police Surgeons Association accept, as is pointed out by Dr Raine Roberts, that it is not the role of police surgeon which is important in this context but the role of a suitably qualified and experienced doctor with the right approach to children. They are strongly of the view of the advantages of joint consultation and joint examination by paediatrician and police surgeon.

The joint working party recommendations are set out in appendix I.

Dr Appleyard and the British Paediatric Association (BPA)

11.68 Dr Appleyard is the Honorary Treasurer of the British Paediatric Association and gave evidence on its behalf to the Inquiry. He told us of the developments in paediatric care and of the increasing number of appointments of consultant paediatricians with a special interest in community child health, who had received specialist training which involved social paediatrics. This specialised training included child abuse and child sexual abuse and some training in forensic aspects of child sexual abuse. He stressed the importance of consultant involvement in child sexual abuse which with the emphasis upon continuing care of the child complemented rather than conflicted with the interests of police surgeons. His association felt that the continuing care of children in such cases would be best provided by 'community paediatricians'.

He provided to the Inquiry a press statement from the Association on the 25th June 1987 and the Agreed Joint Statement of the BPA and the Police Surgeons Association. [in Appendix I] He saw the advantage of the presence of the police surgeon at the examination of the child with the paediatrician, but stressed the importance of not over-emphasising or dramatising the medical examination. He pointed out the danger that a 'negative' medical examination may well result in the case being dropped without other evidence being sought of the need for child protection. We share his view that the medical examination should not play an over-important part in the assessment as to whether sexual abuse has occurred.

He stressed that the interpretation of physical findings needs to be done by highly trained and experienced paediatricians in the field. He said that this was important as some signs may disappear within a few days.

He also spoke of the lack of epidemiology on the whole subject of child sexual abuse and like others who gave evidence stressed the importance of further research, including research on the younger children in whom sexual abuse is now being detected.

There was earlier involvement of the BPA in the problems in Cleveland. During July there were some difficulties in the use of the Regional Reference Group and Professor Sir Bernard Tomlinson sought their help. On the 22nd July, Professor Forfar, the President and Dr Chambers, the Secretary, went at his request to Newcastle; met Dr Higgs and Dr Wyatt and gave some advice to the Region.

After the meeting Professor Forfar wrote both to the Region and to Dr Higgs and to Dr Wyatt. In his letter to the Region Professor Forfar said:—"The role and function of the consultant paediatrician with a special interest in community child health is now well established. The recommendation of the BPA is that each district should have at least one such appointment. Already nearly 100 such appointments have been made.

While there is some overlap between the duties of hospital-based and community-based paediatricians, the latter, more and more, are taking on tasks such as child abuse, case conferences involving children, activities which require to be carried out jointly with social workers, relationships with the police etc. These tasks if they are to be carried out properly, are time-consuming, and paediatricians who are also engaged in routine hospital paediatric practice and neonatal care cannot usually allocate to them the time that is necessary. Dr Higgs and Dr Wyatt told us that they undertake routine hospital paediatric work and neonatal care as well as carrying a heavy load in respect of child abuse cases. It seems possible that they may not have the time to engage fully in the multi-disciplinary activities which problems such as child sexual abuse demand—the frequent on-going consultations with social workers and general practitioners, the joint planning of strategies, the case conferences, the dialogues with the police etc. Pressure of time may be imposing on them the need to take decisions abruptly.

Would it not be possible for the Northern Regional Health Authority to appoint a consultant paediatrician with a special interest in community child health to the Cleveland District, including within the remit of that appointment the community element of the child abuse problem. A community input of that kind would be likely to strengthen the basis of diagnosis and improve the decision making process."

Sir Bernard said that they were grateful for that valuable notion and would give it serious consideration in the near future. We would endorse the suggestion and consider it would be a very helpful step forward.

In his letters to both doctors Professor Forfar made some wise and helpful comments and suggestions. The letter is set out in full at Appendix [G]. We quote from one paragraph:—"The regulation of medical practice is achieved best when it is accomplished within the medical profession. New stances based on a new awareness of clinical signs, or new significances being attached to them, require first to be established within the profession. This takes some time and requires persuasion and scientific evidence of validity, based on the accepted method of communication to professional journals or scientific meetings. It is the dedicated research worker and the pioneering enthusiast who so often change medicine for the better and uncover deficiencies in medical practice and understanding. In the end however, any new development has to be fitted into the complex jig-saw which constitutes balanced medical practice. As well as the benefits, the possible adverse effects of any revision of accepted practices have to be taken into account. Child sexual abuse is a very serious matter which we as paediatricians must seek to eliminate, but removal of children from their parents and forced institutionalism is another very serious matter. The values which different paediatricians and child psychiatrists will attach to these will vary. Perhaps, more importantly, any mistake in pursuing correction of one will cause the other."

CHAPTER 12

Listening to the Child

Introduction

12.1 An essential part of the investigation of an allegation or a complaint of sexual abuse will be an interview with the child if he or she is old enough to say what did or did not happen to them. The child telling of abuse was often referred to as 'in disclosure' and assisting the child to talk of it as 'disclosure work'. The use and potential abuse of 'disclosure work' was the subject of a considerable amount of evidence to the Inquiry. Dr David Jones defined 'disclosure' as:—"a clinically useful concept to describe the process by which a child who has been sexually abused within the family gradually comes to inform the outside world of his/her plight." He defined 'disclosure work' as:—"the process by which professionals attempt to encourage or hasten the natural process of disclosure by a sexually abused child."

When the child speaks of abuse

12.2 The young child may speak innocently of behaviour which an adult recognises as abuse; an older child may wish to unburden and tell of abuse to anyone they may trust and that may occur informally to, for instance, a parent, school teacher, paediatrician on a medical examination or foster mother. Dr Zeitlin told us that:—"There is evidence that material produced spontaneously without prompting is undoubtedly the most reliable form of statements that children make, and often these have been made before disclosure interviews to various people." However as a step in the inter-disciplinary investigation of sexual abuse there needs to be the formal process of interviewing the child.

12.3 During the Inquiry the question as to whether any child involved was or was not telling the truth was not an issue. The problems related to the interpretation by professionals of the comments of children who were not making clear allegations against their parents. Nevertheless, the question of whether or not to believe the child where there is concern about sexual abuse is important and evidence was given to the Inquiry about it.

12.4 What should an adult do when a child speaks of abuse? According to Dr Bentovim, until a few years ago, it was the practice for professionals to disbelieve the child. He said:—"If a child described a sexual experience, you first of all disbelieved and it had to be proven to you, rather than you first of all taking it seriously and saying he is entitled to belief and then obviously investigating it properly and thoroughly."

12.5 In the DHSS paper "Child Abuse—Working Together" (April 1986) it is stated:—"A child's statement that he or she is being abused should be accepted as true until proved otherwise. Children seldom lie about sexual abuse."

This advice follows the present received thinking and research of a number of professionals, many of them in the United States. However not every detail of a child's story particularly a young child is to be taken literally.

Professor Kolvin said that the Royal College of Psychiatrists was not happy with the statement of the DHSS document.:—"They felt that a statement by the child that sexual abuse has occurred should be taken seriously, but you are pre-judging the issue if you say that you believe it; in other words that you believe the child entirely." He went on to say:—"Always listen to the child and always take what they say seriously."

Dr Bentovim said:—"It is safer to say take it seriously. I am glad you reminded me of the phrase we used in the CIBA Foundation booklet: entitled to belief: entitled to be taken seriously is certainly the spirit."

12.6 The importance of this is illustrated by an 11 year old boy of limited intelligence in Cleveland. During 1986/1987 a local child psychiatrist had recorded in the boy's medical records that his revelations about his father were fantasies. Mr Justice Sheldon, in the wardship hearing in early 1988 was satisfied from the wealth of evidence before him,including that of Dr Zeitlin, that the father had sexually abused the boy and his younger sister and that the boy's account was accurate.

Do children tell lies about abuse? Do they fantasise about it?

12.7 In Some Principles of Good Practice it is said:—"It is important to consider the possibility that children may fabricate or that spurious allegations may be made by parents or caretakers, as for example in matrimonial dispute, in order to deny access."

12.8 Dr Cameron told us of research in the United States on false/fictitious complaints, and warned that:—"Grave injustice may be done to a child and to the accused adult, if a false accusation is acted upon as if it were true. The interviewer will avoid such false diagnoses as long as a firm emphasis is maintained on correct interviewing not only of the child, but also of the other adults concerned.".

12.9 Dr Underwager warned us of the risks of children being fed with information provided by adults. He told us of the incidence of false allegations by children in the United States and suggested that 65% of all reports were unfounded. He also suggested that they were not the result of most children telling lies but the effect upon children of the information derived from adults, sometimes as a result of the method of interviewing. Research, particularly in the United States, has shown that the incidence of false accusations appears to be substantially higher in custody and access disputes than in other cases.

The Interview with the child

12.10 When the possibility of sexual abuse is raised the formal interview with a child of sufficient age and understanding is a necessary step in the investigation. Different types of interview must be distinguished and the purposes for which the interview is being held must be clear.

12.11 In Cleveland there was confusion as to whether some interviews were being conducted to ascertain the facts or for therapeutic purposes or a mixture of both. It must also be clear whether it is intended to 'facilitate' or assist the child to speak and if so in what way and using which aids.

The Interviewer

12.12 In most circumstances the initial formal interview will be conducted by a police officer and/or a social worker, but it might be a number of other people. Although the major part of the evidence presented to the Inquiry was from child psychiatrists, for many reasons including practical ones they are not likely to be interviewing more than a small number of children suspected of being abused, and seldom, if ever, at an initial interview. The purpose of the formal interview should be, we suggest, to listen to and to hear what the child has to say. In all but those children with disturbed behaviour or mental disorder or where the child psychiatric team has special expertise, will subsequent interviews, if any, be carried out by child psychiatrists or psychologists. From the evidence of a number of experts it was not always clear that they appreciated this was the situation.

12.13 From all the evidence provided to the Inquiry there is no reason whatsoever to conclude that the police officer, often a policewoman, and the social worker are other than entirely suitable professionals to interview such children, provided they have the appropriate training and communication skills.

12.14 Any interviewer in this delicate field must however be experienced and skilled in interviewing children.

The Surroundings

12.15 To assist children to talk, various materials and techniques were recommended to us, including, toys, play dough, plasticine, drawings and what are described as the 'anatomically correct dolls' They were referred to by a number of experts. Mrs Madge Bray and Miss Debbie Glassbrook both used various methods and explained them to the Inquiry.

12.16 Dr Underwager cautioned about the interpretation of childrens' drawings. Dr Jones warned:—"More fanciful interpretation of play, involving play materials as metaphorical representations of feared or abusive situations would seem quite out of place in the diagnostic, investigative phase of evaluative interviewing."

12.17 It would seem to us that a major consideration should be to create a sympathetic environment for children in this predicament with suitable facilities. Professor Kolvin recommended a place where a child had an opportunity for free play.

Disclosure Work

12.18 The problem arises when there is reason to believe there may be abuse and the child may need help to tell, or where the assessment to that date is inconclusive and then a somewhat different type of interview may take place. This is a second or so-called facilitative stage which needs further consideration. The interviewer at this time may be trying a more indirect approach, with the use of hypothetical or leading questions, or taking cues from the child's play or drawings. According to Dr Bentovim, it should be used sparingly by experts, who may include suitably trained social workers. He said:—"it is worth waiting a couple of days for the people who are really going to have the best skills to interview children. I think a short period of days whilst doing that can save months and months of uncertainty and difficulty."

12.19 There is a great danger, which should be recognised and avoided from the experience in Cleveland, that this facilitative second stage may be seen as a routine part of the general interview, instead of an useful tool to be used sparingly by experts in special cases. In the first stage the child tells the interviewer. The second stage is a process whereby the professional attempts to encourage the child who may be reluctant to tell the story.

Great Ormond Street Clinic

12.20 Some of this approach, initially concerned with therapy, was developed by Dr Bentovim and his colleagues at Great Ormond Street. Dr Bentovim gave us in both his written and oral evidence a helpful insight into the working of his specialised team. Details of their work have been widely published and some professionals from Cleveland had attended their workshops at Great Ormond Street.

12.21 In the late 1970s and early 1980s their work was entirely therapeutic but over the years with increasing referrals to them of children when sexual abuse was only suspected they adapted and developed those techniques for diagnostic purposes. The techniques designed to help the child talk of the experiences suffered were thus in time deployed to ascertain the truth of the allegations made. In a high proportion of cases however seen by them there was clear evidence of abuse.

12.22 Their methods and interviewing techniques have been scrutinised by several Judges in a series of reported judgements (1987 Family Law number 4.) Despite criticisms of individual interviews Judges of the Family Division paid tribute to the skills and expertise of the team. Mr Justice Latey referred to Dr Bentovim as 'an artist in interviewing', and that his clinic "has already done truly valuable work". Mr Justice Waite referred to:—"a team which is doing important pioneering work in the field of the detection of child abuse."

12.23 At the request of Dr Bentovim, Mr Justice Latey made some suggestions in a judgment. He said:—"It would be helpful to the court if the questioners were alert to any indications of an innocent, as well as a sinister, interpretation and recorded them in their notes, reports and evidence."

12.24 Dr Bentovim's team, as a result of the comments of the Judges, have reconsidered their interviewing methods and developed a more structured approach. "We use a variety of open-ended questions to see whether children can speak of their experiences if there is a high index of suspicion of abuse, and we now reserve the use of clinical techniques of interviewing e.g. use of alternative possibilities, hypothetical questions until the latter part of the interview when it is clear that a child is unable to respond to open questions and when there is a high index of suspicion from the behaviour or manifestations or context in which the child is living." He also said:—"It is extremely important that interviews are carried out in a very open way and that is the attitude which the interviewer conveys to the child, which is open-minded and that is the way in which he should conduct the interview." This is equally essential when a child unexpectedly speaks of abuse during therapy.

Dr Jones said:—"A fundamental problem of the 'disclosure' approach is that it is inherent in the concept that there is *something* to disclose. The problem is highlighted by those professionals who consider that the child is either *disclosing* or '*in denial*'. The third, and crucial, alternative possibility, namely that the child has no sexual abuse to disclose, is not considered as a viable option. In the best circumstances, the possibility of no child sexual abuse becomes an extremely unlikely possibility from such 'disclosure work'. The premise that abuse has occurred, yet is hidden and shrouded from discovery, is inherent in the very term 'disclosure work'.

Helping the Child to Tell

12.25 The concept of helping the child to tell is recognised to have its uses in certain circumstances. When embarking upon it for diagnostic purposes, it is important to remember at least three possible situations:

1. The abuse has occurred and the child is speaking of it.

2. The abuse has occurred and the child is unable to speak of it or is denying it.

3. The abuse has not occurred, and the child cannot speak of it.

12.26 It is clearly a difficult matter of judgment to know whether the child is not telling because of some sort of pressure, such as fear of the consequences, or because there is nothing to tell. At the end of a session the professionals may not know which of those two situations is the true position. There may be rare occasions when an abused child does not choose to tell and the adults should respect that view.

Disagreement between the professionals

12.27 The main area of disagreement between the child psychiatrists from whom the Inquiry received contributions, is as to the desirability of and limits upon the facilitative second stage.

12.28 On the one hand, in Dr Bentovim's opinion the use of leading, alternative, hypothetical questions should be available "but it is very important that whoever uses such techniques should be very aware of what the consequences are in terms of the fact that the interviewer immediately has problems in terms of its probability, in terms of evidential value and there is always a balance between those factors.....My reading of the research is that a free statement, a spontaneous statement made by a child is going to be the most acute."

12.29 The experience of his team was that children were usually highly relieved by the interview.

On the other hand, Professor Kolvin said:—"I am uneasy with the concept of disclosure, which really goes hell-bent for trying to get some idea of 'yes' or 'no' on the basis of almost a coercive interview with the child and also does not take into consideration the possibility that perhaps nothing has happened or that perhaps we will not know."

12.30 Some Principles of Good Practice dealt with:—"The value of this concept (disclosure interview) is questionable, as traditionally it incorporates the preconception that non-disclosure is tantamount to denial. It also seems to preclude the possibility that sexual abuse has not occurred. Disclosure techniques include investigative play, the validity and utility of which may be hampered by suggestion, leading questions, and the possibility that the investigative procedure itself may be sexualising and abusive."

12.31 Dr Zeitlin in his paper to the Lancet (October 10, 1987) cautioned against the hazards of over-enthusism and spoke of disclosure having taken on 'almost the character of a crusade'. In his final submission the Official Solicitor said:—"The topic has acquired a mystique; and good sense is not always to be seen amongst the skills which are put to work." These words of caution were strongly endorsed by Dr Underwager.

12.32 Dr Underwager provided the Inquiry with his experience in the United States and warned of the pre-conceptions and biases of adults. He said that children were vulnerable to adult influences and suggestions, such as from leading and suggestive questions. He warned that one should recognise the power of the interviewer compared with the child, and commented that those who interview seem to ignore their own behaviour. He suggested that in the USA some interviewers, 'lie, threaten, fabricate'. The method of assessment contaminates and reduces the reliability of a child's statements. He felt that small children were abused by the interrogation.

12.33 This area of disagreement clearly has to be resolved by the professions in the light of subsequent experience. Dr Bentovim said:—"There is a need for debate about skills and working with children."

Agreement of the professionals

12.34 All those who provided evidence to the Inquiry were agreed on the following points to be observed in conducting all interviews. We endorse their views:

1. The undesirability of calling them 'disclosure' interviews, which precluded the notion that sexual abuse might not have occurred.

2. All interviews should be undertaken only by those with some training, experience and aptitude for talking with children.

3. The need to approach each interview with an open mind.

4. The style of the interview should be open-ended questions to support and encourage the child in free recall.

5. There should be where possible only one and not more than two interviews for the purpose of evaluation, and the interview should not be too long.

6. The interview should go at the pace of the child and not of the adult.

7. The setting for the interview must be suitable and sympathetic.

8. It must be accepted that at the end of the interview the child may have given no information to support the suspicion of sexual abuse and position will remain unclear.

9. There must be careful recording of the interview and what the child says, whether or not there is a video recording.

10. It must be recognised that the use of facilitative techniques may create difficulties in subsequent court proceedings.

11. The great importance of adequate training for all those engaged in this work.

12. In certain circumstances it may be appropriate to use the special skills of a 'facilitated' interview. That type of interview should be treated as a second stage. The interviewer must be conscious of the limitations and strengths of the techniques employed. In such cases the interview should only be conducted by those with special skills and specific training.

Parents at Interviews.

12.35 The professionals who gave evidence to the Inquiry were unanimous about the unsuitability of having a parent present at an interview held because of the suspicion of sexual abuse. Dr Bentovim said the presence of parents made the interview very difficult, but the presence of a person familiar to the child, such as teacher or social worker, may be helpful to the child. However he/she must not take part in the interview.

Disclosure in a therapeutic context.

12.36 According to Dr Jones:—"After the discovery of abuse, at least in outline form, then it is quite possible that there will be further disclosure within the context of therapeutic involvement with the child and the family." This indeed was the way that Dr Bentovim's team was first involved in disclosure work. Dr Jones went on to say:—"The attempt to encourage disclosures while providing therapeutic treatment is fraught with difficulty." He pointed out the "untenable position" of "providing treatment while also attempting to gather information ..Adequate treatment cannot proceed in a vacuum—it must be based on a formulation of what is being treated. .....I am opposed to treatment and 'disclosure' proceeding in parallel."

12.37 Dr Underwager underlined the importance of distinguishing between treatment and investigation of abuse, one of which was in conflict with the other.

12.38 One of the problems for the child psychologist in North Tees, was her belief that she was engaged in a therapeutic process, although the children concerned had not and did not "disclose".

12.39 Other than to endorse the importance of distinguishing between diagnosis or evaluation and therapy, we did not think it appropriate to consider the therapeutic element of disclosure work.

Disclosure Work in Cleveland

12.40 In Cleveland before 1987 sexual abuse had been identified by complaint from the child or from an adult. The need to interview children believed to be sexually abused but reluctant to disclose such abuse was not widely recognised and there was a lack of expertise in the Cleveland area (and almost certainly in many other areas) in this specialised field. A number of social workers had attended conferences and work shops on the subject, some of them at Great Ormond Street.

12.41 During 1987 there appears to have been a immediate response to a suspicion of child sexual abuse that somebody should do disclosure work with the child. It is not clear whether this was intended to listen to the child's account or to use specialised techniques learnt at workshops attended by some professionals.

12.42 There can however be no doubt that there were interviews carried out in Cleveland during 1987 which fall into the type of interviews criticised in the Family Law Reports. It was apparent that various feelings came together at the time of interviewing some at least of these children—anxiety, the need for a solution, beliefs about "denial" and the therapeutic benefits for children of talking about abuse, the perceived need to believe the child and some learnt information about techniques of interviewing. These included matching the pressure on the child not to tell with pressure by the interviewer on the child at the interview. There was in many instances a presumption that abuse had occurred and the child was either not disclosing or denying that abuse. There was insufficient expertise, over-enthusiasm, and those conducting the interviews seemed unaware of the extent of pressure, even coercion, in their approach. There were dangers, which became apparent in some cases, of misinterpretation of the content of the interview. Some interviews we saw would not be likely to be acceptable in any court as evidence of sexual abuse. The Official Solicitor refers to an aspect of this—the dangers with such interviews of costly and protracted litigation. There is also a danger with a great deal of written material available on how to conduct an interview, of the inexperienced interviewer going through each of a number of stages with each child interviewed, rather than considering the best way to interview a particular child.

12.43 The Social Services Department felt the necessity to bring in some expertise from outside, since they had no-one in the Social Services Department with their particular skills. We heard evidence from two experts in this field dedicated to working with children troubled as a result of sexual abuse.[see chapter 4] Whilst not in any way wishing to criticise Social Services for taking that step, we were not entirely happy with the style of the expertise used. We venture to wonder whether it was appropriate at the stage it was employed and whether there was not an element of over-enthusiasm in the approach.

12.44 Dr Higgs and Dr Wyatt were reported as saying that 'disclosure work' was the 'gold standard' in the detection of sexual abuse. Mrs Richardson, other social workers, play therapists, and Mrs Bacon, the North Tees clinical psychologist, all considered it a very important aspect of the assessment of sexual abuse.

12.45 We recognise the importance rightly to be attached to the interview with the child, but the outcome of interviews in Cleveland was considered to be of such importance in the confirmation of the abuse, that the conduct of the interviews became distorted by the anxieties of the interviewers.

Video Recording

12.46 Video recordings have been taken at the Hospital for Sick Children at Great Ormond Street for several years by Dr Bentovim's team and he told us:—"Because the approach to our work is very much an open one for many years now we have video-recorded our work, used video tapes to supervise the quality of our work, and used it for teaching others about skills in interviewing children, carrying out group activities, or family meetings." Video recordings were not intended originally for forensic purposes, but as "clinical notes to enable us to replay an interview at leisure, make an accurate record of what had been said." Video recordings were however introduced in certain wardship proceedings and Mr Justice Latey said that in cases falling into the category:—"where there is nothing more than a combination ('constellation' it is called) of alerting symptoms" which are the ones likely to come to court for decision,:—"there should always be a video recording. The reason is this: where there is a dispute whether there has or has not been abuse the court is anxious whether it should accept the ipse dixit of the interviewer or interviewers, however skilled and experienced. This is because cases have shown (two of them have been referred to during the hearing, and there have been others in my experience) that the precise questions, the oral answers (if there are any), the gestures and body movements, the vocal inflection and intonation, may all play an important part in interpretation. Where there is a dispute, there should be an opportunity for another expert in the field to form a view. Often, no doubt, he would reach the same interpretation and conclusion. In other cases he might not, and in the interest not only of justice between the parties but of doing its best to arrive at the truth of the matter in the interest of the child, the court should have the benefit of such evidence, so informed."

12.47 Not all the Judiciary are in favour of video recordings.

12.48 Dr Cameron made certain helpful comments about the use of video recording. He was sympathetic to their use, but stressed the importance of obtaining an excellent quality of sound and picture, the danger of losing the 'subtle nuances of interaction on video recordings,' the danger of the court itself interpreting the subtleties of a disclosure interview rather than accepting or rejecting the assessment of the professional. But he also pointed out the usefulness of the video recording as an addition to the expert evidence, whereby the professional can point out moments in the recording upon which he bases his conclusions, analogous to the oral evidence in respect of an X-ray.

12.49 "Some Principles of Good Practice" set out advantages and disadvantages.:—"Video tapes are now seen as medical records and as such are subject to conditions similar to those for any other records that may be produced in evidence. Thus, tapes have evidential qualities in addition to their clinical utility. For evidential purposes, detailed and careful recording of all interview material is essential and videotaping is one means of achieving this. Closed circuit television with video recording can reduce the overall number of interviews by allowing the professionals to view the session unobtrusively. However, there are disadvantages: the unavailability of reliable high quality equipment with reproducable sound; the possible interference with the relationship with the child or even the reduction of spontaneity of accounts."

12.50 One major advantage of a video recording is the reduction in the number of necessary interviews with the child. Dr Bentovim said:—"Part of the reason we videoed and thought the videos of interviews were helpful would be to avoid this very fact of continuous interviews. The whole point of having a video of an interview is to obviate the necessity of them going over and over again with a child. ......Indeed one of the things we intend to do is to stop children talking about it and actively prevent that." That was unfortunately not the result in some interview sessions in Cleveland, but in our opinion in future the use of video recording should be with that end in mind.

12.51 We saw a number of video recordings of interviews also seen by those who gave evidence to the Inquiry. The content of such interviews at times may and indeed has called for comment and some criticism. But the presence of the video recordings has been very helpful to us. It also exposes the interview to critical evaluation by others.

12.52 It is important to have sufficiently good equipment and competent use of it for the tapes to be clear and the sound effective. The tapes which we viewed were in some instances difficult to follow and consequently not very helpful.

12.53 We consider that video recordings are a helpful step in the record of the assessment of the child in appropriate circumstances, and with the necessary consents are in the interests of the child.

Anatomically Correct or Complete Dolls

12.54 These dolls were according to Dr Bentovim, imported by his team at Great Ormond Street during 1982/1983 from the United States. They have found the dolls to be extremely helpful to enable children to speak of their experiences, particularly for young children or older children with difficulties in communication. He said:—"Inevitably as accurate diagnosis is the first step in treatment we began to use the dolls increasingly during the diagnostic assessment phase of our work."

12.55 Over the years the Great Ormond Street team have developed a particular expertise in interviewing children generally and in the use of these dolls. The Inquiry does not in any way wish to criticise the use of these dolls in the hands of such experts.

12.56 The problem from the evidence to the Inquiry appears to arise when well-meaning professionals, some of whom have attended Great Ormond Street workshops, or who have read of their work or the work in the United States on the techniques of interviewing children and the use of dolls as an initial part of such interviewing techniques, take to using these dolls as part of the standard interviewing process. There are dangers in their use at too early a stage in the evaluation, in the hands of the inexperienced operator.

12.57 We were concerned to learn of the provision of such dolls as basic equipment for police, social workers or clinical psychologists in Cleveland during the crisis without perhaps sufficient expertise in their use.

12.58 In Some Principles of Good Practice it is said:—"Anatomically correct dolls are often used in the assessment of suspected sexual abuse. They are used by trained professionals as well as, unfortunately, those who are not trained to use them. They should not be used without an understanding of child development, play, fantasising and psychopathology. They should certainly not be used as the first stage method of evaluation. They may be an useful adjunct to the facilative second stage, but in our view there are too many questions concerning the validity and reliability of anatomically correct dolls to recommend their use as a first stage diagnostic aid. They might be useful when a child has indicated sexual abuse at some level, but has then become stuck or wishes to describe a particular detail about sexual abuse and simply does not have the words and concepts, but might be able to show the evaluator. They can be useful with young, barely verbal children when other signs point to a strong liklihood of sexual abuse, e.g. physical findings.''

12.59 In his oral evidence Professor Kolvin said that at his hospital:—"We do not use them initially. We use them for a specific purpose if at all.'' He explained:—"What I am more concerned about is that you give this to untrained professionals in so many settings and there is almost a sense of enthusiasm about the use of these props to play and we really do not know whether we can trust their judgment.''

12.60 Dr Cameron in his paper to the Inquiry said of the dolls:—"These are often sadly misused as the first line of approach to a possibly sexually abused child. These dolls are very potent cues, and it must be borne in mind that the more helpful the cue, the greater the possibility of a false positive result.

It is now accepted that the majority of sexually abused children are likely to make the dolls behave in a sexually explicit manner; in contrast to the majority of non-abused children who use the dolls for non-sexual play (enacting tea parties and other such family gatherings). However it must be borne in mind that some non-sexually abused children will make these dolls pretend to pass urine, and possibly even pretend to have intercourse. This serves to highlight the fact that a 'positive' response to the dolls is only an indicator that the child may have been sexually abused, and is *not* an absolute diagnostic test.''

12.61 Dr David Jones in his paper to the Inquiry said:—"Care should be taken not to 'over-interpret' the child's play and non-verbal responses. This is because there are no reliable norms for the interpretation of play with certainty as to its origin or meaning. Play can be an extremely valuable source of data which confirms or lends support and credence to the verbal account of the child. For instance, the spontaneous play of non-abused children with anatomically explicit dolls is much less likely to contain overt re-enactments of sexual activity than abused children. Hence, if a child re-enacts sexual intercourse with dolls, and describes child sexual abuse by his/her father, the play has lent further support to the verbal account. If, however, the child simply re-enacts sexual activity, this may be a warning sign to professionals, but does not constitute clinical certainty that abuse has occurred. One cannot employ certainty because a very small preportion of non-abused children, in some of the studies, do play in a sexually explicit way with dolls.'' He warned against more fanciful interpretations of play at the investigative stage.

12.62 Both Professor Kolvin and Dr Bentovim considered skilled people suitable to use such dolls include properly trained social workers.

12.63 In the video recordings which we watched we saw the use of these dolls with children of different ages and were concerned as to the suitability of their use in those interviews.

12.64 We are very impressed by the advice from the child psychiatrists on the use of dolls and would urge extreme caution in their use other than by those particularily qualified to do so, for specific purposes and at a later stage. Their use seems highly undesirable as a routine prop in initial interviews.

Consent and confidentiality

12.65 Problems may arise over the issues of consents and confidentiality in notes and video-recordings of interviews with children. The best interest of the child may conflict with that of the parents in cases of sexual abuse within the family. "Some Principles of Good Practice" helpfully sets out some of the problems which arise.:—"With any work with children, the principles of confidentiality are the same. However, in cases of alleged sexual abuse, complex questions of confidentiality inevitably arise because of the conflict between professional ethics and public interest in the detection of child sexual abuse. Much depends on who is the patient and to whom the confidentiality is extended. Nevertheless, the doctor has to reconcile the extent to which confidentiality can be maintained, in the face of best interests of the child. In practice, the welfare and best interests of the child come first even though this may conflict with the best interests of the parents.'' Once formal inquiries have been initiated there is a need to share information on a wider than usual basis with the Police and social workers.:—"Parents need to appreciate that there may be a wider sharing of information by social workers with professionals from many other disciplines; the doctor must also realise this.'' It said:—"Where the child is a patient, parents cannot expect to be accorded the benefits of confidentiality; it must therefore be made clear to them that all relevant information given by them to the doctor concerning the child and any information resulting from the subsequent assessments may need to be shared among professionals working on the case; this also applies to video recordings. The professional has an obligation to alert the family to the extent of this potential sharing of information.''

12.66 Video recordings require proper consultation and the consent, where appropriate, of the parents, child or other suitable person. In particular a child of suitable age and understanding is entitled to be consulted and that child's consent sought. In the submission of the Childrens' Legal Centre to the Inquiry:—"The use of sound or video recording equipment, two-way mirrors, photography etc should in every case be subject to the specific consent of those subjected to the techniques, following a full explanation of the court's powers to view or hear recordings and a full explanation of the uses to which recordings may be put."

12.67 We endorse that submission in respect of those children of an age and understanding to comprehend the explanation.

We were somewhat concerned about evidence of instances where children were told either that the video recording would not be shown to outsiders or to parents or to the court. In pending court proceedings such a promise is unlikely to be capable of being kept and should not therefore be given. Dr Bentovim said:—"I think you cannot promise what you cannot deliver." He saw the issue of confidentiality as one of the problems. He gave as an example of a video recording of an interview where the child was promised it would only be seen by certain people. It was called for by the defence in criminal proceedings and was seen by the alleged abuser.

12.68 The Childrens' Legal Centre in their submission state:—"We are very concerned that the desire for 'inter-agency co-operation' and 'multi-disciplinary team approaches' to child abuse can conflict with childrens' desire, need and right to speak in confidence to others about things that concern them.....The Childrens' Legal Centre believes that childrens' right to and need for confidential advice and counselling has been ignored by many if not all the agencies involved in investigating and seeking to prevent child abuse." It sets out the difficulties inherent in the exchange and pooling of information.

12.69 There is no easy answer to this problem with the responsibilities for protection of children suspected of having been abused, the element of secrecy inherent in family sexual abuse, the likelihood that if true an offence has been committed, the wishes of the child and the duty of confidentiality between doctor and patient.

CHAPTER 13

Social Work Practice

13.1 The Inquiry heard evidence from representatives of professional organisations in the Social Service and social work field, who gave us a view of the social work position nationally, untied to particular localities. Our three witnesses were Mr Brian Roycroft, C.B.E., the President of the Association of Directors of Social Services (ADSS); Mr David Jones, the General Secretary of the British Association of Social Workers (BASW); and Mr Norman Dunning, the Chairman of the British Association for the Study and Prevention of Child Abuse and Neglect (BASPCAN). Whilst there were significant differences of emphasis in the submissions of the different organisations, there was general agreement on the distinctive features of social work practice in relation to child abuse.

Child Protection

13.2 It was a view common to all, that in any social work intervention there must be a clear focus on the needs of the child. The child's welfare, safety and protection must be a primary consideration. There was general agreement that social workers should seek to secure the welfare of the child in consultation and co-operation with the family if at all possible. But if the child's interest could not with confidence be protected by such arrangements, then the appropriate use of statutory protection afforded by the place of safety order would need to be considered.

13.3 We endorse the view that every effort should be made to secure the protection of the child by seeking an agreement with the parents. The emphasis should be on the use of professional skill to secure the co-operation of the parents. Where such co-operation cannot be secured, the use of statutory procedures should be discussed with colleagues in other disciplines rather than applied in an arbitrary manner.

13.4 The removal of a child from the care of parents is an onerous responsibility. Social workers have a duty in law to ensure the protection of children where they have cause to believe that there is a high risk of further immediate abuse. If that risk cannot be mollified by the withdrawal from the home of the person whose behaviour is believed to pose a risk to the child; or the non-abusing parent cannot be relied upon to protect the child; and in the absence of the parents' agreement to the child's admission to hospital, an application to magistrates for a place of safety order may be inevitable.

13.5 Research demonstrates that experiences of children in the care of the Local Authority are significantly fashioned by the manner in which they are initially received into care. Children are best cared for when proper plans are made in relation to their personal needs. It is difficult to achieve these arrangements when children are received into care in an emergency or dramatic manner.

13.6 These considerations should give impetus to social workers' efforts to secure the protection of the child by achieving agreement with the parent or care-giver. They must not, however, consititute a reason for leaving a child in a situation where he is at high risk of further abuse or violence. If that is the social worker's considered view, then their duty must guide them to apply for a place of safety order.

Referral and Response

13.7 Witnesses were reluctant to make generalised statements about the speed of the response to be made by social workers to information suggesting that a child may have been sexually abused. All emphasised that the speed and nature of the response would depend on the way in which the child's needs came to light. Distinctions were drawn between those cases which presented in a clear way with circumstantial or physical signs accompanied by a specific allegation from a child, and those cases where suspicions were raised by a sign or behaviour but there was no complaint from the child or third party. In the latter cases it was agreed that intervention should be planned in a more measured way. We encompass this view in the proposals we make for the introduction of an Specialist Assessment Team to assess such cases (See recommendations). In BASPCAN's view, "one has to act cautiously and take time over such diagnosis".

13.8 It was certainly our view that sexual abuse of children is a problem best managed in a planned and considered manner. Responding on an emergency basis is rarely required and is not likely to be helpful. The emergence or elicitation of an episode of sexual abuse is likely to generate a crisis in family relationships and may unleash or provoke powerful feelings amongst family members. The skills required are those of crisis management, utilising the fluidity of family relationships and potential for more open communication whilst supporting people to control and contain their more powerful emotional responses.

213

13.9 The response to a referral relating to child sexual abuse will be significantly influenced by the nature of that referral. Work with the family of a child admitted to hospital because of a serious genital injury can be planned. The concerns of a foster parent describing the sexualised behaviour of a four year old child can be thought about. A child who has confided serious abuse to a teacher and is afraid to return home is likely to require an urgent visit. An allegation that a child is being physically harmed will need an immediate response. In each case the task is to make an initial assessment of the problem, determine the degree of risk to the child, liaise with other agencies and formulate the first steps in intervention, if intervention is thought to be necessary. Whatever the nature of presentation, whether the response is immediate, prompt or deferred, it should be planned and conducted with professional skill. Children's best interests are rarely served by precipitate action. Initial action in securing the widest possible information about the child's circumstances and family background is an essential pre-requisite to careful judgement and purposeful intervention.

Planning and Co-ordination

13.10 Among the expert witnesses there was clear agreement that intervention should proceed as part of a planned and co-ordinated activity between agencies. Children and families should not be subject to multiple examinations and interviews simply because agencies and their staff failed to plan their work together. The alternative of each agency working in isolation would, in BASW's view, be a damaging, bewildering and destructive experience for families.

13.11 We would emphasise the importance of listening carefully to the initial presentation of information or referral and taking careful notes. A balanced professional judgement must then be made, weighing the indicators of risk or harm suggesting the need for immediate direct intervention against the benefits of exploring the nature of the problem further by seeking information within the agency, cross checking with other agencies or practitioners—interrogating the Child Abuse Register and planning the intervention and follow through in a programmed way.

13.12 Where a child is believed to have been abused within the family, the social worker will need to establish a clear understanding with the Police about how their respective roles are to be co-ordinated. Where unequivocal prima facie evidence of abuse exists, police may wish to interview parents before they are seen by social workers. In many agencies, such an arrangement will be a commonly-agreed practice. Such arrangements should not be open-ended. The needs of the child and decisions over future plans require social workers to interview parents preferably by a visit to their home within a reasonable period. Delay will lead to parents feeling isolated and hostile which may seriously impair the quality of relationships which the social worker can form with the family.

Family Assessment

13.13 The welfare of the child was seen as the first consideration by the professional organisations. The second was full assessment of the family situation. Mr David Jones of BASW put it most firmly "it is absolutely essential that those involved with the family, social workers, and others, conduct the fullest assessment of the family background. A full family history is being shown repeatedly to be of vital importance". He went on to suggest that the broad principles outlined by Henry Kempe in making an assessment of the family should still apply. It was necessary to assess the family by looking at the parents individually, the parents' relationship, the vulnerability of the child, the child's situation in the family, the family's social situation, their contacts with the extended family etc as well as considering and recording the family's perspective of events which set the referral in motion.

13.14 We were told that the need for agencies to work closely together with a clear framework for their inter-action was essential to ensuring that any intervention was not only successful in securing and underpinning the welfare of the child but also respectful to the rights of parents.

Partnership with Parents

13.15 Mr Roycroft emphasised the need to work in partnership with parents or a parent to secure the welfare of the child whilst recognising that, in some cases, statutory intervention must be pursued if the child's welfare could not be secured.

13.16 He saw it as a basic principle of good social work with children that the caring relationship with parents should be maintained. For him it was a principle that held good unless, and until, a decision is made that the child's relationship with either or both parents is preventing normal development and impeding the proper growth of the child.

Working with Parents

13.17 There can be little doubt that the processes of assessing the child and the family following the arousal of suspicion of child sexual abuse demands the careful exercise of professional skills.

13.18 Families who are in a crisis have a heightened emotional response. Anger, aggressive, destructive behaviour and the possibility of violent impulsive reactions may need to be faced. The social worker needs to maintain an open, structured relationship with the family. Whatever the social workers personal feelings, it is important to avoid a judgmental or accusatory attitude towards a parent who is a possible perpetrator. The risk of suicide amongst perpetrators who are able to acknowledge their abusing behaviour to themselves or others must be recognised. Many perpetrators will maintain a position of vehement denial. Social workers must develop the skill of respecting and supporting the person without endorsing or colluding with their acknowledged or suspected patterns of behaviour.

13.19 The principle aim of the social worker's contact with the family at this stage should be to compile a social history, obtaining as comprehensive a picture of relationships and pattern of family life as possible. The quality of the marital relationship and parental skills should be carefully assessed.

13.20 Abusing and non-abusing parents alike need to feel involved in the future plans for the care of their children. For this reason there will be occasions when it is necessary for social workers to work through or with parental hostility in spite of the fact that the nature of the abuse the child has been subjected to makes it unlikely that the child will be returning home.

Risks to Families

13.21 The British Association of Social Workers recognised the risks to families when the agencies of health, social services and police are working in unison—"when these powerful bureaucracies are working together, it poses risk to the family and the family's rights, and their rights to natural justice, their rights to a fair hearing have also to be protected as a group, as a family and as individuals, which is why we so strongly argued throughout the last two decades for legal protection for members of the family, for parents' rights of representation in care proceedings and so on".

13.22 Throughout the phase of initial assessment and preliminary decision making, social workers should be conscious of the fact that the presumption that abuse has taken place can have damaging repercussions for the child and the family. Equally, an abnormally low level of alertness to the possibility of child sexual abuse may deter children from subsequently trusting adults sufficiently to disclosure the fact of abuse to them.

Assessing the Needs of the Child

13.23 Social workers should seek a broadly based assessment of the child. An outline of the child's social development together with information about the important relationships in the child's life is vital information. Where a child is attending playgroup, childminders or school it will be helpful to record the views of those responsible for the child's day to day care.

13.24 In discussing and exploring with the child matters related to the allegation or suspicion of sexual abuse social workers should keep in mind the considerations set out in Listening to the Child (see chapter 12).

Case Conferences

13.25 The issues of parents attending case conferences was more contentious. Mr Dunning of BASPCAN, told us that whilst he personally favoured involving parents for part or whole of the conference, the membership of his organisation was split 50:50 on the issue.

13.26 Where there is the possibility of sexual abuse having occurred within the family there are obvious problems for a case conference, in addressing the needs of the child in a full and frank way, in the presence of distressed and angry parents. The child's interest must be the determining factor and the extent to which the parents can be involved must be tempered by the nature of the matters under discussion and the Chairman's confidence in managing their involvement for all or part of the meeting. On those occasions when parents do not attend the case conference they should be offered the opportunity to discuss the decisions under consideration by the Social Services Department if they so wish.

Medical Opinions

13.27 If a case conference is faced with conflicting medical opinions which have serious implications for the child, or pose fundamental problems in the preparation of legal proceedings—the doctors involved should be asked jointly to review their opinions with the best interest of the child in mind. If they are unable to reconcile their differing views then they should be asked to identify the basic elements of their disagreement. This would then allow the case conference to weigh both opinions in the context of a wider assessment of the child.

13.28 Local Authorities will need to give careful consideration to issues related to the provision of second opinions. This will require them to balance the interests and rights of the child not to be subjected unnecessarily to examinations of an intimate nature and the request of parents to seek second opinions when they cannot accept the diagnosis.

13.29 Second opinions requested by parents need to be carefully considered. Children ought not to be subjected to repeated examinations in support of a search by parents for a medical view with which they could agree. Equally, unless the children have already been subjected to a second, independent medical opinion the report of which could be made available to parents, it would be unreasonable not to agree to the parents' request. Wherever possible, efforts should be made to encourage second opinion or re-appraisal to be based on a review of records rather than further intimate examinations of the children. That ideal will not always be achievable.

13.30 The Local Authority's own request for second opinions may be as equally damaging to the child. Further medical opinions may confuse the position rather than clarify it.

Inadequacy of the Law

13.31 We were told of the inadequacy of the present child care legislation and its failure to balance the interests of the child and the rights of parents. The shortcoming in the legal framework was seen by the Associations to have an effect on the way in which public opinion reacted to issues related to child abuse. The state of current law on place of safety orders and interim care orders was universally seen as unsatisfactory and a review of these arrangements was pressed for as a matter of urgency

Skills

13.32 Whilst agreement between agencies to establish a framework for their interaction was seen as vital, the dangers of placing emphasis on systems rather than skills was another point of common concern. Mr Dunning told us "I think there has been so much professional energy placed into getting the systems right and rather less placed on building up the sort of subtle skills needed in assessments and interview". This theme was reiterated by both BASW and ADSS. Mr Jones, BASW, warned against "the danger of creating an illusion of knowledge that does not exist; sexual abuse and exploitation has gone on since time immemorial, but in terms of awareness of the problem, the numbers of referrals coming to Social Services, and the Police, we are facing really a new scale of problems". He was concerned to point out that social workers are still exploring work and responses in this field and acknowledged that later research could call into question these initial responses which may be found to be wanting. "I think professional people should have a certain modesty about pursuing particular views about professional problems as they emerge".

13.33 He expressed a measured caution which echoed much of the evidence heard during the course of the Inquiry.

Difficulties

13.34 The difficulties which face staff who undertake work with sexually abused children and their families were consistently highlighted. There was a common acknowledgement of the heavy emotional demands and profound impact this area of work has on professionals. Of universal concern was the way in which, if staff are inadequately supported or lack special training, they can quickly lose confidence and become overwhelmed by the complexity of the problems they are seeking to resolve. There was a strong emphasis on the need to ensure that only social workers who were qualified, were suited to the work, were established in their practice and who had received additional training, should undertake work in the field of child sexual abuse.

Training

13.35 Mr Jones of BASW strongly emphasised the need for more training in this field, "I find it incredible that the public are expecting social workers to handle these difficult cases, are ready to hand down sweeping criticisms of the way they are handled, but yet we are not provided with the resources for even updating training, and the training commitment from the Personal Social Services to a post-qualifying level has been poor".

13.36 Mr Roycroft pointed out that in all matters of this nature, the final decision is a judgement: the quality of that judgement must be based on whether people have time to gather together the facts and whether they have the skills and the training. He urged the allocation of resources to ensure that the various agencies involved could discharge their responsibilities with sensitivity and confidence.

13.37 The emphasis placed on the theme of training and the importance given on the need for qualified, experienced staff with a strong sense of personal maturity and competence supported the evidence we heard from social workers from Cleveland expressing the problems which they faced.

CHAPTER 14

Approaches to the Management of Child Sexual Abuse in Different Areas of the Country

14.1 The Inquiry received information from practitioners in different parts of the country as to how child abuse is managed in their areas. The members of the Independent Panel chaired by Professor Kolvin provided us with their views in a paper "Some Principles of Good Practice". We are particularly grateful to Professor Kolvin and his panel for their help. We have set-out in summary and largely in the form it was supplied to us some of the information we found of particular assistance. The selection of examples given here does not of course give a complete picture of all the initiatives taking place throughout the country, they merely represent those examples given to us in evidence which it seemed most useful to set out. Northern Regional Health Authority also made some helpful suggestions as to the management of child sexual abuse, which we have received gratefully and have helped us in forming our recommendations.

Wandsworth

14.2 In the London Borough of Wandsworth the management of child sexual abuse is part of a multi-disciplinary team. St Georges Hospital Tooting provides the medical focus of the team. There are four aims of the intervention practised in Wandsworth:

— The protection of the child

— The physical and emotional treatment of the child

— The assessment of the family with a view to the appropriate intervention or treatment

— The collection of evidence in cases of possible prosecution.

Underlying all of this is a belief that while children may be harmed by being sexually abused they may also be further emotionally harmed if, when the problem is recognised , it is not dealt with in a sensitive and caring way.

14.3 The Wandsworth Borough Review Committee, referred to as a 'strong umbrella committee', was described as being of considerable importance for the success of the procedures. The committee is chaired by a Community Physician (Child Health) and consists of:

Assistant Director, Social Services (Children)

Consultant Paediatrician

Consultant Child Psychiatrist

Child Psychotherapist

Detective Chief Inspector, Police

Assistant Director Education

Principal Physician (Child health—Community)

Police Surgeon

Consultant Gynaecologist

14.4 The procedure for intervention comes in two stages:

1. Preliminary screening

2. Formal interview/examination at St George's Hospital

This procedure is in respect of cases where a child or parent raises the possibility of 'something sexual going on'. The professional involved then contacts the Area Social Work office, and following this a social worker from the Area Office will often visit the family at home to see the child with the following possible outcomes:

— no further action

— referral to a Paediatrician (if signs/symptoms of physical illness)

— referral to family doctor

— referral to a child psychiatrist

— refer for a second stage interview/examination at St George's Hospital, only when evidence is strongly suggestive of sexual interference.

14.5 The second stage takes place in the Nicholls Ward at St George's Hospital. It is first established whether or not the case warrants emergency interviewing (if the alleged offence occurred within 24 hours) or whether a planned interview is preferable (if the activity appears to have taken place over many months or years). We were warned of the dangers of precipitate action and that:
"a more cautious and measured approach may well result in a more effective therapeutic intervention".

14.6 When an interview is due to take place everything else on the ward stops as far as possible, and five rooms are made available for the several people who will need to take part. The five rooms are as follows:

1. An interviewing room with a one way screen;

2. An adjoining room with video and sound facilities;

3. The interviewing social worker's room;

4. A night sister's room for the mother and for meetings to take place;

5. A day sister's office for other people to wait, e.g. police surgeon, a teacher, 'trusted friend' etc

The different professionals involved are

— the disclosure interviewer, a social worker particularly trained in interviewing children

— a woman detective constable in civilian clothes

— a female paediatrician or gynaecologist.

14.7 The first stage in part two is usually the interview, conducted by the social worker, with the policewoman in the consulting room as well. Other professionals will watch from behind a one way mirror. The mother will rarely be present except with very young children.

14.8 It was stressed to us that the interview is always 'child-led' and, if positive information is not forthcoming by the end of an interview lasting one hour, then the interview ceases. In winding up the interview it is often helpful to recapitulate what the child has actually said and to seek confirmation from the child that the statement is correct.

14.9 The physical examination takes place immediately after the interview, and will do so in the presence of a trusted friend or the mother. The paediatrician will discuss with the police surgeon what is needed and will then carry out a full medical examination watched by the police surgeon. The second to last examination is gynaecological and will conclude with an ordinary medical test.

14.10 Four options are then available:

— keep the child on the ward

— send the family to a resource centre run by the Social Services

— if the mother accepts that abuse has taken place, then it may be safe for the child to go home

— in some cases it may be appropriate for the police to go home and immediately arrest the father.

14.11 This system appears to have worked well. Out of 80 cases looked at in the last 10 months, it was felt that inappropriate sexual activity had taken place in the majority of cases, but in only three did the matter result in a court appearance.

14.12 Very few videos or tape recordings are made. Detailed notes are written up immediately after examinations by all the professionals involved.

We were also shown an early edition of some guidelines in use in Wandsworth which referred to the setting up of a Rapid Advice Forum, which consisted of a list of experts in the area to whom professionals could turn for advice.

Southwark and Lewisham

14.13 We were told that in the area of South London covered by the Southwark and Lewisham District Health Authority the Local Authority was seen as the key agency in referral. When the consultant paediatrician was contacted by Social Services we heard it is normal for her to have a full discussion with the referring professional involved before she would agree to a medical examination. Before an examination there is usually some form of planning meeting between the person who had received the disclosure, Social Services, the medical adviser and the Police. The medical examination only takes place as part of a planned examination. The time-scale involved will vary according to the nature of the suspicion. If there is a possibility of collecting forensic evidence, then it is important that the process should begin within hours. If there was no more than an ill-defined suspicion, then things could progress at a slower pace.

14.14 If the child is referred for a complaint to the paediatrician then we were told that the consultant would not examine without having consulted other professionals, and would not do so in the middle of a busy out patient's clinic.

14.15. The physical examination is only a small part of the total investigation, which will be individually tailored to match the circumstances of the case. It was stressed that there was a need to protect other children in the family when child sexual abuse is diagnosed .

14.16 The Inquiry was provided with a valuable pro-forma for the investigating team, which has been developed by police surgeons, the Police and other professionals. This has the advantage of bringing together in one place information collected by the different professionals involved. It is reprinted in full in the appendix F.

Tower Hamlets

14.17 We heard that in Tower Hamlets it was normal for any medical examination out to be carried out jointly by the police surgeon and the paediatrician in a hospital setting. If the police surgeon is not available then forensic kits are on the wards and the police surgeon has demonstrated to the paediatrician the requirements for forensic examination.

14.18 A special room is available for interviewing, equipped with a one way screen. If sexual abuse is diagnosed, even if a subsequent decision is taken not to prosecute, the police surgeon would expect to attend the case conference along with the paediatrician, if he thought he had anything he could usefully contribute in explaining the medical findings to the lay people present at the case conference.

Leeds

14.19 The approach of the Leeds team stressed the need for a multi-disciplinary approach to the investigation of child sexual abuse, with the primary aim of protecting the child. It was stressed that caution is needed on occasion and that precipitate action might not be in the best interests of the child, causing defences to be raised which would hinder further action in the child's interests. The principle of joint interviews between Police and Social Services is accepted, and that this process will involve a heavy commitment in staff time.

14.20 In the case of child sexual abuse within the family, the Leeds team told us there were two types of investigation

1. Where there was clear evidence or an allegation
2. Where information arose from a third party or related incident.

14.21 In the first type of case the emphasis is on stopping the abuse, protecting the child and moving the abuser rather than the child. Social Services or the NSPCC will be the liaising body and will arrange for a medical examination and liaison with the police. Where families are interviewed then this should be in the presence of a social worker as well as the Police. The next stage should be to call a case conference.

14.22 In the second type of case caution is urged. The investigation would begin with a small meeting of those who know the child or the family, including the Police. An appropriate person would be given a watching brief and someone will be appointed to co-ordinate information and liaise with members of the meeting. If further evidence comes to light then the process outlined in the first type of case would begin.

14.23 If a medical examination takes place then it is important that it does so away from the busy setting of a paediatric ward, and if possible it should be joint examination, although we heard that these caused difficulties in practice. The examining doctor should bear in mind requirements for the courts and for police statements. If sexual abuse is diagnosed then the protection of the child is of prime importance. A short admission to hospital might take place—but this is by no means the rule and admission is avoided if possible. The opinion was expressed that hospital was by no means the best place for examination—a suitably equipped house was suggested as an alternative. Siblings should be brought in and examined.

One of the points stressed was the need for caution and careful judgement. The paediatrician may wish carefully to assess, after informal discussion with other professionals, whether it is better to continue to observe a family rather than to make a clear statement of abuse immediately. We were told:
"In cases like this the picture usually becomes clear in several weeks and we have found this a useful method of management. It does however mean a good deal of inter-agency trust."

14.24 The importance of keeping the child's general practitioner informed of developments was stressed. The point was made that this kind of work was stressful and that paediatricians and other professionals need to be part of a support system so that second opinions can be given. The Leeds paediatricians stressed that they had found access to another paediatrician with an interest in child sexual abuse to be invaluable and "to have kept us afloat when the going has been tough."

Manchester

Paediatricians

14.25 We were told that after a child had been referred to a paediatrician in Manchester and physical examination had revealed sexual abuse there were three steps to be taken:

1. The safety of the child should be ensured

2. The Police should be informed

3. The child should be interviewed

14.26 The Social Services Department are consulted where the parents are not co-operative so that a place of safety order can be made and the child can be admitted to hospital. Prompt referral should be made to the police and it is desirable if a room is made available in hospital for an interview to take place. The interviewing of children should not be excessive, and all of the professionals involved discuss who would be the best person to undertake this interviewing. It is important that the paediatrician attend the case conference.

14.27 We were told that the management of the sexually abused child should be unhurried and methodical, and take into account the child's wider needs.

Police surgeon

14.28 In Manchester there are 35 police surgeons, and four of them are women. We were told that these women carry out most of the examinations of cases involving child sexual abuse, usually in their own surgeries, an environment which they regard as being non-threatening and ordinary.

14.29 It was stressed that it was important to spend time with the child in order to let the child settle down. This may involve spending a lot of time with the child.

14.30 Relationships with the paediatricians were described as excellent, based upon "mutual respect and an understanding of each other's roles, together with a commitment to help the child."

The Police

14.31 The Greater Manchester Police Force has one centralised child abuse Liaison Department which is responsible for all administrative matters relating to child abuse. It consists of one Chief Inspector, five Inspectors, one Policewoman Sergeant, two Policewoman Constables.

14.32 Liaison with all ten Area Review Committees in the Greater Manchester area is maintained by the Chief Inspector, who is also a member of the training sub-committee and the guidelines sub-committee of each. All ARCs guidelines have been or are in the process of being amended to take account of child sexual abuse.

14.33 Every case conference is attended by an Inspector from the Department, and there are centralised filing and information systems. The investigation of all allegations of child abuse rests with the Criminal Investigation Department.

14.34. All referrals are reported to the child abuse Liaison Department where a decision is made as to whether or not a police investigation should commence before the initial case conference. In cases involving child sexual abuse an investigation is considered mandatory. When an investigation is started, the investigating officer also attends the case conference.

14.35 Interviews of victims are carried out jointly by a detective and a social worker.

14.36 There are five female police surgeons covering the whole of the Greater Manchester area who examine victims of child sexual abuse. The Force considers that a medical examination is sometimes unnecessary or may not be in the interests of the child's welfare, and therefore a police officer is required to obtain the authority of a Divisional Detective Superintendent before arranging such an examination. Where children are presented to paediatricians it is not uncommon for a female police surgeon to be invited to carry out a joint examination with the paediatrician.

14.37 A number of Force training programmes include child abuse, and the Force also participates in multi-disciplinary training in all ten Health Areas.

Professor Kolvin's Panel

14.38 The panel, when speaking of management, stressed the need for caution, the importance of making the assessment match the intrusiveness and extent of the professional evaluation with the level of suspicion that exists in the individual case and said that there was no need for an emergency response unless:

— there are serious health risks

— samples are needed for forensic purposes and abuse has taken place in the previous 48 hours

— there is a serious psychiatric disturbance

Admission to hospital should be undertaken carefully and should not be automatic. If it takes place as a stop-gap measure the child should be accompanied by a trusted adult.

14.39 Place of safety orders should only be sought by the Social Service Department or the Police and only where there is a high risk of further abuse to the child and there are no alternative methods available, or where the parents refuse all further co-operation.

14.40 The response by Social Services should be a considered exercise rather than an automatic one. "Some Principles of Good Practice" suggests that:

"rarely should any one individual have the power to weigh, sift and filter all the clinical evidence, to diagnose, and to decide the implictions of that diagnosis. Social Services Departments, paediatricians and/or police surgeons and child psychiatrists will all have major roles, different but related, in the assessment of child sexual abuse at a clinical level. Such a system of checks and balances does not dictate any form of group diagnosis or diagnosis by committee—on the contrary, it calls for a recognition of the necessity for multidisciplinary approaches involving professionals with different bases of knowledge, expertise, experience and sharing the results of their assessment. The interests of the child and family will best be served by a sensitive multidisciplinary approach which makes use of all the resources, professional experience and skills available in the local community".

Case conferences should be limited to those professionals most directly concerned with the case, as the concern was expressed that they had been getting rather large.

14.41 Finally, the report recommends that in each region there should be a core group of highly skilled professionals who can provide an assessment of the most contentious cases. The core group could not be expected to look at every case, but would need to be utilised selectively.

Bexley

14.42 The "Bexley Experiment" was a joint initiative by the Metropolitan Police and the London Borough of Bexley which set out to improve methods of investigating allegations of child sexual abuse within the family. The team consists of one detective sergeant and eleven detective constables, four senior social workers and 8 social workers.

14.43 All referrals are made to Bexley Borough Central Child Abuse Service and from there joint investigators—one trained social worker and one trained police officer, are appointed. The preferred mix of joint workers is male/female with the next most desirable female/female. Unilateral action has only been taken by the police in urgent and exceptional cases and that action has been limited to that necessary to protect the child, preserve evidence or prevent the escape of the offender.

14.44 Within three days of the appointment of the joint investigators a co-ordinating meeting is called, involving the investigators and their supervising officers. The purpose of this is to review the case, discuss possible further investigation and consider recommendations for a case conference. At this meeting the need for a further co-ordinating meeting is also considered. There is no specific time limit to the calling of a case conference, but it is considered that it should be called within ten days of the initiation of an investigation.

14.45 Joint interviews of the victim take place in a room specially set aside and equipped in St Mary's Hospital. The interview is video-recorded. Anatomically correct dolls are available. The joint investigating team interviews witnesses together.

14.46 A medical examination room is available in Queen Mary's Hospital adjacent to the interview room. Examinations are normally carried out by police surgeons, usually female police surgeons. Paediatricians at the hospital have committed themselves to respond where the police surgeon requests it. Sexual offences examination kits are provided by the Metropolitan Police.

14.47 Interviews of suspects usually take place at Belvedere Police Station, with the police officer taking the leading role, and the social worker taking part if he or she wishes to do so. Sometimes the video of the interview of the victim may be used in interviewing the suspect.

14.48 A joint training programme lasting 7 days and designed specifically for the project team was introduced and all the members of the team have undergone training.

14.49 The results of the Bexley experiment have been published, and have formed the basis of a code of practice which is being adopted by the Metropolitan Police Force.

Northumbria

14.50 The Northumbria Police have established child abuse Protection Units in each of its 6 territorial divisions. The units comprise one detective sergeant and either two or three woman constables. The role of the members of the units includes liaison with other agencies and the investigation of all allegations of suspected child abuse within the family or extended family.

14.51 The units respond to and are supervised by the heads of the Divisional Criminal Investigation Departments. All case conference minutes are filed on divisions but the Force Headquarters Community Services Department fulfills a central role in collating information, maintaining statistics and representation on Area Review Committees.

14.52 The Force accept that a multi-disciplinary approach to the investigation of child abuse is most desirable.

14.53 While the police surgeons appointed within the force are all male the Force operates a Woman Doctor Scheme and these doctors usually examine the victims of child abuse and when necessary provide the medical evidence to provide the prosecution.

14.54 There is a Force training course which all officers appointed to the child abuse Protection Units undergo.

North Yorkshire

14.55 A multi-disciplinary team was established in the Hambleton/Richmondshire Division of North Yorkshire Social Services in October 1986. The Deputy Divisional Director of Social Services acts as convenor and the members of the team include a paediatrician, 4 social workers, a child psychologist and a policewoman.

14.56 The purpose of the team is to:

— act as a consultancy group for social workers and other professionals involved in sexual abuse cases;

— to accept referrals involving sexual abuse where the child and/or family members require help and counselling;

— to provide a group which may be involved in the initial investigation when allegations of child sexual abuse are made;

— to provide information on up-to-date literature on child sexual abuse and arrange training sessions when such knowledge and expertise can be shared.

14.57 The team concentrate on priority cases. Referrals are through the Area Social Services Officer or case conference.

14.58 Joint interviews are undertaken and this may be police/paediatrician, police/social worker or social worker/police. Interviews take place at hospital, preferably before a medical examination. Initially the interview is directed towards obtaining information which may be used as evidence. If that is not successful then interviewers will ask more specific questions, acknowledging a primary need to discover what has happened so that case work planning and treatment can be determined. Anatomically correct dolls may be used.

14.59 The interview of the victim may be video-recorded, and may be used by the police in the interrogation of a suspect.

14.61 Medical examinations are carried out by a paediatrician, and will always take place in hospital. In appropriate cases the policewoman is present to receive and deal with forensic specimins. Arrangements exist for an experienced police surgeon to give guidance to the paediatrician if this is required.

14.62 Case conferences are attended by the paediatrician, the Detective Chief Inspector and the Deputy Director of Social Services.

14.63 The team use their own cases and experience for training purposes, thereby sharing knowledge and evaluating each other's techniques.

CHAPTER 15

Training

15.1 During the course of the Inquiry we heard a great deal of evidence both from organisations and from individuals about the need for additional training.

15.2 We regard training as an issue of central importance in ensuring that the special needs of children who have or may have been sexually abused are properly recognised and met.

15.3 The individual professional level of suspicion and skill in assessment is a factor of critical importance. If the level of suspicion is high but the assessment only cursory it is likely that many innocent families will be damaged by false accusations. If the skills of assessment are excellent but the level of suspicion or awareness is low then children will go on being damaged. It is therefore important that the development of the necessary professional skills must go hand in hand with an increased level of awareness.

15.4 We heard of the steps taken both in Cleveland and elsewhere to provide training. We were told that before the crisis some social workers had attended courses, together with health visitors, nursing officers, paediatricians, clinical psychiatrists. We heard of joint training seminars for social workers and police which took place during the course of the Inquiry. We heard from Mrs Dunn and Mrs Roach of their efforts to inform professionals in the County on the subject of child sexual abuse.

15.5.From the evidence to the Inquiry and on our visits, we gained the impression that some professionals were not sure what training to look for or where to get it, and others were not always made aware of the need for it.

15.6 It was our overwhelming impression that the training provided nationally is inadequate:

— We learned that child sexual abuse did not form part of the training courses for police surgeons in the Diploma of Forensic Medicine;

— Paediatricians did not have training in child sexual abuse unless they undertook the further training of a community paediatrician;

— A lack of training for General Practitioners;

— Dr Roberts told us of the need for the training of all doctors who will examine children who might have been sexually abused;

— Many social workers experienced difficulty in responding to sexually abused children because they had not received the training necessary to the task they were undertaking.

— Nurses did not have any training in how to manage sexually abused children on the wards and what their needs are.

15.7 Whilst around the country some Authorities are making imaginative efforts to remedy the position of their staff the pattern is a piecemeal one. The impression gained is of small schemes, commendable in themselves but fragmented and diffuse in their outlook and purpose. There is an urgent need for training in child abuse and child sexual abuse to be properly co-ordinated and validated on a national basis. We share and endorse the concern expressed by the national social work organisations that a new initiative and additional resources are needed to ensure adequate training for the various professional groups involved.

CHAPTER 16

The Courts

Introduction

16.1 As a result of the crisis in Cleveland the jurisdiction of courts concerned with care proceedings became of relevance during the Inquiry. Problems arose, as have been seen in Chapter 10, principally in relation to place of safety orders, and other issues some of which have been raised in the Government White Paper, "Law on Child Care and Family Services." We have therefore thought it appropriate to devote a little time to considerations of those issues of general importance which arose in Cleveland.

Place of Safety Orders

16.2 A place of safety order is designed to provide emergency protection for a child at risk. The principal statutory provisions are contained in the Children and Young Persons Act 1933 s. 40 and the Children and Young Persons Act 1969 s. 28. There are other provisions which were not relevant to the issues in Cleveland.

S. 28. refers to "detention of child or young person in place of safety" and states:—

s.28(1) " If, upon an application to a Justice by any person or authority to detain a child or young person and take him to a place of safety, the Justice is satisfied that the applicant has reasonable cause to believe that

(a) any of the conditions set out in s.1(2)(a) to(e) of this Act [including neglect, ill-treatment, risk of moral danger, non-attendance at school] is satisfied in respect of the child or young person; or

(b) an appropriate court would find the condition set out in s.1.(2)(b) of this Act is satisfied in respect of him; or [other grounds]

the Justice may grant the application; and the child or young person in respect of whom an authorisation is issued under this sub-section may be detained in a place of safety by virtue of the authorisation for twenty eight days beginning with the day of authorisation, or for such shorter period beginning with that date as may be specified in the authorisation ...

S. 28(3) A person who detains any person in pursuance of the preceding provisions of this section shall, as soon as practicable after doing so, inform him of the reason for his detention and take such steps as are practicable for informing his parent or guardian of his detention and of the reason for it."

S. 40 of the 1933 Act provides for the issue of a warrant by a Justice on an information laid on oath where there is reasonable cause to suspect assault, ill-treatment or neglect of a child or offences against a child, and the authorisation of a constable to search for the child and to take him to a place of safety. The period of the warrant is 28 days.

A place of safety is defined by s. 107(1) of the 1933 Act as:—"A community home provided by a local authority .... any police station, or any hospital, surgery or other suitable place, the occupant of which is willing temporarily to receive a child or young person."

16.3 The purpose of either order is to ensure the protection of the child and to remove him to a place of safety. S.28 is a wider provision and was the one used in Cleveland and is in common use nationally.

Application for an order

16.4 The application may be made, usually by a social worker, official of the NSPCC or police officer, to a Juvenile Bench or to a single Magistrate. It is generally ex parte, without any requirement for notification in advance to the parent or to the child.

16.5 In some instances no notification to the parents must be an essential element of the application, for instance in cases of physical assault or likely removal of the child on notice. We did however receive interesting evidence from the Clerk to the North Tynside Justices, Mr Paton Webb, about their practice which includes notice to the parents who often attend and the attendance of the Clerk at the hearing of the application for an order. We can see some cases (particularly in the Emergency Protection Order proposed in the White Paper) when the attendance of the parents would be desirable. There is no reason why an applicant should automatically apply ex parte.

The granting of the order is a discretionary judicial act.

Records of orders granted.

16.6 Whether it is practicable or necessary for Clerks always to attend these hearings, sometimes in the early hours of the morning, is a matter upon which we do not wish to express an opinion. We do however consider that it is essential that there should be communication between the Magistrates granting these orders and the Clerk in order to monitor the numbers granted, keep proper records and to have advance notice of the future work of the Juvenile Court.

In so far as the 1986 Home Office Circular 25 does not appear to have sufficient 'teeth' for compliance with its wise provisions, this situation should be reconsidered to achieve greater success.

Appeal or discharge

16.7 There is no right of appeal or discharge of the order granted. However, if the applicant, usually the Local Authority or NSPCC, applies at the end of the period granted for an interim care order under the 1969 Act the parent has the right to oppose it.

Use of order

16.8 There is no inherent right to remove children from their homes. The power in every case derives from specific child care and child protection legislation. Parents alone (except possibly in wardship) have inherent rights and obligations in respect of a child. All rights and obligations in respect of children exercised by others arise either from authority given expressly or by implication by a parent, or by express statutory provision.

16.9 The power under S.28 is to detain for up to 28 days in a place of safety. The extent of the authority to detain must we suggest include the right to do what is necessary to keep the child in a place of safety. S.28 does not however confer upon a Local Authority any of the child care provisions of Part 111 of the Child Care Act 1980, nor does it diminish or extinguish parental rights or obligations save necessarily to the extent that they are incompatible with the authorisation to detain in a place of safety.

Medical examinations

16.10 We would suggest that an initial examination to ascertain the health of a child would be within the authorisation of the agency under the order, and in a case such as physical injury, X-rays and any consequential necessary treatment would follow. It would not however in our view,include repeat examinations for forensic purposes or for information gathering rather than for continuing treatment. Such examinations would require the consent of the parents. A situation might well arise and indeed did arise in Cleveland where there were excessive numbers of medical examinations of certain children. Some control over examinations in the present climate is now highly desirable and is not available under a place of safety order or even under an interim care order.

Access

16.11 Restriction or denial of access to parents, which was a continuing problem in Cleveland in 1987 would not in our view be within the authorisation of a place of safety order, save where the safety of the child required it, for example a violent parent or the likelihood of removal of the child from the place of safety. Common senses dictates that if a child is held in hospital or in a children's home or foster home, unrestricted access by an unreasonable parent might have to be curtailed, and some control by the agency over access would be necessary. Apart from those situations, this order would not appear to confer upon a Local Authority the right to curtail access. Despite the views of some social workers in Cleveland to the contrary, a place of safety order is a very different order from an interim care order.

Disclosure work

16.12 We were concerned that place of safety orders were obtained and access restricted or denied in some cases in order to facilitate 'disclosure work'. The maximum period of 28 days was applied for this purpose, which did not appear to us to be a proper use of the child protection legislation.

Need for an order

16.13 From statistics and evidence before the Inquiry there appeared a wide difference of approach between Local Authorities in their use of place of safety orders. Cleveland used them extensively, others infrequently. In some instances infrequent use may be linked to a greater use of wardship, in other cases to a less interventionist approach.

16.14 The granting of the order imposes upon the child a certain loss of liberty which should not be imposed without very good reasons. We were unhappy to see in Cleveland the acceptance of an automatic response by way of place of safety order to certain sets of facts. If a child is in a safe place, such as a hospital, and there is no immediate fear of the parent removing the child, such as the newborn baby referred to at page 12, the obtaining of the order is likely to cause polarisation of attitudes between social workers and the family at an early stage and may jeopardise co-operation which is much needed at an early stage of investigation. Considerations of wise management suggest that the immediate protection of the child may best be secured by negotiation with the family where possible. Institution of care proceedings may follow. Their purpose can be explained to the family in advance and the parents have the opportunity to be represented at the hearing and can be heard by the magistrates. We were particularily concerned that Mrs Richardson expressed the need for the Social Services Department to use a place of safety order by way of control as the first stage of intervention and management of the family in situations where there was no immediate danger to the child. In our view that is a wholly unjustified use of the place of safety order. We are concerned that measures designed to meet circumstances which threaten the life or safety of a child should not be regarded routinely as the first stage of authoritative intervention.

Emergency Protection Orders

16.15 From the events in Cleveland it has become clear to us that for a number of reasons the place of safety order does not sufficiently meet the needs of a child at risk. We welcome therefore the proposals for a new emergency protection order in the Government White Paper,The Law on Child Care and Family Services, Cm62, 1987. The grey areas would, we hope, be removed and the essential points clarifed. We agree with all the proposals in paragraphs 45 to 47 with the following provisos:—

1. The presumption of access to the parent is desirable, but if the agency obtaining the order for good reasons needs to suspend access thereafter during the 8 day period, we consider the agency should have the obligation of returning to the magistrate for an order to that effect.

2. We would hope that the full implications of the term 'actual custody' would be spelt out to those in charge of the child.

3. Medical examination, as shown in Cleveland, is one example of the need for clear understanding of the rights and duties of all concerned. During the 8 day period of the initial order, we would recommend that decisions as to medical examinations should be made by the agency, but on any extension to the maximum 15 days, and on the hearing of the interim care application, in the case of dispute between the agency and the parents, the court should decide.

4. The need to prove 'exceptional circumstances' to extend to 15 days may create difficulties. With the parents present and able to oppose, we feel that extension should be in the discretion of the magistrates, not lightly to be granted. But many emergencies arise at weekends and Bank Holidays, as they did in Cleveland. If an emergency protection order is taken on Maundy Thursday or Christmas Eve it might on a strict interpretation be difficult to prove 'exceptional circumstances' as the reason for not being able to initiate care proceedings. These Bank Holidays occur every year. We entirely agree with a maximum period of 15 days.

5. Child Protection Order or Medical Assessment Order.

   We do not see the need for a separate order to provide the ability to require the production of a child or the attendance of a child for medical examination. We are in favour of such powers, but consider they would more appropriately be contained within the emergency protection order. A power to make the order but to permit the child to remain at home on condition of being medically examined or being produced to the appropriate agency would be preferable to the creation of a wholly separate order with the potential for confusion. Magistrates might for instance on occasions think it appropriate to adjourn the application, have the parents notified and consider whether to grant the order after hearing what the parents have to say.

6. We strongly support the proposal for an order to disclose the whereabouts of a child. In one case in May in Cleveland, the father attended daily at the police station in accordance with his bail terms and refused to disclose the whereabouts of his children, a place of safety order having been granted. The disclosure order would however require 'teeth' to be effective.

7. The Childrens' Legal Centre in their submission suggest that a magistrate before granting an order should be satisfied that the child's own views have been fully ascertained where practicable. That is a proposal which in suitable cases should be borne in mind.

8. In our view the application for an emergency protection order should as a general rule be made first to the Juvenile Court and only to a single Magistrate if the Court is not sitting.

9. There should be a statutory duty upon the Clerk to the Justices to keep records of emergency protection orders.

10. It would be helpful for a simple explanatory pamphlet to be written and widely circulated to explain the new emergency protection order, the powers and responsibilities under it and its limits. Such a pamphlet would be valuable not only for social workers and NSPCC officials but also for general practitioners, paediatricians, nurses, any other professionals concerned with children, for parents and the general public.

The Jurisdiction of the Juvenile Court in Care proceedings

16.16 Of the various statutory routes by which children may go into care of a Local Authority, the procedure most relevant to the events in Cleveland during 1987 has been that provided by section 1 of the Children and Young Persons Act 1969.

16.17 That section and measures consequent upon and ancillary to it essentially provide a judicial procedure, exercised by the Juvenile Court, for regulating the intervention of a Local Authority Social Services Department into family life.

The grounds upon which an order may be made

16.18 Section 1 of the 1969 Act provides alternative criteria in respect of one of which the Juvenile Court must be satisfied before it can go on to make an order specified by the Act.

16.19 Proceedings are begun by a Local Authority, police constable, or the NSPCC bringing the child or young person before the court, on notice or by summons of which notice is given to the parents. The parties to the proceedings are the Local Authority or police constable or NSPCC and the child. There is a presumption that parents represent the interests of the child, but they are not themselves parties. They may be legally represented, but so far have no right of appeal. The Children and Young Persons (Amendment) Act 1986 is not yet in force.

16.20 The court has power [s.32A CYPA 1969] to order, in an appropriate case, that the parents are not to be treated as representing the child in the proceedings or as authorised to act on the child's behalf. On making such an order, the court is obliged to appoint a guardian ad litem of the child, unless satisfied that that action is not necessary for safeguarding the interests of the child.

16.21 The criteria set out in Section 1(2) (a)-(e) of the Act include reference to the child's proper development being avoidably prevented or neglected or health being avoidably impaired or neglected or being ill-treated, exposed to moral danger, beyond the control of parents or non-attendance at school. Section 1(2)(f) refers to an offence committed by a child or young person of 10 years or more.

In considering children passing through the Juvenile Courts during 1987 the Inquiry has been solely concerned with the civil jurisdiction.

16.22 In addition to being of the opinion that one of these criteria is satisfied, the Court must also be of the opinion that the child or young person is in need of care or control which he is unlikely to receive unless the court makes an order.

Orders which may be made

16.23 When the primary condition and the further condition of need of care or control have been made out, the court has to consider the welfare of the child and has a discretion as to whether to make an order and if so which of the following orders:—

1. An order requiring the parent(s).......to enter into a recognisance to take proper care of and exercise proper control over the child (or young person); or

2. A supervision order or

3. A care order or

4. A hospital order or

5. A guardianship order within the meaning of the Mental Health Acts.

16.24 Between the commencement of proceedings and the court being in a position to decide what sort of order, if any, ought to be made, it has power to make an interim care order which confers upon a Local Authority the same powers and duties as a care order and the interim order may be renewed. If not renewed it expires after 28 days.

16.25 The effect of a care order is to invest the Local Authority with parental rights and duties and a discretion as to the manner in which they are exercised under the provisions of the Child Care Act 1980. Questions such as where and with whom the child lives, education, medical matters, frequency and circumstances of access are all matters for decision by the local authority. Only in the event of a decision to terminate parental access does the court have power, on a separate application to it, to make specific orders, if appropriate, as to access arrangements, by virtue of s12B Child Care Act 1980.

16.26 Having made its determination, the court retains no continuing supervisory role.

The Child concerned

16.27 The child is a party to the proceedings and when care proceedings are instituted he/she must normally attend before the Court. The Justices have the power to dispense with attendance at Court, but save in special circumstances the presence of the child at Court is required for at least part of the hearing. In practice in many if not most courts in contentious proceedings the child is only briefly present.

Wardship—High Court

16.28 It became clear during the Inquiry that wardship is not clearly understood by many who in case conference or otherwise may have important decisions to make over future legal proceedings in respect of children in their care. For that reason we are giving a brief summary of some aspects of the wardship jurisdiction. Some of the wardship files have formed part of the Inquiry documents with the express permission of the Judges hearing the wardship applications and the relevant judgements have been provided to the Assessors and myself.

16.29 The jurisdiction of the High Court over minors has its roots in the ancient prerogative powers and obligations of the Crown as parens patriae to protect the person and property of subjects, particularily those, including infants, who were unable to look after themselves.

16.30 From early times, through the nineteenth century and into the twentieth century, the jurisdiction was essentially based upon considerations of property. However, by the end of the nineteenth century it was recognised that in such cases the minor's interests were of great importance. In 1893 Lord Justice Kay said in The Queen v. Gyngall ([1893] 2 Q.B.232 at p.248) that wardship

"is essentially a parental jurisdiction and that description of it involves that the main consideration to be acted upon in its exercise is the benefit or welfare of the child .... the Court must do what under the circumstances a wise parent acting for the true interest of the child would or ought to do."

16.31 In 1949 the Law Reform (Miscellaneous Provisions) Act removed procedural obstacles which had tended to restrict the use of wardship to cases of rich wards and wayward heiresses. By those reforms and by the provision of an uniform procedure for invoking the jurisdiction, the 1949 Act cleared the way for rapid developments in the use of wardship in the post-war years.

16.32 Further legislation in the field of legal aid, and the reorganisation of the business of the High Court, which in 1971 caused wardship cases to be assigned to the newly designated Family Division of the High Court, have led to the wardship jurisdiction being widely available and comparatively straightforward to use. It is not much concerned today with questions of property, but is habitually exercised in cases of child welfare.

16.33 It is however of the essence of wardship that it is an inherent jurisdiction, flowing from the Crown, and not one created by statute. There are no specific statutory constraints upon its development and few statutory limitations upon the powers of the Court exercising it. [Its procedure is regulated by the Supreme Court Act 1980 and Order 90 of the Supreme Court Rules]

16.34 There are no prescribed criteria for the exercise by the Court of its wardship jurisdiction. [see below for the exercise of wardship in respect of children in care.] Apart from care proceedings, the High Court, adapting to changing social conditions and values, is substantially unconstrained in acting as a wise parent and has very wide powers to achieve that end. In so doing the welfare of the child is the first and paramount consideration. Lord Scarman in Re E ([1984] 1W.L.R.158) said:—"A court exercising jurisdiction over its ward must never lose sight of a fundamental feature of the jurisdiction, namely, that it is exercising a wardship, not an adversarial jurisdiction. Its duty is not limited to the dispute between the parties. On the contrary, its duty is to act in the way best suited in its judgment to serve the true interests and welfare of the ward. In exercising wardship jurisdiction the court is a true family court. Its paramount concern is the welfare of its ward."

Wardship proceedings, begun by originating summons, may be started by anybody with a proper interest in the welfare of the child. Likewise, anyone with a proper interest in the child's welfare may be made a party to the proceedings; be legally represented and have a right of appeal. The Court has power to direct the representation of the child by a guardian ad litem, normally the Official Solicitor [see page 237]. On the issue of the summons the child automatically and immediately becomes a ward of court.

16.35 The Court's wide powers to make specific orders to promote any aspect of the child's welfare include a power to make a care order. The powers and duties of Part iii of the Child Care Act 1980 are thereby invoked but the manner in which the Local Authority carry out the duties imposed upon it by a care order remain at all times subject to the direction of the High Court. So long as a child remains a ward (until 18 or until dewarded by the Court) the Court retains a continuing supervisory role and can make further orders or directions at any stage. Every important decision affecting a child who is a ward, even under a care order, requires the approval of the Court.

Restrictions upon the use of wardship in care proceedings.

16.36 Since the decision of the House of Lords in A v.Liverpool City Council ([1982] A.C. 363) the ability of parents to challenge the activities of Local Authorities by recourse to the wardship jurisdiction has been defined and curtailed. The High Court will not in wardship review the exercise by a Local Authority of its statutory powers and duties in relation to a child in its care. Local Authorities may however invoke the assistance of the High Court for such children and have received judical support for this approach. Anomalies arise from this which stem in part at least from the inability at the present time of either parents or the Local Authority to appeal from a decision of a Juvenile court. In one case in Cleveland last year, the Juvenile Court refused to make a care order and the Local Authority immediately made the children wards of court, a remedy not open to the parents. The point of jurisdiction was conveniently waived by Cleveland County Council during the latter part of 1987 in a situation of crisis and the originating summonses were issued either by the Council or by the parents.

16.37 There is no doubt that the wardship jurisdiction came to the rescue of an otherwise overburdened Juvenile Court. It has proved in Cleveland to be an invaluable procedure to enable extremely difficult, complex and emotive issues to be fully considered and adjudicated upon. Wardship has an ethos which is recognised by those who use and are engaged in the jurisdiction. We see wardship having a role to play in care proceedings in the future.[see also page 235]

Witnesses in wardship

16.38 One matter which was brought to our attention by the Chairman of the Northern Regional Health Authority was the lack of protection that some expert witnesses might have in giving evidence in wardship proceedings where they were not parties. From what we read and heard of the wardship proceedings in Cleveland both Dr Higgs and Dr Wyatt were subjected to detailed and prolonged cross-examination by Counsel on behalf of parents, of a type not endured by other medical witnesses. We recognise the problem raised by Sir Bernard and record his concern. We do not think there is any recommendation we can usefully make.

Comparative Features

The Tribunal

16.39   Care proceedings under the Children and Young Persons Act 1969 are heard by lay magistrates in the Juvenile Court. Wardship is heard in the High Court by High Court Judges or on occasions deputies who may be either experienced Circuit Judges or Queen's Counsel.

16.40   In long and complicated cases there may be difficulties in a Bench being able regularly to sit for several days consecutively and there are even greater difficulties in reconvening a Bench after an adjournment. A High Court Judge almost invariably sits consecutively. There have been cases arising in Cleveland during 1987 where the complexity of the disputed medical evidence and the sheer volume of general evidence to be called, some of which has occupied much time before the Inquiry, would seem to be likely to exhaust the resources and expertise of the Juvenile Bench. One wonders how many Benches would be able to sit for 10 or even 15 days.

The Hearing

16.41   Care proceedings are for the most part heard on oral evidence alone. In wardship a substantial part of the evidence is presented in written form by way of affidavits setting out the issues and often read in advance of the hearing by the Judge.

16.42   Rights of audience, representation and appeal in care proceedings are limited by statute and rules. The wardship court, usually at a preliminary hearing before a Registrar, has a broad discretion to allow representation of all relevant interests at the substantive hearing, such as a putative father or grandparents.

Requirements/Standard of proof

16.43   The way in which the court arrives at the decision as to the best interests of the child depends upon the Act which is invoked. The Juvenile Court must prove two conditions before it looks at the child's best interests. The High Court and the County Court are given the wider powers to regard:—"the welfare of the child as the first and paramount consideration."

16.44   Those who initiate actions which will in due course require proceedings before the courts must be aware of the need to be able to prove the facts to the satisfaction of the particular court. In the criminal jurisdiction of the Magistrates Court and the Crown Court the proceedings are not instituted for the benefit of the child but for the trial of the accused. Our criminal law requires the highest standard of proof that the tribunal trying the defendant shall not convict unless satisfied so as to be sure of his guilt.

All other proceedings are child centred and require the court to consider the welfare of the child on the balance of probabilities. The standard of proof to be applied in wardship cases has been considered from time to time. In the case of Re G ([1988] 1 F.L.R. 314 at page 321) Mr Justice Sheldon in considering the test in a case of allegations of sexual abuse, said:—"a higher degree of probability is required to satisfy the court that the father has been guilty of some sexual misconduct with his daughter than would be needed to justify the conclusion that the child has been the victim of some such behaviour of whatever nature and whoever may have been its perpetrator. In the latter context, indeed, I am of the opinion that the gravity of the matter is such from the child's point of view that any tilt in the balance suggesting that she has been the victim of sexual abuse would justify a finding to that effect. In my view, there may also be circumstances in which the application of a 'standard of proof', as that phrase is commonly understood, is inapt to describe the method by which the court should approach the particular problem; as, for example, where the suspicion of sexual abuse or other wrong-doing, although incapable of formal proof, is such to lead to the conclusion that it would be an unacceptable risk to the child's welfare to leave him in his previous environment; or (more likely in the case of older children) where, although the court may be satisfied that no sexual abuse has taken place, the very fact that it has been alleged by a child against a parent suggests that, in the child's interests, some change in or control over the existing regime is required."

16.45   These words were considered by Mr Justice Hollis in two Cleveland cases and in a judgment given on the 30th July, 1987 he said:—"It seems therefore that if the risk of a child having been sexually abused while in his or her family environment is a real, reasonable or distinct possibility, action should be taken. I think that is really consistent with what Sheldon J. is saying in the case that I have quoted. I do not consider that a probability has to be shown but a real possibility. In that way, the interests of the child will be safeguarded." On appeal to the Court of Appeal (on the 18th December, 1987), Lord Justice Purchas said "The learned Judge applied in my judgment the correct test.....It is clear that the Judge is acting upon a standard of proof which is less than balance of probability and which he describes as a real possibility."

Attendance of child at Court

16.46 The general requirement for a child to attend the Juvenile Court in care proceedings is in contrast to procedures in other cases concerned with the welfare of children. In custody proceedings in the Magistrates' Domestic Court, in the County Court, in wardship and all custody proceedings in the High Court and in applications for access in each of those courts it is widely recognised that it is undesirable for children to attend court at all. In the County Court and High Court it is an almost invariable rule that they do not attend. If they see the Judge they do so privately.

16.47 The reason for the child's attendance in the Juvenile Court is said to be that he is a party. In wardship the child is often a party but the Official Solicitor or other guardian ad litem attends on his behalf. It does appear that the obligatory presence of the child at some part of the court proceedings may owe more to that part of the children's legislation relating to children as offenders rather than as the subjects of court proceedings.

16.48 The degree of media publicity during the Cleveland crisis and the right of the press to attend care proceedings resulted in journalists attending some hearings in great numbers. One small court room had 17 journalists for the hearing of one case. The requirement for a child to attend that hearing, however briefly, with a packed court full of strangers and the parents whom the child may not have seen for some time has caused us considerable anxiety.

We would urge rationalisation and harmonisation of the attendance of children at court. We would prefer that a child in civil proceedings did not attend court at all unless it be to see the tribunal in private, in which case the attendance of the child should be arranged to avoid meeting those attending court. Arrangements could always be made for the older child who wished to be heard. We feel strongly that this procedure is unsuitable and wrong in all care cases and it exhibits a particular lack of sensitivity in the type of case considered by the Inquiry.

Press and Public

16.49 In the Juvenile Court, while the public are excluded, the press are admitted and may publish, even in civil care proceedings particulars, with the exception of names and addresses which might identify the family involved.[CYPA 1933 ss47 and 49]. In custody and access proceedings in the Magistrates, County Court and High Court and in wardship the hearings are in private and both the press and the public are excluded. The extent to which the media may report any details about a child who is a ward of court has been reviewed by the courts from time. In contempt proceedings against national newspapers in a wardship case concerning two Cleveland children who were involved in the crisis, the President of the Family Division specifically considered the right of the press to publish.

16.50 In a judgment given on the 29th April,1988, he held that, in the absence of a specific injunction, facts within the public domain outside the wardship proceedings may be published. He said:—"After an examination of the authorities I feel bound to accept Mr Mumby's contention that it does not constitute a breach of of the restrictions automatically imposed by wardship proceedings in private, to publish the name and address of or to indicate the identity of the ward in the absence of a specific prohibition. Again on the authorities it is not a breach of the provisions of s 12 (Administration of Justice Act 1960) or of the common law to publish the fact that the minor is a ward of court or that wardship proceedings are taking place or have been taking place. What is prohibited by the statute and was prohibited by the common law is the publication of details of the actual proceedings held in private." In that case the press published names, and photographs of the children and their parents.

S. 39 of the Children and Young Persons Act 1933 (as amended) protects the anonymity of children in respect of name, address, identifying particulars, photographs, in criminal courts by direction of the Court. The High Court can of course and does grant injunctions which have a similar effect. The President granted an injunction in the above case, [a copy of which is in appendix K.] The restrictions imposed automatically on the media in the Juvenile Court (by s49 of the 1933 Act) affords greater automatic privacy to the child than the High Court in wardship proceedings.

16.51 We would urge in this area also a rationalisation of the restrictions on reporting by the media of proceedings relating to children in the various courts, with an emphasis upon the need to protect the child from unsuitable publicity even where the parents may seek it. At the very least in our view there should be automatic restriction upon the publication of the names, addresses, photographs and identification of children, who are the subject of civil proceedings.

Orders

16.52 The range of orders available in the Juvenile Court at present is narrow and with little flexibility. The range available to the wardship court is wide and highly flexible. It should however be noted that a Local Authority with a care order in wardship is at present subject to the continued supervision of the court whereas with a care order in the Juvenile Court it is in complete control.

Time and Place

16.53 Under ordinary good management and without either the difficulties experienced in Cleveland in 1987 or general difficulties experienced with the guardians ad litem panel a Juvenile Court ought to be able to hear and determine a care case of ordinary length within a maximum of 3 months. That time span was not possible in Cleveland in 1987 even before the crisis. In circumstances of exceptional urgency a wardship court can hear a case within days. It would however be likely to hear a substantive application normally within 6 to 12 months. There are also constrictions on the time within which difficult wardship applications can be heard out of London.

16.54 The Juvenile Court has the great advantage of being local and accessible unlike wardship which is either heard in London or in the larger towns, in some areas such as Middlesbrough, infrequently. There is power to release wardship to nominated Circuit Judges sitting as High Court Judges which has been extensively invoked in cases arising during the crisis. There is now the ability for wardship applications to be heard in the County Court but that is subject to the directions of the President of the Family Division.

Costs

16.55 Wardship proceedings are likely almost always to be substantially more expensive than Juvenile Court proceedings.

16.56 Comments on the Government White Paper.

1. We welcome the harmonisation of care orders in "family proceedings" with those made in the Juvenile court.

2. We particularily welcome the proposed involvement in the proceedings of "anyone who has a proper interest in the child's future and its welfare."; the proposals to extend the rights of parties and also those who may make representations.

3. We welcome the relaxing of rigid rules, such as by the use of hearsay evidence and the proposal to move from a quasi-criminal model to a civil model. The provision of documents in advance in particular is desirable both to assist the Magistrates to digest in advance complicated reports, particularily medical reports, in cases such as those which arose in Cleveland last year. Disclosure of documents in advance ought also to make better use of court time, if the Bench do not have to rise to read the documents handed in during the hearing.

4. We welcome the recasting of the grounds for an order and the proposal to assimilate them with family proceedings and specifically including 'likely harm,' covering cases of "unacceptable risk in which it may be necessary to balance the chance of harm occurring against the magnitude of that harm if it does occur."

5. The proposed limit of 8 weeks on interim orders is in principle excellent. We are again concerned at the interpretation of 'exceptional circumstances' in order to extend the period for a further 14 days. From the experience we gained in Cleveland some Juvenile Benches are far from achieving the main hearing after 8 weeks, or even 10 weeks.

6. The increasing of the jurisdiction of the Juvenile Court to include custody as one of the possible orders would provide the Juvenile Court with very useful additional powers and give them the right to consider the suitability of other members of the family. One aspect of custodianship, not available in custody is the right of the Local Authority to pay a custodian an allowance. It might be helpful to extend that right to care proceedings to assist for example a suitable grandmother applicant for custody.

7. Access. We welcome proposals that put in to the hands of the Court the right to grant or refuse access. We hope that this will apply to applications for access at interim hearings, in addition to the final hearing. Presumably it would also apply where custody is granted to a third party. Access was one of the most emotive issues arising in Cleveland and it is essential that any dispute over it, whether to restrict, suspend or refuse should be dealt with by the Bench as part of the interim and main care proceedings in addition to any application under s.12 of the 1980 Act.

8. During the course of the interim care proceedings we should like to see problems such as further medical examinations being a matter upon which the Magistrates would have the power to adjudicate. This would provide some protection to children who might otherwise be subjected to repeated medical examinations.

9. We should like to underline the importance of the requirement 'to inform and consult' parents on major decisions and suggest that it should be regarded as necessary in all spheres of the child care legislation.

Comments on the Courts.

16.57 The Juvenile Court designated by the child care legislation as the forum for care proceedings provides in the main a suitable court in which these child cases are heard. It has many advantages. The proposed new grounds for making care applications and the moves towards a civil model of procedure particularily in the broader approach to parties are welcome.

16.58 We do not however believe that these proposed changes will of themselves substantially reduce the reliance of some Local Authorities on wardship.

16.59 There are cases in which the Local Authority properly considers it can gain assistance from the High Court instead of operating the statutory child care procedure in the Juvenile Court.

16.60 Judges of the High Court Family Division have agreed with this view. Mrs Justice Lane said (in Re B [1975] Fam 36 at page 44):—"As a matter of general application it seems to me that there may be various circumstances in which a local authority would be grateful for the court exercising wardship jurisdiction; local authorities are sometimes faced with difficult and onerous decisions concerning children in their charge; responsible officers of their welfare department may be subject to various pressures from within or outside the authority itself. I consider that there would be no abandonment of, or derogation from, their statutory powers and duties were they to seek the guidance and assistance of the High Court in matters of difficulty, as distinct from the day to day arrangements with which as the authorities show, the court will not interfere." Lord Justice Ormrod said (in Re Y [1976] Fam 125 at page 138) "I feel bound to say that I think local authorities might find if they look into it situations in which it would be positively to their advantage to invoke the wardship jurisdiction themselves. It would sometimes avoid their having to take awkward decisions themselves which cause great pain and anguish."

16.61 Local Authorities have been content to issue wardship proceedings despite the subsequent restrictions imposed by the High Court on the control of a Local Authority over the ward in its care. It is not clear from paragraph 36 of the White Paper whether in wardship as in other family proceedings it is envisaged that the Local Authority would have full parental authority. There is a potential for conflict in the wider and undefined jurisdiction in wardship compared with divorce or guardianship jurisdictions. We would be concerned to see general restrictions upon the wardship jurisdiction on this point.

16.62 It is difficult to set out in detail the cases which might be more suited to the High Court. But many of the cases which arose in Cleveland last year and crowded the lists of the Juvenile Court would in our view qualify. Some of them occupied weeks of High Court time to complete and had elements of great complexity.

16.63 A general description of cases better heard in the High Court would be those which were likely to be complex and lengthy to hear. They might include:— elements of complexity of dispute, difficult medical or psychiatric evidence, unusual features; special difficulties affecting a parent or the child; international flavour and competing jurisdictions; length of the projected hearing. Some examples of difficulty have included sterilisation, abortion, surrogacy. One point to consider is the need for the tribunal hearing the case to receive, sift and analyse the evidence of expert evidence, on occasions at length from a number of professional witnesses.

In one Cleveland case before Mr Justice Hollis there were 7 medical experts called. This type of evidence and the evaluation of it makes great demands upon the tribunal called upon to hear it. The Juvenile Bench in Teesside were clearly taken aback by the disputed medical evidence called before them in June.

16.64 There were no submissions to the Inquiry on these points and the proposals are consequently tentative. They are put forward for consideration in the light of the White Paper paragraph 59 and the possible implication that Local Authorities would not in future and ought not to need to invoke the wardship jurisdiction.

16.65 There is an injustice in the ability of a Local Authority to issue wardship proceedings and for the parents not to have that right. In our view the decision in A v. Liverpool City Council [1982] A.C.363 ought to be reconsidered. Parents do of course have the right to apply at six monthly intervals for revocation of the care order.

Family Court

16.66 If that injustice were to be removed and parents were able to issue wardship proceedings in care cases there is a danger that the wardship jurisdiction would be invoked too frequently and unsuitably. It would be necessary to regulate the circumstances in which such applications in care proceedings should be heard in the High Court, in preference to the Juvenile Court. One way would be by review of the case by the Registrar to determine which would be the more suitable forum, in accordance with Directions issued by the President of the Family Division. However under the present procedures there are grave disadvantages to such regulation by the High Court, since the case cannot be transferred but only dismissed and started again in the Juvenile Court, a time-wasting and costly exercise.In situations such as this the setting up of a Family Court with the ability to move cases from one tier of the court to another in a flexible way would significantly assist in the distribution of the individual case to the court best fitted to deal with it.

16.67 At present an understanding of the law relating to each type of child case, each type of court and what is required for each, is needed by all agencies involved in child care and child protection—social workers, NSPCC, police, the medical profession, ali to some degree. It was clear from the experience in Cleveland that many professionals found it incomprehensible; many were very confused; some took inappropriate steps to deal with the children based in many instances on an incorrect or misconceived view of the legal position. The burden on these groups was considerable. It was the children who suffered.

Guardians ad litem

16.68 The circumstances in which the Juvenile Court must, or may if the interests of the child require it, appoint a guardian ad litem in care proceedings (and related proceedings) are contained in sections 32A and 32B Children and Young Persons Act 1969, and in rule 14A Magistrates Court (Children and Young Persons) Rules 1970. There are parallel provisions in rule 21C of the same rules to deal with the appointment of a guardian in proceedings under the Child Care Act 1980. The regulations are contained in the Guardians Ad Litem and Reporting Officers (Panels) Regulations 1983. Resources are provided by section 103 Children Act 1975.

Under the 1983 Regulations:

2.
"(1) There shall be established in the area of each local authority a panel of persons ..... from whom guardians ad litem ..... may be appointed ....

(2) A local authority shall ensure that the number of persons appointed to the panel ..... is sufficient ....

   3. (1) Members of a panel shall be appointed by the local authority in whose area the panel is established ....

   4. (1) Local authorities shall .... defray expenses incurred by members of the panels established in their area and pay fees and allowances for members of each panel."

The panel is often (as in Cleveland) although not invariably administered by a senior member of Social Services staff. Some of the points of criticism made about the role of guardians in Cleveland in 1987 have been met by the DHSS guide on "Panel Administration". The major problem however as expressed to the Inquiry by guardians and social workers both from within Cleveland and outside, was the necessity to demonstate the independence of the panel from the Local Authority who is always a party to the care proceedings. The arrangements made by Cleveland and some other Authorities of entering into an agency agreement with a national child care agency for the provision of a guardian ad litem service goes some way to meet the problem. Other concerns related to the maintenance of good standards of practice, the rate, method and control of remuneration and ongoing training, highlight the problem of establishing a service which can enjoy the confidence of the Court whilst being totally independent of the Local Authority.

16.69 One problem which became apparent in Cleveland was the lack of guidance available to guardians who were appointed in wardship proceedings, unlike in the Juvenile Court. The difficulties which are set out in the sub-chapter Official Solicitor occurred in Cleveland for some of the guardians appointed. In the guide referred to above, helpful advice is given to guardians on wardship, in particular that a guardian appointed is acting in a personal capacity; is not covered by the arrangements for fees and expenses which apply to panel members; the length of wardship proceedings and the effect upon a guardian's other work; the general financial implications.

16.70 In one case in Cleveland a guardian in the Juvenile Court issued wardship proceedings after the Justices discharged a care order with the agreement of the Local Authority. She made the child the Plaintiff and herself as Next Friend.

16.71 A distinction can be drawn between the agreement of all parties that a case proceeding in the Juvenile Court would be better heard in the High Court where the guardian has already appointed and is in possession of the facts, and an adjudication by the Juvenile Court with which the guardian does not agree and thereafter takes wardship proceedings. In the latter situation we doubt the suitability of the procedure other than in rare instances in which it would be appropriate to consult the Official Solicitor before assuming the burden of Plaintiff in the High Court.

16.72 Whether as guardian or as Next Friend it is clear from the following sub-chapter that the Official Solicitor should first be invited to act for the child in these cases.

One area of difficulty for guardians referred to by the Official Solicitor is to be found in Rule 14 A 6(b) in the 1970 Rules which says'' The guardian ad litem..... shall regard as the first and paramount consideration the need to safeguard and promote the the infant's best interests *until he achieves adulthood*. This places upon guardians a duty beyond their capacity to achieve and is likely to cause difficulties. Some more realistic wording which defined their responsibilities within the scope and limits of their duties would be preferable.

16.73 We heard evidence from representatives of BASW and BASPCAN, and from guardians in Cleveland. They were concerned to emphasise their belief that the present arrangement for the administration of guardians ad litem compromised their ability to be seen as independent by parents.

Official Solicitor

16.74 The office of the Official Solicitor may be little known to the public but it is well known to the High Court Judges and much relied upon by them, particularily in the Family Division. The Official Solicitor has various functions, one of which is to act at the request of the Court as Guardian ad litem or Next Friend of a minor. When appointed to act on behalf of the child he is:—"not only an officer of the Court and the ward's guardian, but he is a solicitor and the ward is his client." (See Mr Justice Goff in re R(PM) an infant [1968] 1 All E. R. 691 at p 692.) The Official Solicitor sees :—"his primary role as being to give the child, either through him or Counsel instructed by him, a voice in the proceedings." It was on that basis that the Inquiry asked him to represent children caught up in the crisis in Cleveland. We are extremely grateful to him for the way in which he has carried out his duties to the children during the Inquiry not only in being represented throughout and providing the Inquiry with a dispassionate and objective approach to each aspect of the evidence, but also for the outstanding submission presented to the Inquiry which has been the greatest possible assistance to us.

In looking at the position of the guardian ad litem that of the Official Solicitor is of great importance. He did not, perhaps surprisingly, represent any children in the wardship applications in Cleveland. That situation, which gave him a position of greater detachment may have been of added assistance to the Inquiry, but it was commented upon by Mr Justice Sheldon in a decision on the 20th April 1988. He referred to observations of Mrs Justice Heilbron (reported in re JD [1984] FLR 359 at p360, 361.and approved by Lord Justice Dunn in re C 1984 FLR 419 at 443) She said:—"As to the position of the Official Solicitor, one finds that the implication of almost every reported case and Practice Direction is that the Official Solicitor is the preferred guardian ad litem and the one first to be considered.......It is beyond doubt that the position of the Official Solicitor is unique. Historically, he has been closely involved with wards of court. He provides the expertise and the authority of his office and his department and he is accepted as the person who will form an objective and independent assessment of the ward's interests. As the child's representative in a case where a fresh, unbiased view is required, he can provide invaluable assistance to the court." She went on to say:—"It is also useful to observe that the Official Solicitor's duties as guardian ad litem do not always end at the conclusion of the hearing, because his staff, and indeed he himself may be called upon to assist in working out the order, or to provide a channel of communication between the parties, and there are other functions that he very helpfully can, and often does, perform". A court order may include a provision for the Official Solicitor to continue to play a part after the proceedings in court are over. It would not be unusual for the Official Solicitor to retain an interest in and contact with a ward for 10 years or more. This is in marked contrast to a guardian from the panel whose duties end in the Juvenile Court at the making of the care order and who would in the High Court be hard pressed to be remunerated personally or financed by Legal Aid for a continuing role in a child's life. Mr Justice Sheldon in the Cleveland case referred to the earlier decisions and that the "established principle" was that in wardship cases where the child was made a party "the Official Solicitor should be the first person to be invited to act as guardian ad litem." He pointed out that he may decline to act or ask for further information before coming to a decision, but in the case in question no invitation was extended to him.

He went on to say:—"Questions that the court should always consider before appointing some other person to act as guardian is whether there is some compelling reason why he or she should be preferred to the Official Solicitor; whether the alternative candidate possesses the necessary expertise and experience to undertake the work; and whether he possesses corresponding facilities to those available to the Official Solicitor of obtaining any psychiatric, paediatric or other expert evidence that might be required, particularly at short notice. Further questions that should be considered, not only by the court but also by any prospective guardian, are as to his ability to obtain the legal representation necessary in the high Court and to obtain remuneration, not only for such representation, but also for himself. Nor should it be overlooked that the duties required of a guardian ad litem in wardship (unlike those in the Juvenile Court) may well not end at the conclusion of the hearing and may extend over many years—sometimes until the ward attains his majority—during which time his assistance may be sought in an advisory capacity or developments may occur which may make it necessary, at short notice, to restore the matter to court for further consideration. Again, who, in such an event will be responsible for the guardian's remuneration? The possibility of such continuity of representation, indeed, is regarded as a most important factor in such cases and it is one which the Official Solicitor is particularly well able to provide." The Official Solicitor believes that continuity of representation is one of the most significant advantages that his office possesses in children's cases.

16.75 In the complex and anxious cases such as were seen in Cleveland last year, which are heard in the wardship jurisdiction, the Official Solicitor is often able to provide great assistance to the Court in the difficult decisions that have to be made and in some instances continuing representation for the child.

The Scottish System

16.76 In evidence, Mr Roycroft and Mr Frank Cook MP urged the Inquiry to look at the Scottish arrangements for dealing with children's cases. Professor Forfar suggested that the Scottish system had advantages in his letter to the Northern Regional Health Authority.

16.77 The Official Solicitor made a written submission to the Inquiry on the Scottish system, for which we are very grateful, and the Treasury Solicitor provided the Inquiry with some written information. We did not however receive any wider representation about the arrangements in Scotland and therefore any observations we make or conclusions we reach are tentative.

Procedure and grounds

16.78 The Social Work (Scotland) Act 1968, s32(2) sets out the conditions upon which a child may be made the subject of compulsory measures of care. They are in general not dissimilar from the grounds in s1 of the Children and Young Persons Act 1969, and include: being beyond control, through lack of parental care he is falling into bad associations or is exposed to moral danger, the lack of care is likely to cause him unnecessary suffering or seriously to impair his health or development.

16.79 The major differences between the two systems are to be found in putting the substantive law into practice. The decision about what should happen to a child who may be in need of compulsory measures of care is taken by a Childrens' Hearing.

Childrens' Hearing

16.80 The Secretary of State for Scotland appoints a Children's Panel from which three members constitute a Childrens' Hearing, one of whom acts as Chairman, and both a man and a woman must be among the members. The Children's Hearing does not constitute court proceedings. The parents are expected to attend. Proceedings are informal and conducted in private with the Reporter, the social worker, the child and the parents present, although the child need not be present where attendance would be detrimental to his/her interests. The parties are not normally represented and the rules of evidence do not apply.

16.81 The Children's Hearing has no right to make a determination regarding any dispute as to the grounds of referral. If the parents accept the grounds then the hearing may proceed to consider the question of the need for compulsory measures of care. If there is a dispute over the grounds of referral, the Reporter applies to the Sheriff's Court for a determination of the issue. Application must also be made to the Sheriff's Court if the child is too young to understand what is involved. At the Sheriff's hearing which is held within 28 days and in private, the Sheriff may decide that none of the grounds has been established and dismiss the application. If, however he is satisfied that any grounds of referral exist, he will remit the case to the Reporter for a Children's Hearing to consider the need for compulsory measures of care.

16.82 Like the Juvenile Court at that stage there will be reports prepared for the Hearing. The Childrens' Hearing may withhold certain documents from the parents. The Court of Session has held:—"The principles of natural justice must yield to the best interests of the child."

If no further action is required the referral is discharged. Supervision orders may be made, or the Local Authority may assume parental rights.

The role of the Reporter

16.83 The other major procedural difference from the English system is the role of the Reporter. He is appointed by the Local Authority but is independent of it. A Local Authority with information suggesting that a child may be in need of compulsory measures of care shall cause inquiries to be made and if the suggestion appears justified, give the information to the Reporter.

16.84 His function is to decide whether a child should be brought before a Childrens' Hearing. His discretion is wide; by s.39 of the 1968 Act he is given power to arrange a Childrens' Hearing, or to refer a case to the Local Authority with a view to their making arrangements for advice, guidance and assistance to the child and his family, and he has explicit power to take no further action on the case.

16.85 The Reporter in practice frequently overrules the Local Authority, often for lack of evidence. This emphasises his independent function.

16.86 The Reporter is responsible for obtaining any necessary reports for the Childrens' Hearing.

Safeguarder

16.87 The Chairman of the Childrens' Hearing or the Sheriff may appoint an independent person, termed a Safeguarder, to safeguard the interests of the child where there is a conflict of interest between the child and the parents. This is analagous to the English guardian ad litem.

Comments

16.88 We notice that in common with the English system of the Juvenile Court both criminal and civil proceedings are combined in the same statutory system.

16.89 We do not feel it appropriate in this Report to engage in a discussion over the relative merits of the same tribunal or two different tribunals deciding the issues of referral and disposal of the child. In Cleveland in 1987 all the cases which were disputed would have gone to the Sheriff for determination. The relative advantages and disadvantages of the two systems in the Cleveland perspective would not be easy to evaluate.

Child Protection

16.90 In our view some of the key responsibilities carried out by the Reporter might usefully be adapted to the English system. In the wider considerations of setting up a Family Court these might be considered for inclusion in the new system.

16.91 We would suggest a new Office of Child Protection. The responsibilities of the office would be:

1. To scrutinise the application of the Local Authority and ensure that the prima facie grounds for the Local Authority's application are well founded.

2. The office holder should be able to call for additional reports prior to any hearing of care proceedings. Depending upon the structure of the Family Court he might be empowered to determine the parties to the care proceedings or advise on them.

3. The office-holder should have the power to invite the Local Authority or the Police to reconsider the proposed proceedings in the best interests of the child.

4. Since we are not at this time suggesting the introduction of the Children's Hearing and therefore the proceedings would go to a Court, we do not suggest that the holder of the Office of Child Protection should necessarily have the power to take no further action. There would be a danger that agencies would pass all their problems to the office holder and rely upon his decisions. This is an area which would require careful consideration as to the extent of the powers of the new Office.

   However the requirement to submit the application to the court through the office of Child Protection would provide an useful safeguard in many of the situations which arose in Cleveland and assist Local Authorities in the many and sometimes conflicting duties cast upon them. For instance, it is usual for the Chairman of a case conference to be a senior Social Services manager. He may well be and often is the person responsible for initiating any care proceedings in respect of the child. The introduction of an independent assessment as to whether the proposed proceedings are well founded would provide an impartial check and balance on ensuring that the grounds for proceedings are properly established. There would also be an independent appraisal at an earlier stage than in our system. In Cleveland last year an objective look at the cases would have been a great advantage. From the point of view of the parents there is an intervening step which is independent of the Local Authority proposing the care proceedings.

5. The Office of Child Protection might usefully be considered as the administrator of the guardian ad litem panel and thereby relieve the Local Authority of a duty and create the independence sought by guardians. No doubt Social Services and national child care agencies would continue to have an important part to play in the approval of those placed on the panel.

PART THREE

CONCLUSIONS AND RECOMMENDATIONS

PART 3

Final Conclusions

1. We have learned during the Inquiry that sexual abuse occurs in children of all ages, including the very young, to boys as well as girls, in all classes of society and frequently within the privacy of the family. The sexual abuse can be very serious and on occasions includes vaginal, anal and oral intercourse. The problems of child sexual abuse have been recognised to an increasing extent over the past few years by professionals in different disciplines. This presents new and particularly difficult problems for the agencies concerned in child protection. In Cleveland an honest attempt was made to address these problems by the agencies. In Spring 1987 it went wrong.

2. The reasons for the crisis are complex. In essence they included:

— lack of a proper understanding by the main agencies of each others' functions in relation to child sexual abuse;

— a lack of communication between the agencies;

— differences of views at middle management level which were not recognised by senior staff. These eventually affected those working on the ground.

3. These tensions came out into the open with Dr Higgs' appointment as a consultant paediatrician to the Middlesbrough General Hospital. She was known to have an interest in the problems of child abuse. As a result of her understanding of the work of Dr Hobbs and Dr Wynne in Leeds, she formed the view that physical signs could help to identify sexual abuse and assist those seeking to protect abused children. She referred the first few children in whom she made the diagnosis to Dr Wynne for a second opinion. In each she received confirmation of her diagnosis, and as a consequence she proceeded with increasing confidence. The presence of the physical signs was elevated from grounds of 'strong suspicion' to an unequivocal 'diagnosis' of sexual abuse.

4. Dr Wyatt, another consultant paediatrician at Middlesbrough General Hospital, became equally convinced of the significance of the physical signs and he enthusiastically supported her.

5. Dr Higgs and Dr Wyatt became the centre point of recognition of the problem. Between them in the 5 months, mainly in May and June they diagnosed sexual abuse in 121 children from 57 families. Children were referred to them in various ways; some were brought by social workers because of a suspicion of sexual abuse or allegations or complaints; others were referred by family practitioners, health visitors, or community medical officers because of a suspicion of sexual abuse; a few from within the hospital were referred by junior medical staff or by nurses. In some the diagnosis arose on children attending outpatient clinics with medical conditions in which the possibility of sexual abuse had not been previously raised. Many were siblings of or connected with these children.

6. By reaching a firm conclusion on the basis of physical signs and acting as they would for non-accidental injury or physical abuse; by separating children from their parents and by admitting most of the children to hospital, they compromised the work of the social workers and the Police. The medical diagnosis assumed a central and determining role in the management of the child and the family.

7. It was entirely proper for the two paediatricians to play their part in the identification of sexual abuse in children referred to them. They were responsible for the care of their patients. Nonetheless they had a responsibility to examine their own actions; to consider whether their practice was always correct and whether it was in the best interests of the children and their patients. They are to be criticised for not doing so and for the certainty and over-confidence with which they pursued the detection of sexual abuse in children referred to them. They were not solely nor indeed principally responsible for the subsequent management of the children concerned. However, the certainty of their findings in relation to children diagnosed by them without prior complaint, posed particular problems for the Police and Social Services.

8. The response of the Social Services Department to the diagnoses of the two doctors was determined in the main by the newly appointed Child Abuse Consultant, Mrs Richardson, who supported and agreed with Dr Higgs' approach. She advised that immediately the diagnosis was made the child should be moved to a 'place of safety' for further investigation and evaluation and this was ensured by obtaining a place of safety order from a Magistrate. This practice was confirmed by the issuing of a memorandum by the Director of Social Services which in practice had the effect of endorsing the medical diagnoses of the two

paediatricians. In most cases the social workers' own professional responsibilities required them to make a wider assessment before taking action. The number of children separated from their parents increased dramatically and required both the consultants and Social Services managers to reappraise their practice. This they failed to do. They had a responsibility to look into the numbers of referrals and the method of diagnosis. As the crisis developed, both doctors and social workers had a duty to consider their priorities, particularily with children from families with long-standing problems who were well known to Social Services.

9. Another element was the attitude of the Police encouraged by their senior police surgeon, Dr Irvine, who took the view that Dr Higgs was mistaken in her diagnoses. The Police retreated from the multi-disciplinary approach into an entrenched position. They can be criticised for allowing a rift to develop and taking no effective step to break the deadlock. There was no reaction at senior level to the problems being raised and passed on to them by operational officers. The Police blamed the attitude and approach of Mrs Richardson for their reactions. They should not have allowed personalities to stand in the way of an objective assessment of the situation and the need to resolve it. Their requirement that the diagnoses of Dr Higgs should be reviewed by the senior police surgeon was unhelpful in the circumstances.

10. There was a failure by middle and senior managers in each agency to take action appropriate to the seriousness of the situation. The disagreements between the Police and Social Services were allowed to drift and the crisis to develop. In particular, the Chief Constable and the Director of Social Services failed to understand the depth of the disagreement between their staff and as a consequence failed to take some joint action to bring their two agencies together.

11. The lack of appropriate legal advice at case conferences contributed to the failure of those most closely involved with the children to appreciate that the medical opinions they had acted upon might not provide a satisfactory basis for applications in care proceedings. This deprived them of an useful check in consideration of the advisability of the removal of the children from home.

12. There was an understandable response from parents when the diagnosis of sexual abuse was made. Their child was admitted to hospital; a place of safety order was served on them; access was restricted for the purpose of 'disclosure work'. They were uncertain of their responsibilities, distressed and angry. They did not know what to do or where to turn. They were isolated. As the numbers grew many of them formed themselves into a support group and they then received increasing support from others both locally and nationally. The media reported the situation and the crisis became public knowledge.

13. Most of the 121 children diagnosed by Drs Higgs and Wyatt as sexually abused, were separated from their parents and their home, 70% by place of safety orders. The majority have now returned home, some with all proceedings dismissed, others on conditions of medical examinations and supervision orders. A few children went to one parent or a different parent and a few children were committed to the care of the Council.

14. It is unacceptable that the disagreements and failure of communication of adults should be allowed to obscure the needs of children both long term and short term in so sensitive, difficult and important a field. The children had unhappy experiences which should not be allowed to happen again.

15. It is however important to bear in mind that those who have a responsibility to protect children at risk, such as social workers, health visitors, police and doctors have in the past been criticised for failure to act in sufficient time and to take adequate steps to protect children who are being damaged. In Cleveland the general criticism by the public has been of over-enthusiasm and zeal in the actions taken. It is difficult for professionals to balance the conflicting interests and needs in the enormously important and delicate field of child sexual abuse. We hope that professionals will not as a result of the Cleveland experience stand back and hesitate to act to protect the children.

16. In many Inquiries it is social workers who are under scrutiny for their failure to act in time. We are concerned that in advising a calm, measured and considered approach to the problem of child sexual abuse, we are not seen to imply either that there are never occasions when immediate action may need to be taken or that there is not a problem to be faced and children to be protected. It is a delicate and difficult line to tread between taking action too soon and not taking it soon enough. Social Services whilst putting the needs of the child first must respect the rights of the parents; they also must work if possible with the parents for the benefit of the children. These parents themselves are often in need of help. Inevitably a degree of conflict develops between those objectives.

17. We are also concerned about the extent of the misplaced adverse criticism social workers have received from the media and elswhere. There is a danger that social workers, including those in Cleveland, will be demoralised. Some may hesitate to do what is right. Social workers need the support of the public to continue in the job the public needs them to do. It is time the public and the press gave it to them.

18. Whilst it was important to try and identify what went wrong, it is equally important not to let that identification impede progress in the future, in Cleveland and elsewhere. We make criticisms of individuals. Those criticisms must not be permitted to obscure the wider failings of agencies; nor would we wish to suggest that the identification and management of sexual abuse within the family is easy. It obviously is not.

19. We hope that the troubles of 1987 will recede for those concerned with the protection of children in Cleveland, and that they will work together, to tackle the exacting task of helping children who are subject to sexual abuse to the lasting benefit of the children, the families and their community.

How society acknowledges the existence of, recognises and then handles child sexual abuse poses difficult and complex problems. There are some issues of importance upon which we did not receive evidence and which we have not addressed. These include specifically the nature of abusers and the reasons for sexual abuse of children; the effectiveness and appropriateness of the strategies used once the problem has been identified; and the response of society and the agencies to those who abuse.

There are also some issues upon which we do not make recommendations but which in our view justify further consideration and we set out these with our observations at page 254.

We make the following recommendations:

Recommendations

1. Recognition of sexual abuse

There is a need:

  a. To recognise and describe the extent of the problem of child sexual abuse;

  b. To receive more accurate data of the abuse which is identified.

2. Children

There is a danger that in looking to the welfare of the children believed to be the victims of sexual abuse the children themselves may be overlooked. The child is a person and not an object of concern.

We recommend that:

  a. Professionals recognise the need for adults to explain to children what is going on. Children are entitled to a proper explanation appropriate to their age, to be told why they are being taken away from home and given some idea of what is going to happen to them.

  b. Professionals should not make promises which cannot be kept to a child, and in the light of possible court proceedings should not promise a child that what is said in confidence can be kept in confidence.

  c. Professionals should always listen carefully to what the child has to say and take seriously what is said.

  d. Throughout the proceedings the views and the wishes of the child, particularily as to what should happen to him/her, should be taken into consideration by the professionals involved with their problems.

  e. The views and the wishes of the child should be placed before whichever court deals with the case. We do not however, suggest that those wishes should predominate.

  f. Children should not be subjected to repeated medical examinations solely for evidential purposes. Where appropriate, according to age and understanding, the consent of the child should be obtained before any medical examination or photography.

  g. Children should not be subjected to repeated interviews nor to the probing and confrontational type of 'disclosure' interview for the same purpose, for it in itself can be damaging and harmful to them. The consent of the child should where possible be obtained before the interviews are recorded on video.

h. The child should be medically examined and interviewed in a suitable and sensitive environment, where there are suitably trained staff available.

i. When a child is moved from home or between hospital and foster home it is important that those responsible for the day to day care of the child not only understand the child's legal status but also have sufficient information to look after the child properly.

j. Those involved in investigation of child sexual abuse should make a conscious effort to ensure that they act throughout in the best interests of the child.

3. Parents

We recommend:

a. The parents should be given the same courtesy as the family of any other referred child. This applies to all aspects of the investigation into the suspicion of child sexual abuse, and should be recognised by all professionals concerned with the family.

b. Parents should be informed and where appropriate consulted at each stage of the investigation by the professional dealing with the child, whether medical, police or social worker. Parents are entitled to know what is going on, and to be helped to understand the steps that are being taken.

c. We discuss below the position of parents in case conferences.

d. Social Services should confirm all important decisions to parents in writing. Parents may not understand the implications of decisions made and they should have the opportunity to give the written decision to their lawyers.

e. Parents should always be advised of their rights of appeal or complaint in relation to any decisions made about them or their children.

f. Social Services should always seek to provide support to the family during the investigation. Parents should not be left isolated and bewildered at this difficult time.

g. The service of the place of safety order on parents should include a written explanation of the meaning of the order, the position of the parents, their continuing responsibilities and rights and advice to seek legal advice.

4. Social Services

We make the following recommendations with regard to Social Services:

Place of Safety Orders

a. Place of safety orders should only be sought for the minimum time necessary to ensure protection of the child.

b. Records related to the use of statutory powers on an emergency basis should be kept and monitored regularly by Social Services Departments.

c. A code of practice for the administration by social workers of emergency orders for the purposes of child protection including the provision of information to parents defining their rights in clear simple language should be drawn up (see also recommendations on the courts).

Access

d. Whenever and however children are received into care social workers should agree with parents the arrangements for access unless there are exceptional reasons related to the childs interests not to do so. In either event the parent should be notified in writing as soon as possible of the access arrangements and the avenues of complaint or appeal open to them if they are aggrieved.

Case Conferences

e. Parents should be informed of case conferences and invited to attend for all or part of the conference unless, in the view of the Chairman of the conference, their presence will preclude a full and proper consideration of the child's interests.

f. Irrespective of whether parents attend the conferences, social workers have a primary responsibility to ensure that the case conference has information relating to the family background and the parents' views on the issues under consideration.

g. In complex cases the Chairman of the conference must be able to call upon the attendance of a qualified lawyer to assist in the evaluation of evidence indicative of care proceedings.

h. When a case conference is presented with medical opinions that are in conflict the doctors involved should be asked to review their findings jointly with the interests of the child in mind. If they are unable to establish common ground then they should be asked to identify the basis of their differences. It would then be for the case conference to consider their views in the context of the other information available.

Management

i. Senior managers in Social Services Departments need to ensure that they have efficient systems available to allow accurate monitoring of service activity which will alert them to problems that need to be resolved.

j. Staff engaged in social work practice in the field of child abuse and child sexual abuse need structured arrangements for their professional supervision and personal support. The work is stressful and it is important that their personal needs are not overlooked.

k. We recommend that careful consideration be given to the provision of structured systems of support and supervision for staff undertaking work on Emergency Duty Teams. Operationally such teams should report to a senior line manager.

l. Social Services Departments should maintain an open continuing relationship with the Police to review areas of mutual concern.

5. Police

We make the following recommendations with regard to Police Forces:

a. The Police should examine their organisation to ensure there is an adequate communication network to achieve the recognition and identification of problems at operational level and a system to develop remedies.

b. The Police should develop, monitor and maintain communication and consultation with the other agencies concerned with child protection.

c. The Police should develop and practise inter-agency working, including joint planning and interviews of children in investigation of sexual abuse within the family or caring agency.

d. The Police should recognise and develop their responsibility for the protection of the child as extending beyond the collection of evidence for court proceedings. This should include their attendance at case conferences and assistance to the other child protection agencies.

6. The Medical Profession

We make the following recommendations with regard to the medical profession:

a. They should agree a consistent vocabulary to describe physical signs which may be associated with child sexual abuse.

b. There should be investigation of the natural history and the significance of signs and symptoms which may be associated with child sexual abuse.

c. Consideration be given to inquiring into the significance of the phenomonen of anal dilatation.

d. Doctors engaged in the care of a child in whom the suspicion of sexual abuse is raised must of course give the child the appropriate medical care, but should also recognise the importance of the forensic element.

The doctor concerned should recognise the importance:

i. of taking a full medical history and making a thorough medical examination.

ii. of making where appropriate investigations for forensic purposes, for sexually transmitted diseases and for pregnancy in older girls.

iii. of completing full and accurate medical records which should provide the information for the protective agencies and on occasions the courts.[see appendix F] Those records should be made at the time of examination.

iv. of preparing statements for police purposes and/or for Social Services or NSPCC.

    We understand that the Standing Medical Advisory Committee to the DHSS are in the course of providing guidelines for the medical profession on this subject.

e. On a medical examination for forensic or other evidential purposes unconnected with the immediate care and treatment of the child the informed consent of the parents should be sought. This may present difficulties for the police surgeon or doctor from the approved panel on the specialist assessment team [see below] in cases of suspected sexual abuse within the family. This problem needs to be considered further.

f. Medical practitioners who have examined a child for suspected sexual abuse and disagree in their findings and conclusions should discuss their reports and resolve their differences where possible; in the absence of agreement identify the areas of dispute, recognising their purpose is to act in the best interests of the child.

7. Area Review Committees/Joint Child Abuse Committees

We make the following recommendations in respect of the Area Review Committees/Joint Child Abuse Committees:

a. They should review the arrangements for identifying and monitoring suitable training for professionals working with child sexual abuse;

b. The membership of these committees should include those who have the authority and responsibility to bind their agency to implementing the recommendations of the Committee, and to play a useful part in the decision-making process which accurately reflects the view of the agency they represent.

8. Inter-Agency Co-operation

We strongly recommend:

a. The development of inter-agency co-operation which acknowledges:

i. no single agency—Health, Social Services, Police or voluntary organisation has the pre-eminent responsibility in the assessment of child abuse generally and child sexual abuse specifically. Each agency has a prime responsibility for a particular aspect of the problem. Neither childrens' nor parents' needs and rights can be adequately met or protected unless agencies agree a framework for their inter-action. The statutory duties of Social Service Departments must be recognised;

ii. careful consideration must be given to the detail of working arrangements between doctors, nurses, social workers, police, teachers, staff of voluntary organisations and others responsible for the care of children;

iii. arrangments for collaboration between services must not inhibit prompt action by any professional or agency where this is demanded by the best interests of the child. Agreements over collaborative work should not inhibit or preclude doctors, social workers or policemen from carrying out their primary professional responsibilities. The responsibility for the decisions will remain theirs;

iv. practical issues need to be recognised and resolved at local level in careful discussion between the respective agencies. For example:

— what the level of suspicion of physical or sexual abuse should be before the Police are informed that an offence appears to have been committed;

— when and what parents are told when doctors see signs that may be indicative of sexual abuse;

— in what circumstances social workers should delay seeing parents until they have been interviewed by the Police.

v. managers should accept responsibility for ensuring that agreements reached are implemented in practice. Each agency should give an undertaking not to make unilateral changes in practice or policy without giving prior notice to the others;

vi. the existence of bodies charged with the responsibility to co-ordinate practice between agencies does not relieve Chief Officers such as the Director of Social Services, the Chief Constable, the Director of Education and the Health Service District General Manager of their responsibility to ensure effective co-operation and collaboration between their services or to identify problems and seek solutions.

b. The establishment of Specialist Assessment Teams.

i. The function of the Specialist Assessment Teams (SAT) is to undertake a full multi-disciplinary assessment of the child and the family in cases of particular difficulty. Each member of the team will have direct access to information available within their agency. The completion of a medical examination, a social work assessment, and appropriate inquiries by the Police, carried out in a planned and co-ordinated way should allow the Specialist Assessment Team to present their joint assessment and conclusions to the referring agency or a case conference. Whilst each member of the team has a duty to act with care and undertake the full range of responsibilities normally ascribed to the individual's role—their primary responsibility as a team is to make an assessment. The duty to provide on-going treatment or plan for the future should remain with others.

ii. The team should consist of an approved medical practitioner, a senior social worker, and a police officer with sufficient authority to co-ordinate the investigation of cases.

iii. In each area a list of approved doctors should be drawn up. The process of approval might be adapted from the regulations under the Mental Health Act which provide for the approval of doctors for the purpose of that Act. The doctors on the list should have knowledge and experience of the needs of children and an understanding of child abuse in general and child sexual abuse in particular. They should be prepared, at the request of their medical colleagues, Social Services or the Police, to examine a child and participate in a formal multi-disciplinary assessment of the child's presenting concern. This may include collecting forensic evidence; compiling medical evidence for care proceedings; and involve attendance at case conferences and at Court. The doctors included on such a list might be community or hospital paediatricians, or those who have appropriate experience such as women police doctors, police surgeons etc.

iv. The Social Services will need to appoint to an approved list those social workers who are trained, experienced and competent in work in the field of child abuse and child sexual abuse.

v. The Police will need to appoint to an approved list, police officers trained, experienced and competent in the field of child sexual abuse to undertake the work required.

vi. It is probably not in the interests of either the children, families or professionals or the agency for staff—doctors, social workers, or police, to specialise solely in child sexual abuse. A special interest reflected in allocated time, complemented with other less-demanding work is the most likely arrangement to avoid stress and ensure a balanced perspective.

vii. The existence of the team will have the advantage of building a reservoir of expertise in a difficult area of work. The intention is to foster teamwork and co-ordination of activity without undermining primary professional responsibility or agency function. Such an arrangement would facilitate the development of skills amongst a wider group of people whilst ensuring a reservoir of specialist skill that staff could turn to for assistance with the difficult cases. It should have access to specialist expertise,—for example a child psychiatrist or gynaecologist, who would be consulted or brought in on cases of particular difficulty.

c. The following framework and methods of working.

i. The flowchart gives a general outline. It does not cover every possibility. The framework is intended to allow straightforward cases to be dealt with in a straightforward way. It is not suggested that the Specialist Assessment Team deal with all referrals.

ii. All agencies—Police, Social Services, NSPCC, Health, will receive some referrals where there is a clear account of events by a child and/or an admission of guilt by a perpetrator.

— Social Services will receive information or referrals which present a straightforward pattern of information, clear account by a child, admission by a perpetrator and confirmation by a medical examination. Such cases will require Social Services to work closely with the Police and medical colleagues in a planned intervention. Evidence and information will be collated. A case conference will be called to ensure that all relevant information has been gathered and the conference recommendations are considered in the making of the final decisions in relation to civil or criminal proceedings.

— Referrals to doctors are most likely to arise in relation to an injury or disorder. Where an allegation by a child accompanied by primary medical signs allows a definitive conclusion to be drawn, the case will need to be referred directly to the Police and/or Social Services. In cases

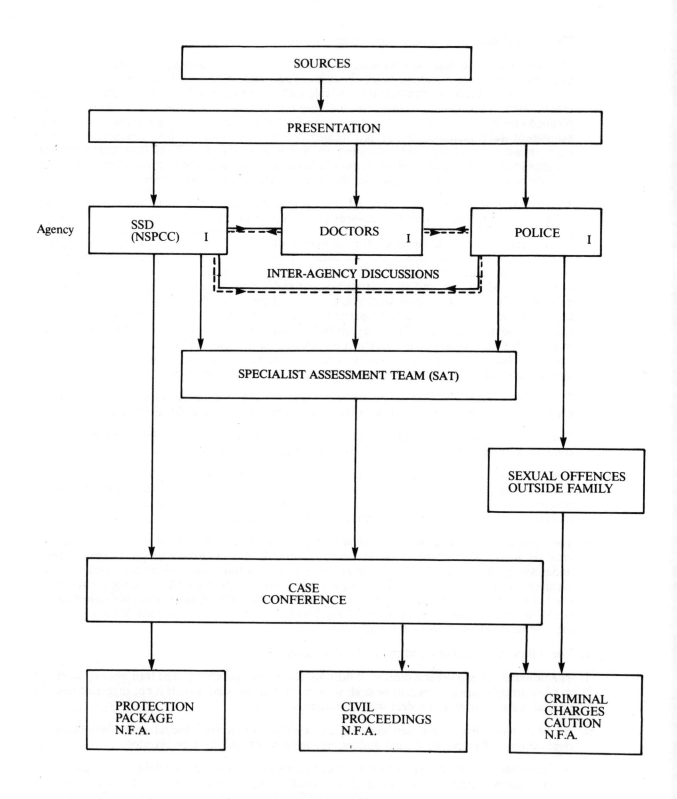

I = INFORMAL INQUIRIES   N.F.A. = NO FURTHER ACTION

A FRAMEWORK FOR INTER-AGENCY RESPONSE

where suspicion is raised by the presence of physical signs without complaints by the child or a third party, a referral should be made to the Specialist Assessment Team for assessment.

— A number of such cases will involve allegations of offences made to the Police by a child or third party relating to events which have taken place outside the family. Such cases will normally be investigated and prosecuted by the Police without the involvement of other agencies. It may be necessary for the Police to draw on the skills of a doctor from the approved list to undertake a medical examination for evidential purposes. If during the course of their investigation, the Police become concerned about the adequacy of care and control the child involved is receiving in his/her own home, then referral to Social Services will need to be considered. Similarly, if the offences alleged to have been committed are such as to raise questions about the safety and welfare of any children within the household to which the alleged perpetrator belongs, referral of that consideration to the Social Services Department may be appropriate.

iii. All agencies, Police, Social Services, NSPCC, and Health, should refer cases to the Inter-Agency Team when they are presented with or become suspicious of the possibility of sexual abuse having occurred on the basis of physical or behavioural signs alone or where there is uncertainty as to whether or not abuse has occurred.

iv. When child sexual abuse within the family comes to the attention of the Police they should inform Social Services and consider the advisability of using the Specialist Assessment Team.

v. There may be other cases of complexity where the use of the Specialist Assessment Team is appropriate.

vi. If there is a suspicion of child sexual abuse in the mind of the professional, the danger of false identification ought not to be forgotten. Therefore when a suspicion arises the professional may elect to:

— take no further action;

— hold a watching brief;

— make further informal inquiries ([I] on the flowchart).

The level of concern may reach a point within the guidance agreed with other agencies—see a.iv above—where it is the duty of all professionals to inform others or refer to the Specialist Assessment Team.

vii. The Specialist Assessment Team would normally be expected to present their findings to a case conference who will consider that information in the overall context of the case and make recommendations as to further action. Whilst professional suspicion may be justified in a particular case, recommendations by a case conference to pursue a statutory intervention under child care law must be firmly based on evidence that can be elicited and brought before a Court. Where such evidence cannot be found but suspicion remains arrangements must be made for the continuing assessment of the child.

9. Training

Training is one of the major needs shown by the Cleveland experience. We recognise that training requirements are different for each profession. We strongly recommend:

a. Those responsible for the educational programmes of all disciplines involved in the care of children immediately consider the introduction of some instruction on the subject of child sexual abuse in basic training at student level.

b. There should be general continuing in-service training for practitioners concerned with child care.

c. There is an urgent need to give immediate in-service training to professionals to bring them up to date on child sexual abuse.

d. The investigation and the management of the child and the family where there is suspicion of sexual abuse needs considerable professional skill. We recommend specialised training for experienced professionals with immediate responsibility for the children and their families.

From the evidence presented to the Inquiry there were particular issues which arose and needed to be addressed.

1. There is a need for inter-agency training and recognition of the role of other disciplines. For example police officers and social workers designated to interview children should have joint training in their approach to this task.

2. Police training needs to be developed well beyond the acquisition of knowledge in respect of the criminal offences involved.

3. The medical profession needs to appreciate the legal implications of and their responsibility for the evidential requirements of their work.

4. Those who work in this field must have an empathy with children and 'their feet on the ground'. They must be able to cope with the stress that is experienced by all who deal with these children. It should not be seen as a failure for some to take the sensible course of saying that he/she is not suited to do that sort of work.

5. In a rapidly changing and difficult area there is a need to review and evaluate the effectiveness of the programmes arranged.

6. All lawyers engaged in this type of work including Judges and Magistrates should have a greater awareness of and inform themselves about the nature of child abuse and the management of children subjected to abuse and in particular sexual abuse.

10. Courts

We make the following recommendations with regard to court proceedings:

a. **Place of Safety Orders.**

i. There should be a statutory duty upon the Clerk to the Justices to keep records of all place of safety orders.

ii. Applications for place of safety orders should normally be made in the first instance to the Juvenile Court during court hours, and only if the court is not sitting or the application cannot be heard within a reasonable time to a single Magistrate.

iii. A simple written explanation of the meaning and effect of a place of safety order should be provided to parents or others served with such an order. This explanation would also be useful for all those who may have the responsibility to care for a child who is the subject of the order. (for example foster parents or nursing officers)

b. Termination of access on an interim care order.

The use of the provisions of section 12B for termination of access and the interpretation of the decision in R v. Bolton Metropolitan Borough Council ex parte B [1985] F.L.R. 343 highlight existing difficulties over access and add urgency to the need to implement the proposals in the White Paper.

c. Consideration should be given to the practice in the Juvenile Courts of attendance of children in court in highly charged cases with members of the press and large numbers of people present. We would urge Magistrates to dispense with the attendance of the child or to arrange to see the child in a private room. It is an appropriate situation to seek the views of the older child as to attendance at court.

The Law on Child Care and Family Services Cm62.

We strongly endorse the proposals set out in the White Paper and believe that it is now urgent that they should be implemented. We have considered that paragraphs 45 to 47, and paragraphs 54 to 68 were relevant to the Inquiry (See appendix J). We make the following recommendations on those paragraphs.

Emergency Protection Orders. (paras 45 to 47)

a. A single Magistrate or the court should decide access if a Local Authority sees need to suspend it after an order has been granted on presumption of reasonable access.

b. Extension for 7 days should be in discretion of Magistrates and not restricted to 'exceptional circumstances'.

c. Application for the disclosure of the whereabouts of a child should include the power to commit to prison for refusal to comply.

d. Any dispute over medical examination during an extension of an emergency protection order should be decided by the court.

e. A simple explanatory pamphlet should be published setting out clearly the rights and duties of 'a person with actual custody'.

Juvenile Court

a. Extension of interim care orders should be at the discretion of Magistrates and not limited to 'exceptional circumstances.'

b. A dispute over access on the granting of and during the continuance of an interim care order should be decided by the Magistrates in the Courts.

c. On the granting of a custody order in care proceedings a Local Authority should have the right to make an allowance to the custodian, as in custodianship proceedings.

d. After care proceedings are instituted the Magistrates should have the power to determine, where necessary, interlocutory matters, such as further medical examinations of children for evidential purposes.

Wardship

a. Wardship should continue to play a role in care proceedings.

b. Parents should have the right to initiate wardship proceedings, subject to paragraph c below.

c. The President should regulate by Practice Direction the type of cases more fitted to be tried in the High Court.

Family Court

We recognise the considerable procedural advantages of the ability to move cases at any time from one tier of the Court to another, which would be achieved by the setting up of a Family Court.

Guardians ad litem

We are concerned that the independence of the guardian ad litem panel should be demonstrated and, in the absence of other arrangements for the administration of the panel, we commend the arrangement made between Cleveland Social Services Department and the Childrens Society.

We further recommend:

a. "Courts should appoint the guardians ad litem. A sufficiently large list of names should be submitted to enable a genuine choice to be made."

b. An amendment to Rule 14A 6(b) Magistrates Court (Children and Young Persons) Rules 1970 to define more closely the role of the guardian.

c. The Official Solicitor should first be invited to act for the child in wardship proceedings before any other guardian is appointed.

Media, Press and Public

We recommend that there should be rationalisation and clarity in:

a. The right of the press to attend court in the absence of the public. To protect the anonymity of the child concerned, the decision whether any particular proceedings or part of proceedings is to be heard in public should be a decision for the tribunal hearing the proceedings in accordance with the usual procedure adopted in the High Court.

b. The right of the press and media generally to report on and publish information about children the subject of civil proceedings.

c. We strongly recommend automatic protection in all civil child proceedings, whether Juvenile or Domestic jurisdiction of Magistrates Court, County Court, or High Court including, matrimonial, guardianship and wardship; such protection should include a ban on publication of names, addresses, photographs or other identification of any child the subject of such proceedings. [see draft injunction in appendix K]

d. We recommend wider recognition by the media that the freedom of the press carries responsibility and consideration as to whether in situations such as arose in Cleveland it is in the best interests of a child to be identified.

11. Issues for further consideration

We wish to raise the following matters for further thought and wider discussion, but not by way of specific recommendation.

1. With the emphasis we place on the need to avoid the necessity of removing a child from home, Social Services Departments should consider the appropriateness of using their powers under s.1 of the 1980 Act designed to prevent the reception of a child into care, to defray for a limited period additional costs incurred by the suspected abuser in leaving home on a temporary basis while initial assessment is completed.

2. Samantha's story [page 9] leads us to advise that there needs to be more sensitive handling of teenagers who have been sexually abused.

3. There is a need to recognise the problem of adults who disclose abuse they suffered as children and the lack of help generally available.

4. There is a need to recognise the problems of an abuser who may wish to confess to the abuse but is inhibited from so doing by fear of the consequences. Some consideration might be given in certain circumstances to the wider interests of the child and the family and whether different arrangements might be made in suitable cases for those abusers who admit their guilt, who co-operate with the arrangements for the child and who are prepared to submit themselves to a programme of control.

5. We suggest that consideration is given to creating a new Office of Child Protection for use in care proceedings in the Family Court with the following responsibilities:

   a. To scrutinise the application of the Local Authority in care proceedings and ensure that it is well founded.

   b. To call for additional investigation or reports.

   c. To invite the Local Authority or the Police to reconsider the civil or criminal proceedings proposed.

   d. To act as administrator of the guardian ad litem panel.

   e. Further consideration should be given to whether the office holder should;

      i. direct who should be parties to the care proceedings

      ii. direct in which tier of the court it should be heard and

      iii. have the power to take no further action.

PART FOUR

APPENDICES

APPENDIX A

COUNSEL FOR THE INQUIRY WERE MR M THORPE, Q.C. AND MR T HARTLEY, INSTRUCTED BY THE TREASURY SOLICITOR

Party	Representatives
The Children	Mr A Kirkwood, instructed by the Official Solicitor
The Parents	Mr S Hawkesworth, QC, and Mr M Taylor instructed by Messrs Spence and Hutchinson
Cleveland County Council	Mr R Stewart, QC, and Mr I Fairwood instructed by Mr R Hinchcliffe, Solicitor County Secretary's Department
Dr Higgs	Mr R Nelson, QC, and Miss N Davies instructed by Messrs Le Brasseur & Bury
North Tees Health Authority	Mr P Hunt instructed by Messrs Darling Heslop & Forster
Police and Police Surgeons	Mr R Bartfield and Miss S Cahill instructed by Cleveland Constabulary Force Solicitor, Mrs C Llewellyn
Regional Health Authority	Miss E Platt, QC, and Mr M Curwen instructed by Messrs. Crutes
Social Services	Mr J Townend, QC, and Miss C Harmer instructed by Messrs Goodswens
South Tees District Health Authority	Mr B Walsh, QC, and Mr L Scott instructed by Messrs. Smith and Graham
Dr Wyatt	Mr R Nelson, QC, and Miss N Davies instructed by Messrs Hempsons
Department of Health and Social Security - Social Services Inspectorate (one day only)	Mr Allan Levy, instructed by DHSS Solicitors Branch
British Association of Social Workers (one day only)	Mr J Trotter, instructed by Messrs Bates, Wells and Braithwate

APPENDIX B

LIST OF PEOPLE WHO GAVE ORAL EVIDENCE (excluding parents, relatives and foster parents)

Mrs Susan Amphlett	Parents against Injustice (PAIN)
Dr William Appleyard	British Paediatric Association
Mrs Gillian Ashdown	Nurse
Mrs Winifred Aston	Nurse
Mrs Heather Bacon	Clinical Psychologist
Mrs Mary Ball	Nurse
Dr Frank Bamford	Paediatrician
Mrs Susan Bareham	Nurse
Mr James Beall	Social Worker
Mr John Beckwith	North Tees District Health Authority
Dr William Beeby	Police Surgeon
Mr Stuart Bell	Member of Parliament
Mrs Jean Bell	Nurse
Dr Arnon Bentovim	Child Psychiatrist
Mr Michael Bishop	Director of Social Services, Cleveland
Mrs Margery Bray	Consultant Social Worker
Mr Malcolm Brown	DHSS, Social Services Inspectorate
Mr Desmond Burnand	Social Worker
Dr Hamish Cameron	Child Psychiatrist
Dr John Canning	Secretary to Cleveland Local Medical Committee
Mrs Olga Caswell	Social Worker
Mrs Iris Chambers	Nursing Officer
Mrs Agnes Chaplin	Nurse
Mrs Barbara Chaytor	Nurse
Dr Alexander Chisholm	Child Psychiatrist
Dr Graham Clayden	Paediatrician
Mrs Audrey Collins	Chairman, South Tees District Health Authority
Mr Francis Cook	Member of Parliament
Mr Alan Cooke	Clerk to the Justices, Teeside Magistrate Court
Mrs Elizabeth Crews	Social Worker
Mrs Deborah Cunliffe	Nurse
Mrs Carol Dargue	Nurse
Mr Leonard Davies	Chairman of Teeside Juvenile Panel
Mrs Alison de Lacey Dunne	Social Worker
Professor Sir John Dewhurst	Gynaecologist
Mr Ian Donaldson	District General Manager, South Tees District Health Authority
Dr Liam Donaldson	Regional Medical Officer, Northern Regional Health Authority

Mrs Judith Drummond	Nurse
Dr John Drury	South Tees District Health Authority
Mr Kenneth Duncan	Social Worker
Mrs Marjorie Dunn	Senior Nurse
Mr Norman Dunning	Chairman, BASPCAN
Dr Mary Ellis-Fraser	Police Surgeon
Mrs Daphne George	Hospital Social Worker
Miss Deborah Glassbrook	Social Work Consultant
Mrs Marguerite Gofton	Social Worker
Mr David Granath	Social Worker
Dr Isabel Grant	Paediatrician
Mr Stanley Green	Social Worker
Mrs Maureen Greig	Social Worker
Dr Ian Guy	South Tees District Health Authority
Mr Douglas Hague	Regional General Manager, Northern Regional Health Authority
Mrs Helga Hanks	Psychologist, Leeds
Mr Richard John Heald	Proctologist
Mr Strachan Heppell	DHSS, Deputy Secretary
Dr Marietta Higgs	Paediatrician
Dr Christopher Hobbs	Paediatrician
Mrs Wendy Hornby	Nurse
Mr Christopher Horne	Social Worker
Mr John Hughes	Social Worker
Dr Alistair Irvine	Police Surgeon
Dr David Jenkins	President, Association of Police Surgeons
Mrs Rose Johnson	Social Worker
Mr David Jones	Secretary, BASW
Mr Henry Keith	Social Worker
Professor Israel Kolvin	Psychiatrist
Mr Donald Laverick	Social Worker
Mr Peh Levine	Social Worker
Dr Margaret Lynch	Paediatrician
Mrs Judith MacMurray	Social Worker, Leeds
Inspector Colin Makepeace	Cleveland Constabulary
Mr McIlvenna	Social Worker
Mrs Patricia McBain	BASW
Mrs Marilyn McConnell	Childrens Society
Mr Tom Mitchie	NSPCC
Mrs Eileen Middleton	Nurse
Mrs Valerie Moore	South Tees District Health Authority

Dr Peter Morrell	Paediatrician
Mr Raymond Morris	Cleveland Social Services Department
Mrs Hilary Morrison	Nurse
Mr Peter Newell	Children's Legal Centre
Dr Jasumati Nirmal	Paediatrician
Dr Nyint Oo	Paediatrician
Mr Aiden Ord	Guardian Ad Litem
Mr John Ord	Deputy Chief Constable, Cleveland Constabulary
Mr Christopher Payne	Chief Constable, Cleveland Constabulary
Mrs Shirley Richardson	Nurse
Mrs Susan Richardson	Child Abuse Consultant Cleveland Social Services Department
Mr Swinborne Ridley	Social Worker
Mrs Freda Roach	Nursing Officer
Mr Colin Roberts	Social Worker
Dr Raine Roberts	Police Surgeon
Professor Sir Martin Roth	Psychiatrist
Mr Brian Roycroft	President, Association of Directors of Social Services
Superintendent Charles Saunders	Cleveland Constabulary
Mrs Regina Shakespeare	South Tees District Health Authority
Mr David Shipman	Guardian Ad Litem
Mr Frederick Smith	Assistant Chief Constable, Cleveland Constabulary
Mrs Susan Smith	Social Worker
Dr Alison Steele	Registrar, Middlesbrough General Hospital
Mrs Rita Summerbell	Social Worker
Mr Peter Thomas	Hospital Social Worker
Mrs Judith Timms	BASW
Professor Sir Bernard Tomlinson	Chaiman, Northern Regional Health Authority
Mr Charles Town	Educational Social Worker
Dr Ralph Underwager	Consulting Psychologist
Mr John Urch	Chairman, Community Health Council
Mr William Utting	DHSS, Chief Inspector, Social Services Inspectorate
Detective Inspector Alan Walls	Cleveland Constabulary
Mr William Walton	Senior Assistant Director, Cleveland Social Services Department
Mr Charles Webb	Clerk to North Tyneside Justices
Detective Superintendent John White	Cleveland Constabulary
Dr Scella Wignarajah	Psychiatrist
Reverend Michael Wright	Priest in Charge, St Cuthberts Church
Dr Geoffrey Wyatt	Paediatrician
Dr Jane Wynne	Paediatrician
Dr Harry Zeitlin	Child Psychiatrist

19 Parents, 1 Grandparent also gave evidence.

APPENDIX C

SELECTED DOCUMENTARY EVIDENCE

British Association of Social Workers—The Management of Child Abuse

British Association of Social Workers—Family Courts

British Association of Social Workers—Report of the project group established by the professional Divisional Committee to respond to the Interdepartmental Working Party on Child Care Law

British Association of Social Workers—Child Care: The Roots of the Dilemma by R A Parker

British Association of Social Workers-Project Group on Guardians/Curators Ad Litem and Reporting Officers

Agreed statement of British Paediatric Association and Association of Police Surgeons

Extract from British Medical Association Journal entitled "BMA approved guidelines on child abuse case conferences"

A Child in Mind—Report of the Inquiry into the Death of Kimberley Carlisle—Mr L Blom-Cooper QC

Child Sexual Abuse—A Study of Prevalence in Great Britain—Dr A W Barker and Dr S P Duncan—Vol 9, pp 457–467, 1985

The Skeleton in the Family's Cupboard—Beatrix Campbell—New Statesman—31 July 1987

Childline—booklet

DHSS—Circular LAC (83) 19—Access to children in care

DHSS—The interim results of the survey of child abuse procedures carried out by Social Services Inspectorate nationally in England and Wales

DHSS—Updated statistics relating to place of safety orders

GP work with Mothers Whose Children have been Sexually Abused—British Journal of Social Work (1978) 17, 285–304

Child Sexual Abuse in the Family and related papers—Sexual Abuse Treatment Project—Hospital for Sick Children (Gt Ormond Street)

A Model for Validation Interviews—NSPCC Child Sexual Abuse Unit, Manchester

Child Sexual Abuse—An Increasing Role in Diagnosis—J Wynne and C Hobbs—The Lancet, 10 October 1987

Investigation of Sexually Abused Children, H Zeitlin, The Lancet—10 October 1987

Reliable and Fictitious Accounts of Sexually Abused Children, D Jones—Journal of Interpersonal Violence, Vol 2, No 1, March 1987, Nos 27–45

Emerging issues in Child Sexual Abuse—D H Schietky—Editorial from unidentified source

Initial and Long Term Effects—A Review of the Research—A Brown and D Finkelhor—Article for unidentified book

Expert Medical Assessment in Determining Probability of Alleged Child Sexual Abuse—C P Herbert— Child Abuse and Neglect, Vol 11, p 213–22

Presentation and Evaluation of Sexual Misuse in the Emergency Department—J S Sepidel, Paediatric Emergency Case Volume 11, No 3, p 157

The Medical Examination in Sexual Offences against children—D M Paul—Medical Science Law Vol 17, No 4, p 251

Home Office—Report of Working Group of Standing Conference on Crime Prevention: The Prevention of Child Sexual Abuse—24 November 1987, Work of an Independent Working Group

Metropolitian Police: The Force response to child abuse: the principles and code of practice (proposed) October 1987 with extract from Home Office Consolidated Circular to Police on Crime

MORI original summary report on Child Abuse

Role of Probation Service in Child Sexual Abuse Cases—Probation Service, Cleveland

A Child in Crisis—Protective Procedure—Child Care Law, N Parton and T Norris—June 1986

Standing Medical Advisory Committee—Epidemiology of Childhood Sexual Abuse in UK

Kidscape—The Facts about Child Sexual Abuse

Kidscape—How to Help them stay safe

APPENDIX D

SELECTION OF STATISTICAL INFORMATION SUPPLIED TO THE INQUIRY

TABLE 1

Number of referrals to Cleveland Social Services Department for Child Abuse/Neglect in 1987

	Sexual Abuse -Index	Sexual Abuse -Sibling	Sexual Abuse -Total	Physical Abuse	Other	Total	Total in Care Jan 1988 for sexual abuse
January	22	3	25	37	25	87	6
February	27	6	33	20	29	82	7
March	25	5	30	39	33	102	2
April	37	6	43	26	31	100	10
May	61	20	81	37	54	172	16
June	89	21	110	31	41	182	17
July	35	4	39	21	68	128	8
August	14	3	17	24	35	76	3
September	11	0	11	26	32	69	1
October	22	3	25	25	16	66	2
November	37	0	37	15	34	86	2
December	13	0	13	20	16	49	2
Total 1987	393	71	464	321	414	1,199	76
Average/ Month	33	6	39	27	35	101	6
Average/ 1st 1/4	25	5	30	32	29	90	5
2nd 1/4	62	16	78	31	42	151	14
3rd 1/4	20	2	22	24	45	91	4
4th 1/4	24	1	25	20	22	67	2
Referrals/ 1,000 pop under 16/ year	2.92	0.53	3.44	2.38	3.07	8.90	

Source: Cleveland County Council Database

TABLE 2

Number of referrals for Child Abuse by month in 1986 and 1987 — figures given during the Inquiry

	1986	1987	% change
January	33	36	9
February	42	42	0
March	32	56	75
April	39	52	33
May	51	87	71
June	40	108	170
July	51	124	143
August	30		
September	31		
October	69		
November	57		
December	42		
Total	517	505	−2
Average	43	42	−2
1st quarter	36	45	25
2nd quarter	43	82	90
3rd quarter	37	41	11
4th quarter	56	—	—
Rate/1000 pop under 16	3.79	3.75	

Note: These figures, and those in the next table, were supplied to us during the Inquiry (Document CC19/1), and include figures for sexual abuse and physical abuse that have been collected differently from the source of Table 1. However, they are the only comparison we have for 1986, and are therefore provided for illustrative purposes only.

TABLE 3

Number of referrals for Child Abuse by District, January–July 1987–figures supplied during the Inquiry

	Langbaurgh	Middlesbrough	Stockton	Hartlepool
January	10	10	9	9
February	13	15	7	7
March	18	10	23	6
April	23	13	15	1
May	34	21	37	5
June	32	60	12	3
July	40	58	18	10
Total	170	187	121	41
Average	24	27	17	6
Av Jan–Mar	14	12	13	7
Av Apr–Jun	32	38	21	5
Rate/1000 pop under 16	4.87	7.14	2.87	1.81

Note: these figures also derive from figures supplied on day 19 of the Inquiry and are provided for illustrative purposes only, as the totals do not match the up to date figures in Table 1.

TABLE 4

Numbers of place of safety orders taken for child abuse in 1986–1987, on a monthly

	1986 (All reasons)	1987 Sexual Abuse	Physical Abuse	Total Other	Total Total
January	21	4	9	10	23
February	14	5	1	9	15
March	24	5	6	2	13
April	29	11	9	12	32
May	30	35	7	15	57
June	32	48	3	1	52
July	18	3	1	7	11
August	10	1	1	5	7
September	18	0	6	2	8
October	34	1	0	0	1
November	24	1	1	0	2
December	23	1	5	0	6
TOTAL	277	115	49	63	227
AVERAGE	23	10	4	5	19
1st quarter	20	5	5	7	17
2nd quarter	30	31	6	9	46
3rd quarter	15	1	3	5	9
4th quarter	27	1	2	0	3

Sources: 1986 figures — document CCC19/1 1987 — Cleveland County Council Database

TABLE 5

Numbers of place of safety orders taken in May 1987 for sexual abuse on a daily basis

Date	Number	Date	Number
1st	3	16th	0
2nd	0	17th	0
3rd	0	18th	1
4th	0	19th	0
5th	3	20th	2
6th	4	21st	0
7th	1	22nd	11
8th	4	23rd	0
9th	0	24th	0
10th	0	25th	0
11th	2	26th	0
12th	0	27th	0
13th	2	28th	1
14th	0	29th	1
15th	0	30th	0
		31st	0
		Total	35

Source: Cleveland County Council Database

TABLE 6

Number of place of safety orders taken in June 1987 for sexual abuse on a daily basis

Date	Number	Date	Number
1st	0	16th	8
2nd	0	17th	1
3rd	0	18th	2
4th	4	19th	0
5th	0	20th	0
6th	4	21st	0
7th	0	22nd	0
8th	1	23rd	0
9th	3	24th	0
10th	1	25th	0
11th	2	26th	0
12th	3	27th	0
13th	12	28th	0
14th	0	29th	0
15th	6	30th	0
		TOTAL	47

Note: One child was referred in June but an order was not taken out until July, hence the total of 47 not 48 as in table 4 on p. 267. Source: Cleveland County Council Database

TABLE 7

Summary of origins of referrals in 1987

	Police	Social Worker	Hospital Doctor	Education	Health Visitor	Relative	Neighbour/Other Friend		Total
January	26	23	5	7	2	7	2	23	95
February	17	6	4	9	4	11	9	27	87
March	14	7	2	9	7	15	7	49	110
April	21	13	12	5	5	14	3	37	110
May	25	20	12	12	6	0	8	94	177
June	25	26	11	14	10	14	12	77	189
July	22	12	8	3	5	26	7	54	137
August	16	3	6	1	4	10	13	29	82
September	8	2	3	9	1	8	8	33	72
October	17	1	5	12	3	2	0	29	69
November	16	2	3	23	0	6	2	40	92
December	12	2	2	5	9	4	1	18	53
Total	219	117	73	109	56	117	72	510	1,273
Average (monthly)	18	10	6	9	5	10	6	43	107
1st 1/4	19	12	4	8	4	11	6	33	97
2nd 1/4	24	20	12	10	7	9	8	69	159
3rd 1/4	15	6	6	4	3	15	9	39	97
4th 1/4	15	2	3	13	4	4	1	29	71

Note: referrals can be from more than one source, hence totals are different from Table 1. Source Cleveland County Council Database

TABLE 8

Summary of Schedule supplied by Dr Higgs and Dr Wyatt

Children seen	165
Families or associated groups	65
Children examined by Dr Higgs	102
Children examined by Dr Wyatt	55
Children examined by other consultant	8

TABLE 9

Summary of conclusions

	Dr Higgs	Dr Wyatt	Others
Cases where no sign of sexual abuse	22	8	4
Cases where signs sufficient for future review	2	4	0
Cases where sexual abuse diagnosed	78	43	4

TABLE 10

Analysis of numbers examined by doctors by month and age

	January	February	March	April	May	June	July
Age							
< 1	0	0	0	0	4	5	0
1	0	0	0	0	5	6	1
2	0	0	1	1	6	11	2
3	0	1	0	2	6	4	3
4	0	0	0	0	2	8	4
5	1	0	0	0	4	12	1
6	0	1	0	1	4	5	2
7	0	0	0	0	4	8	1
8	0	0	1	1	4	5	2
9	0	0	1	0	4	4	0
10	0	0	1	0	1	3	0
11	0	0	0	0	2	3	0
12	0	0	0	0	2	5	1
13	0	0	0	0	2	3	0
14	0	0	0	0	1	1	0
15	0	0	0	0	1	0	0
16	0	0	0	0	0	0	0
NK	0	0	0	0	0	1	0
Totals	1	2	4	5	52	84	17

TABLE 11

Summary of male index children and siblings, whether admitted and orders taken

	Index	Sibling	Non-sib	Admitted	Place of safety orders	Interim care orders
January	1	0	0	1	0	0
February	0	0	0	0	0	0
March	1	1	0	2	2	0
April	0	1	0	0	1	0
May	2	14	4	16	13	0
June	13	22	6	23	20	2
July	3	3	0	2	0	0
Total	20	41	10	44	36	2

TABLE 12

Summary of female index children and siblings, whether admitted and orders taken

	Index	Sibling	Non-sib	Admitted	Place of safety orders	Interim care orders
January	0	0	0	0	0	0
February	2	0	0	2	1	0
March	1	1	0	2	2	0
April	2	2	0	3	2	2
May	15	11	6	25	21	1
June	29	13	1	31	26	4
July	8	3	0	4	3	0
Total	57	30	7	67	55	7

Source Tables 8–12 schedule supplied in evidence by Dr Higgs and Dr Wyatt

TABLE 13

Summary of outpatient attendances at Middlesbrough General Jan–July 1987

Total number of attendances	6,368
Number of referrals for suspected abuse	103
Number of referrals for suspected abuse as % of total	1.60
Attendances seen by Dr Wyatt	2,246
Number of referrals for suspected abuse	53
Number of referrals for suspected abuse as % of total	2.40
Attendances seen by Dr Higgs	560
Number of referrals for suspected abuse	45
Number of referrals for suspected abuse as % of total	8

Source: South Tees District Health Authority

FIGURE 1

DR WYATT – OUTPATIENT ATTENDANCE 1987

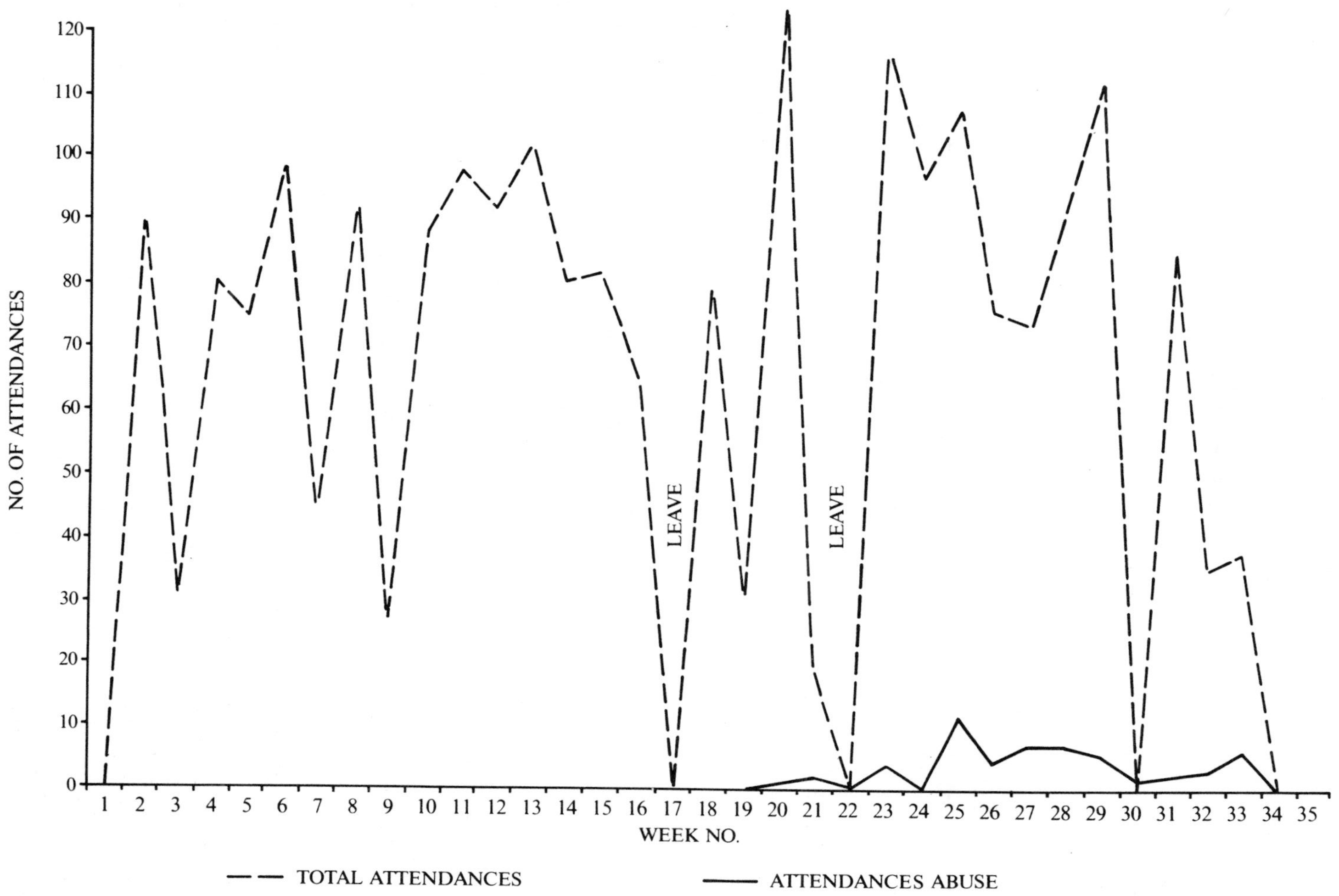

Source: South Tees District Health Authority

269

FIGURE 2

DR HIGGS – OUTPATIENT ATTENDANCES 1987

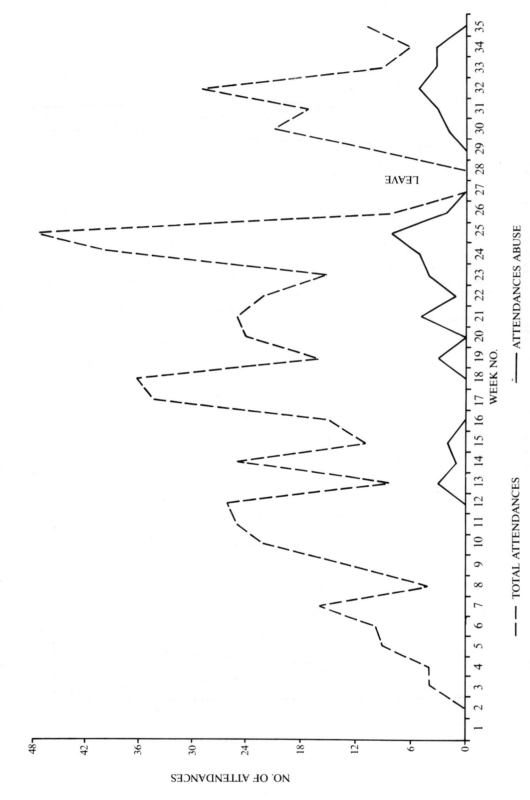

Source: South Tees District Health Authority

FIGURE 3

PAEDIATRIC ADMISSIONS TO MIDDLESBROUGH
GENERAL HOSPITAL FOR ABUSE –
APRIL/JULY 1987

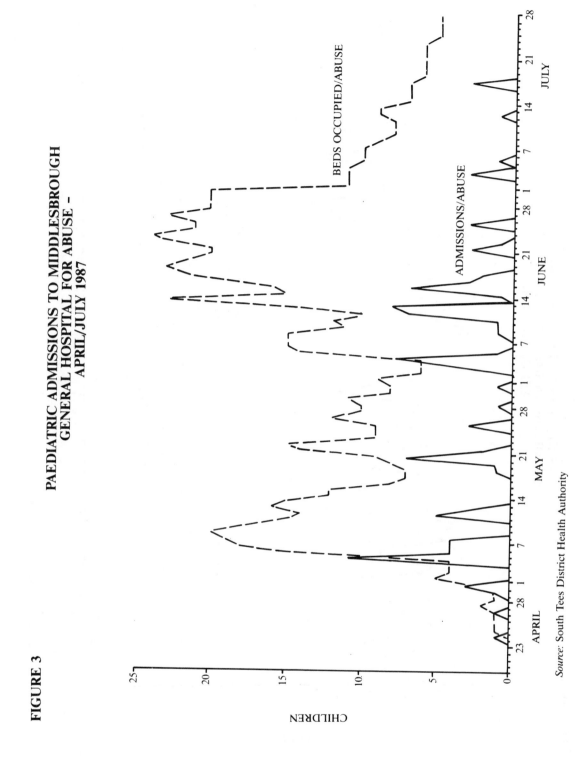

Source: South Tees District Health Authority

271

FIGURE 4

OCCUPATION OF BEDS IN WARDS 9 & 10 MIDDLESBROUGH GENERAL HOSPITAL – APRIL/JULY 1987

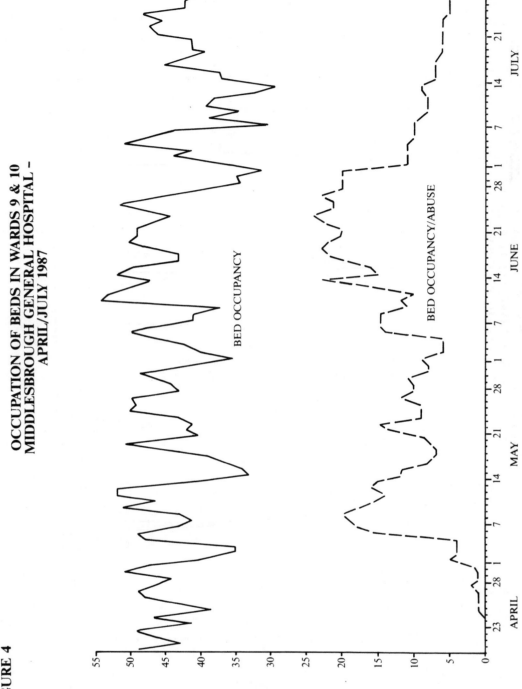

Source: South Tees District Health Authority

272

TABLE 14

Analysis of first 'wave' of referrals to the Social Services Department — 1st to 8th May 1987

	Children	Families
Number referred	50	32
Alleged victims of physical abuse	17	10
Alleged sexual abuse following examination at Middlesbrough General	27	15
Alleged sexual abuse dealt with without referral to hospital	6	6
Referrals to hospital by Social Workers or Guardians ad litem	12	6

TABLE 15

Analysis of the third 'wave' of referrals to the Social Services Department — 12th to 20th June 1987

	Children	Families
Number referred	56	33
Alleged victims of physical abuse	7	5
Alleged victims of sexual abuse	49	29
Referred for medical examination by Social Services	10	6
Identified by Consultants following paediatric out-patients	10	4
Referred by GPs query sexual abuse	6	3
Examined by Drs when nurses raised queries about 2 children already in-patients	10	2
Seen by Drs at mother's request	2	2
Dealt with by Police and Social Services without involving hospital Drs	8	8
Referred from casualty	1	1
Recalled at request of consultant	1	1
Dealt with by Social Services	1	1

TABLE 16

Analysis of children made wards of court from June 1987

	Children	Families	
Total	67	31	
Dewarded	27	12	
Remain wards	40	19	
Care/control to parents	24	10	
Care/control to one parent	4	3	(2 to father not previously living with)
Supervision order	26	12	
Medical/Psychiatric conditions	27	13	
Full Care Order to Cleveland	7	4	(1 child living at home)
Children in care — no access to family	4	3	
Not completed	5	3	(4 children interim care order, 1 child with grandparents)
Total at home	53	24	

TABLE 17

Children on doctors schedule subject to place of safety orders but not made wards

	Children	Families
At home	17	14
At home — with social worker allocated	6	6
Still in care	10	8
Already in care	5	3

TABLE 18

Police records in Inquiry Database analysed by age and result of investigation

Age	Total	Prosecution brought	Caution	No charges	Not known
< 1	20	2	0	10	0
1	27	2	0	15	0
2	36	3	0	24	1
3	32	2	1	15	4
4	41	5	3	19	3
5	37	4	3	17	2
6	28	5	4	11	0
7	28	10	1	10	1
8	22	3	0	13	0
9	27	11	2	11	1
10	23	7	1	7	2
11	25	3	6	10	2
12	21	3	5	7	0
13	15	1	1	7	0
14	21	5	0	10	2
15	30	0	5	5	3
16	14	0	0	8	0
17	3	0	0	0	0
18	1	1	1	0	0
NK	11	0	1	7	2

Source: Database produced by Inquiry from available police, medical and cases conference notes from January–July 1987

TABLE 19

Referrals for Yarm Unit, July–November 1987

	Cases Reported	Satisfied no offence	Charges brought	Caution	Unable to proceed
Anal Abuse	20	14	4	0	2
Indecent Assault	87	42	11	9	12
Incest	10	4	2	0	3
Unlawful Sexual Intercourse	24	4	5	11	2

Source: Cleveland Constabulary

TABLE 20

Age and sex distribution of children in Inquiry database

Age	1. Male Number	2. Female Number
< 1	7	13
1	8	19
2	16	19
3	12	20
4	18	23
5	13	24
6	13	15
7	11	17
8	6	16
9	13	14
10	5	17
11	14	10
12	17	11
13	3	11
14	7	14
15	7	23
16	3	11
17	3	0
18	0	1
NK	7	4
Total	183	282

TABLE 21

Suspected abuse according to age taken from Inquiry database

Age	Inadequate care	Inappropriate chastisement	Failure to thrive	Persistent neglect	Physical Abuse	Sexual Abuse touching	Sexual Abuse vaginal	Sexual Abuse anal	Sexual Abuse other	Indecent assault
< 1	2	0	0	3	7	0	1	4	0	0
1	3	0	1	5	9	0	2	6	0	2
2	3	1	5	4	10	0	4	8	0	4
3	1	0	1	2	7	4	8	10	0	4
4	2	1	4	1	11	4	9	12	0	4
5	4	1	1	2	3	5	5	9	0	7
6	1	0	0	2	5	2	11	8	0	6
7	1	3	2	3	6	6	3	3	1	10
8	2	0	1	1	3	4	7	7	0	4
9	1	0	0	1	8	3	4	4	1	7
10	0	0	0	0	4	1	7	3	0	9
11	0	0	1	2	2	6	2	5	0	7
12	1	1	1	4	7	3	0	2	0	5
13	0	0	0	0	3	2	3	2	0	3
14	0	2	0	3	4	3	2	2	0	5
15	2	1	0	0	4	5	12	1	0	7
16	2	1	0	0	3	4	3	0	0	2
17	1	0	0	0	0	0	2	0	0	1
18	0	1	0	0	0	0	0	0	0	0
NK	0	0	0	0	6	0	0	2	1	2

TABLE 22

Inquiry Database — breakdown by age and district

Age	Hartlepool male	female	Stockton male	female	Langbaurgh male	female	Middlesbrough male	female
< 1	1	1	2	2	0	3	3	7
1	0	2	1	5	5	3	1	8
2	2	4	2	2	2	4	8	9
3	1	3	3	1	3	4	4	10
4	0	2	3	7	3	7	9	5
5	3	3	2	7	5	3	3	9
6	1	1	3	1	3	6	6	7
7	2	3	3	4	4	2	2	7
8	1	0	2	3	1	4	2	9
9	0	10	4	5	3	1	5	5
10	0	2	3	6	1	2	0	0
11	3	0	4	1	6	3	1	0
12	2	4	0	3	1	4	0	6
13	0	1	1	1	0	2	1	6
14	0	2	3	4	2	2	2	4
15	1	0	2	9	1	5	2	7
16	0	1	2	4	0	3	2	5
17	0	0	0	2	0	1	3	7
18	0	0	0	1	0	0	0	3

TABLE 23

Cases in Inquiry database — numbers of case conferences by area by Month

	Hartlepool	Stockton	Langbaurgh	Middlesbrough	Not known
January	7	14	4	6	2
February	8	7	5	3	5
March	1	18	10	5	1
April	4	7	10	8	3
May	5	9	10	14	5
June	3	11	14	29	3
July	3	10	6	20	1

Source of tables 20–23: Database produced by Inquiry from available police, medical and case conference notes January–July 1987

APPENDIX E

CHILD SEXUAL ABUSE WITHIN THE FAMILY

THE CIBA FOUNDATION. EDITED BY RUTH PORTER. PUBLISHED BY TAVISTOCK FOUNDATION 1984

PHYSICAL INDICATORS

GENITAL AND ANAL AREAS

1. Bruises, scratches or other injuries, often very minor, not consistent with accidental injury (masturbation by a child does not cause bruising).

2. Itching, soreness, discharge, or unexplained bleeding.

3. Foreign bodies in the urethra, bladder, vaginal or anal canal.

4. Abnormal dilatation in the urethra, anus, or vaginal opening.

5. Pain on micturition.

6. Signs of sexually transmitted infections.

7. Semen in the vagina or anus or on the external genitalia.

GENERAL

1. Bruises, scratches, bite marks or other injuries to breasts, buttocks, lower abdomen, or thighs.

2. Difficulty in walking or sitting.

3. Torn, stained, or bloody underclothes, or evidence of clothing having been removed and replaced (eg. vest inside out).

4. Semen on skin or clothes.

5. Pregnancy in teenagers, especially where the identity of the father is vague or secret.

6. Recurrent Urinary Tract Infections.

7. Psychosomatic features such as recurrent abdominal pain or headache.

BEHAVIOURAL INDICATORS

SEXUAL

1. A child who hints at sexual activity through words, play or drawings; or at the presence of severe family conflict, family secrets, or puzzling and/or uncomfortable things at home but who seems fearful of outside intervention.

2. A child with an excessive preoccupation with sexual matters and a precocious knowledge of adult sexual behaviour; one who repeatedly engages in inappropriate sexual play with peers; a child who is sexually provocative with adults.

3. An older girl who behaves in a sexually precocious way. Many girls become 'street wise', experienced beyond their age in a manner that isolates them from their peers and attracts censorious or seductive behaviour from adults. Their physical contacts with others have quasi-sexual elements of which they are unaware, with embraces involving breast or buttock caressing, or other body contact. They may wear sexually provocative clothing or adopt revealing postures—the caricature of a 'vamp'. In many cases they have already accepted sexual contacts if not intercourse with people outside the family.

4. Requests for information about contraception are rare but may be a cry for help.

GENERAL

1. Sudden change in mood.

2. Regressive behaviour, eg. sudden onset of bed-wetting or its persistence into the later school years.

3. Change in eating patterns: loss of appetite, faddiness, or excessive preoccupation of food.

4. Lack of trust in familiar adults or marked fear of men.

5. Disobedience, attention seeking or restlessness, aimless behaviour and poor concentration.

6. Severe sleep disturbance with fears, vivid dreams or nightmares sometimes with overt or veiled sexual content.

7. Social isolation; the child plays alone and withdraws into a private world.

8. Girl takes over the 'mothering' role in the family whether or not the mother is present.

9. Inappropriate displays of affection between fathers and daughters or mothers and sons, who behave more like lovers than parent and child. The father may be over-concerned about his daughter and may insist on accompanying her to the doctor for, say, contraceptive advice.

BEHAVIOUR ESPECIALLY NOTICEABLE IN SCHOOL

1. Poor peer group relationships and inability to make friends.

2. Inability to concentrate, learning difficulties, or a sudden drop in school performance. (For some sexually abused children school may be a haven; they arrive early, are reluctant to leave, and generally perform well).

3. Marked reluctance to participate in physical activity or to change clothes for physical education, games, swimming.

4. Regular avoidance and fear of school medical examinations.

BEHAVIOUR IN OLDER CHILDREN

1. Anti-social behaviour or delinquency in young teenagers. The sexually precocious behaviour already described. Promiscuity and involvement in prostitution may be ways of drawing attention to sexual abuse. In addition, the following may occur:

(a) Hysterical attacks;

(b) Truancy or running away from home;

(c) Suicide attempts and self-mutilation;

(d) Dependence on alcohol or drugs.

METROPOLITAN POLICE
AND
LONDON BOROUGH OF
MEDICAL EXAMINATION OF ABUSED CHILDREN

CONTENTS   PAGE

This proforma is to be printed X3 on NCR paper.
The top copy will be for retension by the Paediatrition.
The second copy will be for the Forensic Medical Examiner.
The third copy (in book form) will be for the use of Police and Social Work investigators.

For the purposes of this trial photocopies are to be provided for the Paediatrician and the Forensic Medical Examiner.
The completed book is to be retained by the investigating team.

Where alternatives are given in the text circle as appropriate. ? = uncertain, NA = not applicable.

INVESTIGATING TEAM

SOCIAL WORKERS

1. _____ Tel. _____

Employed by _____

2. _____ Tel. _____

Employed by _____

POLICE

INVESTIGATING OFFICER _____ Tel. _____

INTERVIEWING OFFICER _____ Tel. _____

STATION _____ Ref. _____

MEDICAL EXAMINERS

1. _____ Tel. _____

2. _____ Tel. _____

PART I   PATIENT'S DETAILS

SURNAME _____ MALE/FEMALE

FORENAMES _____

DATE OF BIRTH   /   /   , and AGE _____ years _____ months

ADDRESS _____
_____
_____

GENERAL PRACTITIONER   _____
_____
_____

ACCOMPANYING PERSONS   1.   _____
(Name and relationship to child)   _____

2.   _____
_____

FAMILY COMPOSITION   _____
_____
_____
_____
_____
_____
_____

CHILD PROTECTION REGISTER

THIS CHILD ON REGISTER   YES/NO

OTHER FAMILY MEMBERS ON REGISTER

Names   1. _____ YES/NO

2. _____ YES/NO

3. _____ YES/NO

4. _____ YES/NO

Completed by _____ Date   /   /

Name _____ Police Office/Social Worker

Child's name _____

PART II HISTORY REFERRAL AND DISCLOSURE DETAILS AS AVAILABLE
(Circle as appropriate and enter details)

1 | REFERRAL THROUGH GP/SCHOOL/SOCIAL WORKER/COMMUNITY PAEDIATRICIAN/ HOSPITAL PAEDIATRICIAN/POLICE/OTHER, details

2 | REASONS FOR REFERRAL

3 | SYMPTOMS/BEHAVIOUR/DISCLOSURE OR OTHER ALERTING SUSPICIONS

4 | HAS ANYONE ELSE INTERVIEWED THE CHILD?
Give names and telephone numbers

5 | DISCLOSURE INTERVIEW
DATE   /   /
LOCATION

INTERVIEWERS   NAME AND PROFESSIONAL STATUS
1. _____
   _____
2. _____
   _____

OTHERS PRESENT   NAME AND RELATIONSHIP TO CHILD
1. _____
2. _____

VIDEO/TAPE RECORDING MADE   YES/NO

Completed by   Date   /   /

Child's name _____

PART II HISTORY, REFERRAL AND DISCLOSURE DETAILS AS AVAILABLE

6 | DETAILS OF ANY FURTHER INTERVIEWS, give date, location and interviewers

DETAILS OF ABUSE AND ACTIONS AFTER

7 | NATURE OF ABUSE
DATE OF LATEST/SINGLE ASSAULT   /   /   , DAY
TIME
LOCATION
NUMBER OF ASSAULTS (if known)
NUMBER OF ABUSERS
IDENTITY OF ABUSER AND RELATIONSHIP TO CHILD

8 | WAS ANYONE ELSE IN THE HOUSE?   YES/NO? if yes give details

DID THEY ATTEMPT TO RESTRAIN THEM? YES/NO?   If yes give details

9 | WHAT CLOTHES WERE WORN BY THE CHILD DURING THE ASSAULT/ABUSE?,
describe

WHAT HAPPENED TO THEM AFTERWARDS?

10| THREATS USED
VERBAL THREATS USED YES/NO?
WAS A DOOR LOCKED? YES/NO?
TRICKS USED, YES/NO? If yes give details

Completed by   Date   /   /

Child's name _____

PART II HISTORY, DETAILS OF ABUSE AND ACTIONS AFTER CONTINUED

11 FORCE USED, if any   Where on body?

Restraints (ligatures etc.)   YES/NO? _____

Blows   YES/NO? _____

Kicking   YES/NO? _____

Tight hold/grabbing   YES/NO? _____

Bites   YES/NO? _____

Knife threats   YES/NO? _____

Hand over mouth   YES/NO? _____

Attempted strangulation   YES/NO? _____

12 OFFERED/GIVEN/INVOLVED   ANY DETAILS AVAILABLE

·DRUGS   YES/NO? _____

ALCOHOL   YES/NO? _____

SWEETS/FOOD   YES/NO? _____

GLUE SNIFFING   YES/NO? _____

PHOTOGRAPHS TAKEN   YES/NO? _____

MADE VIDEO RECORDING   YES/NO? _____

13 ABUSER CLOTHED,   YES/NO?, (give any details available)

14 ABUSER TOOK ALCOHOL/DRUGS, YES/NO?

If yes, give any details available

Completed by _____   Date   /   /

Child's name _____

PART II HISTORY, DETAILS OF ABUSE AND ACTIONS AFTER CONTINUED

---

15 **CHILD'S ACTION DURING ASSAULT**

WAS THE CHILD LYING/SITTING/STANDING DURING THE ASSAULT?

WHERE WAS THE CHILD? give details

DID THE CHILD TOUCH THE ABUSER?   YES/NO?, If yes, where?

WAS BOY'S PENIS ERECT?   YES/NO?

DID BOY EJACULATE   YES/NO?

---

16 **ABUSER'S ACTS ON CHILD** — Vagina/Vulva

a) Penis rubbed between thighs	YES/NO?
b) Touching/fondling of vulva/vagina	YES/NO?
c) Fingers inside vulva/vagina	YES/NO?
d) Penis in vulva area	YES/NO?
e) Vaginal intercourse attempted	YES/NO?
f) Object inserted in vagina (details if available)	YES/NO?
g) Licked/spat on vulva/vagina	YES/NO?
h) Lubricant used, (give any details known)	YES/NO?

---

17 **ABUSER'S ACTS ON CHILD** — Anus

a) Anal intercourse attempted	YES/NO?
b) Penis rubbed between buttocks	YES/NO?
c) Touching/fondling of anus	YES/NO?
d) Fingers inserted in anus	YES/NO?
e) Object inserted into anus (details if available)	YES/NO?
f) Licked/sucked spat on anus	YES/NO?
g) Lubricant used on anus	YES/NO?

Completed by   Date   /   /

Child's name _____

PART II HISTORY, DETAILS OF ABUSE AND ACTIONS AFTER CONTINUED

---

18 | <u>ABUSER'S ACTS ON CHILD</u> — Face, Mouth, Breasts, Penis, other parts of body

    a) Penis inserted in child's mouth   YES/NO?

    b) Ejaculated in child's mouth   YES/NO?

    c) Licked/spat on child's face   YES/NO?

    d) Licked/spat on child's mouth   YES/NO?

    e) Touching/fondling of breasts   YES/NO?

    f) Licked/sucked/spat on/bit breasts   YES/NO?

    g) Touching/fondling of child's testicles   YES/NO?

    h) Touching/fondling of child's penis   YES/NO?

    i) Licked/sucked/spat on child's penis   YES/NO?

    j) Was the child's penis erect?   YES/NO?

    k) Was there ejeculation?   YES/NO?

    l) Penis rubbed on child's body   YES/NO?
       (where on body?)

    m) Ejaculated on child's body   YES/NO?
       (where on body?)

    n) Other acts involved

---

19 | <u>SPECIFIC ACTS OF ABUSER AND CHILD NOT COVERED BY SECTIONS 1–18</u>

Completed by   Date   /   /

Child's name _____

PART II HISTORY, DETAILS OF ABUSE AND ACTIONS AFTER CONTINUED

20 | IF ANY INJURIES NOTICED AFTER ASSAULT GIVE LOCATION ON BODY

Location

BRUISES   YES/NO? _____

SORENESS   YES/NO? _____

BITES   YES/NO? _____

SCRATCHES   YES/NO? _____

BLEEDING   YES/NO? _____

21 | CHILD'S ACTIONS AFTER ASSAULT (for recent assaults)

a) Changed clothes   YES/NO/Not applicable
   (If yes, ascertain if these clothes are unwashed and still available)

b) Washed/showered/bathed,   YES/NO/NA

c) Defecated   YES/NO/NA

d) Used sanitary towel/tampon   YES/NO/NA

e) Cleaned teeth/used mouth wash   YES/NO/NA

f) Taken medicines/drugs,   YES/NO/NA
   (If yes, enter details and time when taken)

NB   If assault happened in bed, on sofa etc consider the examination of sheets, under
      blankets, mattress covers, duvet covers, blankets, quilts, cushions, covers etc. for the
      presence of seminal stains and other material, provided that the items have not been
      washed.

Completed by   Date   /   /

Child's name _____

PART III   CONSENT TO MEDICAL EXAMINATION

I hereby consent to a complete medical examination and to the recording of findings for legal purposes.

I authorise the collection of all necessary specimens for laboratory tests and for the taking of necessary photographs of injuries related to the reason for this examination.

I also authorise the use of the medical records, including any necessary photographs and relevant laboratory reports as requested by The Metropolitan Police, The London Borough of and The Crown Prosecuter for Medical-legal purposes.

SIGNED _____ Date   /   /

NAME _____

RELATIONSHIP TO CHILD _____

WITNESSED BY _____ Date   /   /

NAME _____ POLICE OFFICER/
SOCIAL WORKER/MEDICAL PRACTITIONER

Child's name _____

PART IV MEDICAL HISTORY

To be completed by the doctor undertaking the Forensic Medical Examination.

To be asked of the child's mother or other close relative or person responsible for the care of the child.

PERSON SUPPLYING INFORMATION

NAME _____

RELATIONSHIP TO CHILD _____

1	**HAS THE CHILD SUFFERED FROM ANY OF THE FOLLOWING?** (If yes, enter details)

a) <u>Allergies</u>   YES/NO?

<u>NB</u> Does the child use any type of bubble bath/bath oil? If yes, is brand known? Was any redness/reaction noticed afterwards.

b) <u>Skin diseases</u>   YES/NO?
   If yes, where on body.

c) <u>Nappy rash</u>/soreness/redness in anal-genital area   YES/NO?

d) <u>Urinary tract infection</u>   YES/NO?

e) <u>Incontinence</u>   YES/NO?

f) <u>Constipation</u>   YES/NO?

g) <u>Diarrhoea</u>   YES/NO?

h) <u>Vaginal discharge</u>   YES/NO?

i) <u>Genito-Urinary infection</u>   YES/NO?

j) <u>Threadworm/Tapeworm infections</u>   YES/NO?

Completed by   Date   /   /

Child's name _____

PART IV   MEDICAL HISTORY CONTINUED

2 | ACCIDENTS (give dates and where treated)

a) in genital area,

b) fractures

c) burns

d) other accidents

3 | MENSTRUAL HISTORY Applicable/Not applicable

a) age at onset

b) frequency

c) duration

d) associated symptoms

e) regularity

f) last menstrual period

g) does she use sanitary towel or tampon?

h) birth control

i) pregnancies

j) any children

l) abortions

4 | ANY OTHER INFORMATION

e.g. alcohol, drugs, glue sniffing — known or suspected.

Completed by   Date   /   /

PART V   FORENSIC MEDICAL EXAMINATION

To be completed by the doctor undertaking the Forensic Medical Examination

---

1 | **EXAMINATION**   DATE   /   /

NAME OF CHILD _____

HOSPITAL/VENUE _____

---

2 | **PERSONS PRESENT**   Relationship to child/Professional Status

1. _____

2. _____

3. _____

4. _____

---

3 | **MENTAL DEVELOPMENT OF CHILD**

---

4 | **PHYSICAL DEVELOPMENT**

Age   years   months, DOB   /   /

Looks age   ☐   looks younger   ☐   looks older   ☐

Height .... Weight .... HC ....

Percentiles ....

Abnormalities

State of puberty

Pubic hair present   Yes/No
If yes, indicate if sparce/abundant, straight/curly.

Completed by   Date   /   /

V FORENSIC MEDICAL EXAMINATION CONTINUED

QUICK REFERENCE CHECK LIST FOR BODY INJURIES PARTICULARLY ASSOCIATED WITH 'STRANGER ATTACKS'

In all assaults on children preserve any loose pubic hairs, noting where they were found.

In stranger attacks preserve all loose debris, e.g. hairs textile fibres, vegetation found on body.

	Examine for:
HEAD	
1. HAIR	a) loose debris, b) dried matted patches (from dried blood or seminal staining),
2. SCALP	a) examine for possible cuts and bruises, b) feel and examine for possible bruising,
3. EYES	a) petechial haemorrhages (attempted strangulation) b) dilated or pinpoint pupils etc (drugs/alcohol)
4. CHEEKS	bruising (from gag and forced opening of mouth, re. oral masturbation and forced opening of the mouth), associated scratches,
5. MOUTH O/S I/S	a) bruising (hand held over mouth or gag), b) scratches, c) damage to inside of lips (from hand over mouth), d) bruising to inside of cheeks (from forced opening of mouth), e) hairs and textile fibres, f) soreness to roof of mouth (from pressure and rubbing during oral assault/masturbation/ejaculation),
6. NECK	a) fingertip bruising (attempted manual strangulation), b) bruising from ligature, c) scratch marks, d) pressure marks from clothing of jewelry (from pulling child or from attempted strangulation),
ARMS	a) bruising (from pulling, restraining), b) ligature marks, particularly on wrists,
THIGHS	bruising, particularly fingertip bruising on inner thigh region,
ANKLES	gripmark bruising (particularly if more than one perpetrator is involved.
GENERALLY OVER BODY	Bitemarks and dried stains of blood, semen, saliva and faeces. Traces of lubricants and oils.

Child's name _____

PART V   FORENSIC MEDICAL EXAMINATION CONTINUED

5 | GENERAL APPEARANCE clothing worn and hygeine
NB If the crutch of the pants becomes soiled and hard, this is likely to cause soreness, also if nylon pants are worn in hot weather they may cause redness.

6 | CHILD'S ATTITUDE AND BEHAVIOUR DURING EXAMINATION

PAIN ON EXAMINATION, OR TURNING,   Yes/No

If yes, give details

PHYSICAL EXAMINATION AND FINDINGS

Use diagrams on pages 14–17 to show position of all injuries

Use numbered arrows and state in words the size, shape, colour, type, possible age etc.

ASSESSMENT OF FINDINGS

a) Probable cause _____

_____

_____

_____

b) Dating of injuries _____

_____

_____

_____

c) Consistent with history _____

_____

_____

PHOTOGRAPHS

Not required ☐ , taken by, name _____

Requested to be taken by police photographer ☐

Instructions

Completed by   Date   /   /

Patient _____ Date _____ Examiner _____

INJURIES ASSESSMENT FORM 1AG
(GENERAL)

RECENT INJURIES

OBSERVATION	LOCATION
EDEMA (Swelling)	
ERYTHEMA (Redness)	
LACERATIONS/ABRASIONS	
ECCHYMOSIS (Bruising)	
BROKEN BONES/FRACTURES	
ORAL INJURIES	
SPECIFIC TRAUMA Bite marks, rope burns, object imprints, etc.	
RECTAL BLEEDING	

SUSTAINED INJURIES

HEALED SCARS	
HEALED FRACTURES/BONES	
BURNS	
ADDITIONAL OBSERVATIONS	

Patient _____ Date _____ Examiner _____

INJURIES ASSESSMENT FORM
(FEMALE) 1AF

RECENT INJURIES

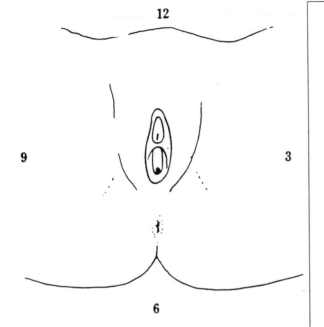

12

9   3

6

12

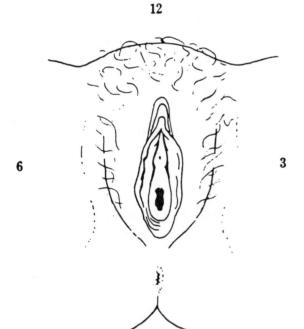

6   3

6

Permission to reproduce is granted provided
copyright statement always appears.

EDEMA (Swelling)

Vulva _____
Perineal Zone _____
Posterior Fourchette _____

ERYTHEMA (REDNESS)

Vulva _____
Perineal Zone _____
Posterior Fourchette _____

LACERATIONS/ABRASIONS

Vulva _____
Perineal Zone _____
Posterior Fourchette _____
Hymenal Ring _____

HYMEN RECENT INJURIES _____
_____
_____

ECCHYMOSIS (BRUISING)

Vulva _____
Perineal Zone _____
Posterior Fourchette _____

**SEPIFIC TRAUMA (Finernail or Bite
marks, object imprints, etc.)**
_____

GENERAL INTERNAL TRAUMA

INTRA-ABDOMINAL WALL _____

PUBOCOCCYGEUS MUSCLE _____

VAGINA WALL _____

URETHRA _____

ABNEXAE CERVIX _____

SUSTAINED INJURIES

SYNECHIAE (Internal or External) _____
_____

**HYMEN DESCRIPTION (Scarring, laxity,
general tone, perforations, etc.)** _____
_____

**PUBOCOCCYGEUS MUSCLE - Laxity or
Integrity** _____
_____

ADDITIONAL OBSERVATIONS _____
_____

Patient _____ Date _____ Examiner _____

INJURIES ASSESSMENT FORM
AAR (ANAL RECTAL)

RECENT INJURIES

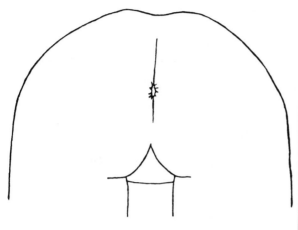

FIGURE AAR

OBSERVATION	LOCATION
EDEMA	
ERYTHEMA	
LACERATIONS/ABRASIONS	
ECCHYMOSIS	
SPECIFIC TRAUMA - MARKS, etc.	
RECTAL BLEEDING	
FISSURES	
PETCHIAE	
SUBMUCOUS HEMORRHAGE	

SUSTAINED INJURIES

LOSS OF PUCKER	
THICKENING OF SKIN (perianal)	
HEALED FISSURES	
RECTAL SPHINCTER TONE	
ADDITIONAL OBSERVATIONS	

Patient _____ Date _____ Examiner _____

INJURIES ASSESSMENT FORM
(MALE) 1AM

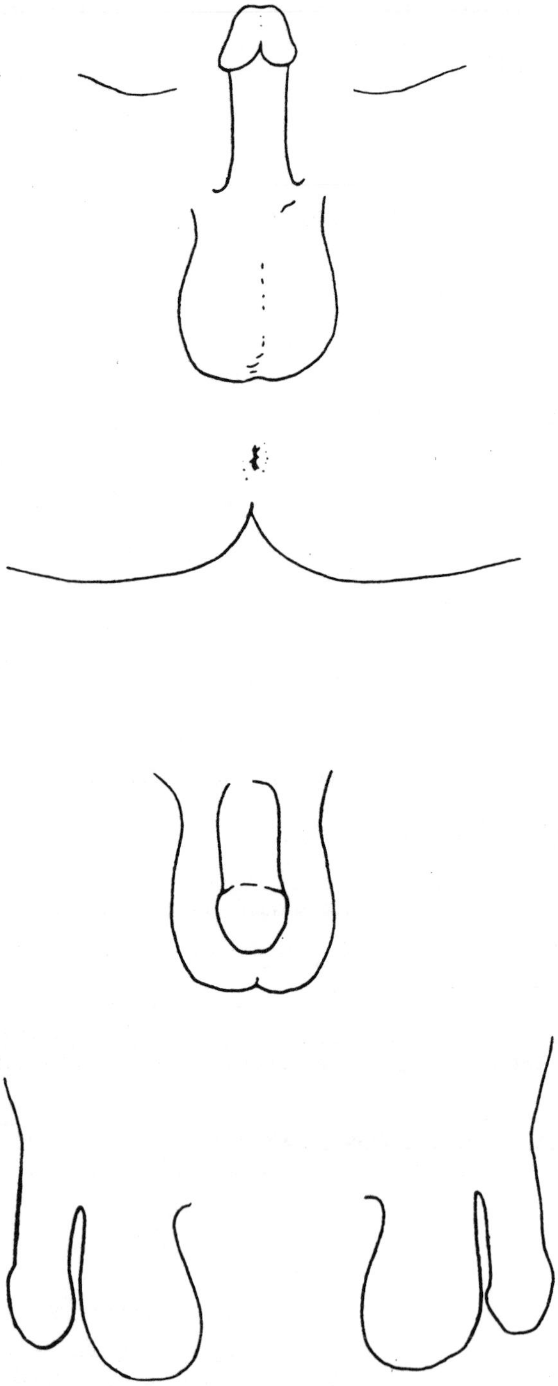

RECENT INJURIES

EDEMA (Swelling)

Penis _____
Scrotum _____
Perineal Zone _____

ERYTHEMA (REDNESS)

Penis _____
Scrotum _____
Perineal Zone _____

LACERATIONS/ABRASIONS

Penis _____
Scrotum _____
Perineal Zone _____
Urethra _____

ECCHYMOSIS (BRUISING)

Penis _____
Scrotum _____
Perineal Zone _____

SPECIFIC TRAUMA (Fingernail or Bite
marks, object imprints, etc.)

_____
_____
_____

SUSTAINED INJURIES

SCARRING _____
_____

PIGMENTATION _____
_____

OTHER INJURIES _____
ADDITIONAL OBSERVATIONS _____
_____

PART VI   FORENSIC SAMPLES

Packing, storage and transfer of exhibits

Exhibit type	Packing to use	Seal with	Storage in
Dry clothes/shoes	Paper bags	Sellotape	Cool room
Damp/wet items	Paper bags	Leave open	Cool room
Paper	Polythene bag	Sellotape	Cool room
Fragments from wounds (may also be taken on swabs)	Polythene bag	Sellotape	Refrigerator
Fingernail samples	Polythene bag	Sellotape	Refrigerator
Hair Combings	Leave on comb and return to bag	Sellotape	Cool room or refrigerator
Hair sample	Polythene bag	Sellotape	Cool room or refrigerator
Blood—PLAIN Urine	Glass universal bottle	Freezer tape	Freezer
Saliva	Glass universal bottle	Freezer tape	Freezer
Swabs	Swab pack tube	Freezer tape	Freezer
Sanitary towel/Tampon	Polythene bag	Freezer tape	Freezer
Blood—PRESERVED	Glass universal bottle	Freezer tape	Freezer—If glue sniffing or solvent abuse suspected Refrigerator—otherwise

Labelling example

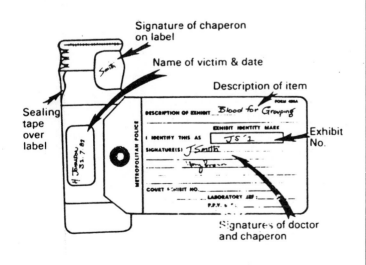

Notes on packing and sealing

a) Seal each item first with a signed sealing label and then with the correct type of tape (see chart above) fixed OVER the lable.

b) Make sure that "420" labels are not caught under tape or sealing label.

c) **To fasten bags securely:**
Turn over top 3 cm. of bag and then turn over again.

Fix flap with signed sealing label.

Apply strip of tape (which goes over the label) to seal flap, allowing 3 cm. overhang at each end.

Stick overhanging ends to back of bag.

Child's name _____

PART VI   FORENSIC SAMPLES TAKEN

Check list for samples which may be relevant. Use containers and swabs in the Metropolitan Police Kit.		
	✓ if Taken	Exhibit Number
1. CLOTHING (if thought to have been worn during the assault)		
_____	[ ]	[/]
_____	[ ]	[/]
_____	[ ]	[/]
_____	[ ]	[/]
_____	[ ]	[/]
_____	[ ]	[/]

2. URINE, (routine sample for drug/alcohol analysis)	[ ]	[/]
Enter date and time if sample taken,	/ / ,	am/pm

3. BLOOD (plain) for grouping	[ ]	[/]
BLOOD (preserved)	[ ]	[/]
Enter date and time if samples taken	/ / ,	am/pm

4. SALIVA (for grouping and detection of semen)	[ ]	[/]

5. SKIN SWABS (for removal of stains e.g blood, semen, saliva, lubricant, grease)	[ ]	[/]
_____	[ ]	[/]
_____	[ ]	[/]
_____	[ ]	[/]
_____	[ ]	[/]
_____	[ ]	[/]

Completed by _____   Date   /   /

Child's name _____

PART VI   FORENSIC SAMPLES TAKEN CONTINUED

	✓ if Taken	Exhibit Number

6. VAGINAL SWABS (for semen, saliva, lubricants)

	✓ if Taken	Exhibit Number
External _____	[ ]	[/]
Internal 1 _____	[ ]	[/]
2 _____	[ ]	[/]
Enter date and time if sample taken,	/ / ,	am/pm

7. ANAL SWABS (for semen, saliva, lubricants)

	✓ if Taken	Exhibit Number
External 1 _____	[ ]	[/]
External 2 _____	[ ]	[/]
Internal _____	[ ]	[/]

8. PENILE SWABS (for semen, saliva, lubricants)

	✓ if Taken	Exhibit Number
External _____	[ ]	[/]

9. HEAD HAIR SAMPLES (needed in 'stranger' assaults)

	✓ if Taken	Exhibit Number
Combed (use comb in kit, leave hairs on comb)	[ ]	[/]
Cut sample (10−25, cut next to scalp)	[ ]	[/]

10. PUBIC HAIR SAMPLES (if present)

	✓ if Taken	Exhibit Number
	[ ]	[/]
Combed (use comb in kit, leave hairs on comb)	[ ]	[/]
Cut sample (10−25 hairs if possible, cut next to skin)	[ ]	[/]
Retain all loose pubic hairs found on child and list under other samples		

11. OTHER SAMPLES (enter description)

	✓ if Taken	Exhibit Number
_____	[ ]	[/]
_____	[ ]	[/]
_____	[ ]	[/]
_____	[ ]	[/]

Completed by _____   Date   /   /

Child's name _____

PART VII   HOSPITAL INVESTIGATIONS   To be completed by the Paediatrician

---

1. | SEXUALLY TRANSMITTED DISEASES

Examination for the presence of discharge, sores, skin lesions, warts and infestations

Record of Findings

MOUTH/THROAT _____

ANUS _____   _____

VAGINA _____

PENIS _____

Samples taken   From   Identification   Result
                                                    mark

1. _____

2. _____

3. _____

4. _____

5. _____

6. _____

7. _____

8. _____

9. _____

10. _____

---

2. | PREGNANCY TESTING   YES/NO

RESULT

---

3. | BLOOD GROUP STUDIES/PATERNITY TESTING

Record samples taken and transfer to police officer for examination at the Metropolitan Police Forensic Laboratory

SAMPLE FROM   DATE   EXHIBIT NO. TRANSFERRED TO   DATE

_____

_____

Completed by   Date   /   /

Child's name _____

PART VII   HOSPITAL INVESTIGATIONS CONTINUED

4. | FURTHER MEDICAL EXAMINATIONS ADVISED   YES/NO

HOSPITAL/CLINIC _____

DATE AND TIME OF NEXT APPOINTMENT _____

5. | PSYCHIATRIC ASSESSMENT RECOMMENDED   YES/NO

HOSPITAL/CLINIC _____

DATE AND TIME OF APPOINTMENT _____

6. | FURTHER INFORMATION

Completed by _____   Date   /   /

BRITISH PAEDIATRIC ASSOCIATION
5 St Andrews Place, Regents Park, London NW1 4LB
Telephone 01-486 5151

PERSONAL

FROM THE PRESIDENT

JOF/HWC

31 July 1987

Dr Marietta Higgs
Consultant Paediatrician
Paediatric Department
Middlesborough General Hospital
Ayresome Green Lane
Middlesborough
Cleveland TS5 5AZ

Dear Dr Higgs

Dr Chambers and I were very pleased to have the opportunity of meeting you a few days ago and appreciated your willingness to travel to Newcastle at the end of a long day.

After such a meeting when we ranged over so many issues connected with child sexual abuse there are always a few after-thoughts.

Let me say first that Dr Chambers and I came only as officers of the professional association to which you belong and with the sole objective of seeing whether we would be of any help to you and also to the Health Authority in dealing with the problem of sexual abuse in your area.

Before seeing you we had a meeting with the Chairman of the Northern Regional Health Authority (Professor Tomlinson) and the Regional Medical Officer (Dr Donaldson). Both allowed us to question them freely about the Health Authority's responses to the various problems which the Cleveland child sexual abuse problem posed. We concluded that the Authority had acted with good sense and responsibility and with considerable understanding of your position. Health Authorities, being political instruments, are very susceptible to political pressure but it was quite obvious that the Authority was supporting you and refusing to bow to any demand which it considered an improper interference with your work or status.

We are aware of a number of complaints which have been made against your clinical examination of child patients. It seemed to us that these were essentially irrelevant and based on a fundamental misunderstanding of the nature of a normal paediatric examination. No doubt when you examine 'controls' you ensure that you have parental and, if appropriate, patient consent and obtain ethical committee approval.

The regulation of medical practice is achieved best when it is accomplished within the medical profession. New stances based on a new awareness of clinical signs, or new significances being attached to them, require first to be established within the profession. This takes some time and required persuasion and scientific evidence of validity, based on the accepted method of communication to professional journals or scientific meetings. It is the dedicated research worker and the pioneering enthusiast who so often change medicine for the better and uncover deficiencies in medical practice and understanding. In the end, however, any new development has to be fitted into the complex jig-saw which constitutes balanced medical practice. As well as the benefits, the possible adverse effects of any revision of accepted practices have to be taken into account. Child sexual abuse is a very serious matter which we as paediatricians must seek to eliminate, but removal of children from their parents and forced institutionalisation is another very serious matter. The values which different paediatricians and child psychiatrists will attach to these will vary. Perhaps, more importantly any mistake in pursuing correction of one will cause the other. Where medical practice has a definitive interface with the law, as with child abuse, there is particular difficulty because laws, once established, are rigid and inflexible and relate to accepted practice of the time. Laws are established on consensus views and do not easily accommodate evolving, developing medical practices. Once established they are likely to encode and impose the accepted practice of today and may well inhibit the development of better practice for tomorrow. The more they are kept out of medical practice the better.

The law is now entering in a major way into the Cleveland child sexual abuse affair. It is likely that the legal conclusions which will be reached will be guided by and represent the consensus views of a cross section of paediatricians and child psychiatrists. It would be unfortunate if the 'Cleveland affair' resulted in a legal brake being put on developing better and surer methods of recognising and dealing with child sexual abuse not only in Cleveland but throughout the whole country. From your own point of view the confidence of your professional paediatric colleagues is important. Their support will be important in achieving recognition of the type of service which you feel should be established.

It would not be appropriate for Dr Chambers or me to comment on individual items in the scheme of management of child sexual abuse in which you are involved. The British Paediatric Association, however, does have an important role to play in seeking to achieve effective national guidelines. Its Standing Committee on Child Abuse (a joint committee with the British Association of Paediatric Surgeons) has already, on BPA initiative, met with the Association of Police Surgeons and produced the AGREED JOINT STATEMENT (subject to ratification by the parent bodies) of which I gave you a copy. The BPA will also be involved closely in advising the DHSS Standing Medical Advisory Committee, which is seeking further advice on establishing better guidelines for recognising and managing child sexual abuse. The BPA is also likely to be involved in other ways.

The Children's Panels in Scotland appear to be a better way of dealing with the problem of suspected child abuse than the system which pertains in England and Wales. They provide a means by which, in conjunction with selected informed lay advisers and under the chairmanship of a professional assessor, paediatricians and other doctors dealing with children can interview parents and children (jointly or separately) along with representatives of social work departments and the law. This provides a means of appreciating and assessing a multidisciplinary problem in a multidisciplinary way. It reduces the risk of arbitrariness and provides a means of achieving a more cooperative and flexible approach. The system, where necessary, allows effective sanctions to be taken against parents but the broader base on which decisions on such sanctions are taken makes them more acceptable.

The BPA is, of course willing to respond to any further requests for help and if I can assist in a personal way I am very willing to do so.

With kind regards,

Yours sincerely

John O Forfar

APPENDIX H

DISCIPLINARY PROCEDURES INVOLVING CONSULTANT MEDICAL STAFF

1. Doctors may be considered in a disciplinary framework by their employing authority where there is concern about them in any of 4 main areas.

1. Professional competence

—This concerns a consultant's exercise of clinical judgement in the investigation, diagnosis, treatment and care of patients.

2. Professional conduct

—This involves the consultant's behaviour in relation to accepted standards during contact with patients or in any other aspect of his professional life.

3. Personal Conduct

—This is often difficult to distinguish from Professional misconduct, but usually it takes the form of undesirable behaviour which does not involve patients—examples could be abusive behaviour towards other staff, assault, drunkenness, theft or fraud.

4. Contractual commitments

—This could include failure properly to undertake duties and responsibilities in relation to contract of service.

Disciplinary Action

2. The formal disciplinary action open to an employing authority when allegations have been made which involve professional incompetence or professional misconduct of a serious nature which could result in dismissal is set out in DHSS Circular HM(61)112. There is no other formal mechanism in existence for serious disciplinary action against consultant medical staff in respect of professional incompetence of misconduct.

3. No formal procedure exists for matters which, though serious, are not serious enough to result in dismissal.

4. In practice, many employing health authorities have devised approaches of their own for investigating and dealing with such matters. In many cases, they will be resolved by counselling or the issuing of warnings. There are no effective sanctions for consultants who do not fulfill their contractual commitments.

Complaints procedure

5. The procedure for dealing with complaints about the clinical judgement of consultants is set out in DHSS circular HC(81)5, and allows for three stages:

i. The consultant in question should try to resolve the complaint within a few days, preferably by offering to see the complainant to discuss the matter and to seek to provide a satisfactory explanation. If the complaint is addressed to the District General Manager, then it should be for him or her to contact the consultant, referring any clinical aspects to him, and then to send a written reply on behalf of the Health Authority.

ii. If the complainant is not satisfied then he or she can ask for complaint to be referred to the Regional Medical Officer. The Regional Medical Officer will then discuss the matter with the consultant and if necessary the complainant and will decide whether or not to set in motion the third stage of the procedure.

iii. Two consultants from outside the region, nominated by the Joint Consultants Committee of the British Medical Association, will visit, examine the case notes, discuss the case with the consultant and talk to the complainant. A confidential report will then be sent to the Regional Medical Officer, and the main findings will be communicated to the complainant via the District General Manager.

6. About 15 such reviews are carried out in the Northern Region each year.

(Abridged from evidence given by Dr Donaldson)

BRITISH PAEDIATRIC ASSOCIATION
5 St Andrews Place
Regents Park
London NW1 4LB
Tel: 01-486 6151

ASSOCIATION OF POLICE SURGEONS OF GREAT BRITAIN
Creaton House
Creaton
Northampton NN6 8ND
Tel: 060-124 722

AGREED JOINT STATEMENT:
from a Working Party of the
Association of Police Surgeons of Great Britain and
the British Paediatric Association

CHILD SEXUAL ABUSE

1. Child sexual abuse may present to professionals either as:

(a) a "crisis" or:

(b) as an incidental finding with:

    (i) An allegation by a parent or "third party", or disclosure by a child;

    (ii) A pattern of physical features;

    (iii) Behavioural, developmental or psychiatric problems in a child.

2. As part of the initial full assessment of the child, where there is a need for a forensic examination, there should only be one such examination. It may be appropriate to delay this examination until further information is obtained and the child interviewed. It should be carried out in a paediatric environment by an appropriately trained doctor. There are advantages in a joint consultation being carried out eg. between a paediatrician and an experienced police surgeon.

3. The medical examination, although providing corroboration, may in many cases neither support nor contradict the diagnosis of sexual abuse.

4. Any examining doctor(s) should provide a written report for the medical and statutory agencies responsible for the care of the child including police statements when requested.

5. The diagnosis thus necessitates full and continuing consultation with other professionals involved with each child, eg. family doctor, social worker, child psychiatrist, clinical psychologist and an experienced police officer.

6. These views need to be coordinated in a case conference which should be attended by examining doctor(s) who should be prepared to attend any court hearing to present and be cross examined on the forensic evidence.

7. Each Health District has a multi-disciplinary Child Protection Committee, (previously known as the Area Review Committee), concerned with the management of child abuse. A working party of this committee should establish local procedures and utilise the available experience and skills for the development of child sexual abuse teams. These multi-disciplinary child sexual abuse teams should include inter alia: consultant paediatricians, including those with a special interest in community child health, and/or senior clinical medical officers (SCMOs) and police surgeons.

8. The continuing paediatric care of the child should be supervised by a consultant paediatrician who should attend further case conferences and support the Social Services Department and the family doctor, health visitor and other members of the primary health care team. Apart from any emergency treatment, police surgeons are not responsible for continuing care of the child who should be referred to the GP.

9. Both Associations recognize the need for further training and research.

10. The British Paediatric Association of Police Surgeons of Great Britain are available to provide joint advice on any difficulties between members of our two Associations arising out of these agreed procedures.

London 10 July 1987

Approved by the Executive Committee on behalf of the Council of the British Paediatric Association on 11 September 1987.

APPENDIX J

FROM: THE LAW ON CHILD CARE AND FAMILY SERVICES, 1987 (CM 62)

CHAPTER FOUR

PROTECTION OF CHILDREN AT RISK

40.   This chapter sets out the Government's proposals to protect children at risk of harm. These include a revised investigative duty on local authorities and the introduction of an emergency protection order to replace the current place of safety order.

Investigation

41.   There has been particular public concern derived from some recent tragic cases of child abuse that the law may be inadequate to provide the protection that children at risk may require. Since publication of the Review, the Jasmine Beckford Report—"A Child in Trust"*—has been published and the Government have taken this and other enquiry reports into consideration in assessing whether this aspect of the law can be improved.

42.   Under existing legislation the local authority have a duty to investigate cases where information is received which suggests that there are grounds for care proceedings. The Review proposed that this should be replaced by a more active duty to investigate in any case where it is suspected that the child is suffering harm or is likely to do so. The Government endorse that proposal and accept that the enquiries made should be such as are necessary to enable the local authority to decide what action, if any, to take.

43.   The Jasmine Beckford Report declared that there were powerful reasons why the duty on local authorities or health authorities to co-operate under section 22 of the NHS Act 1977 should in the context of child abuse be made more specific, to include the duty to consult and the duty to assist by advice and the supply of information so as to help in the management of such cases. Such a duty would, it was argued, operate as a positive and practical step to promote multidisciplinary working in this area, which is important not only at the stage of identification of abuse but also in subsequent follow-up action. The Government accept this view, and therefore intend to make legal provision for co-operation between statutory and voluntary agencies in the investigation of harm and protection of children at risk.

44.   The Government accept the Review's recommendation that, save for the NSPCC, only local social services authorities should be able to bring care proceedings since they will be responsible for the child if a care or supervision order is made. The exception for the NSPCC reflects their specialist role in child abuse cases and they will be expected to act in concert with the local authority. Thus the present powers of the police and local education authorities to initiate care proceedings will be removed. However children who are the subject of care proceedings may have a history of poor school attendance and in such cases the social services department will be required to consult the local education authority when initiating proceedings. In other cases of school non-attendance where care proceedings are not appropriate the local education authority will be able to apply for a supervision order relating to educational need and the legislation will provide for a suitable means of enforcement.

Emergency protection orders

45.   Under existing statutory provisions any person may apply to a magistrate for removal of a child to a "place of safety". The "place of safety order" is unsatisfactory in various ways; for example the grounds do not address the emergency nature of the need to remove the child. It is proposed to replace it by an "emergency protection order". The new order will deal with circumstances where there is reasonable cause to believe that damage to the child's health or well being is likely unless he can immediately be removed to or detained in a place of protection for a period up to the duration of the order. The responsibility for the child during this period, which is not defined in the present place of safety order, will be with the applicant for the order. It will be explicit that he will have the responsibilities of a person with actual custody of the child in the interests of the child's well being. A local authority with this responsibility would be expected to comply with such regulations, for example, on boarding out, as are appropriate to the circumstances. The order will include a specific requirement to notify the parents of the making of an order. There will be presumption of reasonable access to the child unless specified otherwise by the magistrate. If the applicant for the order is other than a local authority, he will have to inform the relevant local authority of the order giving details of the child's address and who has charge of the child. The local authority will then be able to apply for the emergency order to be transferred to them if it would be in the child's interest.

---

* A Child in Trust: The Report of the Panel of Inquiry into the circumstances surrounding the death of Jasmine Beckford, published by London Borough of Brent 1985 ISBN 0-9511068-0-5.

46. A place of safety order may last up to 28 days. The Review proposed that an emergency protection order should last for 8 days only, following the House of Commons Social Services Select Committee's proposal. This elicited widespread comment. After detailed examination it is accepted. The Government recognise that there is a need to keep to a practicable minimum the period that the child is detained during which there is no provision for challenge by the parent or child. During this period a local authority should normally have time to investigate the case, decide whether or not to initiate care proceedings and obtain sufficient evidence to enable the court to decide whether to make an interim care order. However there may be some occasions when the local authority are not ready to proceed. In exceptional circumstances the local authority will be permitted to apply for an extension of an emergency protection order for a further period of up to 7 days to provide continued protection for the child. There will be on this occasion an opportunity for the parents or child to challenge the extension, such a challenge being based on the ground that there is no risk to the child which justifies an extension of the emergency protection order. Within 15 days it should always be possible for the court to decide the case for an interim care order.

47. It has been suggested that a new type of order would be appropriate in circumstances where removing the child would be too drastic a step, but there is nevertheless serious although not urgent concern about the health and well-being of the child, for example where there is difficulty in gaining access to see the child. The concerns which prompted this proposal will be addressed in the context of the new proposals for emergency protection orders. These will allow for the child not to be removed if, when seen, this proves not to be necessary. Provision will also be made to require the disclosure of the whereabouts of the child. As at present a search warrant will be necessary if entry cannot be obtained by agreement.

Police powers

48. The police will retain their existing power to detain a child without recourse to a magistrate in a place of protection, but this will in future be limited to 72 hours not 8 days as at present. There will be provision for a single magistrate or court to allow an extension of up to 8 days from the beginning of the initial detention provided that there is satisfactory evidence of the grounds. The parents and the child, if of sufficient age to understand the implication, would be notified of the application and could attend if they wished. The police should endeavour to hand over the child, and responsibility for applying for any further order, to the local authority if possible.

Absconding of a child subject to a care order or emergency protection order

49. The present law relating to children who abscond or who are unlawfully taken away or detained is complicated and applies only to certain children in care. The new proposals set out below would apply to children in care under a care order or an emergency protection order, but not children in a local authority's care as part of a voluntary arrangement as described in Chapter 2.

50. The Government propose that there should be a single offence consisting of knowingly and without reasonable excuse or lawful authority:

(a) taking the child or;

(b) detaining or harbouring him or;

(c) assisting, inducing or inciting him or her to run away.

There are a number of agencies who carry out useful work in looking after children who have run away for short periods until alternative arrangements can be made. It is proposed that these organisations could be specified and then exempted from liability for the offence in defined circumstances.

51. Present powers for *recovery* of children who abscond or are abducted also need to be rationalised. The Government agree with the Review that the current power to arrest such a child without warrant should be discontinued in respect of children committed to care in civil proceedings. The authority should be able to seek an order authorising a constable, an officer of the court or a person specified by the authority to take charge of a child subject to a care order who has absconded. This proposal follows the model in section 34(1) of the Family Law Act 1986 for children subject to custody orders. The Government also intend to adopt from that Act a power for the local authority to apply to the court to compel disclosure by a person who there is reason to believe may have relevant information concerning the child's welfare. His answers will not be admissible in evidence against him in criminal proceedings for an offence other than perjury.

52. Additionally, the court will be able to authorise a constable or an officer of the court to enter and search any named premises where there are grounds to believe that the child may be found. Such a person will be able to use such force as may be necessary to give effect to the purpose of the order. The current power to order a person, reasonably believed to be able to do so, to produce an absent child will be retained. The Government also accept the review proposal that the court should be able to order any person who it has reasonable grounds to believe intends to remove or detain a child without permission, not to do so.

53. Consideration will be given to permitting court orders for the recovery of children to be served and enforced throughout the UK, Isle of Man, and Channel Islands. The Islands authorities will be consulted about this.

CHAPTER FIVE

THE ROLE OF THE COURT, ITS PROCEDURES AND ORDERS

54. Care proceedings are a central area of child care law and the Government's proposals to improve them in the interests of a better outcome for the children involved will be a major feature of the new legislation. In particular new improved grounds for the making of a care order and its discharge will be provided in addition to strengthened supervision orders and a new custody order for those cases where reponsibility for the child can be satisfactorily assumed by someone other than the local authority, such as a grandparent. A fairer way of resolving disputes over parental access to a child in care, wider rights of participation in proceedings and rights of appeal will also be provided together with changes in the court process itself designed to align it more with other civil proceedings and less with criminal trials. The administrative procedure of transferring parental rights by local authority resolution will be abandoned.

Parties

55. The Government recognise the advantages of involving in the proceedings anyone who has a proper interest in the child's future and his welfare. Some movement has been made in that direction by the Children and Young Persons (Amendment) Act 1986, under which a parent or grandparent can, in certain circumstances, be made a party to the proceedings in addition to the child and the applicant. That change in the law removed the more obvious shortcomings in the present arrangements. For the future, the position will be further improved. Anyone whose legal position could be affected by the proceedings will be entitled to party status. Hence, those who already have legal responsibility for the child, normally parents or the child's legal guardian, will be parties. In addition, anyone who is permitted to seek and is seeking legal responsibility for the child in the proceedings will be able to be a party. This will include anyone seeking a custody order such as a parent or stepparent or a person who is qualified to apply for a custodianship order. If the first two limbs of the proposed grounds for a care order (see paragraph 59) are satisfied, anyone who establishes he has a proper interest in the child and who wishes to have custody of the child will be able to be a party.

56. As a general rule party status in civil cases is accorded only to those whose legal position could be affected by the proceedings. Those people would be covered by the categories set out above. Others who may have evidence, opinions or views to contribute are adequately provided for without granting them party status by allowing them to take such part in the proceedings as the court directs, short of full party status. Thus it is intended that the court should be able to allow such persons to make representations or itself call them as witnesses and if the court thought fit, they would receive some or all of the documents and reports in the case. The court also might allow them to ask questions of witnesses, as it thought fit. Grandparents who wish to retain or take over custody of a child would be able to be parties and there would be no need for a specific provision such as that in the Children and Young Persons (Amendment) Act 1986.

Procedure including disclosure

57. The Review also made a number of other recommendations on procedure and participation. The aim was to move care proceedings away from the quasi-criminal model towards a civil model with more advance disclosure, so that the respondents—ie, the child or the child and his parents—know the elements of the case for an order; and also to allow the use of hearsay evidence as under the Civil Evidence Acts 1968 and 1972. It is also proposed that the use of guardians *ad litem* should no longer be restricted to those care proceedings where a conflict of interest between the parents and the child is identified. The Review recommended that the court should be under a duty to appoint a guardian *ad litem* in all cases except where

it appears unnecessary to do so in order to safeguard the child's interests. The Government consider all these to be important proposals and accept them with two modifications:

(a) Some concern was expressed that the applicant (normally the local authority) would be required to disclose their case automatically but the respondent only on the direction of the court. It is proposed to require the respondents as a minimum to give an outline of their reasons for contesting the application, when practicable.

(b) The Review canvassed the idea of discovery of documents, a process by which parties can have access to other parties' records (even though they may not be produced in court). This is not practicable in present circumstances but it is important that the guardian *ad litem* for the child has access as a statutory right and this will be provided. All documents on which each party is to rely in court should be disclosed in advance.

Privilege

58. The Review drew attention to the fact that most of the records relevant in care proceedings would be those of the local authority and would be covered by privilege in respect of local authority files on children. Thus while the local authority could themselves use whichever of those records they thought proper as evidence, they could prevent other parties from doing so. The Government recognise the need for confidentiality in this area but nonetheless believe that the partial relaxation of the privilege rule proposed by the Review for care proceedings only would be desirable. Where a person, for example, already has a document or copy of a document which would be covered by that privilege he would be able to use it as evidence at the hearing.

Grounds for a care order

59. A major proposal in the Review which will be implemented is a re-casting of the grounds for an order in care proceedings and an assimiliation to them of the grounds in family proceedings other than wardship. This involves the removal of specific grounds for making a care order such as the committing of an offence or non-attendance at school. There will be three elements in the grounds each of which must be satisfied for an order to be made. These are:

(a) evidence of harm or likely harm to the child; and that

(b) this is attributable to the absence of a reasonable standard of parental care or the child being beyond parental control; and

(c) that the order proposed is the most effective means available to the court of safeguarding the child's welfare.

The current grounds are largely confined to an examination of the present and past defects in the development or well-being of the child. Where future harm is at issue, the local authority often make application to the High Court for wardship. It is intended that the inclusion of likely harm in the new grounds should allow those cases to be heard in juvenile courts in future and will cover children who are being cared for by the local authority on a voluntary basis where a return home is likely to harm them.

60. The three tests will each need to be satisfied. It is intended that "likely harm" should cover all cases of unacceptable risk in which it may be necessary to balance the chance of the harm occurring against the magnitude of that harm if it does occur. However the test is worded, the court will have to judge whether there is a risk and what the nature of the risk is. The court will also have to make a decision as to whether the harm was caused or will in future be caused by the child not receiving a reasonable standard of care or by the absence of adequate parental control. This is not intended to imply a judgment on the parent who may be doing his best but is still unable to provide a reasonable standard of care. The intention behind the third limb of the grounds—that the order contemplated is the most effective means available to the court of safeguarding the child's welfare—is to direct the court's mind to all the options (including making a supervision order, no order at all or, where it has power, a custody order) in deciding what will be in the child's best interest, or whether the situation will be satisfactorily handled without compulsory measures. It will be essential for the local authority to give the court an idea of their general plans for the child. The amount of detail in the plan will vary from case to case depending on how far it is possible for the local authority to foresee what will be best for the child at the time. There is no intention however to involve the juvenile courts themselves in deciding how the child is to be treated if and when he enters the care of the local authority.

Interim care orders

61. The Government accept the Review's proposal that the court should have the power to make an interim care order only after care proceedings have been initiated and under strict rules as to grounds and duration. The limits on duration were the subject of extensive comment but the Government have concluded that they should be maintained because of the crucial importance of determining the child's future as soon as possible. There will be two changes to the grounds from those in the Review. It would be necessary for there to be reasonable cause to believe that only the first two limbs of the grounds for a full order may exist (ie harm or likely harm, attributable to the absence of a reasonable standard of parental care or adequate control) and secondly that *the power* to remove or detain the child is necessary in order to safeguard his or her welfare during the interim period. Thus, the local authority under an interim care order could, as under a full order, allow the child to remain at, or return home. The maximum duration of an interim care order will be 8 weeks though it will be possible to apply for extensions of up to 14 days in exceptional circumstances. The local authority will be expected to say how they intend to manage the care of the child during this period.

Supervision orders

62. The Review made a number of recommendations to combat serious shortcomings in supervision orders which a court can make in care proceedings, eg, that conditions can only be imposed on the child, and not on the parent. The Government accept them. Further consideration is being given as the Review recommended to supervision orders in family proceedings.

Custody orders

63. An important recommendation of the Review was that in care proceedings the court should be able to make custody orders as between parents or spouses, or in favour of a third party such as a grandparent if either the party is qualified to apply for custodianship or the first *two* elements of the new grounds are satisfied and a custody order is the most effective means of protecting the child's welfare. The first of these provisos is straightforward but the second needs some qualification. In those cases where the court has found that the first two elements of the new grounds are satisfied it is intended to couple a supervision order with the custody order unless the court decides that it is unnecessary to do so. In those cases where a supervision order is also made the local authority could work with the family and supervise the child's care and progress and come back to the court if it is unsatisfactory.

Access

64. In accordance with the Review the Government propose significant changes in the resolution of disputes about parental access to children in care. To begin with there is to be a presumption of reasonable access enshrined in legislation. Local authorities are to be encouraged where possible to agree on access with the parents at an early stage, so that in the few cases where agreement cannot be reached, the dispute can be dealt with by the court at the time the care order is made. The court will also have the power to determine subsequent disputes about what is "reasonable access". Thereafter, the local authority will be able to propose variations in access arrangements specified in an order but if a parent or child objects the local authority will either have to refer the matter to a court or maintain the previous arrangements. These proposals will lead to some additional court work but they will mark an important step in making the legal framework fairer to parents who disagree with a local authority's restrictions on access to a child subject to a care order. The Government believe that this will be in the interests of all the parties.

Discharge of care orders

65. The present ground for discharge of a care order is simply that in the court's view it is appropriate and, if the child is in need of care and control that he will receive it after the order has been discharged. The Government intend that the court should be satisfied that discharge of the order would be in the best interests of the child and that in reaching its decision the court should satisfy itself, that if control is needed (which may be to protect the public as well as the child) it would be provided.

Appeals

66. The Government propose that appeals from care and related proceedings should be to the same court. This would be within the Family Court should a decision be made to introduce one; under the present arrangements it means that those appeals which are not at present heard in the High Court should be referred to that court not to the Crown Court. The Review recommended that parents and local authorities

should have a right of appeal in care and discharge proceedings consistent with their party status. The Government intend to go further, however, and give all parties to the original proceedings the right to appeal against decisions of the court; thus parents and local authorities (amongst others) will enjoy that right, and the latter will no longer need to seek to resort to wardship where a care order is refused.

67.   The Review did not deal with the position of the child pending appeal. Usually pending any appeal in care and related proceedings the child's position would conform with the decision which is being appealed. Thus, where a court, for example, refuses an order in care proceedings or discharges a care order the child should generally be free of any compulsory local authority powers or care pending an appeal. On the other hand, where the court, for example, makes a care order or refuses to discharge such an order generally the child should enter or remain in care.

68.   The fact that a decision, such as a refusal to make a care order, was reached would not prevent an application for an emergency protection order if there appeared to be an immediate risk to the child and in addition, the appellate court will have a power to grant an interim care order. However where a court of first instance reaches a decision which would result in a child who is already subject to a care order or interim order leaving care, pending an appeal, it is proposed that the court should have power to stay its decision. That power will be exercised only where it is in the child's best interests and its purpose will be to risk unnecessary interruptions in the continuity of his care. There will be a time limit governing such stays.

APPENDIX K

DRAFT INJUNCTION ON PUBLICITY

IN THE HIGH COURT OF JUSTICE
FAMILY DIVISION

Before The Honourable Mr Justice .... in Chambers

In the matter of .... a minors

and in the matter of the Supreme Court Act 1981

and in the matter of the Guardianship of Minors Acts 1971 and 1973

Between .... Plaintiff
and .... Defendant

IT IS ORDERED THAT:—

and an Injunction is hereby granted restraining until further Order any person (whether by himself or by his servants or agents or otherwise howsoever or in the case of a company whether by its directors or officers servants or agents or otherwise howsoever) from publishing in any newspaper or broadcasting in any sound or television broadcast or by means of any cable programme service the name, address or school of any of the above-mentioned Minors wards of this Court (being the children whose names and addresses are set out in third Schedule hereto) and from publishing in any newspaper or broadcasting in any television broadcast or by means of any cable programme service any picture being or including a picture of any of the said children the said wards in each case in a manner calculated to lead to the identification of such child as being a ward of this Court.

(5) copies of this Order endorsed with a penal notice be served by the Plaintiff (a) on each of the parties herein in each case by personal service and (b) on each of the national daily or Sunday newspapers and on such other newspapers and sound or television broadcasting or cable programme services as the Plaintiff or the Official Solicitor may think fit in each case by facsimile transmission or pre-paid first class post addressed to the editor in the case of a newspaper or senior news editor in the case of a broadcasting or cable programme service.

AND the parties and any person affected by the Injunction in paragraph (2) above are to be at liberty to apply.

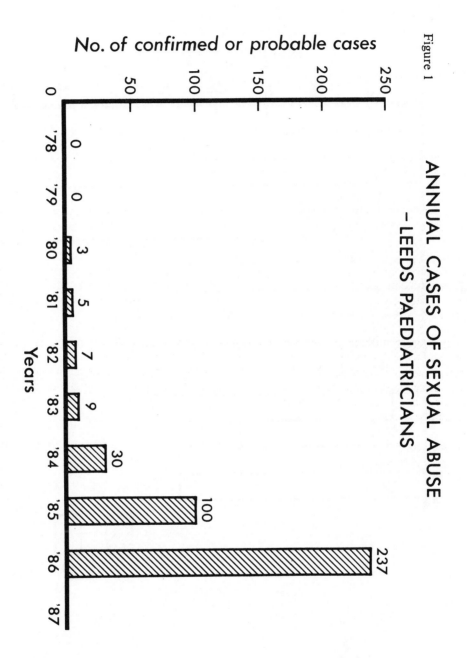

Figure 1

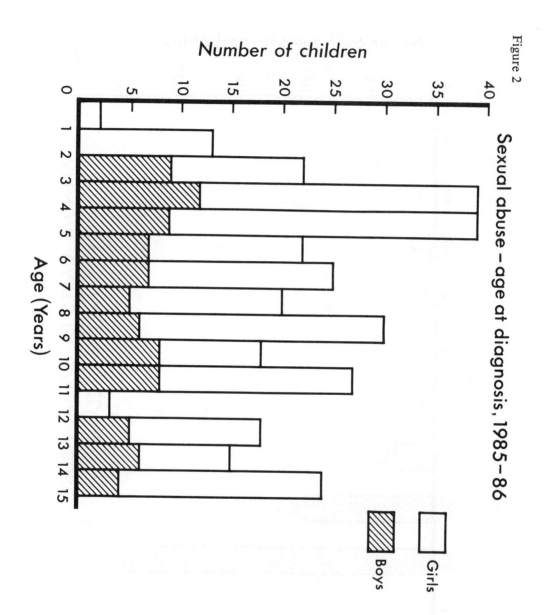

Figure 2

Sexual abuse – age at diagnosis, 1985–86

314

MODE OF PRESENTATION

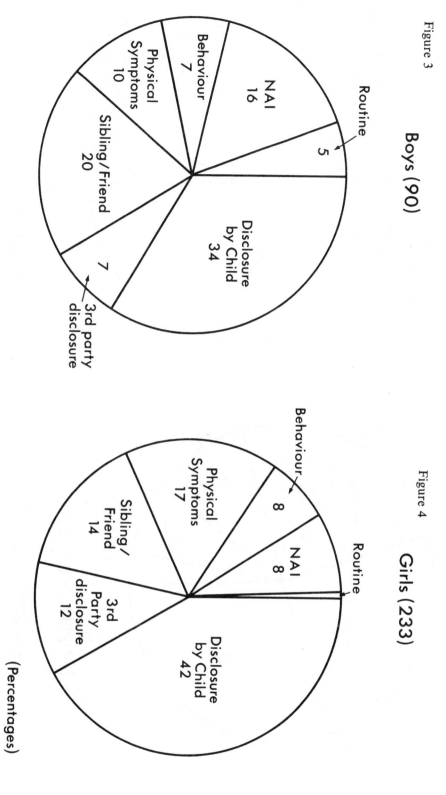

Figure 3

Boys (90)

Figure 4

Girls (233)

(Percentages)

315

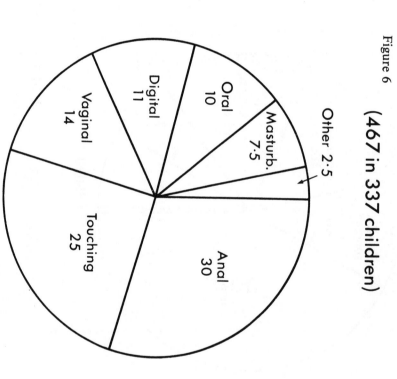

Figure 5

Sexual abuse – referral agency

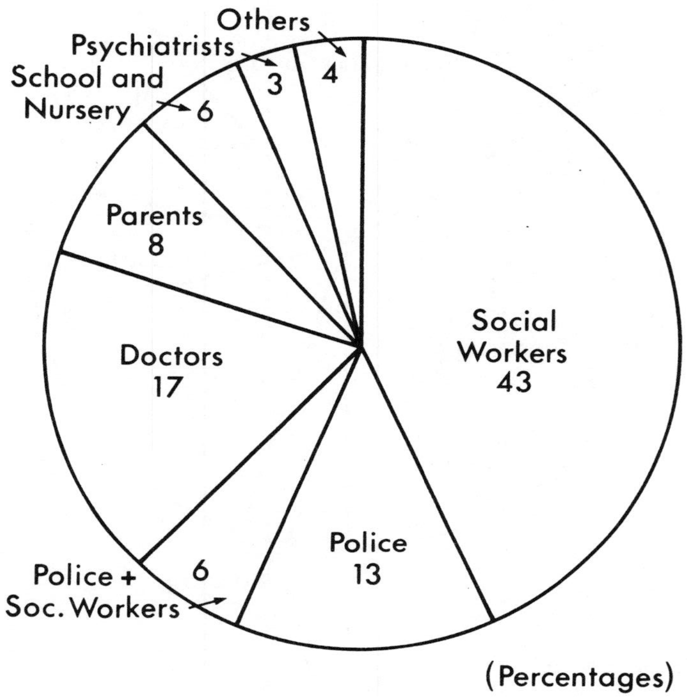

Psychiatrists
School and
Nursery

Others

Parents
8

6

Doctors
17

3

4

Police +
Soc. Workers
6

Police
13

Social
Workers
43

(Percentages)

Figure 6

TYPES OF ABUSE
(SEXES COMBINED)
(467 in 337 children)

Oral
10

Masturb.
7·5

Other 2·5

Digital
11

Vaginal
14

Anal
30

Touching
25

(Percentages)

316

Figure 7

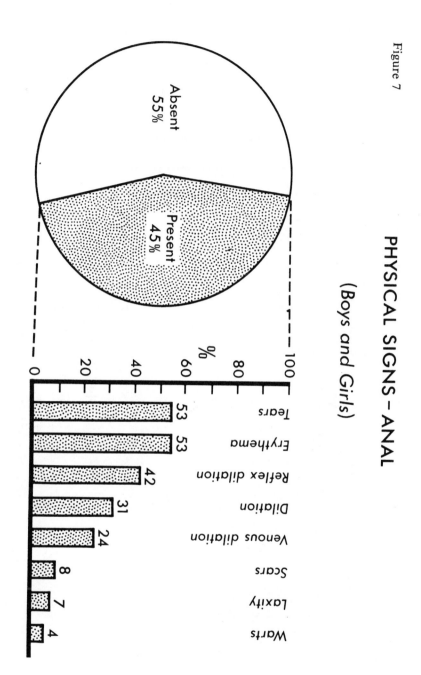

PHYSICAL SIGNS – ANAL

(Boys and Girls)

317

Figure 8

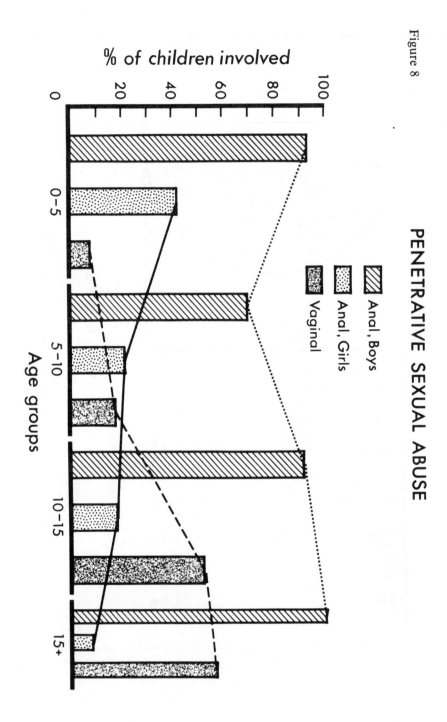

PENETRATIVE SEXUAL ABUSE

% of children involved

Age groups

Anal, Boys

Anal, Girls

Vaginal

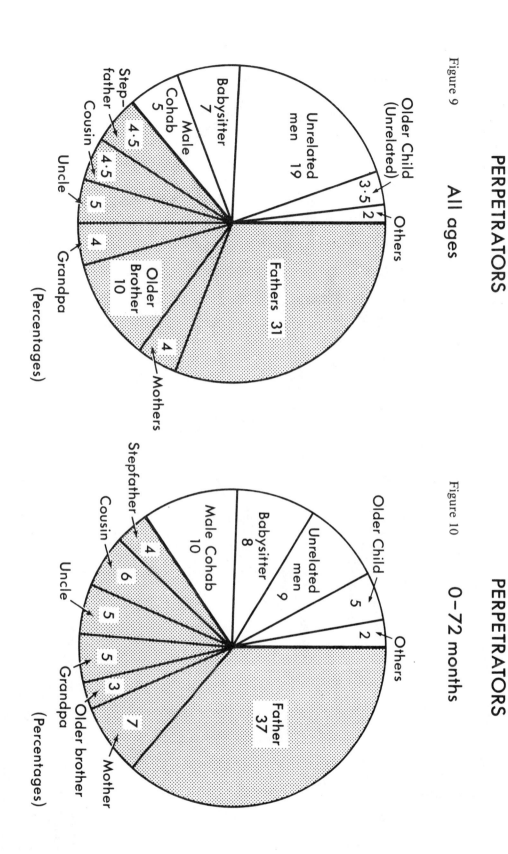

PERPETRATORS

Figure 9   All ages

Older Child
(Unrelated)

Babysitter
7

Male
Cohab
5

Step-
father
4·5

Cousin
4·5

Uncle
5

Grandpa
4

Older
Brother
10

Mothers
4

Fathers 31

Unrelated
men
19

3·5 2

Others

(Percentages)

PERPETRATORS

Figure 10   0–72 months

Older Child

Babysitter
8

Unrelated
men
9

Male Cohab
10

Stepfather
4

Cousin
6

Uncle
5

Grandpa
5

Older brother
3

Mother
7

Father
37

5

2

Others

(Percentages)

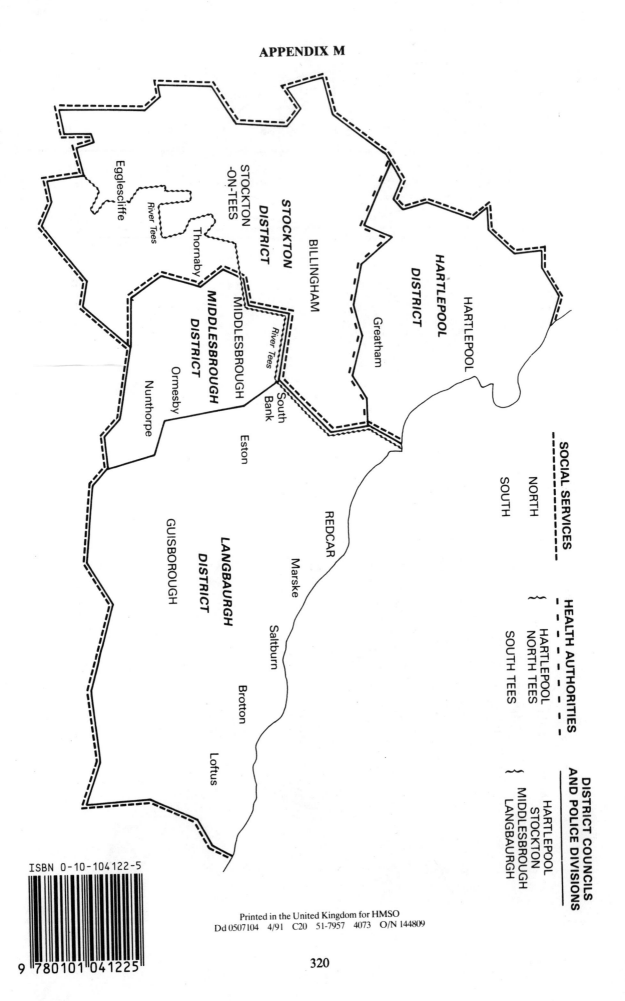

SOCIAL SERVICES

NORTH

SOUTH

HEALTH AUTHORITIES

HARTLEPOOL
NORTH TEES
SOUTH TEES

DISTRICT COUNCILS
AND POLICE DIVISIONS

HARTLEPOOL
STOCKTON
MIDDLESBROUGH
LANGBAURGH

ISBN 0-10-104122-5

Printed in the United Kingdom for HMSO
Dd 0507104   4/91   C20   51-7957   4073   O/N 144809

9 780101 041225